EVERYMAN IN EUROPE
Essays In Social History

The Preindustrial Millennia

VOLUME 1

EVERYMAN IN

Allan Mitchell

University of California, San Diego

Istvan Deak

Columbia University

EUROPE

ESSAYS IN
SOCIAL HISTORY

The Preindustrial Millennia

PRENTICE-HALL, INC., *Englewood Cliffs, New Jersey*

Library of Congress Cataloging in Publication Data

MITCHELL, ALLAN, COMP.
  Everyman in Europe.

  CONTENTS: v. 1. The preindustrial millenia.
  Bibliography: v. 1, p.
  1. Social history—Modern—Addresses, essays,
lectures. I. Deák, István, joint comp. II. Title.
HN13.M58   914'.03   73-21800
ISBN 0-13-293563-5

Allan   Mitchell and *Istvan Deak*

EVERYMAN IN EUROPE:
ESSAYS IN SOCIAL HISTORY

Volume 1   The Preindustrial Millennia

Printed in the United States of America

10 9 8 7 6 5

PRENTICE-HALL INTERNATIONAL, INC., *London*
PRENTICE-HALL OF AUSTRALIA, PTY. LTD., *Sydney*
PRENTICE-HALL OF CANADA, LTD., *Toronto*
PRENTICE-HALL OF INDIA PRIVATE LIMITED, *New Delhi*
PRENTICE-HALL OF JAPAN, INC., *Tokyo*

To Four Women
Gloria, Catherine, Alexandra, and Éva

CONTENTS

Part II

Manors and Manners In Medieval Times   105

Part III

Inertia and Motion
In Early Modern Times   205

PREFACE

Historians ordinarily record the major events of the past. They attempt to tell us what happened, and when, and if possible why. No one would deny that these are important things to know, and few would dispute that it is a proper and necessary function of historians to be concerned with the impact of such events. Yet there has been for some time a realization among professional historians, as well as among students, that history needs to be something more than an analysis of dramatic events, however crucial they may have been. If we are really to understand the past, we ought also to know about the daily lives of the many people who endured rather than instigated the events of which we so often read in books. It is the special concern of these volumes, then, to study how most people lived rather than how a few acted.

Most men and women who populate this world have always been poor and uneducated. This is not to say that they have been altogether powerless and inarticulate. What it does mean is that they have tended to express themselves and their interests in social groups, of one sort or another, rather than as individuals. To comprehend their behavior it is therefore more useful to think in terms of social types than of personalities. In the pages that follow, proper names will consequently figure only infrequently. As important as they are, it is not Pericles, Julius Caesar, Henry VIII, and Napoleon Bonaparte who stand here in the foreground; rather it is the peasant, the worker, the woman, and the youth. In short, our chief protagonist is Everyman.

By the careful selection of articles and excerpts we have attempted to trace the changing circumstances and activities of ordinary people from Greek civilization to the present time. Our focus is Europe; and we have defined Europe as broadly as possible, drawing our examples from Ireland to Russia. Too often Europe is conceived largely in terms of what is most familiar to us and to the majority of Western historians: Britain and France. By giving the areas of central and eastern Europe their due, we hope to redress the balance and to suggest a truer picture of European society as a whole.

The attentive reader will quickly perceive that generalizations about Everyman in one area of Europe at a given time are not universally applicable. Can we nonetheless say that the various social types under consideration have something in common? Is there any constant factor among so many people in such a multitude of times and places? If so, it is certainly *not* that they have been deaf and dumb throughout European history. To the contrary, in their own way they have often and unmistakenly expressed enthusiasm, or dissatisfaction, or indifference. Even the ostensibly most random forms of violence and deviant modes of behavior have sometimes spoken eloquently as to the character of European society. Yet Everyman has hardly been the master of his own fate and what has emerged as the salient characteristic of most people's behavior is this: they usually take rather than give orders. They do not command, they obey—or at least they are expected to do so.

Is this, then, a history of the oppressed? That is a question which the reader must finally answer for himself. There is certainly much evidence to support an affirmative reply. Still, the reader cannot remain unaware of the relativity of such a notion as "oppression." What degree of consciousness must the oppressed person attain of his deprived social status before he can be considered enslaved? What degree of personal liberty is required in order to protest or to escape oppression? These are not simple issues, and they are not much clarified by dogmatic assertions of whatever political persuasion. The historian is always on the side of complexity and the social historian emphatically so; the dogmatist will therefore find little support here for his terrible simplifications.

We have kept two objectives well in view: to select essays which are adequate to the difficulty of the subject rather than to choose brief and random fragments, and to achieve a sense of variety by drawing on a representative sample of historical techniques. The reader should gain the altogether legitimate impression that social history which we believe is still its adolescence, is far from becoming a monolithic discipline.

The notion that European society was transformed in modern times by an "industrial revolution" need not be accepted without reservation. In the first place, the term "revolution" implies a rapid and thorough change, whereas the development of an industrial society in Europe has been slow, uneven, and incomplete. The transformation was, moreover, not exclusively a matter of industry; one must also take into account demographic, agricultural, and technological innovations of considerable magnitude and complexity. To separate cause from effect, or symptom from correlation, is no simple task.

Another preliminary word of caution. We are perhaps unduly conditioned to believe that history consists of winners and losers. Thus we may be inclined, without a flicker of protest, to accept the assertion that modern times were marked by the "triumph" of the bourgeoisie. Yet we would do well to recall that the results of a protracted social evolution are seldom to be measured by box scores or body counts, as if history were an athletic contest or a formal military engagement. Even if we could derive a precise definition of "bourgeois"—which would hardly hold for the entire European continent—we cannot be quite certain what "to win" really means in social terms. We know only that industrialization has meant an important alteration in the quality of life for most Europeans. A careful study of the essays in this volume should enrich our understanding of that complex phenomenon.

The preparation of this volume, as well as the preceding one, was greatly facilitated by the superb editorial care of Patricia Albano, Gloria Deak and Claire Nolte. We are also extending our heartfelt thanks to Robert P. Fenyo, Assistant Vice President of Prentice-Hall, Inc., who brings to the publishing world infinite patience and foresight.

COMMON PEOPLE IN CLASSICAL TIMES

part I

1. SLAVES AND LABORERS

For those of us now living in the twentieth century it is difficult to imagine the circumstances and attitudes of a society in which slave labor was a commonplace. Yet Greek and Roman civilizations both utilized and accepted slavery as a matter of course. Not that slavery altogether escaped criticism from certain intellectuals and protest from some of the slaves themselves. But it was a part of everyday life, and those societies could scarcely have existed without it. The articles that follow illustrate how little the institution of slavery actually changed from the fourth century B.C. to the fourth century A.D. They also raise some nagging questions. To what extent can it be said that slavery was "fundamental" to classical civilization? What proportion of the population was regarded and treated as chattel? What social function did the slaves perform? What possibilities existed for their escape from the status of a slave?

Gustave Glotz describes the practice of slavery in Greece and attempts to answer some elementary queries. How were slaves recruited? What rights and protection did they have? What roles did they perform? His analysis provides an excellent introduction to the subject.

M. I. Finley writes with a more polemical bite. He argues that Greek society and economy were founded on the institutionalized exploitation of slavery. He examines the fragmentary evidence of the mentality of slaves, both those who willingly submitted and those who attempted to escape. And he suggests why less attention ought to be paid to the alleged political effects of slavery and more to its social function.

P. A. Brunt confirms that Roman attitudes toward slave labor hardly

3

differed from the Greek; and he shows how the practice of slavery was altered only very slowly in a society which remained overwhelmingly agricultural. Unlike Finley, Brunt raises the question of morality and finds it worthwhile to ask whether slavery affected the decline and collapse of classical civilization.

The careful reader will easily note the variation of scholarly opinion on these issues. But more importantly, he should gain some impression of how deeply rooted in Western society is the notion that some persons are by birth inferior to others, an assumption which has survived in one form or another well into modern times and which has not disappeared up to the present day.

GUSTAVE GLOTZ

The Slaves

In the eyes of the Greek no healthy, lasting society could dispense with slaves. To devote his forces and intelligence to the city, the citizen must be relieved of domestic occupations and manual labour. Slavery was a necessary institution. That it might be a legal institution there must be creatures made for servitude by a natural inferiority. These born slaves existed; they were the barbarians. So the life of the city necessitated and justified slavery. No one would see, neither philosopher nor common man, that the rights invoked were merely wants.

1. THE RECRUITING AND
CONDITION OF THE SLAVES

Slavery came from three sources—birth, war, and judicial condemnation. The slaves "born in the house" were not very numerous. In the deeds of manumission found at Delphi, out of 841 slaves freed there are 217 of this class; and it should be noted that a master was more willing to free

Gustave Glotz, *Ancient Greece at Work: An Economic History of Greece from the Homeric Period to the Roman Conquest*, trans. M. R. Dobie (New York: Alfred A. Knopf, Inc., 1926), pp. 192–207.

servants whom he had known since their childhood. The reason was that the breeding of human livestock was not a good speculation. Most of the newborn infants were killed or exposed; those who had the most chance of surviving were those who owed their birth to a caprice of the master.

The vast majority of slaves came from war. After a pitched battle those prisoners who could not buy their freedom were sold; after the assault of a city the men were put to the sword and the women and children divided among the victors by lot. To barbarians these laws were applied in all their brutality; after the Eurymedon campaign Cimon threw more than twenty thousand prisoners on the market. Towards Greeks certain scruples were felt, and neutral public opinion made mercy necessary. Furthermore, in barbarian countries slave-raiding was always allowed, and occasionally a little poaching was done on Greek soil. Wherever the power of the State did not make itself felt with energy, in Thessaly, in Ætolia, brigands and pirates acted as purveyors to the dealers in men.

Lastly, private law itself contributed to the recruiting of slaves. Athens caused individual liberty to be respected in almost all circumstances, but elsewhere subordination easily became servitude. Even in philanthropical Athens the father had a right to expose his children, and newborn infants were hardly ever picked up on roads and public places except to be made into slaves. In most cities a father could get rid even of the children whom he had brought up (a horrible temptation in time of need); Athens forbade this abominable traffic, but authorized the sale of a guilty daughter. The insolvent debtor fell into the power of his creditor, with his wife and children; Athens almost alone forbade loans on the person. Everywhere the State, arrogating to itself the right which it allowed to individuals, maintained penal slavery in the code of law; Athens confined this to the Metic who usurped the rank of citizen, but most cities made much use of it, and some made civic degradation or *atimia* an ingenious preliminary to slavery.

In general, most slaves came into their master's house by way of purchase. They were of very varied origins. Few were Greeks; these were often wastrels, criminals sold abroad. In 415 one set of sixteen slaves was composed of five Thracians, three Carians, two Syrians, two Illyrians, one Scythian, one Cholcidian, one Lydian, and one Maltese. To meet the increasing demand the recruiters gradually extended their field of operation, and procured Bastarnæ and Sarmatians, Persians and Arabs, Egyptians and Libyans. In origin the slaves were more or less equally distributed between the rude countries of the North and the more civilized East. In other words, the Greeks had almost as much need of strong arms for the mines and workshops as of pliant natures and quick wits for domestic service and business.

So the slave trade was very busy in Greece. Dealers rushed after the armies or entered into relations with the pirates. They operated chiefly in the neighbourhood of the barbarian lands. Chios, Ephesos, Byzantion, and Thessaly, these were the great markets of supply. The recruiters sometimes formed a syndicate covering a district. The importers sent almost all the goods to Attica. A monthly fair was held on the Agora of Athens. Part of the cargoes was sent to Sunion for the mines. The surplus of imports was re-embarked for Sicily. So Athens was the centre of this business. The slave-dealers there were very rich; they ordered their bust from the fashionable sculptor, and would one day be sufficiently powerful to give financial backing to a revolution. . . .

The ideas of the Greeks on the necessity and lawfulness of slavery determined the legal status of the slave. He was a living instrument. He belonged to another man, he was his chattel. But this chattel was alive and had a soul. According as the master's right was absolute and uncompromising, or took into account the exceptional nature of this kind of property, there were notable differences in law, and still more in practice; for we can hardly say that slavery had a legal position in the city; it was subject to household law, which the master interpreted according to his own ideas.

On principle the slave had no personality. He had no real name of his own. If two slaves cohabited this union, though tolerated, was not a marriage. Their issue was merely an increase in livestock which belonged to the owner of the woman. Not being a person, the slave had not the free disposal of his body. He might be made over to another or confiscated; he might become immovable property through the use to which he was put. Being property himself, he was incapable of exercising the right of property. He was allowed to save his earnings; sometimes he plied his trade outside and had the use of part of his salary; he might even make a fortune and show off his wealth. But his enjoyment of his property always depended on a permission which might be recalled. In law the master's authority came between the legally disqualified slave and third parties, whether they were private individuals or representatives of the State. The slave could not lodge an accusation without the master. But his responsibility also was very limited. He was covered by the orders which he had received. Since he owned nothing in law, he could not be subjected to pecuniary penalties; for him there was, instead, the whip. If a sentence for damages was given, it fell on the master; he paid the damages, or else gave up the slave altogether by noxal surrender.

The interest of the master was the slave's only safeguard. For Aristotle the slave is an instrument, and "one must take care of the instrument in the measure which the work requires." If a man has a good servant he will be wise to feed and dress him better, to allow his rest, to let him form a family, and to hold out a prospect of the supreme reward, freedom. Plato is hard enough on the "brute" who revolts against a natural inequality; but such a difficult piece of property must be treated well, "for our own advantage rather than for his."

One might suppose that in societies in which the law kept down the slaves with implacable logic, and philosophy sought no alleviation of their lot but in a better utilization of their labour, nothing could lighten the weight of their chains. Yet the Athenian people had the merit of introducing humane contradictions into its law and improving the condition of the slaves. It acted in obedience to economic and political necessities. In a country where there were many slaves, public safety required that they should not be kept in a permanent state of exasperation. But above all the democratic idea had its own special virtue, that thoughtful tenderness for the humble which is designated by the essentially Athenian word "philanthropy." From the citizens this idea went on to shed its blessing on those who had not the right of citizenship, nor any right at all. Aristotle observes contemptuously that "democracy is adapted to the anarchy of slaves"; but, an Athenian retorts, "it was not for the slaves that the lawgiver felt so much concern, . . . he considered that the man who in a democracy does outrage to anybody whomsoever is not fit to take part in civic life." So the slaves had a better time in Athens than in any other city, and it was said that they enjoyed there an amount of freedom which the poor citizens of many an oligarchic State might have envied them.

By a series of fine inconsistencies the law of Athens went so far as to regard the slave as a human being. The master had a very extensive right of correction, but he had no longer the right of life and death. The slave was armed against arbitrary and continuous cruelty; he could take refuge in certain sanctuaries and, under the ægis of the deity, call upon his master to sell him. Elsewhere the slave was exposed to the violence of all free men. Plato thought this an excellent plan. There was nothing like it in Athens. There the aristocrat was furious because he could not thrash the swine in the street and make them get out of his way.

The criminal code safeguarded the life of the slave. It was one of the boasts of the Athenian. "Among you," the Hecuba of Euripides says to the Greeks, "the free man and the slave are alike protected by the laws of murder." It is of the law of Athens that the poet is thinking. Incidentally he exaggerates its range. The murderer of a slave could never be tried by the Areiopagos, nor condemned to death. He was sentenced to temporary exile, and might be dispensed from this by the legal champion of his victim; he was at the mercy of the slave's master, and had only to pay him for the necessary permission to settle the blood price. But the eulogy bestowed on the Athenians at least proclaims the ideal at which reality, still imperfect, was aiming.

Athens protected even the honour of the slave. Every grave act coming within the definition of "outrage" was a menace to public order, and the penalty was made very severe if it appeared that the cause of a weak man was that of the whole city.

But the most novel idea, that which was most full of promise, was that of giving the slave guarantees even against the officials who embodied the State. All over Greece the police regulations carried as penalty the fine for free men and the whip for slaves. As a rule the length of the flogging was left to the magistrate or the executioner. In Athens the slave received fifty strokes, as the citizen paid fifty drachmas; both penalties were alike limited. The law recognized that the slave had a right, even under the whip of the city. This was the beginning of a legal revolution, and the Greeks were so well aware of it that the people which dared to set foot on this road was never followed along it.

In law, then, the condition of the slave was comparatively good in Athens. But it was not good enough to make his life other than abominable. Everything depended on the master. Everywhere there were despots whose every word was accompanied by a lash. But on the whole manners were mild in Greece, especially in Athens. "Philanthropy" would not have been in the spirit of the law if it had not pervaded the whole soul in private relations. When he came into the house the slave was initiated into the family worship. Showers of figs, nuts, and other fruit were poured on his head as a presage of the joys which his work would bring him. Henceforward he was one of the family. Nothing in his costume distinguished him from the free worker. He talked in his free way with everybody. He sometimes overdid this, and in the comedy Daos is appallingly impudent. But, take it all round, freedom of speech, which did not damage industry or loyalty, was preferred to silent, hypocritical hostility. A "boy" born in the house and his master who had played with him might be bound by genuine affection; a nurse might be surrounded with tenderness and deference. Many slave families were formed without opposition, and the parents kept their children. The thrifty worker heaped up his savings without fear of filling a money box for his master. An intelligent landowner or manufacturer knew that he had every interest in giving a decent position to the men who worked his land or ran his factory. In certain cases manumission was no more than a moral satisfaction.

All these features together give a picture which is no doubt too idyllic. Beneath the few slaves who were on familiar terms with their masters there were thousands of squalid creatures vegetating, especially in the mines, fed just enough to prevent their strength from diminishing, and resting from work only when they were beaten. We cannot forget that the slaves of the Athenians used to flee to Megara, that the appearance of the Spartans was for the workers of Laurcion the signal for desertion in a mass, and that in Attica itself many wretches bore on their forehead the brand of the runaway. But it is something that, in a realistic theatre, we hear slaves uttering grateful praises of their masters.

2. SLAVE LABOR

It would be very interesting to be certain of the number of slaves in the various cities of Greece. We hear of 470,000 slaves in Ægina, of 460,000 in Corinth, of 400,000 in Athens. The exaggeration is obvious. It may at least be taken as a rule that in the commercial and manufacturing cities the slave population was greater than the free. On the other hand, those districts which still lived by agriculture and stock-breeding had few slaves. When in the middle of the fourth century a landowner in Phocis had a thousand there was an outcry. Slavery, then, appears in Greece as a concomitant of trade and industry, varying according to their development. At the same points, once in Ionia, now on the Saronic Gulf, economic life and slave labor were concentrated.

If we cannot know the number of the slaves we should at least like to know the proportion of the sexes in this class. We should then have exact information for the relative importance of the servile occupations; we could compare the total amount of domestic labor with that of industrial and commercial labor. Unfortunately the information which we possess on the subject refers chiefly to freedmen. Now the slaves who most easily obtained their liberty were those who had most opportunity for making themselves pleasant. In this the women were at a great advantage, for they attended to the cares of the household and had still other means of winning the good graces of the master. Of the 1,675 manumissions known from the inscriptions 927 refer to women (55 percent) and 748 to men (45 percent). It does not follow that the female element predominated among slaves. Moreover, even in the deeds of manumission, the preponderance of the women is not constant. At Chæroneia it is enormous; out of 104 slaves freed 65 are women (62.5 percent) and 39 are men (37.5 percent). It is almost as great at Delphi; figures covering 841 cases give 510 women (60.6 percent) as against 331 men (39.4 percent). But in Athens, according to the vases dedicated to the Goddess by former slaves (the manumission *phialai*), the proportion is the other way; out of 233 donors the women number 105 (45 percent) and the men 128 (55 percent). Moreover, on the lists of slaves confiscated by the Athenians in 415 the women are not many; a set of 16 slaves contains 4 or 5 females (25 or 31 percent). Therefore it seems that in Greece as a whole domestic service and family industry required rather more women than the fields, workshops, and commercial houses required male slaves. But, although the female element of the slave class was in a considerable majority in communities which got their resources from the soil and remained attached to the econ-

omy of old times, the male element predominated in the same proportion
in cities where trade and industry were highly developed.

The whole of Greece needed slaves for domestic service. Almost all the
work of providing food was done by the women. The maidservants made
the bread and did the cooking. For big dinners special dishes were ordered
from professional cooks, or else one of these artists was engaged for the
day; and one or two great personages had a chef of their own. We hear
of the chef of Alcibiades; and the story goes that the cook of Demetrios
of Phaleron made enough in two years to buy three tenement houses.
Round about the master cook there was a busy staff of slaves, scullions,
bakers, and pastry cooks.

The clothing of the family was also made at home. Under the eye of
their mistress the slave girls spun, wove, and embroidered. Their chief
occupations were the manufacture of materials and sewing; that is why,
once free, they generally lived by the textile industry.

Women in easy circumstances had several slaves in their service, and
even the humblest always had one. The speeches of the orators give us
some typical examples. Ciron, a landowner with a fortune of more than
twenty-thousand drachmas, had three domestics. An honest farmer, whose
wife had one single child, kept a cook (a woman), a chambermaid, and
a nurse maid. The ordinary middle-class townsman had a serving man and
women of two classes, those of the ground floor, who did the house work,
and those of the first floor, who made the clothes. Diogenes Laertios takes
us into the homes of the philosophers. Plato freed a woman in his will
and left four slaves to his heirs. Aristotle, who found that with too many
servants it was hard to organize work, nevertheless had nine slaves, not
including children. Theophrastos, too, had nine. Straton's will mentioned
seven, and Lycon's twelve. In sum, a man of average fortune employed
in his house from three to twelve slaves of the two sexes. But three was
on the small side. There were families in very difficult circumstances who
could not do with less. Stephanos, who lived on his wits with his concubine and three children, placed at the disposal of this household a male
slave and two servant women. In the *Plutos* of Aristophanes, when poor
old Chremylos groans over his wretched lot he confides his woes in his
serving man. People used to point out, as "characters," Diogenes, who did
not need any one to keep his tub in order, Hippias, who made his own
clothes and shoes, and Chrysippos, who took Odysseus for a model in the
art of fending for himself.

The rich were obliged by the progress of luxury to live in great style,
with chambermaids, wet-nurses, dry-nurses, housekeepers, lady's maids,
valets, footmen, coachmen, grooms, and pedagogues. "Use slaves like the
members of the body, one for each purpose." The precept comes from a

philosopher. The division of labor which it proclaims produced in very wealthy families an extreme diversity of servile functions. That servants might be well trained they were sent to take lessons at the school of house-keeping or from a certificated master in the culinary art.

In houses with a large domestic staff it was found necessary to place a trustworthy person over them. Pericles had a steward who managed his estates and had charge of the personnel. Big landowners even had a female housekeeper in addition to the steward. Such a post was well suited to slaves; it was easy to get back from them anything which they should take improperly. For this very reason citizens looked down on it. Eutheros, to whom Socrates suggests this means of earning a living, thanks him for nothing. It was an important and delicate decision, to choose out of your slaves the man or woman who should be put over them. Xenophon gives minute advice on the subject. As housekeeper you must choose "the woman who seems least inclined to gluttony, drink, sleep, and running after men; she must also have an excellent memory, and she must be ca-pable of either foreseeing the punishment which neglect will cost her or of thinking of ways of pleasing her masters and deserving their favor." But the masters too must treat her with sympathy, and interest her in her work and in their property, "by keeping her informed of their position and shar-ing their happiness with her." As steward, also, you must reject the idler, the drunkard, and the dissolute man, and look for intelligence, industry, loyalty, experience, and authority, without being too much afraid of love of gain, which is a stimulus.

Apart from this, the Greeks never attained the frightful squandering of labor of which the Roman town houses and villas were to boast. It is true that in the sixth century a Sybarite appeared at the court of Sicyon with a retinue of a thousand slaves; but these Greeks from the colonies wanted to dazzle the old world. It is also true that, two centuries later, a man in Phocis formed a troop of slaves who were likewise reckoned at a thousand head, but he meant them to work in the fields; the proof of it is that he was accused of taking the bread from the mouths of so many free men, and in the same country the wife of Philomelos attracted attention the first time she walked out accompanied by two servant-women. So it is not in thousands, nor even in hundreds, that we must count the slaves in the houses which were most largely supplied with them. It was even held, with Aristotle, that too many servants spoiled the service. Plato compares to "tyrants" (we should say, to princes) those private individuals who own fifty slaves or more. We find one rich Metic, in 415, with only sixteen slaves. In the next century the ostentatious Meidias perhaps owned more; he had three or four footmen following him and kept a number of servant-women; but if he had had a "tyrannical" household staff his opponent Demosthenes would have made the most of it, and he says nothing about it. The Athenians, who loved money in order to employ it usefully, took good care not to sink large capital in an over-grand style of housekeeping.

Agriculture did not make a very great use of slave labor. In the countries of big estates, Laconia, Messenia, and Thessaly, the lords of the land had it worked by serfs who must pay a fixed revenue. Countries of small farms are notoriously ill-adapted to slavery. Corn growing furnished only intermittent work. To feed slaves all the year round in order to employ them usefully for about seven weeks is bad business. If costs of this amount are not to absorb the return in advance, the estate must be extraordinarily fertile and very extensive. In Greece, where the soil was poor and the fallow in alternate years reduced the sown land by a half, the production of corn by slave labor could not be remunerative. The cultivation of the olive and vine requires great care and knowledge. It suited the small proprietor working his own land. One or two slaves, employed in the house when there was no work in the fields—no more were needed. And indeed, as Aristotle says, "with the poor, the ox takes the place of a slave." In other words, to have more than two slaves the farmer had to be in comfortable circumstances.

Therefore the slave population was insignificant in the agricultural districts. In the fifth century there were hardly any slaves in central Greece. In 431 Platæa could not make up a troop of a hundred and ten female slaves. In the fourth century the slave element barely came to one third of the total population in Bœotia. Even at Thebes, in 335, the number of slaves was far from being equal to that of free men. In Locris and Phocis slavery was almost unknown until the looting of Delphi brought gold pouring into those rural districts. In agricultural regions, then, slavery was a late institution. Sometimes it progressed suddenly through the sudden development of wealth; but wherever the development took place naturally it was very slow. Here and there an isolated agriculturist turned to slaves for the help which was indispensable, and sometimes for the family which he lacked. If, in the environs of Delphi, the farmer is very ready to free his slaves, and if the freedman in one case out of ten bears the name of his master, it is because work in common and concubinage brought master and slaves together.

Even in the manufacturing and commercial countries the abundance of slave labor was of no benefit to agriculture. Attica had few rural slaves. Xenophon's model farm employs slave labor almost entirely, but it is economical with it. Not number but quality was sought; for the difference in productivity between the good and the bad worker was reckoned at nine tenths. Agricultural science already fixed the return to be expected per team of oxen and per worker; each knew exactly how many beasts and men he needed. Among the condemned men whose goods were sold in 415 only one possessed sixteen slaves, and he was a Metic from the Peiræeus, who could not own land. All the others, those whose lands or crops, standing or ingathered, had been confiscated, either had no slaves at all or had one, two, three, or at the most four. In a list of 131 freedmen whose occupations are known there are 62 women, none of whom worked on the land, and 69 men, of whom 9 were farmers (almost all market-gardeners) and 2 vine-growers. A wise landowner did not keep permanently the whole staff needed at the time of the oil-pressing; he took on hired men by the job or the day. They were not always free men, it is true; they were often slaves, but they were hired out. Going from one farm to another, and doing different tasks as the seasons came round, these slaves brought their masters a return which was sufficiently regular to be remunerative. One Arethusios had two men whom he hired out for all agricultural tasks; his own part was confined to making the contracts and drawing his share of their wages. The organization of labor by the hiring of slaves, which did great service in industry, was also applied, but in a limited form, in agriculture.

For industry was what required far the most slaves. The industrial system was such that it could not work without the motive power of slave labor. The division of labor in the crafts required an ever greater variety of manual operations. But for want of machines, "instruments working by themselves" as Aristotle calls them, all the work was done by man power. The slave was an animated tool; a gang of slaves was a machine with men for parts. The more arduous or delicate a task was, the more need it had, failing powerful or ingenious machines, of numerous or skillful slaves. An Athenian could not imagine that any industry could keep going without them.

The smallest craftsman had a few slaves as workmen or at least one slave as mate. Whether the work was done in the workshop, on the site, or at the customer's place, whether the master worked with his men or no, it was to him that the fruit of their labor came. One Athenian who sends mattress-makers to private houses lives on their salaries. In a comedy a mother and daughter have no means of subsistence but the money earned by their slave. A craftsman must be very badly off to say, like Lysias' cripple, "I have a trade which brings me a small income, and I carry it on myself, for I cannot afford a slave to whom I could entrust it."

The building industries employed slaves in the most varied fashion. In the accounts of the Erechtheion we find slaves of all kinds. One is a laborer at a drachma a day. Others are skilled workers, but are told off in case of need to set up or remove scaffolding. The majority work only at their own trade. Out of thirty-five marble workers about twenty are slaves; half of these work with their master, and one is the foreman of a gang. All are paid at the same rate as the free men and their master himself; but, if their pay is entered under their name, it does not follow that they keep it.

Slave labor, extensively used by small employers, held an almost exclusive place in those industries which were organized in workshops and factories. In Socrates' day the miller Nausicydes, the baker Cyrebos, the chiton-maker Demeas, and the cloak-maker Menon made their fortunes without employing one free man. Timarchos owned a shoemaking establishment with workers and foreman of slave condition. The orators tell us of slaves plying the trade of metal-workers, embroiderers, druggists, and perfumers. Sophocles' father had them in his forge and Isocrates' father in his lyre manufactory. On a vase painting the potter is surrounded by slaves whom he threatens or chastises. The patrimony of Demosthenes included a bed factory and an armor works, which were chiefly valuable for the personnel with which they were supplied. Manufactories of shields like those of Cephalos and Pasion owed their importance less to the premises and the stock than to the human machinery. There are abundant examples of the kind from Athens, and they are not lacking from other cities. In Megara dressmaking was done entirely by barbarian labor.

But, though the total number of industrial slaves was large, they were never grouped in masses. There was nothing comparable to the great factory of the present day. The absence of machinery, the necessity for keeping the permanent staff proportionate to the constant, certain demand, the difficulty of keeping effective control over workmen who had not the incentive of pay, everything prevented the concentration of industry and the collection of large bodies of labor. The shoemakers of Timarchos numbered nine or ten, Demosthenes' workshops contained twenty cabinet-makers and thirty-two or thirty-three armorers, and the great factory of Cephalos employed a hundred and twenty men.

The only industries which could employ multitudes of workers were those which required neither vast buildings nor skilled labor, the transport business and the mines. The transport of heavy material needed an enormous train of wagons and oxen; to load the wagons and to drive the beasts at least one man was needed for each team. At Laureion, both for extraction and for smelting, labor was entirely servile. A concession or a workshop was hired, complete with personnel. The normal concession included a gang of thirty miners, but a man could obtain a large number of concessions and employ a whole army of slaves. Nicias hired a thousand to Sosias, Hipponicos hired out six hundred, Philomenides three hundred. When the Spartans occupied Deceleia twenty thousand fugitive slaves came running up to them. Xenophon proposed that the State should buy and let out miners up to ten thousand; the project may be fantastic, but the figure is significant.

To sum up, industrial slavery is inevitably confined within fairly narrow limits. It assumes a certain development only when the division of labor ceases to be rudimentary, and it does not progress beyond a certain point. For the tasks which require only physical strength the number of slaves can always be increased until it is sufficient. But if complicated articles have to be manufactured in quantities, it is indispensable that each man should specialize in one operation, in one motion. This is only possible with machinery, for to turn the human tool into an automatic machine a course of training would be necessary which would cost too much for too little result. Now so long as a society enslaves man power, being ignorant of the use of machine power, it has such opportunity for obtaining plentiful, docile labor that it does not feel the necessity of supplementing it artificially. The absence of machinery is at once the cause and, to a certain extent, the effect of industrial slavery; the result is that slavery is an obstacle to industry and even prevents itself from extending indefinitely.

MOSES I. FINLEY

Was Greek Civilization Based on Slave Labor? [1]

I.

Two generalizations may be made at the outset. First: at all times and in all places the Greek world relied on some form (or forms) of dependent labor to meet its needs, both public and private. By this I mean that dependent labor was essential, in a significant measure, if the requirements of agriculture, trade, manufacture, public works, and war production were to

M. I. Finley, "Was Greek Civilization Based on Slave Labor?" *Historia,* 8 (1959): 145–64.

[1] This is a slightly enlarged and revised version of a paper read at the triennial meeting of the Joint Committee of Greek and Roman Societies in Cambridge on 11 August 1958. No effort has been made to annotate fully or to provide more than a handful of modern references. I am grateful to Professors A. H. M. Jones and M. Postan in Cambridge, and Mr. G. E. M. de Ste. Croix of New College and Mr. P. A. Brunt of Oriel College, Oxford, for much helpful criticism.

be fulfilled. And by dependent labor I mean work performed under compulsions other than those of kinship or communal obligations.[2] Second: with the rarest of exceptions, there were always substantial numbers of free men engaged in productive labor. By this I mean primarily not free hired labor but free men working on their own (or leased) land or in their shops or homes as craftsmen and shopkeepers. It is within the framework created by these two generalizations that the questions must be asked which seek to locate slavery in the society. And by slavery, finally, I mean roughly the status in which a man is, in the eyes of the law and of public opinion and with respect to all other parties, a possession, a chattel, of another man.[3]

How completely the Greeks always took slavery for granted as one of the facts of human existence is abundantly evident to anyone who has read their literature. In the Homeric poems it is assumed (correctly) that captive women will be taken home as slaves, and that occasional male slaves —the victims of Phoenician merchant-pirates—will also be on hand. In the seventh century B.C., when Hesiod, the Boeotian "peasant" poet, gets down to practical advice in his *Works and Days,* he tells his brother how to use slaves properly; that they will be available is simply assumed.[4] The same is true of Xenophon's manual for the gentleman farmer, the *Oeconomicus,* written about 375 B.C. A few years earlier, an Athenian cripple who was appealing a decision dropping him from the dole, said to the Council: "I have a trade which brings me in a little, but I can barely work at it myself and I cannot afford to buy someone to replace myself in it." [5] In the first book of the Pseudo-Aristotelian *Oeconomica,* a Peripatetic work probably of the late fourth or early third century B.C., we find the following proposition about the organization of the household, stated as baldly and flatly as it could possibly be done: "Of property, the first and most necessary kind, the best and most manageable, is man. Therefore the first step is to procure good slaves. Of slaves there are two kinds, the overseer and the worker." [6] Polybius, discussing the strategic situation of

[2] I also exclude the "economic compulsion" of the wage-labor system.

[3] It is obviously not a valid objection to this working definition to point out either that a slave is biologically a man none the less, or that there were usually some pressures to give him a little recognition of his humanity, such as the privilege of asylum or the de facto privilege of marriage.

[4] I believe that the ἔριθος and perhaps the θῆς of ll. 602–3 were slaves, from the context, peculiar as that use of the two words may be. But even if one rejects my interpretation of these two lines, slaves are so repeatedly taken for granted in the poem that it is incorrect to imply a balanced alternative, as does W. L. Westermann, The Slave Systems of Greek and Roman Antiquity (Philadelphia 1955), 4, when he writes: "The peasant of modest means of the type of Hesiod might well have slaves but he also used hired labor."

[5] Lysias 24.6.

[6] Ps.-Aristotle, Oec. 1.5.1,1344a22.

Byzantium, speaks quite casually of "the necessities of life—cattle and slaves" which come from the Black Sea region.[7] And so on.

The Greek language had an astonishing range of vocabulary for slaves, unparalleled in my knowledge.[8] In the earliest texts, Homer and Hesiod, there were two basic words for slave, *dmos* and *doulos,* used without any discoverable distinction between them, and both with uncertain etymologies. *Dmos* died out quickly, surviving only in poetry, whereas *doulos* remained the basic word, so to speak, all through Greek history, and the root on which were built such words as *douleia,* "slavery." But Homer already has, in one probably interpolated passage, the word (in the plural form) *andrapoda,* which became very common, and seems to have been constructed on the model of *tetrapoda.*[9] Still another general word came into use in the Hellenistic period, when *soma* ("body") came to mean "slave" if not otherwise qualified by an adjective.

These words were strictly servile, except in such metaphors as "the Athenians enslaved the allies." But there was still another group which could be used for both slaves and freemen, depending on the context. Three of them are built on the household root, *oikos—oikeus, oiketes,* and *oikiatas*—and the pattern of usage is variegated, complicated, and still largely unexamined. In Crete, for example, *oikeus* seems to have been a technical status term more like "serf" than any other instance known to me in Greek history. It was archaic even in Crete, however, and it dropped out of sight there in post-fifth-century documents. Elsewhere these *oikos-* words sometimes meant merely "servant" or "slave" generically, and sometimes, though less often, they indicated narrower distinctions, such as house-born slave (as against purchased) or privately owned (as against royal in the Hellenistic context).[10]

If we think of ancient society as made up of a spectrum of statuses, with the free citizen at one end and the slave at the other, and with a considerable number of shades of dependence in between, then we have already discovered two lines of the spectrum, the slave and the serf-like *oikeus*

[7] Polyb. 4.38.4.

[8] I am not considering the local helotage words here, although the Greeks themselves customarily called such people "slaves."

[9] Homer, Il. 7.475.

[10] The terminology needs systematic investigation in terms of a range of unfree and semi-free statuses. I have given only some examples. On the regional and dialectal variations, see Erika Kretschmer, "Beiträge zur Wortgeographie der altgr. Dialekte. 1. Diener, Sklave," Glotta XVIII (1930), 71–81. On the interchangeability of the terms in classical Athenian usage, see Siegfried Lauffer, Die Bergwerkssklaven von Laureion (2 vols., Akad. Wiss. Mainz, Abh. Geistes- u. Sozialwiss. Kl. 1955, no. 12; 1956, no. 11), I 1104–8; cf. E. L. Kazakevich, "The Term δοῦλος and the Concept 'Slave' in Athens in the Fourth Century B.C." (in Russian), VDI (1956), no. 3, pp. 119–36, summarized in Bibl. Class. Or. II (1957), 203–205. (A former student, Mr. Jonathan Frankel, kindly abstracted the latter article for me.)

of Crete. At least four more can easily be added: the helot (with such parallels as the *penestes* of Thessaly); the debt-bondsman, who was not a slave although under some conditions he could eventually be sold into slavery abroad; the conditionally manumitted slave; and, finally, the freed-man. All six categories rarely, if ever, appeared concurrently within the same community, nor were they equal in importance or equally significant in all periods of Greek history. By and large, the slave proper was the decisive figure (to the virtual exclusion of the others) in the economically and politically advanced communities; whereas helotage and debt-bondage were to be found in the more archaic communities, whether in Crete or Sparta or Thessaly at an even late date, or in Athens in its pre-Solonian period. There is also some correlation, though by no means a perfect one, between the various categories of dependent labor and their function. Slavery was the most flexible of the forms, adaptable to all kinds and levels of activity, whereas helotage and the rest were best suited to agriculture, pasturage, and household service, much less so to manufacture and trade.

II.

With little exception, there was no activity, productive or unproductive, public or private, pleasant or unpleasant, which was not performed by slaves at some times and in some places in the Greek world. The major exception was, of course, political: no slave held public office or sat on the deliberative and judicial bodies (though slaves were commonly em-ployed in the "civil service," as secretaries and clerks, and as policemen and prison attendants). Slaves did not fight as a rule, either, unless freed (although helots apparently did), and they were very rare in the liberal professions, including medicine. On the other side, there was no activity which was not performed by free men at some times and in some places. That is sometimes denied, but the denial rests on a gross error, namely, the failure to differentiate between a free man working for himself and one working for another, for hire. In the Greek scale of values, the crucial test was not so much the nature of the work (within limits, of course) as the condition or status under which it was carried on.[11] "The condition of the free man," said Aristotle, "is that he does not live under the restraint of another."[12] On this point, Aristotle was expressing a nearly universal Greek notion. Although we find free Greeks doing every kind of work, the free wage-earner, the free man who regularly works *for* another and therefore "lives under the restraint of another" is a rare figure in the sources, and he surely was a minor factor in the picture.[13]

[11] See A. Aymard, "L'idée de travail dans la Grèce archaïque," J. de Psych. XLI (1948), 29–45.

[12] Rhet. 1.9, 1367a32.

[13] This statement is not invalidated by the occasional sally which a smallholder or

The basic economic activity was, of course, agriculture. Throughout Greek history, the overwhelming majority of the population had its main wealth in the land. And the majority were smallholders, depending on their own labor, the labor of other members of the family, and the occasional assistance (as in time of harvest) of neighbours and casual hired hands. Some proportion of these smallholders owned a slave, or even two, but we cannot possibly determine what the proportion was, and in this sector the whole issue is clearly not of the greatest importance. But the large landholders, a minority though they were, constituted the political (and often the intellectual) elite of the Greek world; our evidence reveals remarkably few names of any consequence whose economic base was outside the land. This landholding elite tended to become more and more of an absentee group in the course of Greek history; but early or late, whether they sat on their estates or in the cities, dependent labor worked their land as a basic rule (even when allowance is made for tenancy). In some areas it took the form of helotage, and in the archaic period, of debt-bondage, but generally the form was outright slavery.

I am aware, of course, that this view of slavery in Greek agriculture is now strongly contested. Nevertheless, I accept the evidence of the line of authors whom I have already cited, from Hesiod to the pseudo-Aristotelian *Oeconomica*. These are all matter-of-fact writings, not utopias or speculative statements of what ought to be. If slavery was not the customary labor form on the larger holdings, then I cannot imagine what Hesiod or Xenophon or the Peripatetic were doing, or why any Greek bothered to read their works.[14] One similar piece of evidence is worth adding. There was

---

petty craftsman might make into the labour market to do three days' harvesting or a week's work on temple construction; or by the presence in cities like Athens of a substantial number of men, almost all of them unskilled, who lived on odd jobs (when they were not rowing in the fleet or otherwise occupied by the state), those, for example, who congregated daily at Κολωνὸςμἶσθιος (on which see A. Fuks, in *Eranos* XLIX, 1951, 171–73). Nowhere in the sources do we hear of private establishments employing a staff of hired workers as their normal operation. Public works are frequently adduced as evidence to the contrary, but I believe without sufficient cogency. In the first place, the more common practice seems to have been a contract with an entrepreneur (even if he worked alone), not hire for wages; see P. H. Davis, "The Delian Building Accounts", *Bull. Corr. Hell.* LXI (1937), at pp. 110–20. Second, such evidence as we have—most fully from Delos—argues that such work was spasmodic and infrequent, and quite inconceivable as a source of livelihood for any but a handful of men. All this is consistent with the view that most of the craftsmen appearing in the accounts were independent masons and carpenters who occasionally accepted a job from the state just as they accepted orders from private clients. The key to the whole question is the absence of entrepreneurs whose regular labour force consisted of hired free men.

[14] Scholars who argue that slavery was unimportant in agriculture systematically ignore the *Hausvaterliteratur* and similar evidence, while trying to prove their case partly by weak arguments from silence (on which see G. E. M. de Ste. Croix in *Class. Rev.*, n. s. VII, 1957, p. 56), and partly by reference to the papyri. One

a Greek harvest festival called the Kronia, which was celebrated in Athens and other places (especially among the Ionians). One feature, says the Atthidographer Philochorus, was that "the heads of families ate the crops and fruits at the same table with their slaves, with whom they had shared the labors of cultivation. For the god is pleased with this honor from the slaves in contemplation of their labors." [15] Neither the practice nor Philochorus' explanation of it makes any sense whatever if slavery was as unimportant in agriculture as some modern writers pretend.

I had better be perfectly clear here: I am not saying that slaves outnumbered free men in agriculture, or that the bulk of farming was done by slaves, but that slavery dominated agriculture insofar as it was on a scale that transcended the labor of the householder and his sons. Nor am I suggesting that there was no hired free labor; rather that there was little of any significance. Among the slaves, furthermore, were the overseers, invariably so if the property was large enough or if the owner was an absentee. "Of slaves," said the author of the *Oeconomica,* "there are two kinds, the overseer and the worker."

In mining and quarrying the situation was decisively one-sided. There were free men, in Athens for example, who leased such small mining concessions that they were able to work them alone. The moment, however, additional labor was introduced (and that was the more common case), it seems normally to have been slave. The largest individual holdings of slaves in Athens were workers in the mines, topped by the one thousand reported to have been leased out for this purpose by the fifth-century general Nicias.[16] It has been suggested, indeed, that at one point there may have been as many as thirty thousand slaves at work in the Athenian silver mines and processing mills.[17]

Manufacture was like agriculture in that the choice was (even more exclusively) between the independent craftsman working alone or with members of his family and the owner of slaves. The link with slavery was so close (and the absence of free hired labor so complete) that Demosthenes, for example, could say "they caused the *ergasterion* to disappear" and then he could follow, as an exact synonym and with no possible misunderstanding, by saying that "they caused the slaves to disappear." [18] On the other hand, the proportion of operations employing slaves, as against the inde-

---

cannot protest strongly enough against the latter procedure, since the agricultural regime in Ptolemaic and Roman Egypt was not Greek; see M. Rostovtzeff, The Social & Economic History of the Hellenistic World (3 vols., Oxford, repr. 1953), I 272–77.

[15] Philochorus 328 F 97, ap. Macrob. Sat. 1.10.22.

[16] Xenophon, Poroi 4.14.

[17] See Lauffer, op. cit., II 904–16.

[18] Dem. 27.19,26; 28.12; see Finley, Studies in Land and Credit in Ancient Athens (New Brunswick 1952), 67. For another decisive text, see Xen. Memorab. 2.7.6.

pendent self-employed craftsmen, was probably greater than in agriculture, and in this respect more like mining. In commerce and banking, subordinates were invariably slaves, even in such posts as "bank manager." However, the numbers were small.

In the domestic field, finally, we can take it as a rule that any free man who possibly could afford one, owned a slave attendant who accompanied him when he walked abroad in the town or when he travelled (including his military service), and also a slave woman for the household chores. There is no conceivable way of estimating how many such free men there were, or how many owned numbers of domestics, but the fact is taken for granted so completely and so often in the literature that I strongly believe that many owned slaves even when they could not afford them. (Modern parallels will come to mind readily.) I stress this for two reasons. First, the need for domestic slaves, often an unproductive element, should serve as a cautionary sign when one examines such questions as the efficiency and cost of slave labor. Second, domestic slavery was by no means entirely unproductive. In the countryside in particular, but also in the towns, two important industries would often be in their hands in the larger households, on a straight production for household consumption basis. I refer to baking and textile making, and every medievalist, at least, will at once grasp the significance of the withdrawal of the latter from market production, even if the withdrawal was far from complete.[19]

It would be very helpful if we had some idea how many slaves there were in any given Greek community to carry on all this work, and how they were divided among the branches of the economy. Unfortunately we have no reliable figures, and none at all for most of the *poleis*. What I consider to be the best computations for Athens suggest that the total of slaves reached 80–100,000 in peak periods in the fifth and fourth centuries B.C.[20] Athens had the largest population in the classical Greek world and the largest number of slaves. Thucydides said that there were more slaves in his day on the island of Chios than in any other Greek community except Sparta,[21] but I suggest that he was thinking of the density of the slave population measured against the free, not of absolute totals (and in Sparta he meant the helots, not chattel slaves). Other places, such as Aegina or Corinth, may at one time or another also have had a higher ratio of slaves than Athens. And there were surely communities in which the slaves were less dense.

More than that we can scarcely say about the numbers, but I think that

[19] On the importance of the domestic slave as nursemaid and pedagogue, see Joseph Vogt's rectoral address, "Wege zur Menschlichkeit in der antiken Sklaverei", Univ. Tübingen Reden XLVII (1958), 19–38. (Dr. V. Ehrenberg kindly called my attention to this publication.)
[20] Lauffer, op. cit., II 904–16.
[21] Thuc. 8.40.2.

is really enough. There is too much tendentious discussion of numbers in the literature already, as if a mere count of heads is the answer to all the complicated questions which flow from the existence of slavery. The Athenian figures I mentioned amount to an average of no less than three or four slaves to each free household (including all free men in the calculation, whether citizen or not). But even the smallest figure anyone has suggested, twenty thousand slaves in Demosthenes' time [22]—altogether too low in my opinion—would be roughly equivalent to one slave for each adult citizen, no negligible ratio. Within very broad limits, the numbers are irrelevant to the question of significance. When Starr, for example, objects to "exaggerated guesses" and replies that "the most careful estimates . . . reduce the proportion of slaves to far less than half the population, probably one third or one quarter at most," [23] he is proving far less than he thinks. No one seriously believes that slaves did all the work in Athens (or anywhere else in Greece except for Sparta with its helots), and one merely confuses the issues when one pretends that somehow a reduction of the estimates to only a third or a quarter of the population is crucial.[24] In 1860, according to official census figures, slightly less than one third of the total population of the American slave states were slaves. Furthermore, "nearly three-fourths of all free Southerners had no connection with slavery through either family ties or direct ownership. The 'typical' Southerner was not only a small farmer but also a nonslaveholder." [25] Yet no one would think of denying that slavery was a decisive element in southern society. The analogy seems obvious for ancient Greece, where, it can be shown, ownership of slaves was even more widely spread among the free men and the use of slaves much more diversified, and where the estimates do not give a ratio significantly below the American one. Simply stated, there can be no denial that there were enough slaves about for them to be, of necessity, an integral factor in the society.

There were two main sources of supply. One was captives, the victims of war and sometimes piracy. One of the few generalizations about the ancient world to which there is no exception is this, that the victorious power had absolute right over the persons and the property of the vanquished.[26] This right was not exercised to its full extent every time, but

[22] A. H. M. Jones, Athenian Democracy (Oxford 1957), 76–79; cf. his "Slavery in the Ancient World", Econ. Hist. Rev., 2nd ser., IX (1956), at p. 187.

[23] C. G. Starr, "An Overdose of Slavery", J. Econ. Hist. XVIII (1958), at pp. 21–22.

[24] It is remarkable how completely Starr misses this point in his very belligerent article. Although he says over and over again that slavery was not "dominant" or "basic" in antiquity, I can find no serious argument in his article other than his disproof of the view that slaves did all the work.

[25] Kenneth M. Stampp, The Peculiar Institution: Slavery in the Ante-Bellum South (New York 1956), 29–30.

[26] See A. Aymard, "Le partage des profits de la guerre dans les traités d'alliance antiques," Rev. hist. CCXVII (1957), 233–49.

it was exercised often enough, and on a large enough scale, to throw a continuous and numerous supply of men, women, and children on to the slave market. Alongside the captives we must place the so-called barbarians who came into the Greek world in a steady stream—Thracians, Scythians, Cappadocians, etc.—through the activity of full-time traders, much like the process by which African slaves reached the new world in more modern times. Many were the victims of wars among the barbarians themselves. Others came peacefully, so to speak: Herodotus says that the Thracians sold their children for export.[27] The first steps all took place outside the Greek orbit, and our sources tell us virtually nothing about them, but there can be no doubt that large numbers and a steady supply were involved, for there is no other way to explain such facts as the high proportion of Paphlagonians and Tracians among the slaves in the Attic silver mines, many of them specialists, or the corps of three hundred Scythian archers (slaves owned by the state) who constituted the Athenian police force.

Merely to complete the picture, we must list penal servitude and the exposure of unwanted children. Beyond mere mention, however, they can be ignored because they were altogether negligible in their importance. There then remains one more source, breeding, and that is a puzzle. One reads in the modern literature that there was very little breeding of slaves (as distinct from helots and the like) among the Greeks because, under their conditions, it was cheaper to buy slaves than to raise them. I am not altogether satisfied with the evidence for this view, and I am altogether dissatisfied with the economics which is supposed to justify it. There were conditions under which breeding was certainly rare, but for reasons which have nothing to do with economics. In the mines, for example, nearly all the slaves were men, and that is the explanation, simply enough. But what about domestics, among whom the proportion of women was surely high? I must leave the question unanswered, except to remove one fallacy. It is sometimes said that there is a demographic law that no slave population ever reproduces itself, that they must always be replenished from outside. Such a law is a myth: that can be said categorically on the evidence of the southern states, evidence which is statistical and reliable.

III.

The impression one gets is clearly that the majority of the slaves were foreigners. In a sense, they were all foreigners. That is to say, it was the rule (apart from debt bondage) that Athenians were never kept as slaves in Athens, or Corinthians in Corinth. However, I am referring to the more basic sense, that the majority were not Greeks at all, but men and women

[27] Herod. 5.6.

from the races living outside the Greek world. It is idle to speculate about proportions here, but there cannot be any reasonable doubt about the majority. In some places, such as the Laurium silver mines in Attica, this meant relatively large concentrations in a small area. The number of Thracian slaves in Laurium in Xenophon's time, for example, was greater than the total population of some of the smaller Greek city-states.

No wonder some Greeks came to identify slaves and barbarians (a synonym for all non-Greeks). The most serious effort, so far as we know, to justify this view as part of the natural arrangement of things, will be found in the first book of Aristotle's *Politics*. It was not a successful effort for several reasons, of which the most obvious is the fact, as Aristotle himself conceded, that too many were slaves "by accident," by the chance of warfare or shipwreck or kidnapping. In the end, natural slavery was abandoned as a concept, defeated by the pragmatic view that slavery was a fact of life, a conventional institution universally practised. As the Roman jurist Florentinus phrased it, "Slavery is an institution of the *ius gentium* whereby someone is subject to the *dominium* of another, contrary to nature." [28] That view (and even sharper formulations) can be traced back to the sophistic literature of the fifth century B.C., and, in a less formal way, to Greek tragedy. I chose Florentinus to quote instead because his definition appears in the *Digest,* in which slavery is so prominent that the Roman law of slavery has been called "the most characteristic part of the most characteristic intellectual product of Rome." [29] Nothing illustrates more perfectly the inability of the ancient world to imagine that there could be a civilized society without slaves.

The Greek world was one of endless debate and challenge. Among the intellectuals, no belief or idea was self-evident: every conception and every institution sooner or later came under attack—religious beliefs, ethical values, political systems, aspects of the economy, even such bedrock institutions as the family and private property. Slavery, too, up to a point, but that point was invariably a good distance short of abolitionist proposals. Plato, who criticized society more radically than any other thinker, did not concern himself much with the question in the *Republic,* but even there he assumed the continuance of slavery. And in the *Laws,* "the number of passages . . . that deal with slavery is surprisingly large" and the tenor of the legislation is generally more severe than the actual law of Athens at that time. "Their effect, on the one hand, is to give greater authority to masters in the exercise of rule over slaves, and on the other hand to accentuate the distinction between slave and free man." [30] Paradoxically,

---

[28] Dig. 1.5.4.1.

[29] W. W. Buckland, The Roman Law of Slavery (Cambridge 1908), v.

[30] Glenn R. Morrow, Plato's Law of Slavery in Its Relation to Greek Law (Univ. of Illinois Press 1939), 11 and 127. Morrow effectively disproves the view that

neither were the believers in the brotherhood of man (whether Cynic, Stoic, or early Christian) opponents of slavery. In their eyes, all material concerns, including status, were a matter of essential indifference. Diogenes, it is said, was once seized by pirates and taken to Crete to be sold. At the auction, he pointed to a certain Corinthian among the buyers and said: "Sell me to him; he needs a master." [31]

The question must then be faced, how much relevance has all this for the majority of Greeks, for those who were neither philosophers nor wealthy men of leisure? What did the little man think about slavery? It is no answer to argue that we must not take "the political theorists of the philosophical schools too seriously as having established 'the main line of Greek thought concerning slavery'." [32] No one pretends that Plato and Aristotle speak for all Greeks. But, equally, no one should pretend that lower-class Greeks necessarily rejected everything which we read in Greek literature and philosophy, simply because, with virtually no exceptions, the poets and philosophers were men of the leisure class. The history of ideology and belief is not so simple. It is a commonplace that the little man shares the ideals and aspirations of his betters—in his dreams if not in the hard reality of his daily life. By and large, the vast majority in all periods of history have always taken the basic institutions of society for granted. Men do not, as a rule, ask themselves whether monogamous marriage or a police force or machine production is necessary to their way of life. They accept them as facts, as self-evident. Only when there is a challenge from one source or another—from outside or from catastrophic famine or plague —do such facts become questions.

A large section of the Greek population was always on the edge of marginal subsistence. They worked hard for their livelihood and could not look forward to economic advancement as a reward for their labors; on the contrary, if they moved at all, it was likely to be downward. Famines, plagues, wars, political struggles, all were a threat, and social crisis was a common enough phenomenon in Greek history. Yet through the centuries no ideology of labor appeared, nothing that can in any sense be counterposed to the negative judgments with which the writings of the leisure class are filled. There was neither a word in the Greek language with which to express the general notion of "labor," nor the concept of

---

"Plato at heart disapproved of slavery and in introducing it into the *Laws* was simply accommodating himself to his age" (pp. 129–30.) Cf. G. Vlastos, "Slavery in Plato's Thought", *Philos. Rev.* L (1941), 293: "There is not the slightest indication, either in the *Republic,* or anywhere else, that Plato means to obliterate or relax in any way" the distinction between slave and free labour.

[31] Diogenes Laertius 6.74. On the Cynics, Stoics, and Christians, see Westermann, op. cit., pp. 24–25, 39–40, 116–17, 149–59.

[32] Westermann, op. cit., p. 14 n. 48.

labor "as a general social function." [33] There was plenty of grumbling, of course, and there was pride of craftmanship. Men could not survive psychologically without them. But neither developed into a belief: grumbling was not turned into a punishment for sin—"In the sweat of thy face shalt thou eat bread"—nor pride of craftsmanship into the virtue of labor, into the doctrine of the calling or anything comparable. The nearest to either will be found in Hesiod's *Works and Days,* and in this context the decisive fact about Hesiod is his unquestioning assumption that the farmer will have proper slave labor.

That was all there was to the poor man's counter-ideology: we live in the iron age when "men never rest from toil and sorrow by day, and from perishing by night"; therefore it is better to toil than to idle and perish—but if we can we too will turn to the labor of slaves. Hesiod may not have been able, even in his imagination, to think beyond slavery as *supplementary* to his own labor, but that was the seventh century, still the early days of slavery. About 400 B.C., however, Lysias' cripple could make the serious argument in the Athenian *boule* that he required a dole because he could not afford a slave as a *replacement*.[34] And half a century later Xenophon put forth a scheme whereby every citizen could be maintained by the state, chiefly from revenues to be derived from publicly owned slaves working in the mines.[35]

When talk turned to action, even when crisis turned into civil war and revolution, slavery remained unchallenged. With absolute regularity, all through Greek history, the demand was "Cancel debts and redistribute the land." Never, to my knowledge, do we hear a protest from the free poor, not even in the deepest crises, against slave competition. There are no complaints—as there might well have been—that slaves deprive free men of a livelihood, or compel free men to work for lower wages and longer hours.[36] There is nothing remotely resembling a workers' programme, no wage demands, no talk of working conditions or government employment measures or the like. In a city like Athens there was ample opportunity.

---

[33] See J. P. Vernant, "Prométhée et la fonction technique", J. de Psych. XLV (1952), 419–29; "Travail et nature dans la Grèce ancienne", J. de Psych. LII (1955), 18–38.

[34] Lys. 24.6: τὸν διαδεξ ὁμενον δ'αὐτὴν οὔπω δύναμαι χτήσασθαι.

[35] Xen. Poroi 4.33; cf. 6.1. The best examples of Utopian dreaming in this direction are, of course, provided by Aristophanes, in Eccl. 651–61 and Plut. 510–26, but I refrain from stressing them because I wish to avoid the long argument about slavery in Attic comedy.

[36] This generalization stands despite an isolated (and confused) passage like Timaeus 566 F 11, ap. Athen. 6.264D, 272B, about Aristotle's friend Mnason. Periander's prohibition of slave ownership (Nicolaus of Damascus 90 F 58) sounds like another of the traditional tyrant's measures designed (as Nicolaus suggests) to keep the citizens of Corinth occupied. If there is any truth in it, the "slaves" may actually have been debt-bondsmen, for the background of Periander's programme was an archaic rural one; see Édouard Will, Korinthiaka (Paris 1955), 510–12.

The *demos* had power, enough of them were poor, and they had leaders. But economic assistance took the form of pay for public office and for rowing in the fleet, free admission to the theatre (the so-called theoric fund), and various doles; while economic legislation was restricted to imports and exports, weights and measures, price controls.[37] Not even the wildest of the accusations against the demagogues—and they were wholly unrestrained as every reader of Aristophanes or Plato knows—ever suggested anything which would hint at a working-class interest, or an anti-slavery bias. No issue of free versus slave appears in this field of public activity.[38]

Nor did the free poor take the other possible tack of joining with the slaves in a common struggle on a principled basis. The Solonic revolution in Athens at the beginning of the sixth century B.C., for example, brought an end to debt bondage and the return of Athenians who had been sold into slavery abroad, but not the emancipation of others, non-Athenians, who were in slavery in Athens. Centuries later, when the great wave of slave revolts came after 140 B.C., starting in the Roman west and spreading to the Greek east, the free poor on the whole simply stood apart. It was no issue of theirs, they seem to have thought; correctly so, for the outcome of the revolts promised them nothing one way or the other. Numbers of free men may have taken advantage of the chaos to enrich themselves personally, by looting or otherwise. Essentially that is what they did, when the opportunity arose, in a military campaign, nothing more. The slaves were, in a basic sense, irrelevant to their behavior at that moment.[39]

In 464 B.C. a great helot revolt broke out, and in 462 Athens dispatched a hoplite force under Cimon to help the Spartans suppress it. When the revolt ended, after nearly five years, a group of the rebels were permitted to escape, and it was Athens which provided them refuge, settling them in Naupactus. A comparable shift took place in the first phase of the Peloponnesian War. In 425 the Athenians seized Pylos, a harbor on the west coast of the Peloponnese. The garrison was a small one and Pylos was by no means an important port. Nevertheless, Sparta was so frightened that she soon sued for peace, because the Athenian foothold was a dangerous centre

[37] There is, of course, the argument of Plutarch, Pericles 12.4–5, that the great temple-building activity in fifth-century Athens was a calculated make-work programme. I know of no similar statement in contemporary sources, and the notion is significantly missing in Aristotle, Ath. Pol. 24.3. But even if Plutarch is right, public works at best provided supplementary income (see n. 13) and they made use of slave labour, thus serving as further evidence for my argument. Nor could Plutarch's thesis be applied to many cities (if any) other than Athens.

[38] I doubt if any point can be made in this context of the fact that citizens and slaves worked side by side in the fields and workshops and on public works, or that they sometimes belonged to the same cult associations. Such phenomena are widespread wherever slavery existed, including the American South.

[39] See Joseph Vogt, Struktur der antiken Sklavenkriege (Mainz Abh. 1957, no. 1), 53–57; cf. E. A. Thompson, "Peasant Revolts in Late Roman Gaul and Spain", Past & Present, no. 2 (1952), 11–23.

of infection, inviting desertion and eventual revolt among the Messenian helots. Athens finally agreed to peace in 421, and immediately afterwards concluded an alliance with Sparta, one of the terms of which was "Should the slave-class rise in rebellion, the Athenians will assist the Lacedaemonians with all their might, according to their power." [40]

Obviously the attitude of one city to the slaves of another lies largely outside our problem. Athens agreed to help suppress helots when she and Sparta were allies; she encouraged helot revolts when they were at war. That reflects elementary tactics, not a judgment about slavery. Much the same kind of distinction must be made in the instances, recurring in Spartan history, when helots were freed as pawns in an internal power struggle. So, too, of the instances which were apparently not uncommon in fourth-century Greece, but about which nothing concrete is known other than the clause in the agreement between Alexander and the Hellenic League, binding the members to guarantee that "there shall be no killing or banishment contrary to the laws of each city, no confiscation of property, no redistribution of land, no cancellation of debts, no freeing of slaves for purposes of revolution." [41] These were mere tactics again. Slaves were resources, and they could be useful in a particular situation. But only a number of specific slaves, those who were available at the precise moment; not slaves in general, or all slaves, and surely not slaves in the future. Some slaves were freed, but slavery remained untouched. Exactly the same behavior can be found in the reverse case, when a state (or ruling class) called upon its slaves to help protect it. Often enough in a military crisis, slaves were freed, conscripted into the army or navy, and called upon to fight.[42] And again the result was that some slaves were freed while the institution continued exactly as before.

In sum, under certain conditions of crisis and tension the society (or a sector of it) was faced with a conflict within its system of values and beliefs. It was sometimes necessary, in the interest of national safety or of a political programme, to surrender the normal use of, and approach to,

---

[40] The relevant passages in Thucydides are 4.41, 55, 80; 5.14; 5.23.3; 7.26.2. The "slave-class" (ἡ δουλεία) here meant the helots, of course. In my text in the pages which follow immediately (on slaves in war), I also say "slaves" to include the helots, ignoring for the moment the distinction between them.

[41] Ps.-Demosthenes 17.15. For earlier periods, cf. Herod. 7.155 on Syracuse and Thuc. 3.73 on Corcyra (and note that Thucydides does not return to the point or generalize about it in his final peroration on *stasis* and its evils).

[42] See the material assembled by Louis Robert, Etudes épigraphiques et philologiques (Bibl. Éc. Hautes Ét. 272, Paris 1938), 118–26. Xenophon, Poroi 4.42, uses the potential value of slaves as military and naval manpower as an argument in favour of his proposal to have the state buy thousands of slaves to be hired out in the mines. Cf. Hypereides' proposal after Chaeronea to free all the Athenian slaves and arm them (see fragments of his speech against Aristogeiton, Blass no. 18, and Ps.-Plut., Hyper. 848F–849A).

slaves. When this happened, the institution itself survived without any noticeable weakening. The fact that it happened is not without significance; it suggests that among the Greeks, even in Sparta, there was not that deep-rooted and often neurotic horror of the slaves known in some other societies, which would have made the freeing and arming of slaves en masse, for whatever purpose, a virtual impossibility. It suggests, further, something about the slaves themselves. Some did fight for their masters, and that is not unimportant.

Nothing is more elusive than the psychology of the slave. Even when, as in the American South, there seems to be a lot of material—autobiographies of ex-slaves, impressions of travellers from non-slaveholding societies, and the like—no reliable picture emerges.[43] For antiquity there is scarcely any evidence at all, and the bits are indirect and tangential, and far from easy to interpret. Thus, a favorite apology is to invoke the fact that, apart from very special instances as in Sparta, the record shows neither revolts of slaves nor a fear of uprisings. Even if the facts are granted—and the nature of our sources warrants a little scepticism—the rosy conclusion does not follow. Slaves have scarcely ever revolted, even in the southern states.[44] A large-scale rebellion is impossible to organize and carry through except under very unusual circumstances. The right combination appeared but once in ancient history, during two generations of the late Roman Republic, when there were great concentrations of slaves in Italy and Sicily, many of them almost completely unattended and unguarded, many others professional fighters (gladiators), and when the whole society was in turmoil, with a very marked breakdown of social and moral values.[45]

At this point it is necessary to recall that helots differed in certain key respects from chattel slaves. First, they had the necessary ties of solidarity that come from kinship and nationhood, intensified by the fact, not to be underestimated, that they were not foreigners but a subject people working their own lands in a state of servitude. This complex was lacking among the slaves of the Greek world. The Peripatetic author of the *Oeconomica* made the sensible recommendation that neither an individual nor a city should have many slaves of the same nationality.[46] Second, the helots had property rights of a kind: the law, at least, permitted them to retain everything they produced beyond the fixed deliveries to their masters. Third, they outnumbered the free population on a scale without parallel in other Greek communities. These are the peculiar factors, in

---

[43] See Stampp, op. cit., pp. 86–88.
[44] Ibid., pp. 132–40.
[45] Vogt, Sklavenkrieg.
[46] Ps.-Arist., Oec. 1.5, 1344b18; cf. Plato, Laws 6.777C–D; Arist., Pol. 7.9.9, 1330a 25–28.

my opinion, which explain the revolts of the helots and the persistent Spartan concern with the question, more than Spartan cruelty.[47] It is a fallacy to think that the threat of rebellion increases automatically with an increase in misery and oppression. Hunger and torture destroy the spirit; at most they stimulate efforts at flight or other forms of purely individual behavior (including betrayal of fellow-victims), whereas revolt requires organization and courage and persistence. Frederick Douglass, who in 1855 wrote the most penetrating analysis to come from an ex-slave, summed up the psychology in these words:

"Beat and cuff your slave, keep him hungry and spiritless, and he will follow the chain of his master like a dog; but feed and clothe him well,— work him moderately—surround him with physical comfort,—and dreams of freedom intrude. Give him a *bad* master, and he aspires to a *good* master; give him a good master, and he wishes to become his *own* master." [48]

There are many ways, other than revolt, in which slaves can protest.[49] In particular they can flee, and though we have no figures whatsoever, it seems safe to say that the fugitive slave was a chronic and sufficiently numerous phenomenon in the Greek cities.[50] Thucydides estimated that more than twenty thousand Athenian slaves fled in the final decade of the Peloponnesian War. In this they were openly encouraged by the Spartan garrison established in Decelea, and Thucydides makes quite a point of the operation. Obviously he thought the harm to Athens was serious, intensified by the fact that many were skilled workers.[51] My immediate concern is with the slaves themselves, not with Athens, and I should stress very heavily that so many skilled slaves (who must be presumed to have been, on the average, among the best treated) took the risk and tried to flee. The risk was no light one, at least for the barbarians among them: no Thracian or Carian wandering about the Greek countryside without credentials could be sure of what lay ahead in Boeotia or Thessaly. Indeed, there is a hint that these particular twenty thousand and more may have been very badly treated after escaping under Spartan promise. A reliable fourth-century

[47] Note that Thucydides 8.40.2 makes the disproportionately large number of Chian slaves the key to their ill-treatment and their readiness to desert to the Athenians.

[48] My Bondage and My Freedom (New York 1855), 263–64, quoted from Stampp, op. cit., p. 89.

[49] Stampp, op. cit., ch. III: "A Troublesome Property", should be required reading on this subject.

[50] I am prepared to say this despite the fact that the evidence is scrappy and has not, to my knowledge, been properly assembled. For mass flights in time of war, see e.g., Thuc. 7.75.5; 8.40.2.

[51] Note how Thucydides stressed the loss in anticipation (1.142.4; 6.91.7) before actually reporting it in 7.27.5.

historian attributed the great Theban prosperity at the end of the fifth century to their having purchased very cheaply the slaves and other booty seized from the Athenians during the Spartan occupation of Decelea.[52] Although there is no way to determine whether this a reference to the twenty thousand, the suspicion is obvious. Ethics aside, there was no power, within or without the law, which could have prevented the re-enslavement of fugitive slaves even if they had been promised their freedom.

The *Oeconomica* sums up the life of the slave as consisting of three elements: work, punishment, and food.[53] And there are more than enough flogging and even tortures, in Greek literature, from one end to the other. Apart from psychological quirks (sadism and the like), flogging means simply that the slave, as slave, must be goaded into performing the function assigned to him. So, too, do the various incentive plans which were frequently adopted. The efficient, skilled, reliable slave could look forward to managerial status. In the cities, in particular, he could often achieve a curious sort of quasi independence, living and working on his own, paying a kind of rental to his owner, and accumulating earnings with which, ultimately, to purchase his freedom. Manumission was, of course, the greatest incentive of all. Again we are baffled by the absence of numbers, but it is undisputed that manumission was a common phenomenon in most of the Greek world. This is an important difference between the Greek slave on the one hand, and the helot or American slave on the other. It is also important evidence about the degree of the slave's alleged "acceptance" of his status.[54]

IV.

It is now time to try to add all this up and form some judgment about the institution. This would be difficult enough to do under ordinary circumstances. It has become almost impossible because of two extraneous factors imposed by modern society. The first is the confusion of the historical study with moral judgments about slavery. We condemn slavery, and we are embarrassed for the Greeks, whom we admire so much; therefore we tend either to underestimate its role in their life, or we ignore it altogether, hoping that somehow it will quietly go away. The second factor is more political, and it goes back at least to 1848, when the

[52] Hellenica Oxyrhynchia 12.4.

[53] Ps.-Arist., Oec. 1.5,1344ª35.

[54] The technical and aesthetic excellence of much work performed by slaves is, of course, visible in innumerable museums and archaeological sites. This is part of the complexity and ambiguity of the institution (discussed in the following section), which extended to the slaves themselves as well as to their masters.

Communist Manifesto declared that "The history of all hitherto existing society is the history of class struggles. Free man and slave, patrician and plebeian, lord and serf, guild-master and journeyman, in a word oppressor and oppressed, stood in constant opposition to one another. . . ." Ever since, ancient slavery has been a battleground between Marxists and non-Marxists, a political issue rather than a historical phenomenon.

Now we observe that a sizable fraction of the population of the Greek world consisted of slaves, or other kinds of dependent labor, many of them barbarians; that by and large the elite in each city-state were men of leisure, completely free from any preoccupation with economic matters, thanks to a labor force which they bought and sold, over whom they had extensive property rights, and, equally important, what we may call physical rights; that the condition of servitude was one which no man, woman, or child, regardless of status or wealth, could be sure to escape in case of war or some other unpredictable and uncontrollable emergency. It seems to me that, seeing all this, if we could emancipate ourselves from the despotism of extraneous moral, intellectual, and political pressures, we would conclude, without hesitation, that slavery was a basic element in Greek civilization.

Such a conclusion, however, should be the starting-point of analysis, not the end of an argument, as it is so often at present. Perhaps it would be best to avoid the word "basic" altogether, because it has been pre-empted as a technical term by the Marxist theory of history. Anyone else who uses it in such a question as the one which is the title of this paper, is compelled, by the intellectual (and political) situation in which we work, to qualify the term at once, to distinguish between *a* basic institution and *the* basic institution. In effect what has happened is that, in the guise of a discussion of ancient slavery, there has been a desultory discussion of Marxist theory, none of it, on either side, particularly illuminating about either Marxism or slavery. Neither our understanding of the historical process nor our knowledge of ancient society is significantly advanced by these repeated statements and counter-statements, affirmations and denials of the proposition, "Ancient society was based on slave labor." Nor have we gained much from the persistent debate about causes. Was slavery the cause of the decline of Greek science? or of loose sexual morality? or of the widespread contempt for gainful employment? These are essentially false questions, imposed by a naive kind of pseudo-scientific thinking.

The most fruitful approach, I suggest, is to think in terms of purpose, in Immanuel Kant's sense, or of function, as the social anthropologists use that concept. The question which is most promising for systematic investigation is not whether slavery was the basic element, or whether it caused this or that, but how it functioned.[55] This eliminates the sterile attempts to decide which was historically prior, slavery or something else; it avoids imposing moral judgments on, and prior to, the historical analysis; and it should avoid the trap which I shall call the free-will error. There is a maxim of Emile Durkheim's that "The voluntary character of a practice or an institution should never be assumed beforehand." [56] Given the existence of slavery—and it is given, for our sources do not permit us to go back to a stage in Greek history when it did not exist—the choice facing individual Greeks was socially and psychologically imposed. In the *Memorabilia* Xenophen says that "those who can do so buy slaves so that they may have fellow workers." [57] That sentence is often quoted to prove that some Greeks owned no slaves, which needs no proof. It is much better cited to prove that *those who can,* buy slaves—Xenophon clearly places this whole phenomenon squarely in the realm of necessity.

The question of function permits no single answer. There are as many answers as there are contexts: function in relation to what? And when? And where? Buckland begins his work on the Roman law of slavery by noting that there "is scarcely a problem which can present itself, in any branch of law, the solution of which may not be affected by the fact that one of the parties to the transaction is a slave." [58] That sums up the situation in its simplest, most naked form, and it is as correct a statement for Greek law as for Roman. Beyond that, I would argue, there is no problem or practice in any branch of Greek life which was not affected, in some fashion, by the fact that many people in that society, even if not in the specific situation under consideration, were (or had been) slaves. The connection was not always simple or direct, nor was the impact necessarily "bad" (or "good"). The historian's problem is precisely to uncover what the connections were, in all their concreteness and complexity, their goodness or badness or moral neutrality.

I think we will find that, more often than not, the institution of slavery turned out to be ambiguous in its function. Certainly the Greek attitudes to it were shot through with ambiguity, and not rarely with tension. To the Greeks, Nietzsche said, both labor and slavery were "a necessary disgrace, of which one feels *ashamed,* as a disgrace and as a necessity at

---

[55] Cf. Vogt, "Wege zur Menschlichkeit", pp. 19–20: "What we lack is a clear picture of the functions maintained by slavery in the organism of ancient society, and a critical evaluation of its role in the rise, development, and decline of the culture."

[56] E. Durkheim, The Rules of Sociological Method, transl. from 8th ed. (repr. Glencoe Ill., 1950), 28.

[57] Xen., Mem. 2.3.3.

[58] Op. cit., p. v.

the same time." [59] There was a lot of discussion: that is clear from the literature which has survived, and it was neither easy nor unequivocally one-sided, even though it did not end in abolitionism. In Roman law "slavery is the only case in which, in the extant sources. . . ., a conflict is declared to exist between the *Ius Gentium* and the *Ius Naturale*." [60] In a sense, that was an academic conflict, since slavery went right on; but no society can carry such a conflict within it, around so important a set of beliefs and institutions, without the stresses erupting in some fashion no matter how remote and extended the lines and connections may be from the original stimulus. Perhaps the most interesting sign among the Greeks can be found in the proposals, and to an extent the practice in the fourth century B.C., to give up the enslavement of Greeks.[61] They all came to nought in the Hellenistic world, and I suggest that this one fact reveals much about Greek civilization after Alexander.[62]

It is worth calling attention to two examples pregnant with ambiguity, neither of which has received the attention it deserves. The first comes from Locris, the Greek colony in southern Italy, where descent was matrilineal, an anomaly which Aristotle explained historically. The reason, he said, was that the colony was originally founded by slaves and their children by free women. Timaeus wrote a violent protest against this insulting account, and Polybius, in turn, defended Aristotle in a long digression, of which unfortunately only fragments survive. One of his remarks is particularly worth quoting: "To suppose, with Timaeus, that it was unlikely that men, who had been the slaves of the allies of the Lacedaemonians, would continue the kindly feelings and adopt the friendships of their late masters is foolish. For when they have had the good fortune to recover their freedom, and a certain time has elapsed, men, who have been slaves, not only endeavour to adopt the friendships of their late masters, but also their ties of hospitality and blood; in fact, their aim is to keep them up even more than the ties of nature, for the express purpose of thereby wiping out the remembrance of their former degradation and humble position, because they wish to pose as the descendants of their masters rather than as their freedmen." [63]

---

[59] The Greek State: Preface to an Unwritten Book, in Early Greek Philosophy & Other Essays, transl. by M. A. Mügge (London & Edinburgh 1911), 6.

[60] Buckland, op. cit., p. 1.

[61] See F. Kiechle, "Zur Humanität in der Kriegführung der griechischen Staaten", Historia VII (1958), 129–56, for a useful collection of materials, often vitiated by a confusion between a fact and a moralizing statement; and even more by special pleading of a familiar tendency, as in the argument (p. 140 n. 1) that reports of mass enslavement or massacre must not be taken too literally because some always managed to escape, or in the pointless discussion (pp. 150–53) of the supposed significance of Polybius' use of ἀναγχάζουσιν instead of κελεύουσιν in 5.11.3.

[62] See Rostovtzeff, op. cit. I 201–208.

[63] Polyb. 12.6a (transl. by E. S. Shuckburgh).

In the course of his polemic Timaeus had said that "it was not customary for the Greeks of early times to be served by bought slaves." [64] This distinction, between slaves who were bought and slaves who were captured (or bred from captives), had severe moral overtones. Inevitably, as was their habit, the Greeks found a historical origin for the practice of buying slaves—in the island of Chios. The historian Theopompus, a native of the island, phrased it this way: "The Chians were the first of the Greeks, after the Thessalians and Lacedaemonians, who used slaves. But they did not acquire them in the same manner as the latter; for the Lacedaemonians and Thessalians will be found to have derived their slaves from the Greeks who formerly inhabited the territory which they now possess, . . . calling them helots and *penestae,* respectively. But the Chians possessed barbarian slaves, for whom they paid a price." [65] The quotation is preserved by Athenaeus, whose *floruit* was about 200 A.D. and who went on to comment that the Chians ultimately received divine punishment for their innovation. The stories he then tells, as evidence, are curious and interesting, but I cannot take time for them.

This is not very good history, but that does not make it any less important. By a remarkable coincidence Chios provides us with the earliest contemporary evidence of democratic institutions in the Greek world. In a Chian inscription dated, most probably, to the years 575–550 B.C., there is unmistakable reference to a popular council and to the "laws (or ordinances) of the *demos.*" [66] I do not wish to assign any significance other than symbolic to this coincidence, but it is a symbol with enormous implications. I have already made the point that the more advanced the Greek city-state, the more it will be found to have had true slavery rather than the "hybrid" types like helotage. More bluntly put the cities in which individual freedom reached its highest expression—most obviously Athens—were cities in which chattel slavery flourished. The Greeks, it is well known, discovered both the idea of individual freedom and the institutional framework in which it could be realized.[67] The pre-Greek world—the world of the Sumerians, Babylonians, Egyptians, and Assyrians; and I cannot refrain from adding the Mycenaeans—was, in a very profound sense, a world without free men, in the sense in which the west has come to understand that concept. It was equally a world in which chattel slavery played no role of any consequence. That, too, was

[64] 566 F 11, ap. Athen. 6.264C; cf. 272 A–B.

[65] 115 F 122, ap. Athen. 6.265B–C.

[66] For the most recent discussion of this text, see L. H. Jeffery in Annual of the Brit. Sch. Athens, LI (1956), 157–67.

[67] It is hardly necessary to add that "freedom" is a term which, in the Greek context was restricted to the members of the *koinonia,* always a fraction, and often a minor fraction of the total male population.

a Greek discovery. One aspect of Greek history, in short, is the advance, hand in hand, of freedom *and* slavery.

PETER A. BRUNT

Work and Slavery

Agriculture was the chief source of income and the chief occupation in all ages and lands of the ancient world. Trade and industry were by modern standards little developed. For this there were many reasons. Technology was backward and fuel scarce. Legal and social institutions did not favor the accumulation of liquid capital. Above all, transportation was slow and costly. Under Diocletian's tariff of maximum prices the cost of moving a bushel of grain fifty miles by wagon would have absorbed two-fifths of the permitted retail price. It was less expensive to move goods by sea or inland waterway. But ships were small and slow, there were few navigational aids, and voyages were normally suspended in the winter. Italy, in particular, has few good harbors or navigable rivers. As most people lived near the subsistence level, there was no effective demand for most goods that had to travel a long distance. Some indispensable raw materials like iron might have to be imported despite the costs, but consumer goods could not have found a world-wide market, as Lancashire cottons did in the nineteenth century, and this alone can explain why there were no large factories. Industry catered for local needs or for the production of high-class goods which could stand the costs of transport. Trade was chiefly in luxuries or semi-luxuries. One great exception must be noted. The large population of Rome and later of Constantinople was fed with grain imported from overseas, especially from Africa and Egypt. But much of it was paid for by the Imperial treasury out of provincial revenues. Other cities without similar resources could not rely on imports of food. In general each community, indeed each large estate, aimed at self-sufficiency, and the result of a local failure of crops was famine.

Peter A. Brunt, "Work and Slavery," in *The Romans*, ed. J.P.V.D. Balsdon (New York: Basic Books, Inc., 1965), pp. 177–91.

Even by ancient standards Italy was not important for industry, nor, except for a short period, for commerce. Rome itself was never a manufacturing center; it was only some Campanian, Etruscan and north Italian towns that were noted for armaments and certain fine products. Thus in the time of Augustus the ware of Arretium in Etruria was the most prized in the Mediterranean world; but it was soon imitated elsewhere, and lost its imperial market. In the first century B.C. Italian business men were dominant in the east. As a result of the great conquests Rome had made, enormous capital flowed into Italy, and Italians became the financiers of the Greek cities. They also traded in grain which the Italian tax-farmers had collected in kind. These were temporary advantages which faded when Rome ceased to exploit her subjects so ruthlessly; Syrians or Gauls replaced Italians in imperial commerce. Italy herself had little to export except wine and oil; her available surplus of timber had vanished with deforestation, and she had virtually no mineral wealth. It is for the fertility of her land that the highest praises are heaped upon her by ancient writers.

The Romans and the other Italians were thus primarily agriculturists. They themselves were convinced that they owed their empire to their hardy peasant stock. They loved to tell how in the early days of the Republic Cincinnatus was called from the plough to command the army. "It is from the farming class" wrote Cato in the second century B.C. "that the bravest men and sturdiest soldiers come, their calling is most highly respected, their livelihood is most assured . . . and those who are engaged in that pursuit are least inclined to be disaffected." It is characteristically Roman that Virgil's great poem, the *Georgics,* is devoted to describing the hard, almost unremitting labour and rustic festivities of the farmer's life

> But still the farmer furrows the land with his curving plough:
> The land is his annual labour, it keeps his native country,
> His little grandson and herds of cattle and trusty bullocks . . .
> Such was the life the Sabines lived in days of old,
> And Remus and his brother: so it was beyond all question
> That Tuscany grew to greatness, Rome became queen of all the world,
> Ringing her seven citadels with a single wall.[1]

The old-style peasant had just enough land on which to raise and support a family; he was not producing for the market, except to the extent that he needed to buy tools and a few other things he could not make for himself. The women spun and weaved; even great ladies in later times are commended for their wool-making, and the Emperor Antoninus Pius was proud to wear home-spun clothes.

Of course there were also skilled craftsman. The second of the Roman

[1] C. Day-Lewis's translation.

Kings, Numa, is said to have organized guilds of flute-players, gold-smiths, carpenters, dyers, cobblers, tanners, copper-workers and potters, and of the 193 centuries into which the Roman people in arms were divided (the Comitia Centuriata) two were appointed for the makers of arms, who enjoyed, it seems, a position of some honor. In the early period such craftsmen in Rome were evidently for the most part free citizens, and presumably this was true elsewhere.

The great majority of Romans and of other Italians, however, must have lived on the land. Their life was never easy. In a bad year they had to borrow, and if they could not repay, their creditors could reduce them to a form of bondage. Roman conquests in Italy probably did more than remedial legislation to improve the position of the small man. Rome confiscated part of the territory of the Italian cities she subdued and used it to settle her own citizens, a policy which at once increased her population and military strength and provided the poor with lands. But from the beginning of the second century B.C. onwards wars overseas contributed to ruin the peasantry. While the ploughman was doing military service, perhaps for six years on end, in Spain, his farm was neglected. Other factors helped to promote the concentration of landed property in the hands of a few rich men who sought to accumulate it because it was both the safest and the most honorable investment and who did not scruple to secure it even by force or fraud. Pasturage, which required relatively little labor, was often the most lucrative way of exploiting their lands, and they often preferred slaves to free workers.

Thus the old yeomanry gradually diminished. Many displaced farmers sought shelter in the city of Rome. We must not exaggerate the extent or speed of the process. At the lowest and probably correct estimate the free population of Italy under Augustus did not exceed five millions, and probably under one million lived in Rome. In 37 B.C. Varro spoke of large numbers of the poor who tilled their lands with the help of their children, smaller owners, or, perhaps, tenants of the great proprietors, who were recommended by the experts to lease farms, if they could not supervise them closely or if they were situated on unhealthy land, where slaves would suffer heavy mortality. It was also uneconomic to maintain enough slaves for seasonal operations, harvest or vintage for which gangs of free laborers were employed, probably men who eked out subsistence at other times on their own little plots or by casual work in the towns. In the late Republic some two hundred thousand free Italians were often under arms; these soldiers came from the country and sought allotments of land as a reward for their service. But numerous assignations of land to the rural poor seem to have done no more than retard the concentration of property. The process went on, and in the late Empire we hear of enormous estates in Italy called *massae*.

It is indeed generally held that under the Augustan peace the supply of slaves dwindled and that the large proprietors had to rely more on free labor and, in particular, on leasing farms to tenants. This is dubious. Certainly fewer slaves were made by war, piracy and brigandage, but we cannot be sure that Italian slaveowners did not then breed them in large numbers, like the owners of plantations in the Southern states. Even tenants often worked their farms with the help of slaves, who might be supplied to them along with other expensive equipment by the land-lords. Nor were the tenants themselves prosperous; they were often in debt, and by the time of Constantine they had come to be tied to their lands and were little better than serfs. Probably, in most periods of Roman history, there must have been perennial under-employment and near starvation among the agricultural poor.

Driven from the land, what could the Roman peasant do? Unlike his successor in the England of the industrial revolution, he could not readily find alternative employment in the towns. This was not merely due to the absence of a large-scale industry; there was also slave competition. The freeborn poor in the towns had to depend in large part on public corn doles and on the bounty of the great houses. There were also casual earnings, especially in the building trade, where the operations were not sufficiently continuous to warrant the employment of slaves who had to be fed and clothed, whether they were working or not. The Emperor Vespasian was a lavish builder; once when an engineer came to him with a labor-saving device, he was rewarded—but Vespasian refused to adopt his invention. "You must let me feed my poor commons" he said. The Colosseum and his other great monuments were evidently constructed by free labor.

One result of the improverishment of the masses from the second century B.C. onwards was decline in the birth rate. Many of the poor were unable to raise children. This was a source of concern to many statesmen from Tiberius Gracchus to Trajan. That Emperor made public funds available to feed poor children under a scheme which endured for a century. Its success is uncertain; plague, endemic malaria and famine helped to reduce the population, and in Marcus Aurelius' reign parts of Italy were desolate and could be used for settling barbarians.

What has already been said indicates the importance of slavery in Roman society. As in all other ancient lands it was an institution of im-memorial antiquity, which no one ever proposed to abolish. Greeks who were accustomed to question everything had challenged its legitimacy and evoked a powerful defence from Aristotle; the slave was in his view a man who had only enough rationality to understand and obey orders, and it was as much in his own interest as the master's that he should be subject to rational government. (Slightly modified, this argument is familiar today from the writings of imperialist apologists.) But this controversy was in the realm of theory. Even when slaves rebelled, they did not object to slavery as such: they merely wanted to be free themselves. A Roman jurist said that by natural law all men are born free, but he hastened to add that slavery existed by the law of nations. The Stoics, who were influential at Rome, taught that all men were brothers, including slaves; but in their philosophy man's welfare is purely spiritual, and material conditions irrelevant to it; true misery lies in being a slave to one's own passions, and legal servitude does not stop a man from being master of himself in the moral sense. The Christian attitude was much the same. Slaves, according to Paul, are not to worry about the condition in which they were called; and he did not recommend Philemon to liberate Onesimus. Hence it is no surprise that when Christianity became the official religion, the Church did not advocate abolition: on the contrary, it acquired slaves of its own. In the breakup of the Empire slavery gradually dwindled, for reasons that are not clear; but as great numbers of free men were reduced to serfdom, from which it was often harder to escape, the net gain to human freedom was not large.

The children of slave mothers were born slaves, but free men could be made slaves by capture in war, by piracy and by kidnapping. Legally a Roman citizen or a free subject of Rome could not be reduced to servitude within Rome's jurisdiction, but this rule may have been often evaded; in particular, exposure of free-born infants was not forbidden until Christian times, and when such foundlings were reared as slaves, there would seldom have been evidence of their original status. In primitive Rome, a poor community, there can have been few slaves, but there was a vast influx as a result of Rome's wars of conquest from the middle of the third century B.C. In one campaign in 167 B.C. the Romans are said to have made fifty thousand slaves in Epirus. Trade across the frontiers always swelled the numbers, and so did piracy by sea and brigandage by land until the time of Augustus. In the heyday of piracy the mart at Delos was reputed to be capable of handling twenty thousand in a single day. Never before had slaves been so cheap and plentiful as in Cicero's Italy, and nowhere else in the Empire did the economy become so dependent on slave labor. A comparison may be drawn with the Old South in the United States. There, in 1850, only eleven owners had more than five hundred slaves apiece. But in Nero's reign one senator had four hundred serving him in his own town house—and how many more working in the fields to support this establishment of unproductive mouths? Augustus thought it necessary to forbid owners to manumit more than a hundred by testament. It can be conjectured that in his time there were three slaves for every five free men in Italy.

The slaves were of all nations, including Celts and Germans from the

north and Asiatics from the east; many, born in slavery or illegally enslaved, came from Italy or the provinces. These were not only sturdy
laborers for the fields or mines, but craftsmen or men with professional
talents who brought new skills to Italy. Shrewd owners trained slave
boys to be secretaries, accountants and doctors. It was such trained scribes
in Atticus' publishing house who copied the works of Cicero. The master
and preceptor of a young mathematical genius records with sorrow his
death at the age of twelve. The fine pottery of Arretium was made by
slaves. Hundreds of epitaphs prove that in such industries as the making
of lamps, pipes, and glassware eighty percent of the workmen were of
servile stock; the same is true of goldsmiths and jewellers. Most of these
men died as freedmen; they had been presumably employed in the same
way as slaves, but manumission was the normal reward for their services.

In Roman law the slave was a chattel. Varro classifies the equipment
of the farm as articulate, inarticulate and mute, that is to say, the slaves,
the cattle and the ploughs. The slave can be bought, sold or hired out,
mated or not (the Elder Cato allowed no women to his farm-hands),
fed, clothed and in general punished at the master's will. All that he
earns is legally for the master's account. The child of the slave mother
is the master's property.

From the first, however, the law was not consistent, and could not be.
It had to take account of the slave's humanity, if only in the interests of
the free citizens themselves. He might commit a crime; the state would
then punish him and more severely than if he were free. He might witness a crime and then he should give evidence. The slave might denounce
a plot against the State, and then the State would free him. Moreover
the law provided formal procedures under which the master himself
might manumit his slave. Manumission is always a concomitant of slavery,
but under Roman law, unlike Greek, the freedman of a Roman citizen
became a citizen himself, if he was emancipated by the proper formalities.

The interests of the master too required him to care for the slave's
welfare. He had to be fed and clothed even when the free poor went
hungry and naked. The harsh Cato recommends for farm-hands about as
much wheat as the soldier got, with a little wine, oil, olives or pickled
fish and salt; they should have shoes and a tunic and cloak every other
year; blankets may be made of the discarded clothes. The master was
for long empowered to put his slave to death, but only a very capricious
owner would destroy his property without strong cause. He could have
him flogged, but Varro, for one, preferred verbal rebukes—if they were
equally effective. Rewards often served the master's interest better than
punishments. He might pay his slave a wage or set him up in business
and let him retain part of the earnings. The money or other property
he then acquired, though legally his master's, was in practice treated as

his own (*peculium*); it might even include other slaves. With his savings he could buy his freedom, "defrauding his belly," as Seneca puts it. But freedom often came as a gift. Owners, especially if they died without natural heirs, were particularly ready to emancipiate slaves by their wills; this gave them posthumous acclaim for generosity. But manumission in the owner's lifetime was also frequent—astonishingly at first sight, but it is not hard to explain. Freedom was the greatest spur to good work, and probably no other incentive sufficed for slaves employed in skilled work and trusted posts. Moreover the former owner now became the patron of his old slave and retained a right to respect and services of many kinds; he might actually impose on the freedman the obligation to work for him without pay to an extent limited only by the proviso that he must either maintain him or allow him enough time to maintain himself. We do not know how usual this practice was; certainly it was not universal, for many freedmen became rich.

Of course kindly, humane feelings and the philosophic doctrine that a master was custodian of his slave's welfare often fortified the self-interest which by itself dictated good treatment of the slave and even his emancipation. But the chief beneficiaries from all these motives were the skilled slaves and the domestics whose duties brought them into close contact with the masters. Farm-workers on distant estates did not benefit; they were often chained together in work or sleep, and Pliny calls them men without hope. Even the farm manager was normally a slave, not a freedman.

Jefferson, writing from experience, declared that

> the whole commerce between master and slave is a perpetual exercise of the most boisterous passions, the most unremitting despotism on the one part and degrading submission on the other.

How far was this true in Rome? We cannot generalize either from instances of kind and friendly relations or from recorded atrocities. But Seneca says that masters notorious for cruelty were pointed at in the streets, and the development of the law, which is apt to lag behind the best opinion of its day rather than lead it, is significant. From the first century A. D. for instance it was murder for a master to kill his slave without cause, and a slave who was starved or subjected to savagery and debauchery could take asylum at one of the Emperor's statues and had a right to be sold to another master. It is not likely that the protection of the law was very efficacious, any more than in the Old South, where masters accused of slave-murder were always acquitted by their peers. The Christian Emperor, Constantine, moreover, ruled that where a master was charged with murdering his slave, it had to be proved that he intended to kill him; it was not enough if he died under a flogging. But the provisions of the law do at least reveal the moral climate of opinion.

Humanity was not indeed the only reason for protecting slaves against the cruelty of individual masters. Antoninus Pius declared that such protection was in the interest of masters and designed to prevent uprisings. Centuries before, the philosopher-historian Posidonius had pointed out that ill-treatment of some slaves had been the cause of the great revolt which desolated Sicily from 134 to 132 B. C. This was not the last slave revolt. In the seventies before Christ, slaves led by Spartacus devastated many parts of Italy and routed Roman armies. The Principate was better able to keep order, but the sense of insecurity persisted. *Quot servi tot hostes*—"Every slave is an enemy"—was a Roman proverb. Slaves were always running away, and the murder of masters was a constant danger. Under a savage Augustan enactment, which gave rise to much case law, when a master was murdered, all his slaves "under the same roof" were to be executed; if not accomplices, they were at least guilty of not preventing his death. One slave-girl pleaded that the assassin of her mistress had terrified her into silence; Hadrian ruled that she must die, for it was her duty to cry out at the cost of her own life. Still, harsh repression was at least accompanied by some attempts to curb the excesses of masters.

For many who could attain freedom slavery was not a hopeless lot. Petronius depicts a Sicilian who sold himself into slavery (illegally) because he preferred the chance of becoming a Roman citizen to remaining a provincial taxpayer. The freedman could more easily be integrated into society because there was no color prejudice; there were seldom marked differences of skin to give rise to it. His rights were indeed limited; he could not serve in the army, nor hold state or municipal offices, and he might have onerous obligations to his patron. But if he had economic independence and some little talent and enterprise, he might grow wealthy. His political disabilities, like those imposed in later times on Jews or Quakers, channelled his energies into business, where freedmen were often dominant. They might be assisted by their patron, like the freedman of an Augustan nobleman who managed all his business affairs and received from him ample gifts for himself, a dowry for his daughter and a commission in the army for his son. Another freedman of this time boasted in his will that he left 4,116 slaves, 3,600 pairs of oxen and 257,000 head of other cattle. Petronius' Trimalchio, whose estates in Italy stretched from sea to sea, is no mere figment of a novelist. These are extreme examples, but many other freedmen secured a modest competence, and were able to advance their children, who suffered no legal disabilities, further in the social scale. The poet Horace was the son of a freedman who could give him the education of a gentleman and help to make him the court laureate, and Horace was not ashamed to recall his origin. In Nero's time it could be alleged that most senators had servile blood in their veins and a century later, Marcus Helvius Pertinax, the son of a freedman, rose by military and administrative capacity so high that in 193 he was proclaimed Emperor.

The most favored of slaves and freedmen were the Emperor's, who were employed in the Imperial administration. Under Tiberius a slave who was paymaster in Gaul took sixteen of his own slaves with him on a visit to Rome; of these two were needed to keep his plate. Claudius' freedmen secretaries are said to have been the wealthiest men of their day and the real rulers of the Empire; the brother of one was that Felix who governed Judaea in Paul's day and married a descendant of Cleopatra. In some later reigns, chamberlains, often eunuchs, who had the Emperor's private ear, were to exercise power no less great.

The enormous importance of slavery in the economy of ancient Italy raises a large historical question. Obviously if the technical advances of even the early modern period of European history had been anticipated in the Graeco-Roman world, the Empire must have been too strong for the barbarians, whose invasions were at least the proximate cause and the necessary condition for its disruption. Can the extensive use of slavery be held responsible for technological backwardness and economic stagnation?

It has been argued that because slave labour was abundant and cheap the ancient world had no incentive to technological invention and that slavery so far abased the dignity of labor that the best minds turned away in disgust from everything connected with manual tasks; hence the backwardness of the Greeks and Romans in all scientific investigations which, unlike mathematics, demanded any approach other than that of abstract thinking. At the same time, to quote Cairnes' famous judgement on American slavery, slave labor "is given reluctantly; it is unskilful; it is wanting in versatility"; it must therefore be assumed that it was inefficient.

Even on these premises slavery cannot have been a prime cause of Rome's decline. After Augustus the Empire drew its strength increasingly and in the end exclusively from the provinces, where slavery was not predominant as it was in Italy. Not only did the provinces furnish soldiers; some of them, notably Gaul and Egypt, were economically more prosperous, and it is certain of Egypt and probable of Gaul that slavery there was on a small scale. Yet these regions were no more inventive or progressive than Italy. We must therefore look elsewhere for reasons that will explain scientific or technological stagnation. Some have already been given; and we must add that progress was to depend on the formulation of fertile scientific hypotheses or on crucial inventions like optical glass; it is perhaps no more easy to understand why these happen in one age and not in another than to account for the flowering of poetical genius.

And was slave labor so inefficient? Roman experts on agriculture assumed that on good land and adequately supervised it brought in higher profits than free labor. We lack ancient evidence to test this assumption, and modern analogies yield no clear conclusion; the latest analyses of the economy of the Old South seem to show that its backwardness compared with the North cannot be certainly ascribed to slavery. In trade and industry the slaves were skilled workers spurred on by the hope of freedom; they are actually credited with minor inventions (like American negro slaves) and, if other factors had permitted mechanization, they were clearly capable of minding machines; indeed negroes too were used successfully in factories, although they were at a lower cultural level and lacked such strong incentives. (Similarly in the last world war German productivity actually increased with the extended use of what was in all but name slave labor.) However cheap Roman slaves were, and we do not know just how cheap, the owners still had no motive to be indifferent to devices that might have increased their output.

It is thus on moral rather than on economic grounds that Roman slavery merits opprobrium. And many Roman slaves were no worse off than the mass of the peasantry who, though free in name, found it hard to assert their rights or defend their interests and never lived far from starvation. In a preindustrial and poor society, of course, the poverty of the masses is the price to be paid if even a few are to enjoy leisure and civilization and the opportunity of promoting further progress. But in the Roman world such inevitable inequality was carried too far, further, for instance, than in democratic Greek communities. Hence, in the first century B. C. agrarian discontent in Italy helped to bring the Republic down, and in and after the third century A. D. the peasantry, unconscious of the benefits that accrued even to them from the Roman peace, often showed themselves indifferent and sometimes hostile to an empire in which the interests of the wealthy, *beati possidentes,* were always preponderant. This was no doubt one reason why despite its immensely superior resources the Empire succumbed to the inroads of barbarians.

BIBLIOGRAPHY

Much of the evidence is collected and translated in *An Economic Survey of Ancient Rome,* 5 volumes, edited by TENNEY FRANK, and interpreted by Frank in his *Economic History of Rome* and by M. ROSTOVTZEFF, *Social and Economic History of the Roman Empire.* For agricultural labor *see* W. E. HEITLAND, *Agricola;* for freedmen, A. M. DUFF, *Freedmen in the Early Roman Empire.* The useful but inaccurate compilation of W. L. WESTERMANN, *The Slave Systems of Greek and Roman Antiquity (see* my criticisms in *Journal of Roman Studies,* 1958) has not wholly superseded H. WALLON, *Histoire de l'esclavage dans l'antiquité* (1879). Some valuable essays are republished in *Slavery in Classical Antiquity,* edited by M. I. FINLEY.

2. EXPLOITATION BEGINS AT HOME

Family life is a special concern of social historians. The rules and procedures concerning marriage and divorce, birth and death, tell us much about a society. Specifically, we can learn from such a study about the fate of women who make up slightly more than half of the world's population. The readings in this section provide many interesting details but few real surprises about the status of women in Greece and Rome.

Robert Flacelière contends that, outside of their own home, most Greek women enjoyed little more political and legal rights than slaves. To be sure there were differences from city to city and, obviously, class distinctions made the daily condition of women far from uniform. Still, the social behavior, personal freedom, and potential accomplishments of women were largely dependent on the station of their husbands. The French scholar adds, however, that the highest born were not necessarily the freest of women.

W. K. Lacey enters into the details of marital and extramarital custom in classical Greece: marriage and divorce, inheritance regulations, concubinage and adultery. He concentrates on Athenian law and shows both its complexity and flexibility. He indicates, at least so far as the well born were concerned, that women were not left totally unprotected by the law, since the punishment for violating their person and rights was often severe.

Frederik Poulsen extends the foregoing discussion. He seeks to describe the evolving condition of women in Roman times which he sees, quite optimistically, as a period of increasing emancipation for them. But his discussion centers on the happy few so often portrayed in literature and iconography; he virtually ignores the lot of the many who only endured.

Clearly, classical times were a man's world. Not only does the available evidence point to the fact that the legal status of women was narrowly circumscribed, but the striking thing is how little evidence can be gathered from classical sources about women. That they were so frequently ignored by writers and legislators is probably the best indication of their true social position.

ROBERT FLACELIÈRE

Women, Marriage, and the Family

THE STATUS OF WOMEN

In Athens, the wives of citizens enjoyed no more political or legal rights than did their slaves. Women had lost the important role they formerly played in Minoan society,[1] and which, as it seems, they had at least partially preserved during the Homeric period.[2] Yet though a married Athenian woman might be confined to her house, here at least she enjoyed absolute authority—subject always to the consent of her lord and master: to her slave-girls she was the *despoina,* the mistress. In any case, her husband was so busy with other matters—in the country, hunting or farming; in the city, his profession, and political or legal affairs of state—that he was compelled, more often than not, to leave his wife to run their home as she pleased.

The dependent and subordinate position of Athenian women can be deduced, first, from the life led by young girls, and the way in which

Robert Flacelière, *Daily Life in Greece at the Time of Pericles,* trans. Peter Green (New York: The Macmillan Publishing Co., Inc. 1965), pp. 55–59, 66–69, 71–76.

[1] See G. Glotz, *La Civilisation égéenne,* pp. 166–70.
[2] See E. Mireaux, *La Vie Quotidienne au temps d'Homère,* pp. 204–27.

they came to be married. There was no question of a girl being free to meet other young people, since she scarcely ever left the women's apartments, the *gynaikeion.* Whereas married women seldom crossed the thresholds of their own front door, adolescent girls were lucky if they were allowed as far as the inner courtyard, since they had to stay where they could not be seen—well away, even, from the male members of their own family. There is nothing in fifth-century Athens corresponding to the 'school' for well-connected girls which the poetess Sappho conducted, at the beginning of the sixth century, on the island of Lesbos. Nor do we find anything in Athens resembling the physical training given to young Spartan girls, in short tunics which "exposed their thighs," and concerning which Euripides wrote:

> Spartan maidens, allowed out of doors with the young men, running and wrestling in their company, with naked thighs and girt-up tunics.[3]

In this respect, and this alone, disciplinarian Sparta was more tolerant than Athens; and Euripides chooses just this aspect of Lacedaemonian *mores* to criticize as scandalous, for the simple reason that here he has a direct contrast with accepted Athenian custom.

Everything a young Athenian girl learnt—which meant, basically, domestic skills such as cooking, spinning, and weaving, with perhaps a little reading, music and arithmetic thrown in—she would be taught by her mother, or her grandmother, or some family slave-girl. The only occasions on which girls normally went out were during certain religious festivals, when they assisted at the sacrifice and took part in the procession, as we learn from the Panathenaic frieze on the Parthenon. Still, some of them must have been trained to sing and dance, in order to join the festival choir—though in such choirs boys and girls were always kept strictly apart.

In Xenophon's *Oeconomica* Ischomachus says of his young bride:

> What can she have known about life when I married her, my dear Socrates? She was not yet quite fifteen at the time she crossed my threshold; and till that moment she had lived under the most cramping restrictions, trained from childhood to see and hear as little as possible, and ask an absolute minimum of questions.[4]

This was, indeed, the ideal aimed at when giving girls a good education.

Here is another statement on the subject by Ischomachus. This time it is his wife he is addressing:

[3] Euripides, *Andromache* 597–598.
[4] Xenophon, *Oeconomica* 7.5.

Do you now understand why it was I married you, and why your parents bethrothed you to me? There would have been no difficulty in finding another girl to share my bed: I am quite sure you realize *that*. No; the decision was only taken after a great deal of thought—both by me on my own account and by your parents on yours—as to the best helpmeet each of us could find for the care of our home and future children. Eventually I picked on you, just as your parents settled for me—probably after considering various other potential husbands.

It was, in fact, the girl's *kyrios* (that is, her father, or, failing him, a blood-brother, or a grandfather, or, in the last resort, her legal guardian) who chose a husband for her and decided when she was to be married. Doubtless in many cases her own wishes were ascertained; but we have no evidence to suggest this, and her consent was not in the slightest degree necessary. Herodotus, it is true, tells a very strange anecdote about one sixth-century Athenian: "His treatment of his three daughters was as follows: when they reached marriageable age, he gave them the most magnificent dowry, and then let each of them choose—from the whole body of Athenian citizens—the man she desired for a husband; to whom, in due course, he married her off." [5]

Herodotus, who was himself a product of the fifth century, appears to find this paterfamilias' behaviour admirable, and certainly quotes it in an approving manner. But he also makes it clear that it was the exception rather than the rule. The rule was that formulated in verse by a much later author: "Girl, wed the man your parents wish you to." [6]

An Athenian citizen married, primarily, to have children: he expected them not only to care for him in his old age, but also—more important— to bury him with the full appropriate rites and keep up the family cult after he was gone. The first and foremost reason for marriage was thus a religious one, and on this point the conclusions of Fustel de Coulanges, in his *Cité antique,* have lost none of their validity. A man married, above all, in order to have male children: one son at least, to perpetuate the line and guarantee him the cult-honors which he, the father, performed for *his* ancestors, and which were regarded as indispensable for the well-being of the dead in the nether world.

At Sparta, confirmed bachelors were liable to legal sanctions; there was no such law of enforcement in Athens, but the pressure of public opinion was strong, and any unmarried male found himself subjected to much scornful censure. Despite this, a man whose elder brother had married and produced children found it somewhat more socially permissible to remain single himself.

[5] Herodotus, 6. 122.
[6] Naumachius *ap.* Stobaeus Vol. 3 pp. 22, 68, 234 [ed. Gaisford]: his poem *Advice to the Married* 12.

It looks very much as though the majority of Athenians married for religious and social convenience rather than from personal choice. According to the poet Menander, writing at the end of the fourth century, they regarded marriage as a 'necessary evil'.[7] At any rate, we have no evidence of love between the engaged couple prior to the New Comedy. Besides, how could an Athenian have conceived a passion for a girl whom, in most cases, he had never so much as set eyes on? We know that the Greeks of the fifth and fourth centuries used the word *erôs* (love) in the first instance to describe the passion linking an *erastés* with his *erômenos*—in other words, just that type of relationship which we mean when we talk of "Greek love." . . .

All this, of course, does not mean that love could not subsequently come about between husband and wife. Xenophon makes Socrates say, in his *Symposium*: "Niceratus, from what I hear, is passionately in love with his wife, and she with him." [8] The poet Euripides, though he was commonly regarded as a misogynist, made a play out of the sublime self-sacrifice and devotion of Alcestis, who gave up her own life for love of her husband; and even Plato, the theorist of ideal pederasty, once wrote: "Only those who love can ever be willing to die for another's sake: and this applies to women no less than men." He cites the instance of Alcestis, "whose case impressed the gods so much that they allowed her to return from Hades and behold the light of heaven once more." [9] The works of Aristotle, who had married the niece of his friend Hermias, and found his wife eminently satisfactory, are full of passages in which marriage is regarded, not as a mere alliance, the sole function of which is to perpetuate one's line, but as a relationship full of affection and mutual tenderness, capable of satisfying all the moral and emotional demands that life may make on it. Nevertheless, it was only through late Stoicism—probably under the influence of Roman *mores*—that conjugal love was to be finally rehabilitated in Greece. The philosophical tradition favoring all-male love was strong and persistent; even at the beginning of the second century A. D. Plutarch, before embarking on the apologia for marriage, feels constrained to demonstrate that young girls are just as capable of arousing the passions as young boys! [10]

Incest was not legally forbidden in Athens, but unions between parent and child were regarded as an abomination that called down the wrath of the gods: Sophocles' *Oedipus Rex* is ample demonstration of this. The same religious taboo was extended to unions between brother and sister

---

[7] Menander, *The Arbitration* 490 ff., and fr. 651.

[8] Xenophon, *Symposium* 8.3.

[9] Plato, *Symposium* 179 b–c.

[10] Cf. Plutarch, *Amatorius, passium,* and R. Flacelière, *Les Epicuriens et l'amour,* in *Rev. Et. Gr.* Vol. 67 (1954), pp. 69–81.

born of the same mother, but a half-brother could marry his sister if the common strain came through their father. For instance, a daughter of Themistocles named Mnesiptolema, born to the great statesman by his second wife, married her own brother Archeptolis, he being the child of a different mother.[11] Similarly we find a plaintiff referring to his grandfather's marriage—the old man wed his sister, but they had different mothers.[12] The principle of endogamy, that is to say marriage within a limited social group, results in unions between close relatives being not only tolerated but actively encouraged. We find one Athenian admitting, in the course of a lawsuit, that he married his daughter off to his nephew rather than to some stranger, so as to preserve and reinforce family ties. Marriages between first cousins, or even uncle and niece, are by no means rare: in the latter case the bridegroom's brother would also become his father-in-law. An *epikléros,* that is, a daughter who inherited her defunct father's estate in the absence of any male heir, was obliged to marry her father's closest relative who would agree to the match. Here we have an unmistakable instance of the primitive urge to ensure the continuity of race and family cult alike. . . .

THE GYNAIKEIA

Marriage did not put an end to the confined and sedentary existence that women led before it. In Athens, it is true, the *gynaikeia* were not locked up (except at night) and did not have barred windows; but customary usage sufficed to keep women within doors. This rule was strictly enforced, and gave rise to various categorical aphorisms such as: "Respectable women should stay at home: the street is for worthless hussies." [13] Even those who lingered on their doorsteps, out of sheer curiosity, were treated as suspect. It was husbands or slaves who normally went to market and did the daily shopping.

Nevertheless, it is important to distinguish, in this respect, between the various social classes. Poor Athenians, with nothing but cramped lodgings at their disposal, were more inclined to allow their wives out. In any case, the wives often had to take a job in order to make ends meet: we know, for instance, that many of them worked as stallkeepers in the market. Athenians of the middle class, on the other hand, and those with large incomes, seem to have been far more strict in the seclusion of their women; but then the wives of such citizens possessed a far more ample *gynaikeion,* often provided with an inner courtyard where they could take the air, safe from the inquisitive eyes of the multitude.

[11] Plutarch, *Life of Themistocies* 32.
[12] Demosthenes, *Against Eubulides* 20–1.
[13] Menander, fr. 546.

Still, every woman, even one from the ranks of the bourgeoisie, on occasion needed to do some essentially personal shopping, e.g., for clothes or shoes, which meant that she had to go out. On such occasions she was obliged to take one of her attendants with her—that is, one of her slaves. But the main occasions on which women were allowed away from their homes were during the various city festivals, or for special family events. Athens was remarkable in having one festival specially reserved for married women, the Thesmophoria.[14] We find a deceived husband, who has killed his wife's lover, telling the court: "To begin with, my wife was a paragon of marital virtue—she ran the house efficiently and economically, in short she was a first-class domestic manager. But then I lost my mother, and her death was the cause of all my subsequent misfortune. You see, it was while walking in her funeral procession that my wife was first spotted by Eratosthenes, who managed, in course of time, to seduce her: he lay in wait for the slave-girl who did her shopping, used this girl as a go-between to make contact with her mistress, and finally achieved the latter's ruin." The same plaintiff later reveals how he was tipped off about his wife's infidelity by the slave of yet another married woman who had succumbed to Eratosthenes' advances, and how, by means of threats, he made his own wife's maid tell him the whole truth: "She told me how he had accosted her after the funeral . . . and finally how, at the time of the Thesmophoria, when I was away in the country, she had gone to the sanctuary with his mother." [15]

Women were not even supposed to take any interest in what went on outside the house: that was strictly the men's business. Nor did they have much opportunity for talking at any great length to their own husbands, since the latter were nearly always out, and do not seem to have been in the habit of taking meals with their wives. "Is there anyone of your acquaintance with whom you have less conversation than your wife?" Socrates asks Critobulus, and the latter replies: "Hardly anyone, I think." [16] When an Athenian invited friends to his home, his wife never appeared in *andrón,* the banqueting-chamber, except perhaps to supervise the slaves waiting at table; nor did she accompany her husband out when he was a guest in his turn. It was only at family festivals that men and women mingled.

Yet it was the wife who held supreme authority within the home, where she was responsible for everything: Xenophon's *Oeconomica* acquaints us in detail with the duties that developed on the mistress of the house. These instructions, laid down for his wife by Ischomachus, will suffice to give us some idea of her responsibilities:

14 Eg Aristophanes in the *Thesmophoriazusae.*
15 Lysias, *On The Murder of Eratosthenes* 7–8, 20.
16 Xenophon, *Oeconomica* 3.12.

You are to stay in the house, and ensure that all those servants whose work takes them out of doors leave at the same time. You are also responsible for supervising those who remain, and who perform their duties in the house itself. You must personally take charge of all goods brought into the house, and issue what is needed for necessary outgoings—budgeting in advance for a reserve, and taking care not to squander in a month what should last a full year. When your slaves bring you spun wool, you must see to it that this wool is used to make clothes for those who need them. You must keep a constant eye on the grain in the store-room, and make sure it remains fit to eat . . . When a servant falls ill, you must always ensure that he is receiving proper care and attention.[17]

The wife did not bake bread herself except in the very poorest families. When Alexander's envoys accompanied the Athenian Phocion to his home, Plutarch tells us, "they found his domestic arrangements austere indeed: his wife was busy kneading dough, and Phocion himself took a bucket off to the well to get water for washing his own and his guests' feet." [18] Normally such tasks were performed by slaves, under the supervision of the *despoina*—as in Homeric times, when Eurycleia washed the feet of Odysseus.[19]

A wife's badge of authority consisted of the keys she carried about with her, in particular those to storeroom and cellar. Theophrastus' picture of the Distrustful Man contains these words: "When he is in bed he will ask his wife if she has locked up the big chest and the silver cabinet, and whether the back door is properly bolted." [20] Gluttony, drunkenness, or prodigality in a wife might lead her husband to withdraw the keys from her.

It is hard to evaluate Aristophanes' evidence on the social life of women, since we can never be quite sure where realism ends and caricature begins. Yet the overall impression one gets from his comedies is that by the end of the fifth century the traditional seclusion of women was giving rise to numerous exceptions, and it is not hard to understand why. The Peloponnesian War meant that Athenian menfolk, whether serving in some expeditionary force or manning the ramparts of Attica, were absent from their homes for even longer periods than in peacetime. The chorus of women in the *Lysistrata*—free women, certainly, and Athenians—observe: "At crack of dawn I went and filled my water-pot from the fountain —and what a business it was! All that crowd, and the noise, and jars banging against each other, and a mob of servants and branded slaves elbowing past you . . ." [21]

[17] *Ibid.* 7.35–7.
[18] Plutarch, *Life of Phocion* 18.
[19] Homer, *Odyssey* 19. 350–94.
[20] Theophrastus, *Characters* 18.
[21] Aristophanes, *Lysistrata* 327.

According to Aristophanes, women went not only to the fountain, but down to the market as well, to do their shopping and sell their own produce: like Euripides' mother, who was, it seems, some sort of green grocer.[22] We also hear, in a plaintiff's brief, of one Athenian woman who was in turn a ribbon-seller and a paid nurse;[23] but whereas freeborn Athenian women only took jobs in the last resort, as a matter of extreme necessity, the wives of metics were often wool-weavers, shoemakers, dressmakers, and so on. Some of them seem to have been genuine "businesswomen."[24] . . .

CONJUGAL AND FAMILY LOVE

It seems fairly clear, then, that there was little intimacy, intellectual contact, or even real love between husband and wife in classical Athens. Men constantly met and entertained one another: in their homes, in the Agora or the law courts of the Assembly, about their business affairs. Women, by contrast, lived a wholly secluded life. The *gynaikeion* was always kept well away from the *andrôn*. Many Athenians must have held opinions on marriage such as Montaigne was later to express: "In this discreete match, appetites are not commonly so fondling; but drowsie and more sluggish . . . A man doth not marry for himselfe, whatsoever he aleageth; but as much or more for his posteritie and familie . . . Nor is it other than a kinde of incest, in this reverent alliance and sacred bond, to employ the efforts and extravagant humor of an amorous licentiousnes . . . A good marriage (if any there be) refuseth the company and conditions of love."[25]

But these carnal or emotional needs that the Athenian did not satisfy at home (since he saw his wife merely as the mistress of his house and the mother of his children) he tended to find an outlet for elsewhere, in the company of boys or courtesans. Here we must make a distinction between the fifth and the fourth centuries. The Athenian family, as a social unit, seems to have stood firm throughout the greater part of the fifth century; but the Peloponnesian War, a savagely fought conflict which lasted for thirty long years, brought about fundamental changes in Athenian *mores*. The terrible Plague of 430–429, which claimed Pericles among its victims, was directly attributable to the war, and Thucydides thus describes its effect upon public morality:

[22] Aristophanes, *Wasps* 497; *Thesmophoriazusae* 387.
[23] Demosthenes, *Against Eubulides* 34, 35.
[24] See M. Clerc, *Les Métèques athéniens* (1893) p. 395, and G. Glotz, *Le Travail dans la Grèce ancienne*, pp. 218, 221.
[25] Montaigne, *Essays*, Vol. 3 Ch. 5 (Florio's translation).

> These sudden changes of fortune which people witnessed—the wealthy struck dead overnight, paupers inheriting their riches—made them the more willing to indulge openly in such pleasures as they would before have taken care to conceal. They sought quick returns for their money, and saw immediate self-gratification as the one reasonable pursuit in a world where they, and their wealth, were liable to perish at any moment.[26]

Many women acquired more free and easy habits, following the example of Spartan wives, who lived a far less secluded life than did their Athenian counterparts, and spent a good deal more time in men's company. The resultant disorder led to the appointment of a special magistrate, whose job it was to control the behavior and, in particular, the extravagance of women—a problem to which Solon, too, had already bent his mind. This magistrate was known as the *gynaikonomos*.[27] To read the *Lysistrata,* which dates from 411 B.C., and the *Women in Parliament,* performed as late as 392, one might be forgiven for inferring that many Athenian women, having seen an exclusively masculine government carry the city headlong to disaster, were convinced that things might go a little better if *they* expressed their views and gave their husbands advice, but these two plays by Aristophanes are wildly exaggerated fantasy-farces, which afford us no evidence that there existed what today we would term a "feminist movement"—something quite inconceivable in ancient Athens.

Besides, Praxagora herself, disguised as a man and speaking in that capacity, draws an interesting contrast between women's placid traditionalism and the restless, never satisfied urge for change and discovery which characterizes men (the speech is taken from *Women in Parliament*):

> Women's methods are much better than ours, as I shall show you. To begin with, they invariably dye their wool by boiling it, in the good old-fashioned way; you won't catch *them* trying any new-fangled methods. And wouldn't it have been better for Athens if *she'd* let well alone, instead of messing about with a lot of novel ideas? Women roast their barley sitting, just as they always have; they carry loads on their heads, just as they always have; they keep the Thesmophoria, just as they always have; they bake cakes, just as they always have; they nag their husbands, just as they always have; they sneak their lovers into the house, just as they always have; they buy themselves little tit-bits, just as they always have; they prefer their wine unwatered, just as they always have; and they enjoy a good fuck—just as they always have.[28]

As for their husbands, this interminable war meant that they were constantly away from their wives and homes, and therefore also less hesitant about giving free vent to their appetites. It was a plaintiff from the fourth,

[26] Thucydides, 2. 53.
[27] Aristotle, *Politics* 6. 15 [p. 1299 a]
[28] Aristophanes, *Women in Parliament* 214–28.

not the fifth, century who one day declared in open court: "We have courtesans for pleasure, concubines to perform our domestic chores, and wives to bear us legitimate children and be the faithful guardians of our homes." [29]

We do, indeed, find in the fifth century such an irregular liaison as that between Pericles and Aspasia. At the time of his first meeting with the beautiful Milesian he was already married to a distant cousin of his, and the father of two sons. However, he put away his wife in order to live with Aspasia. Divorce was permissible in Athens, and Pericles could have married Aspasia *en secondes noces* if she had been Athenian-born, or from a town to which Athens had granted the right of *epigamia* (intermarriage between states). But this right was not enjoyed by Aspasia's city of origin, Miletus. So she became Pericles' mistress, and lived with him—on terms of great intimacy, it would seem—until his death. She was an intelligent and highly cultured woman, and Socrates (if we can trust Xenophon and Plato) [30] thought the world of her. The comic poets, on the other hand, attacked her with immense virulence, going so far as to portray her as a prostitute and a brothel-keeper.[31]

As Marie Delcourt wrote in her study of Pericles: "No one would have thought the less of Pericles for making love to young boys, or for treating his first wife so shabbily; but they *were* shocked by his treating her successor like a human being—by the fact that he *lived* with her instead of relegating her to the *gynaikeion,* and included his friends' wives when he issued invitations to dinner. It was all too amazing to be proper; and Aspasia was so brilliant she could not possibly be respectable." [32] There may be much truth in this; but my own feeling is that what people found it hard to forgive Pericles, the first citizen of Athens (and therefore one who should have set an example in his private conduct), was the way he put away an Athenian wife and replaced her by a foreigner.

In the fourth century, it would appear, many Athenians kept a concubine without considering this a reason to dismiss their legitimate wives. But did these concubines (who might equally well be Athenians, slaves, or freeborn foreigners) enjoy any legal, publicly recognized status? From the advocates' speeches in which allusions to them occur, we might well doubt it.[33] But custom, if not the law, looked on them with remarkable tolerance, and a large number of Athenians seem to have been, to all intents and purposes, bigamous. Socrates is supposed to have had a second wife called

[29] Ps-Demosthenes, *Against Neaera* 122.
[30] Cf. Xenophon, *Oeconomica* 3. 14, and Plato, *Menexenus, passim,* though allowance must be made here for Platonic irony.
[31] Aristophanes, *Acharnians* 526–7.
[32] Marie Delcourt, *Périclès* (1939) p. 77.
[33] E.g. in particular Demosthenes, *Against Boeotus,* I and II, and Isaeus, *On the Succession of Pyrrhus.*

Myrto, as well as the acidulous Xanthippe; but this story may well be pure fiction. The misogynist streak which Euripides reveals in several of his plays was explained by the assertion that he, too, was bigamously married, and therefore had twice as much opportunity as most men to study feminine malice! Some authorities—late ones, it must be said—also inform us that during the Peloponnesian War, as a measure designed to counter the slump in population, every male Athenian was authorized to have another woman, over and above his legally married wife, to bear him children: the woman might be a foreigner, and all offspring of such a union were treated as legitimate.

But long before this we find the case of Themistocles, whose father, it is true, was an Athenian citizen but whose mother was a Thracian slave, one Abrotonon: his illegitimacy had proved no bar to a successful career. "When one's legal wife becomes intolerable," Plutarch wrote, "is not the best solution to take a companion like Abrotonon of Thrace or Bacchis of Miletus, without any *engyésis*—just buy them outright, and scatter a few nuts over their head?" [34] But if the concubine was an Athenian, how could one make a distinction between her and one's legal wife, especially if the children she bore were likewise considered Athenian citizens? Isaeus informs us that "even those parents who give their own daughters into concubinage negotiate a fixed sum, payable to the concubine." [35] We may well suppose that some poor Athenians, who could not provide a dowry for their daughters, made them contract an alternative union of this nature instead, asking nothing on their behalf except some financial recompense in case of a separation. A legally married wife, on the other hand, normally brought her husband a dowry.

As for the *hetairai,* or courtesans, they were for the most part slaves. Many of them were content with the modest enough fee of one obol, though some—the top-grade *hetairai*—cost their lovers a pretty penny. During the Hellenistic epoch certain courtesans even managed to marry reigning princes, and thus become queens: "Flute-girls, dancers from Samos, an Aristonica or an Agathocleia or an Oenanthe with her tambourine—all these have trodden a royal diadem underfoot." [36] Even as early as the fourth century the celebrated Phryne, a Boeotian from Thespiae, had managed to make a really rich killing. Her actual name was Mnesarete, which means "mindful of virtue"; "Phryne" was a nickname, given her on account of her yellowish complexion (the word in fact means "toad"; though this, apparently, did not make her any the less beautiful). It is well known what methods the orator Hyperides, himself one of her lovers, is supposed to have employed in order to secure her acquittal on an impiety charge

[34] Plutarch, *Amatorius* 753 D.
[35] Isaeus, *op. cit.* 28.
[36] Plutarch, *op. cit. ibid.*

that had been brought against her; but this anecdote is highly suspect.[37] [Hyperides is said to have made her bare her bosom before the court, an argument which proved irresistible. (Trs.)] She was also Praxiteles' mistress, and served as the model for several statues he made of Aphrodite. Her personal fortune was so immense that it enabled her to set up her own statue, in gold, in the sanctuary at Delphi, amongst those of generals and kings. Plutarch, himself a priest of Pythian Apollo, was to take great exception to this centuries later: he described the statue as "a trophy won from the lechery of the Greeks." [38]

Brothels had existed in Athens at least since Solon's day, in the Ceramicus and, particularly, the Piraeus; [39] a percentage of the profits had gone to build the temple of Aphrodite Pandemos.[40]

Were these courtesans (whether freelance or institutionalized) really, as is sometimes claimed, better educated and more culturally aware than respectable Athenian matrons? To judge from those whom we can observe in conflict with legitimate wives, during various court hearings, the matter is at least open to doubt. Consider Alcé the brothel-madam, who gobbled up poor old Euctémon,[41] or Neaera, who lived with Stephanus, or her daughter Phano, who managed to hook an Athenian holding the office of King-archon, and later took part with him in various highly sacred rituals: [42] none of these women would appear to have received a refined education. Neaera was reared by a procuress "who was highly skilled in picking out future beauties on the strength of their appearance in infancy"; but her education seems to have consisted, first and foremost, in learning the secrets of dressing and make-up, and other aids to physical seduction. We hear that Phryne was beautiful; no one suggests that she was clever or cultivated, like Aspasia. It was by their compliant ways and willingness to please that these *hetairai* kept their lovers. As one comic poet put it: "Is not a mistress always more loving than a wife? Indeed she is, and for a very good reason. However unpleasant your wife may be, you are legally bound to keep her. A mistress, on the other hand, knows that a lover can only be kept by constant attentiveness, failing which he will turn elsewhere." [43]

It is quite likely, however, that many courtesans received a somewhat freer and wider education than the middle-class ladies of Athens, especially in such fields as music, singing, and dancing: numbers of them had been

[37] See G. Colin's introduction to his edition of Hyperides (Coll. G. Budé) pp. 10–12.
[38] Plutarch, *On the Pythian Oracles* 401 A.
[39] Cf. Aristophanes, *Peace* 165.
[40] Athenaeus, 13. 569 d.
[41] Isaeus, *On the Succession of Philoctemon* 19–20.
[42] Ps-Demosthenes, *Against Neaera, passim.*
[43] Amphis, *ap.* Athenaeus, 13. 559 a.

trained to perform on the flute (*aulos*), and were employed to play, sing, and dance at banquets. . . .

W. K. LACEY

Marriage and the Family in Athens

AGE OF MARRIAGE

. . . The normal age for men to marry seems to have been about thirty, an age approved by the philosophers as suitable,[1] but there were sound family reasons as well as those of imaginary eugenics. These lay in the Athenian custom of old men retiring from the headship of (or at least from economic responsibility for) their families in favor of their sons, and the son's marriage was an appropriate moment for this to occur. . . . A man who married at about thirty would be about sixty when his son reached thirty; fifty-nine was the age at which a man's military service ended and he was therefore considered an old man.[2]

Girls were married much younger; philosophers and other writers recommended about eighteen or nineteen as suitable.[3] Plutarch relates that Spartan girls were married when they were ripe for it, not when they were small and unready for it.[4] In Athens, girls were presented to the phratry *

W. K. Lacey, *The Family in Classical Greece* (London: Thames and Hudson, 1968), pp. 106–16.

[1] Plato, *Laws* 721B, 785B; *cf. ib.* 772D, *Republic* 460E (25 or over); Arist. *Politics* VII, 14, 6 (1335A) (37 or a little before; girls at 18).

[2] They then were said to be ὑπὲρ τοῦ καταλόγου or ἔξω τοῦ καταλόγου. They became arbitrators (διαιτηταί) for one year (*Ath. Pol.* LIII, 4), but did not necessarily retire into oblivion—Socrates was even a member of the Council, and president of the Assembly after that age, since he was aged 70 in 399 and had been president in 405 (Xen. *Mem.* I, 1, 18 with Plato, *Apology* 32B–C). He was also married rather late in life, since his three sons were still under age in 399, two being described as merely little children (παίδια) at his death (Plato, *id.* 34D.)

[3] See note 1 above. Hesiod, *W. and D.* 695 ff and in art, *Pl.* 24.

[4] Plut. *Lycurgus* XV, 3; they were . . . οὐ μικρὰς οὐδὲ ἀώρους πρὸς γάμον . . . ἀκμαζούσας καὶ πείπερους.

* A group in Athens of obscure origin, but great importance, at least in the social field.

on the *koureotis* day (the third day) of the Apatouria, when a sacrifice was made by their (new) husband; this is associated with the boys' sacrifice on the same day, made on the occasion of their cutting their hair as indicating the end of their childhood.[5] Therefore it will have been not later than about sixteen, and the Greeks' fanatical emphasis on premarital virginity will have made it tend to be earlier than this rather than later.[6]

FREEDOM OF CHOICE

A few instances are known in which a woman is said to have chosen her own husband, but in every case it is clear that it was most unusual; in the instance he cites, Herodotus says so specifically and clearly;[7] Plutarch regards it as one of the remarkable things about Elpinice, sister of Cimon, that her marriage was in accordance with her own free will;[8] Peisistratus' daughter is said to have married for love. It is important to stress that all these women belonged to the highest social class, in which the women have always had markedly more independence than the bulk of the population.

Society demanded that a man procure marriages for his daughters, and, if necessary, sisters; it was regarded as a slight on his excellence if he did not do so.[9] Nature, however, ordained (always until the twentieth century) that more girl-babies than boys should survive infancy, and battle casualties were at least as numerous as deaths in childbirth; the excess of brides seeking husbands therefore created a competitive situation for the fathers of girls, which ensured that a dowry was an invariable accompaniment (though by no means a legal requirement) of a marriage. Girls who had no dowry could not get married, and therefore to marry a girl without a dowry, or with only a very small one, was to do her a very great honor, and was a matter for self-congratulation by orators, especially when the

---

[5] Pollux VIII, 107 (s.v. Φράτορες). 'They brought boys (κόρους) and girls (κόρας) to the *phrateres,* and at the age of young adulthood (εἰς ἡλικίαν προελθόντων) on the so-called *koureotis* day they sacrificed, for the boys the boys' sacrifice (τὸ χούρειον), for the girls the wedding sacrifice' (τὴνγαμηλίαν). For the association with the cutting of the hair, *SIG* 921, and commentary. Deubner, *AF* 232 ff for an account of the Apatouria.

[6] For a modern illustration in primitive parts of the Peloponnese, Sheelagh Kanelli, *Earth and Water* (1965), 121/2.

[7] Hdt. VI, 122. The fact that the chapter is generally condemned as spurious does not affect this argument much, since, even if it was not Herodotus who thought it most unusual, it was another writer.

[8] Plut. *Cimon* IV, 7; *cf. ib.* 9 for Cimon himself, and Dem. XL, 27 for a man said to be in love with his wife (probably a second one in this case).

[9] Isaeus I, 39 on the obligation to see to the marriage of cousins had they been left orphans by their father's death. In Athens it would be taken as a mark of his miserliness if a man did not procure husbands for his daughters or sisters; *cf.* Lysias XIII, 45, XII, 21 for deprivation of marriage as a grievous wrong.

girl was an *epikleros* *.[10] Unmarried girls had either to remain at home, or enter the world of the demimondaines if they were destitute orphans.[11] After marriage, however, a girl seems to have had more ability to determine her lot. The only evidence that there was any special cachet attached to a first, or lifelong, marriage is in the religious sphere; we are told that from the earliest times it had been necessary for the wife of the King Archon (the Basileus) to be a citizen, and a virgin at her marriage; [12] she had the duty of being 'married' to the god Dionysus and spending the night with him in his temple. But for most married couples divorce was easy, and widows were often remarried.

In the choice of their second husband widows were certainly sometimes able to exercise some element of choice; Demosthenes' mother did not marry Aphobus, despite her betrothal; Demosthenes speaks of her disputing with him, and his retaliating by refusing to supply her with food, and in another speech declares that "she inflicted on herself a life of widowhood for the sake of her children." [13] The prosecutors of Lycophron had alleged that a widow had promised herself to her (alleged) lover and had sworn that she would refuse to have intercourse with her husband when her brother gave her to another man.[14] There can be little doubt, however, that young widows, even if they had children, were expected to remarry.[15]

Moreover, Athenian women had as much right to divorce their husbands [16] as their husbands had to divorce them,[17] and we even hear of a father taking his daughter away when he quarreled with his son-in-law; [18] divorce by consent was also possible, especially in connection with a suit for an *epikleros*.[19] In all cases, however, the woman's dowry had to be

* Girl (or woman) without living brothers at the time of the father's death.

[10] Elpinice, Plut. *Cimon* IV, 7; Dem. LIX, 8, 'Who would ever have married the daughter of a state debtor who was utterly without means—and she without a dowry?'; cf. id. XXVIII, 21, XL, 56, XLV, 74. Lysias XIX, 14–16, choosing a poor but honest bride.
[11] Suggested by the comic fragment in Athenaeus XIII, 572A.
[12] Dem. LIX, 75–6; cf. *Ath. Pol.* III, 5. The shrine was at Limnae and open only once a year, on the occasion of this women's rite at the Anthesteria.
[13] Dem. XXVII, 13–15, id. XXIX, 26.
[14] Hypereides, *Lycophron* I, 7 with *ib.* 3.
[15] Demosthenes' mother is an example, also Hagnias' mother, Isaeus XI, 8; cf. id. VII, 7–8, IX, 27 etc.
[16] By ἀπόλευψις; see (e.g.) Isaeus III, 8, 35, 78; Dem. XXX *passim*, Plut. *Alcibiades* VIII, 3–5. The only legal provision was that the woman must get the divorce registered in the Archon's court, Dem. XXX, 17 and 26, Plut. *loc. cit.*, Andocides IV, 14 etc.
[17] By ἀπόπεμψις; e.g. Dem. LIX, 81–3; the speaker claims the reason was her illegitimacy. For varying formulae in divorce, Wyse, *S.I.*, note on III, 8, 5.
[18] Dem. XLI, 4.
[19] Isaeus II, 7–9; Dem. LVII, 40–41.

repaid to her *kyrios,** and a large dowry is said to be something which protects a woman and prevents her being divorced. It is therefore alleged [20] that a woman whose citizenship was doubtful would necessarily have a large dowry so that her husband would not easily get rid of her.

THE DOWRY

The dowry was a field in which it is accepted that a man would express his self-esteem: "nobody," says Isaeus, "would give a dowry of twenty minae to a man of property"; in another speech [21] he asks if ten minae is a dowry suitable for a free-born girl being given in marriage to a man worth three talents. Demosthenes argues [22] that dowries of two talents and eighty minae must have come from a large estate, since nobody would leave his son's estate destitute. Nobody failed to give a dowry if he could help it; an uncle, it is said, guardian to four nieces and one nephew, would be sure to see that the girls were given dowries; friends gave dowries to the daughters of the poor; the daughters of *thetes,* the lowest financial class, who lacked brothers had by law to be given dowries by their relatives in accordance with their means; [23] even the state stepped in very occasionally (in return for outstanding public services) to dower a man's daughters; examples include those of Aristeides in the fifth century and, in the late third century, those of Timosthenes.[24] Dowries consisted of cash, or real estate valued in cash; apart from sums of cash we hear of a tenement house in Cerameicus valued at forty minae, and of thiry minae in cash and ten minae promised on the bride's father's death—a sum later secured by attachment to a claim on a house.[25] Widows on their remarriage received dowries in exactly the same way as unmarried girls, and this is only natural since a woman's dowry was deemed to be her share of her paternal estate, a share set apart for her maintenance, and it is an unfailing principle of Athenian law that the head of the family who had a woman's dowry in his possession had to maintain her.[26]

* The person who has the legal power to dispose of the property or to manage the affairs of a person who is not fully his (or her) own *kyrios,* such as a woman or a minor. Hence *kyrieia* is full ownership or headship of a family.

[20] Isaeus III, 28; *cf. ib.,* 49–51: less than one tenth of an estate is 'outrageously small.'

[21] Isaeus XI, 40 (in effect), III, 49 *et al.*

[22] Dem. XXVII, 42–5; *cf.* Archippe's huge dowry, *id.* XLV, 28.

[23] Isaeus XI, 38–9, Dem. XXVII, 69, law quoted in *id.* XLIII, 54.

[24] Aeschines, III, 258; *cf.* Plut. *Aristeides* XXVII, 4; Aristogeiton's granddaughter was given a dowry by the state (fifth century). For Timosthenes, *SIG* 496, 18: ὅσα ἄν βούληται (in 229/8).

[25] Examples above; *cf.* Isaeus VIII, 8, V, 26, Dem. XLI, 5. For money secured by real property as a form of dowry, Finley, *SLC,* 79 ff *et al.*

[26] Wolff, *MLAA,* 61–2. Examples of widows' dowries, Dem. XXVII, 5, 13–4, 13 with *id.* XLV 28, Isaeus VIII, 8; Lysias XXXII, 6; Hypereides, *Lycophron,* I, 5—an

Household furniture is stated in one passage to belong to a dowry,[27] but it must be assumed that this had been bought with the dowry, since there is evidence that a law of Solon's prevented dowries being constituted of elaborate personal effects.[28] It was in these, given to the bride, over and above the dowry, that Athenians showed goodwill towards their sons-in-law, since these were not valued, and could not be recovered if the marriage broke up in rancour.[29] As in our day, friends also appear to have made wedding gifts to a bride. It is possible that quite large sums of money may have passed undeclared as well—since Athenians also concealed their wealth in order to avoid taxation—because Aphobus was able to allege that Demosthenes' father had four talents of silver buried in the floor of the house, of which his mother had control[30]—a charge which the orator refutes, but which must have been at least credible.

As remarked above, a dowry was intended primarily for a woman's maintenance. It remained in her husband's control while he lived; if he predeceased her and there were no children, it returned with her to her own family; if there were children, it was part of the children's inheritance provided that they supported their mother if adult, or their guardian did if they were infants.[31] Hence in one speech we hear that a widow's assets and liabilities were formally examined when her husband died, and that he had counted among his assets a debt to her. But, in this family at least, the wife had *de facto* made arrangements for her daughters' benefit, and had spent half a mina on a funeral;[32] clearly there were occasions on which

---

exceptionally interesting case in that her *kyrios* (her brother) arranged her marriage, but her child's guardian, who had charge of her first dowry, provided her with a dowry.

[27] Dem. XLVII, 56–7.

[28] Plut. *Solon* XX, 4; that this is the meaning of the passage, Wolff, *MLAA*, 58.

[29] Isaeus III, 35. For gifts of garments and jewels as a mark of goodwill, Isaeus II, 9: 'When Menecles (who had divorced his young wife by consent) paid back (ἀποδίδωσι) the dowry, and gave to her (δίδωσι) the garments she had when she came to the house and the jewels which there were . . .' Isaeus VIII, 8, should be punctuated in this sense as well: ἐκδίδωσιν αὐτὴν Ναυσιμένει Χολαργεῖ σὺν ἱματίοις καὶ χρυσίοις, πέντε καὶ εἴκοσι μνᾶς ἐπιδούς.

[30] Dem. XXVII, 53–5; he describes her as in control of them (κυρία), and says: 'If he distrusted his son's guardians, it was sheer madness to tell them about what lay concealed if he had no intention of putting the property into their charge. If he trusted them, surely he would not have given into their hands the bulk of his money without giving them charge of some more. Nor would he have given my mother this money to look after and given her herself to one of the guardians to be his wife; it is not rational to try to preserve the money through my mother and to put one of those whom he did not trust in charge of her and the money alike.' G. E. M. de Ste. Croix, *Classica et Mediaevalia*, 1953, 34, note 17, provides examples of concealment of wealth.

[31] Or he might provide her with a new dowry, as in Hypereides, *Lycophron* I, 13.

[32] Dem. XLI, 9 and 21; *cf. ib.*, 11.

a wife could dispose of property, though doubtless her husband's assent was obtained.

CHILDREN

After the betrothal came the wedding, at which the bride was brought to the bridegroom's house and the marriage really began (*Pl. 24*), so that the various songs of the wedding were then appropriate.[33] It was living together which made a marriage a marriage; its existence was therefore essentially a question of fact. Living together [34] is the Greek for being married, and the procreation of children was its explicit object. Xenophon's Socrates says: "Surely you do not suppose that it is for sexual satisfaction that men and women breed children, since the streets are full of people who will satisfy that appetite, as are the brothels? No, it is clear that we enquire into which women we may beget the best children from, and we come together with them and breed children"; [35] Neaira's accuser says: "This is what cohabitation is; it is when a person breeds children, and presents his sons to the *phrateres* * and demesmen, and gives in marriage his daughters to husbands as legitimately begotten by himself." [36]

The view that girls had a right not merely to marriage but also to children is clearly implied in what one speaker says of Menecles: "Menecles said that he viewed with anxiety the passing of his vigour and his wife's childlessness; it was not right that she should be rewarded for her virtues by being made to grow old with him in childlessness." [37] Support comes from another passage,[38] where it is clearly implied that a wife who was still of an age to have children could have, and should have, been given a

---

* Members of a phratry (see above).

[33] For the ceremonies at a marriage, 'Hans Licht', *Sexual Life in Ancient Greece* (1932), (*SL* hereafter) 42–56.

[34] Dem. XXVII, 45 says of Demophon's betrothing his infant sister that Demophon got possession of her dowry (2 talents) 'though he was not yet going to live with my sister': οὔπω μέλλοντι . . . συνοικήσειν. *Cf.* Pollux, III, 44–5.

[35] Xen. *Mem.* II, 2, 4: φανεροὶ δ' ἐσμὲν σκοπούμενοι ἐξ ὁποίων ἂν γυναικῶν βέλτιστα ἡμῖν τέκνα γένοιτο· αἷς συνελθόντες . . . τεκνοποιούμθα. I doubt if *LSJ* is right in translating συνελθεῖν as 'have sexual intercourse'; it is equivalent to συνοικεῖν rather, which, it is true, implies this, but has prime reference to the establishment of an *oikos*. *Cf.* what Isomachos says (Xen. *Oec.* VII, 11–12, 18–19)—he and his wife's parents both sought 'the best partner in the *oikos* and children.'

[36] Dem. LIX, 122; *cf.* Isaeus VI, 2–4, where, despite the husband's age, children were to be sought.

[37] Isaeus II, 7–9; *cf.* Xen. *Mem.* I, 4, 7: the desire for children is natural alike in men and women. On this question I should regard the evidence of tragedy as useful support; it is unequivocal, *e.g.* Sophocles, *Electra* 164–5 and 959–62, *O.T.* 1492 ff, *Antigone* 810 ff and 916–18, whether the latter is spurious or not, as Dindorf amongst others thought. See Jebb *ad loc.*

[38] Isaeus VIII, 36.

new husband, but avoided this by repeatedly pretending she was pregnant.

The Athenians were even a bit sentimental about children, if about anything; weeping children were a stock-in-trade of the defendant at a trial— Socrates refused to countenance such behavior at his trial; [39] the emotional appeals of Sositheus in his peroration [40] were obviously accompanied by the boy pleading in person before the court. "Even when people's estates are confiscated by the court for some offence," says Demosthenes,[41] "you, the people, do not confiscate all they have, but out of pity either for their womenfolk, or for their little children, you always leave something even to them" (*i.e.* criminal offenders). "When we are dying," says Xenophon's Socrates,[42] "if we want to commit to someone the duty of educating our sons, guarding our virgin daughters and preserving our money, shall we think the intemperate man worthy of our trust?" Xenophon was clearly thinking of a man's most important responsibilities.

Formal marriage and the birth of children from it also had a public side; this was due to the importance of asserting the child's legitimacy. With this in view a marriage was registered with the *phrateres,* the husband's *phrateres* in most cases, but also, when the girl was an *epikleros,* with her family's.[43] Similarly, when a child was born, it was exhibited at least to relatives on the tenth day festival, at what seems to have been a big celebration; and on this occasion the father named him.[44] It was possibly on this occasion that the child was introduced to the *phrateres,* but this seems usually to have happened later; the father swore "that he knew that the child had citizen-status, being born to him from a citizen mother, properly (*i.e.* formally) married." [45]

Children who could not substantiate their claim to legitimacy were bastards; they not only lacked rights of succession after 403—their maximum inheritance was a thousand drachmae—they were also excluded from the family religious observances, and they did not enjoy citizen-rights.[46]

[39] Aristophanes, *Wasps* 568–71, 976–8 etc. Plato, *Apology* 34D–35B; *cf.* Dem. LIII, 29, XXI, 99 etc. for accusations that the opponent will do this.

[40] *Id.* XLIII, 81–4; *cf.* XL, 56–7; Mantitheus' daughter was clearly in court.

[41] *Id.* XXVII, 65, reading γυναῖκας with the MSS. *Id.* LIII, 28 shows a mother claiming that part of an estate was not liable to be confiscated by the state.

[42] Xen. *Mem.* I, 5, 2.

[43] Isaeus VIII, 18, *id.* III, 75, 79; Pollux VIII, 107.

[44] Dem. XXXIX, 22, XL, 28; Isaeus III, 30, relatives (uncles) attended; Aristophanes, *Birds* 494, 922; *cf.* the comic fragment in Athenaeus XV, 668D for an all-night celebration. For family names, Dem. XLIII, 50, 74 and 77 etc.

[45] *Id.* LVII, 54; ἀστὸν ἐξ ἀστης ἐγγυητης ἑαυτῷ γεγενημένον εἰδώς; Isaeus VIII, 19, suggests it was very early in life, *id.* XII, 3, somewhat later. Adopted sons were also introduced at their adoption, Dem. XLIII, 13, etc., Isaeus VII, 13 and 27–8 etc.

[46] 1000 drachmae = 10 minae = τὰ νοθεῖα, the bastard's portion. This meant that other (citizen) relatives could claim the rest of their family property, Dem. LVII, 53; *cf.* Hypereides, *Lycophron* I, fr. 5 and Isaeus III, *passim,* a speech which is intended to prove the rival claimant a bastard. For religious rights, Dem. XLIII, 51, citizen rights, Wolff, *op. cit.* 76–8.

This did not mean that they had no rights; our legal sources, being, as they are, mainly disputes about inheritances, give a distorted view. Bastards resembled outsiders (*xenoi*) in that they lacked the right to claim citizens' estates,[47] but they must have had rights at law, as did *xenoi*, in whose interests one of the state's chief magistrates, the Polemarchos, was responsible for the administration of justice.[48] *Xenoi* had duties too; metics certainly served in the army and there is no reason to suppose that bastards (if they were rich enough) did not do so likewise.[49] Metics paid extra taxes too; [50] having the duties but not the rewards of citizenship, it is not surprising that they sometimes tried to usurp it—we hear in the orators of "the tricks of those who try to claim citizenship." [51] The state was therefore very severe on attempts to obtain citizenship clandestinely.[52]

WIVES AND CONCUBINES

In his speech against Neaira, Apollodorus cites a law forbidding a foreigner to live with a citizen woman as his wife, and a foreign woman to

[47] This is the point of the joke against Heracles in Aristophanes, *Birds* 1641–69. In Dem. LVII, 53–5, it is clear that bastards (νόθοι) were not the same as *xenoi*, but from the point of view of claiming citizens' estates, they had similar disabilities. *Xenoi* were themselves of several classes: ξένοι (true *xenoi*), who were merely temporarily in Athens, ξένοι *metoikoi* (metics) who lived semi-permanently in Athens, ξένοι *isoteleis*, and *proxenoi* who were specially privileged metics. In what spheres bastards were underprivileged citizens, and in what they were exceptionally-privileged *xenoi* we do not know. It is important to remember that *xenos* means 'the outsider who has been allowed into the circle though not a member of it.'

[48] *Ath. Pol.* LVIII, Dem. XLVI, 22.

[49] For metics, *e.g.* Thucydides II, 31, 2, 3000 metic hoplites. Among bastards, Themistocles certainly served, so did Ctesias son of Conon, Demosthenes LIV, 26 with 3 and 7. Poorer metics might have had to serve in the fleet; no doubt bastards did the same.

[50] Hommel, *RE*, XV, (1932) 1413 ff. sv. μέτοικοι; metics paid a special tax of 12 drachmae a year (μετοίκιον) unless they were raised to the status of *isoteleis* (*i.e.* those who (only) pay the same taxes as citizens). *SIG* 346, an inscription in honour of Nicandrus and Polyzelus, records payments of 10 talents in *eisphorai* between 347/6 and 323/2 (lines 14–18), as well as military service (lines 37–41); in return they were made *isoteleis* and granted γῆς καὶ οἰκίας ἔγκτησις, leave to purchase real-estate, and to pay *eisphorai* and serve on campaign with the Athenians—*i.e.* only when the citizens were called out.

[51] Dem. LVII, 55; 'What have I done of the things that those who are not genuinely citizens are always revealed as having done, and where did I do it?' From this speech it may fairly be deduced that they bribed the officer in charge of the deme's roll of citizens (ληξιαρχικὸν γραμματεῖον) to insert their names, giving them a spurious parentage; they may also have tried a number of different demes.

[52] Dem. LIX, 16–7; in his next sentence Apollodorus makes it clear that the point of the law was to prevent illegal pseudo-marriages: 'the law does not allow a foreigner to live with a citizen or *vice versa* nor to procreate children'—οὐκ ἐᾶ . . . συνοικεῖν . . . οὐδὲπαιδοποιεῖσθαι. Men who openly kept a concubine were not said συνοικεῖν and παιδοποιεῖσθαι, though concubines had a fully-recognized status under the law, *id.* XXIII, 55–6, etc.

with a citizen, on pain of enslavement or a heavy fine; clearly this did not mean a prohibition of sexual intercourse across these boundaries, nor a prohibition on keeping a concubine, or, in the case of a woman, a lover, but it prohibited such people from pretending that they were formally married, and from claiming to breed citizen children. Similar prohibitions barred attempts to marry a daughter born of one citizen-parent to an Athenian as if she were free-born.[53] Thus Apollodorus can maintain that his opponent Stephanus must either claim that Neaira (the woman in question) is a citizen, and his wife in conformity with the laws, or admit that Neaira is a concubine in his house and not his wife, in which case the children claimed to be citizens must be the offspring of another woman, a relative of his own, whom he had earlier married. This is the context of the often misquoted dictum [54] on the courtesan, the concubine and the wife: "we have courtesans for pleasure, concubines to look after the day-to-day needs of the body, wives that we may breed legitimate children and have a trusty warden of what we have in the house"; it does not state that we cannot have either pleasure or care of our persons from our wives— quite the reverse; the services to a man of the three classes of woman are intended cumulatively, and it is the purpose of the argument merely to stress that you can beget legitimate children only from a properly married wife. . . .

ADULTERY

The importance of being able to prove legitimacy had two principal results; it made adultery a public as well as a private offence, and it made the Athenians excessively preoccupied with the chastity of their women-folk, with the result that they were guarded in a manner nowadays thought to be intolerable.[55]

Adultery in Athens (it is sometimes said) meant "the sins of a wife." The evidence is not quite so unequivocal; in the first place, the punishment

[53] Dem. LIX, 51–53; she cohabited (συνώκει) with her husband, pretending she was a citizen.

[54] *Id.* LIX, 118–122. For a wife as higher in standing than a concubine or courtesan, *cf.* Plut. *Solon* XXII, 4, Lysias I, 30 Xen. *Mem.* II, 2, 4, *Oec.,* I, 13, Menander, *Dyskolos* 58–66 etc. This testimony across three centuries should be sufficient evidence to deny the validity of the traditional interpretation.

[55] It is legitimate to wonder how far the remarkable ease with which Homeric and heroic ladies (except Penelope) could be seduced influenced men's thought. Dem. XLVII, 53, for the extreme impropriety of even entering the presence of an Athenian woman in the absence of her husband—the opponents (of course) did not hesitate, whereas a witness would not do so (*id.* 60), and of course the speaker did not do himself; though he entered the opponent's house 'he knew he was not married' (*id.* 38). See also p. 158 ff below.

of death is prescribed for the adulterer and not the adulteress—she was punished, naturally, but it is odd that, if the offence was only hers, her lover should be put to death, not she.

Secondly, in the version of the law which we have, it is stated [56] that a man may with impunity kill an adulterer caught in the act with any of the women in his *kyrieia*—his mother, sister and daughter are mentioned as well as his wife. If the law is correctly reported, and there are no good grounds for believing it is not, this must disprove the idea that the right to kill was to protect a man's own marriage, and that it was because a woman was married that her paramour was able to be punished by her *kyrios;* the man concerned therefore committed an offence as well as the woman.

The punishment of death for adultery is said by Euphiletus to be universally demanded by all states; Lycurgus the orator declares that the adulterer is "one who betrays nature's instincts," and Xenophon compares the man who cannot control his lust to a silly bird, pointing out that the needs of nature can be satisfied without committing adultery.[57] Plato's laws on sexual matters are revealing. They were intended to be as severe for men as for women, but, as he admitted, he had to compromise; though he wished to brand all sexual intercourse with anyone other than a wife as adultery, and claimed that the law of nature was to preserve virginity until the age of procreation, then to remain faithful to one's mate, he admitted that most men, both Greeks and non-Greeks, did not do this; he therefore fell back on 'the possible,' which was to prohibit all sexual intercourse with free-born or citizen women other than a man's wedded wife, to forbid sodomy, and impose secrecy on intercourse with any other (*i.e.* nonfree) woman on pain of disfranchisement.[58] Obviously Plato was reacting against contemporary attitudes, which did allow men extramarital sexual relations provided that they were not with women in the *kyrieia* of other citizens. This is to say that adultery was not *solely* an offence by a female; a man was punishable as an adulterer if he seduced a woman he was forbidden to seduce, and his punishment was apt to be more severe, as his liberty of action was greater.

Athenian women had no sexual liberty, but the explanation of the Athenians' attitude was primarily civic, not moral. Euphiletus says that

[56] *Id.* XXIII, 53–6; *cf. Ath. Pol.* LVII, 3 for lawful killings.

[57] Lysias I, 2; Plut., *Solon* XXIII, says that Solon prescribed a fine of twenty drachmae for seduction of a free woman, one hundred drachmae for rape; this hardly agrees with Demosthenes. The likeliest explanation is that Plutarch has either misunderstood his source, or expressed himself badly, and free but noncitizen women are in question here. The fact that his next sentence is about prostitutes adds to this impression, since kept women are virtually always slaves or freedwomen, Isaeus VI, 19–22, Dem. LIX, *passim,* Lycurgus, fr. 96 (= Stobaeus II, 30) (we must remember that fragments lack their context), Xen. *Mem.* II, 1, 4–5.

[58] Plato, *Laws* 838E–841E.

"the lawgiver prescribed death for adultery" (though not for rape) [59]
". . . because he who achieves his ends by persuasion thereby corrupts
the mind as well as the body of the women . . . gains access to all a man's
possessions, and casts doubt on his children's parentage." This was the
point; if an Athenian had an affair with a citizen-woman not his wife, a
baby would not have any claim on his property or family or religious associations, nor impose on them a bogus claim for citizenship; but the
woman would be compelled to claim that her husband was the father, and
his kinship-group and its cult was therefore deeply implicated, since it
would be having a non-member foisted upon it, and if she were detected,
all her husband's children would have difficulty in proving their rights to
citizenship if they were challenged. An unmarried Athenian girl who had
been seduced could be sold into slavery according to Solon's laws; Hypereides implies that it was more usual 250 years later merely to keep her
at home unmarried—when he hints that neither she nor a widow who had
been seduced would be able to get a husband. [60]

Death for an adulterer, even if caught in the act, was quite certainly not
always demanded; comedy speaks of payment, depilation and other hu-
miliating, vulgar but comical indignities being inflicted on an adulterer,
which would prevent him appearing in public, certainly from appearing
in the wrestling-school, for some time. [61] Divorce for a woman taken in
adultery was compulsory, [62] but we may be pretty certain that the demand
was not always complied with; a woman with a large dowry would have
to have it repaid, and this might be impossible for her husband, or be something he was unwilling to do. Hypereides declares [63] that an adulterer
causes many women to live with those with whom legally they ought not
to be living, but there is no certainty that the orator is speaking of those
known to be adulteresses.

An interesting compromised case of adultery is revealed in the speech
against Neaira. [64] A man who had slept with Neaira's daughter was accused

---

[59] Lysias I, 33; *cf.* I, 4: 'He corrupted my wife, he brought shame on my children,
he insulted me myself.'

[60] Implied by Plut. *Solon* XXIII, 2, a virgin could not be sold; Hypereides,
Lycophron I, 12–13; the seducer is accused that [πολλὰς μὲν γ]υνα[ῖκας ποιῶ] ἀγάυον[ς
ἔνδον κα]ταγηρ[άσκειν] and the same is said to happen to widows: ἀνέκδοτον ἔνδον
καταληρ̣άσκειν. Aechines I, 183, shows that it was deprivation of the pleasure of
dressing-up for festivals that was what "made life not worth living". Was this
more savage than Victorian fathers putting their seduced daughters out on the street?
Aeschines, *loc. cit.*, knows of even more barbarous punishments, but they may well
be apocryphal, as Hans Licht is inclined to think (*SL* 62).

[61] Kallias, frag. 1; κέρδος αἰσχύνης ἄμεινον. ἔγκε μοιχὸν ἐς μυχόν. *Cf.* Aristophanes, *Plutus* 168, *Ach.* 849 (shaving), *Clouds* 1079–1084 (depilation and
ῥαφανίδωσις); Xenophon, *Mem.* II, 1, 5 for his Socrates' view.

[62] Dem. LIX, 86–7.

[63] Hypereides, *Lycophron* I, 12.

[64] Dem. LIX, 64–71.

of adultery with her, and was allowed to buy himself out by giving security of thirty minae, being kept under constraint until he paid; he subsequently sued for wrongful imprisonment (because the girl, he said, was an *hetaira,* not a citizen-girl), the condition being that if he were to be convicted of adultery he could be abused before the court as the accuser wished, save that weapons were barred. In fact the case was settled out of court for a payment of ten minae, "because he had slept with the girl and owed her a good turn." In return he was to have access to her whenever he was in Athens; she became in fact a concubine with the maximum endowment permitted by law for one who was not a legitimate wife. Other cases of concubinage are rare; one is mentioned by Isaeus, when the orator says, "even those who give their womenfolk for the purposes of concubinage make in every case an arrangement in advance about the endowment which will be given to the concubines"; [65] this "concubine," claimed by the orator to be an illegitimate daughter of a citizen, had, like Neaira's daughter, the maximum bastard's portion from her father's estate.

Noncitizens could contract legally valid marriages and dower their daughters to noncitizens,[66] and the Athenian law upheld their contracts; [67] what the Athenian law was concerned to prevent was noncitizens claiming to be citizens, and making claims on the property of citizens, the *oikoi* which comprised the demes. . . .

---

[65] Isaeus III, 39; the passage has been hotly disputed, Wyse, *SI,* note *ad loc.*— but quite unnecessarily, unless we start with preconceptions as to what the Athenians ought to have done. The girl in this speech was married ὡςἐξ ἑταίρας οὖσα with a dowry of 10 minae (τὰ νοθεῖα)—according to the speaker. He may be lying, but what he says must have sounded credible at least.

[66] Hypereides, *Athenog.* 29 (a very fragmentary passage) shows a metic marrying his daughters off; the orator employs the word (ἐξέδωκε) which is used for citizen-fathers also.

[67] *Ath. Pol.* LVIII. Dinarchus (*in Dem.* 23) also cites examples of Athenian courts punishing citizens severely for personal offenses against non-citizens—keeping a free boy imprisoned, raping a Rhodian lyre-girl, sending an Olynthian maid-servant to a brothel—but there may have been more in the cases than we are told.

FREDERIK POULSEN

The Roman Woman

. . . The Roman woman was marriageable at the age of twelve, even if sensible doctors advocated the age of eighteen as being more suitable. Under Augustus' strict laws against the unmarried state and barrenness a twenty-year-old woman without husband and children was liable to punishment. The husband was selected by the family, and the two young people knew as little of each other as the bridal couple in the modern Orient, so that Seneca had some reason to say: "We subject our animals, slaves, clothes and kitchen utensils to a careful inspection before buying them. The bride alone is not examined, so that it will not be known if she displeases the bridegroom before he has taken her home. Only after the wedding will he learn if she is a shrew, stupid or misshapen, or has a bad breath, or whatever her blemishes may be." During the reign of the Caesars this was altered, and Salvius Julianus, the great jurist, characterises the juridical position like this: "In the case of marriage, the agreement of the contracting parties is required, and the consent of the bride."

This notion is bound up with a total change with regard to the legal basis of conjugal relations. The Republic had the patriarchal system, which invested the father with absolute authority over wife and children—the wife was loco filiae, i.e. in the position of a minor daughter. Under the Emperors there were quite modern freedom and independence. In a people like the Roman, of course the emancipation was first and foremost of a financial nature. The wife had absolute control of her fortune; the husband could not even dispose of the dowry. It might happen that, in a moment of weakness, the wife shared her fortune with the husband, or spent a considerable sum of money on procuring him the rank of Knight or Senator; but generally the ladies were rather hard-fisted. This was a great advantage if the husband became bankrupt and his creditors were eager to clap their hands on the money of the wife, too.

For the management of her fortune the wife would engage a legally trained steward, a procurator, often one of the freedmen of the family,

Frederik Poulsen, *Glimpses of Roman Culture,* trans. J. Dahlmann-Hansen (Leiden: E. J. Brill, 1950), pp. 200–208.

72

whom she trusted, as Martial puts it, with "her precious stones, her golden vessels, wine, and favorite slaves," indeed, according to Martial again, even with her virtue sometimes.

"Who is the curly-haired, little man?" Martial asks an indulgent husband, "who does not withdraw from the side of your wife, but incessantly whispers something in her ear, placing his right arm on the back of her chair? You say he is in charge of your wife's business? Indeed! He is really a reliable and strict man, whose face reveals the procurator.—He is in charge of your wife's business? Oh, you fool, it is your business he is taking care of." Among those who accompany the bride into her new home, Seneca in his book on marriage also mentions the curly-haired procurator, under whose mask a lover is disguised, and the holy Hieronymus warns Christian women against being seen in the company of curly-haired procurators.

The next step in the emancipation of woman was that the wife "wore the breeches" and henpecked her husband, for which they already had a word in ancient Rome. "You ask me why I won't marry a rich woman?" says Martial, and he answers: "Because I am not interested in becoming my wife's wife."

With the right to live independent lives came naturally enough easy access to divorce. The men practised successive polygamy—on a tombstone a seventh wife is mentioned—and there were women who contracted three or four, or even five marriages, like Statilia Messalina, who married Nero. That this state of affairs ripened the married woman very early, making her conscious and self-conscious like the modern American lady, is proved by several instances from the days of the Roman Emperors. A Stoic author of the Flavian times, Musonius Rufus, declares the intellectual equality of the sexes. It is true that according to the jurist Ulpian women were excluded from all civic and public functions—they could neither be judges nor hold office, and they could more easily be pronounced unfit to manage their own affairs "on account of the innate improvidence of woman," an argument which the jurist Gaius finds completely unreasonable. On the other hand, the number of independent, masterful Empresses in the second and third centuries: the noble Plotina, the scrupulous Sabina, the two beautiful and passionate Faustinas, and the learned Julia Domna, all those serve to give us an idea of the thoughts and behavior of the "modern" Roman lady.

Of course, the men of that time, like those of our days, sighed for the goodness and virtue of the woman of a still older Rome, in the days when the ideal was: lanifica et linifica matrona, (the spinning and weaving matron). Augustus forced his female relatives into "familiarize themselves with wool-work." Epitaphs bear witness to this, too, and the epigram of a tombstone proclaims:

"All that parents have generally wished to find in their daughters was awarded to you, Caesia, and you deserved it: The spinner's shining fidelity, which is the foster-child of piety, and above all—honour for old-time chastity."

The contrast is explained by an agricultural author of the early years of the Emperors, Columella, when he deplores that the women of his time are so addicted to luxury and frivolity that they despise the spinning of wool and view homemade clothes with a scornful eye. "Their taste is so depraved that they prefer to buy that which costs much money, often very much money."

The injustice of this complaint is evident. Roman evidence is available to the effect that the homemade dresses were very ugly (really only fit for slaves) and comparatively dearer than the clothes made in factories. But it would indeed be unreasonable to expect women to dress without taste, even at considerable expense, and the correct disposition was not influenced by the fact that a few women bought much too expensive clothes.

The Roman writers were fond of rhetorical exaggerations. Velleius Paterculus writes (II, 1): "The Elder Scipio paved the way for the power of Rome, the Younger for her luxury. When the fear of Carthage had been removed, the transition from virtue to vice was not a gradual development, but a headlong fall." Such expressions must be borne in mind when we find censure of the "fall" of woman from the virtues of the home to the gadding about of the flirt. Bringing the individuality of woman to life entailed some drawbacks—and sometimes excesses, but quite as often did it bring about improvement of quality and refinement of intellect. In the midst of praises sung to the old-time virtue, characterised by the term, domiseda, sit-at-home, a woman of a completely different mould appears; Cornelia, the mother of the Gracchi, of whom Plutarch says (C. Gracchus 19): "She had many friends, and kept a good table that she might show hospitality, for she always had Greeks and other literary men about her, and all the reigning kings (of the Hellenistic countries) exchanged gifts with her."

Here we find the typical woman of the world in Roman society, as early as the middle of the second century B.C., and no one among her contemporaries or in later ages called in question Cornelia's purity of mind or the firmness of her character.

Outcries about the depravity of woman find their most violent expression in the poet Juvenal, who lived under the Emperors Domitian and Trajan and far into the reign of Hadrian. When he asserts that virtue has completely left this earth of ours, he reminds us of modern wits who maintain that the lur-players on the column at Raadhuspladsen (the Town-Hall Square) of Copenhagen will blow their horns whenever a virgin crosses the square: but so far they have never given a sound. In Juvenal we hear of women who beat all American records and have enjoyed eight husbands within five seasons; we witness the evening atmosphere after bedtime, when the wife gives tongue so that there is little chance of sleep. She will cry, upbraid the husband about some rival of her own creation and his other reprehensible doings, and by degrees she will grow fiercer than a tigress robbed of her whelps.

Alas! the virtuous, old days are past, when the Romans lived in humble dwellings and narrow circumstances, when the hours of sleep were few, and there was no time for squabbling and vice, when hands were hardened with wool and spinning-wheel, etc. Now we are suffering all the evils of long-continued peace. Luxury more ruthless than war broods over Rome, and exacts vengeance for a conquered world. Certainly a singular way to express thankfulness for Pax Romana!

There are many vicious types among the wives, says Juvenal: The opulent woman, whom the husband married out of avarice; for which reason she thinks she is entitled to have the pleasures of a widow. There is the learned wife, who matches and compares Homer and Virgil, whose speech teems with rhetoric, who tackles any definition whatsoever like a philosopher, prefers the Greek language, and will only be loved "in the Greek fashion."

The indefinite woman lingers far into the evening in the thermae. She cannot leave the caldarium until her languid arms sink down, or the crafty anointer has passed his hand down her body and given her a final slap on the buttocks. In the meantime her poor guests are dying of hunger and weariness. Finally she puts on an appearance in her home, flushed and with a tremendous thirst. She drains the goblets of wine so senselessly that at last she drinks and vomits just as when a snake has glided into a cask.

In the heroic days of yore, Alcestis encountered death for her husband. Were a similar exchange allowed to the women of our time, they would gladly purchase a lapdog's life by the sacrifice of their husband's.

We recognize all this from modern attempts to reduce woman within the compass of a formula, or to characterise her by a slogan. It must also be called false wit when some people of today have tried to apply to Rome and the Roman lady the words of a Viennese diplomat, uttered shortly before the first Great War: "Austria will be ruined by her women." It was really the diplomats of Austria who plunged the country into war and disaster, and in the same way the women of Rome are not responsible for the destructive wars of the third century, which became the beginning of the end.

The only really striking statement about women is that of the shrewd reasoner of Louis XIV's time, La Bruyère, who writes (Les Caractères): "Les femmes sont extrêmes; elles sont meilleures ou pires que les hommes." (Women always go to extremes; they are either better or worse than men). Bearing these sage words in mind, we will follow in the wake of Roman ladies—take a bath of human beings, as Kierkegaard has it—and begin by surprising the Roman woman where she is most herself—at her morning toilet.

After the carousal of the night, many Roman ladies and damsels were naturally enough suffering from the aftereffects, and vented their spleen on those who were nearest at hand, the chambermaids. Even the love-poet, Ovid, uses that motif several times. He says somewhere: "Yet I forbid you not to let your locks be combed before them, so that they lie rippling adown your back: at that time, especially, beware of being ill-tempered, nor often unbind your fallen tresses. Let the tiring-woman be safe; I hate her who tears with her nails her handmaid's face, or seizing a needle stabs her arms. That maid curses, as she touches it, her mistress's head, and weeps the while, bloodstained, over the hated locks."

In the "Amores," the poet has a splendid panegyric on his beloved one's hair, which, when unbound, reaches her waist.

"Add to this, that it flows with a hundred natural waves and has never given you any cause for annoyance. No pin, and no rampart of a comb ever plagued your tresses. Never did the maid who braided your hair suffer injury. Often did she curl it in my presence, and a hairpin never wounded her arms."

The coiffures of Ovid's time were so "easy" that the storms of fury of the mistress failed to culminate. But under the Emperor Trajan, the styles of hair became so complicated that the subject recurs very often in the poets of that time. A bust of a plump Roman lady in the Ny Carlsberg Glyptotek gives the necessary color to the descriptions of the poets. Above a low border of curls we see three tiers of plaits, reminding one of diadems, each braid decorated at the top with small snail-like or cylindrical curls. If it is no wig, but natural hair with an addition of artificial curls, we quite understand the worries of the poor lady's maid, and the impatience of the mistress, which according to Martial might rise to such a pitch, that they knocked the maid on the head with the bronze mirror, and the poor girl fainted on the marble floor.

The most faithful description of the morning toilet and its central figure, the distinguished lady, is given by Juvenal in the sixth satire, the longest, most carefully elaborated and most famous of his sixteen great poems. A passage of it ends with these lines: (v. 474 ff.). "It is worthwhile to find out exactly what their occupation and pursuits are through the live-long day. If her husband has gone to sleep with his back to her, the housekeeper is half killed, the tire-women are stripped and whipped, and the Liburnian slave is accused of having come behind his time, and has to pay the penalty of another's sleep (the husband's). One has rods broken about him, another bleeds from the whips, a third from the cowhide. Some women pay a regular salary to their torturer. While he lashes she is employed in enamelling her face. She listens to her friend's chatter or examines the broad gold of an embroidered robe, and while he flogs, she reads the morning paper, which is written criss-cross, until at length, when the torturer is exhausted, she thunders out: "Begone!".

The government of her household is no more merciful than that of a Sicilian Court. If she has made an assignation in one of the parks or rather near the chapel of the Isiac procuress, and is anxious to be decked out more becomingly than usual, the unhappy Psecas (the slave) will be arranging her hair, herself with dishevelled locks, naked shoulders and naked breasts. "Why is this curl too high?" screams the mistress. Instantly the white-hot, lyre-shaped curling-iron avenges the heinous crime of the misplacing of a hair. What has poor Psecas done? What crime is of hers? Is it her nose that displeases you? Another, on the left hand, draws out and combs her curls and rolls them into a band. An aged matron, who has served her due period at the needle in the time of the mistress's mother, is the first to be asked for her opinion on the coiffure. Then those who are her inferiors in years and skill will vote in order, as though their mistress's good name or life were at stake. So great is the desire for beauty! Into so many tiers she forms her curls, so many stages high she builds her head. In front you will look upon an Andromache (Hector's proud wife), behind she is a dwarf—you would imagine her another person.—No thought meanwhile about her husband, not a word of her ruinous expenditure; she lives as though she were merely a neighbor of her husband's, and in this respect alone is nearer to him—that she hates her husband's friends and his slaves, and makes grievous inroads on his purse."

Peculiarly enough, it is generally the Roman law that gives us the clearest picture of the equipment of the distinguished Roman lady. A sharp distinction is made between the wardrobe of a lady, especially her trinkets, and what is called mundus muliebris, "the female world," i.e. the paraphernalia of the toilet-table: bowls, scent-bottles, and the different tubs with water for baths.

Among the trinkets we shall mention the engagement-rings, which the ladies of ancient Rome, like the women of modern Sweden, wore on the fourth finger of the left hand. Aulus Gellius, a Roman author of the second century A.D., explains this by a very ingenious myth. He alleges that the Egyptians—he probably means the doctors of Alexandria—had discovered in their studies of anatomy an especially delicate sinew, passing from that finger to the heart, the seat of love. That was why they chose the fourth finger as the bearer of the symbol of love. This anatomical hypothesis is more romantic than convincing.

Let us now piece together with the assistance of the Roman authors a description of what took place at the morning-toilet of the Roman lady, besides the difficult arrangement of the coiffure. Before braiding her hair, she had it dyed blonde, by means of a kind of soap made from goat's tallow and buck ashes. If she wished to appear with demoniacally black locks, she would affect one of the wigs, black as ebony, which were imported directly from India and on which very high duty was paid at the frontiers of the Roman Empire. Then the tiring-maid would proceed to a most painful operation: that of plucking all the hairs of her mistress's arms and legs. Next the forehead and arms were painted with chalk or white lead, the cheeks with ochre, the lips with lees of wine, lashes and eyebrows with ashes or powder of antimony. The teeth were brushed chalk-white with crushed horn. In addition there were all the touches with the brush that gave character to all the feaures for which purpose there were different liquids in bowls and bottles. In his witty epigram on a modern, little lady Martial says: "You are disturbed, oh Galla, in a hundred bottles, and the face you show us is not the one that sleeps with you at night."

But let us by no means imagine, that everyone was of Galla's type. An examination of the collection of Roman portraits in the Ny Carlsberg Glyptotek will show us, throughout four centuries, women of different mentality, among them noble and strong women whose features contradict all the nonsense served out by the authors of satires and epigrams, and by Suetonius in his Imperial Biographies. At the very time when Juvenal was composing his satires, there was a reaction among the circle of distinguished Roman ladies, a return to ancient Roman austerity. The model was Plotina, Trajan's excellent wife, whom Pliny the Younger characterizes like this: "Who is more pious, who more old-fashioned than she?"

The same Pliny tells us of an old friend of his who lived with his wife for thirty-nine years without quarrelling. And how bravely many Roman wives accompanied their husbands into exile, even unto death, when the Triumviri or the Emperors condemned them!

Velleius Paterculus relates that when numerous noblemen were proscribed or sent to death by Antonius and Octavianus, their sons forsook them, some of their freedmen too, but their wives stood by them with admirable loyalty. From the first years of the Roman Emperors, a long list could be made of brave wives. Most famous is Arria, who infused courage into the breast of her husband, condemned to death by Claudius. Plunging a dagger into her bosom, she drew it out, and handed it to him with these words: "Paetus, it does not hurt." Pliny the Younger relates of an excursion on Lake Como, during which the ship passes a villa. An elderly friend then tells him of a wife who had drowned herself there with her husband, when a painful disease made life unbearable to him.

Starting from La Bruyère's words, we can go one step further and assert that the Roman lady was both better and worse than the modern woman;

worse, because she knew no humane and social inhibitions in her cruelty; better, because it was not for nothing that she was the daughter of the first heroic people of antiquity and brought up to dread neither danger nor death. . . .

3. MOMENTS OF LEISURE

Throughout history both rich and poor have found time for amusement. Sports, games, festivals, and religious holidays have always been a part of Everyman's existence. But not all people have participated in them to the same extent; and often, it seems, one person's fun has proved to be another's hardship. The diversion of the wealthy meant only more work, and in some cases even death, for slaves and servants. Without dwelling on extreme cases, however, we can probably posit that the lower classes usually participated on the fringes and derived at least some vicarious pleasure from the spectacles that were presented.

Emile Mireaux demonstrates how Greek festivals and religious symbolism were closely connected with the cycle of nature. Thus the harvest and the funeral were major social institutions for all walks of society. The notion of "funeral games" may seem strange to us, but for the early Greeks they were events more frequent and hardly less elaborate than the celebration of victories in battle.

J. P. V. D. Balsdon relates many details of everyday life in Rome, a society which notoriously devoted so much of its wealth and energy to amusement. Some of this assumed a bizarre character—dancing girls from Cadiz, performing monkeys, half-naked priests running through the streets with leather whips—but much of it is also thoroughly familiar to us. We discover that the public extravaganzas were organized by and for the rich; yet, even the poor occasionally looked on at the circus.

W. Warde Fowler examines the Roman notion of "holiday" in both its religious and secular aspects. Any modern person whose Sundays are regularly devoted to the rituals of professional football can easily appreciate the ordinary Roman's fanaticism for sports. At least in this regard, social custom has changed remarkably little in two thousand years.

If societies can be judged by their forms of leisure, then classical civilization would seem to be closer to our own than many of the intervening eras. The Greeks and Romans probably knew a degree of formalization in sports and public festivals not equaled again until the twentieth century. With them we share the reverence for the arena and the gymnasium: and the revival of the Olympic games in our time may be symptomatic of the lessening significance which is now given to the focal institution of Christianized Europe: the Church.

EMILE MIREAUX

Popular Festivals, Funeral Rites, Public Games

. . . In all rural cultures each of the principal actions of the farmer's year, seed time, harvest, threshing, grape harvest, has been and sometimes still is accompanied by festivities which are designed to favor those natural forces that promote fertility, to celebrate their metamorphoses, their seasonal death and resurrection, to ward off hostile influences and raise the ban that weighs on every new creation.

These festivals usually permitted of dancing, music and songs, the magic virtue of which was universally recognized. The Homeric poems tell us very little of them; but there is a revealing picture of grape harvest in the description of the shield of Achilles. The grapes are gathered by young men and girls. In the midst of them a boy is playing the cithara and in a reedy voice singing a *linos,* or funeral lament. The others strike the earth in cadence and accompany him with cries and dances. There is no doubt that we have here a case of agrarian magic, a harvest ritual, which normally includes a lament for the god's death. Some few centuries later

Emile Mireaux, *Daily Life in the Time of Homer,* trans. Iris Sells (London: George Allen and Unwin Ltd., 1959), pp. 227–40.

Theocritus [1] tells us how once, on the isle of Cos, he took part in the Thalysia, a rural ceremony in which, at the time of threshing, one offered the first fruits to Demeter. The celebrants lay on a bed of freshly plucked rushes singing alternate songs in honor of an effigy of the goddess. This was adorned with stalks of wheat and poppies and stood on the threshing-floor beside a pile of yellow wheat in which a threshing-shovel had been planted. One may take account of this recent text because it certainly describes a very ancient ceremonial.

The present writer has conjectured and tried to show that the various episodes of Odysseus' sojourn among the Phaeacians represent a transposition, on to the plane of myth, of the successive rites of a Springtime festival of rebirth. This, like many ceremonies that have survived into our own day, began with a "quest" for the spirit of the Tree, or of Vegetation, a spirit drowsy and overwhelmed by winter; it ended, after a victorious ordeal, with the revelation of the god rejuvenated or resuscitated, with a recitation of his trials, and the expulsion, on a boat by night, of a person who played the part of a scapegoat.

A certain number of these popular festivals of a rural character took place during the winter months. The enforced leisure and an abundance of provisions were at that time favorable to festivities. Winter was related to the world of night, and also the reign of the subterranean and infernal powers, permanent sources of fertility and dispensers of wealth. And, finally, winter was the season of the dead, when they once more came in contact with the living who evoked them in masquerades and displayed their presence in processions of masks.

Of these winter festivals we are fairly well acquainted with those that were celebrated in Athens and which at an early date were placed under the patronage of Dionysus.

The 'Rustic Dionysia' took place at the end of our autumn and the beginning of winter. They were village festivals strung out through the course of the month Poseideon and consisting mainly of a procession which carried a large phallus and was no doubt designed to promote fertile harvests. The procession was accompanied with sacrifices, songs and games. The most popular contest consisted in balancing oneself on a wine-skin oiled for the purpose, and the young man who contrived to stand on it longest without slipping carried off the skin and the wine. There were also gay processions, marching to the sound of the flute, of young men wearing masks and disguises; in the course of these diversions, two of the youths came to grips in a grotesque sort of combat. These processions, interspersed with comic episodes [2]—the *comoi*—later gave birth to Comedy.

During the months that followed, but this time outside the city itself, a

[1] *Idyll,* VII.
[2] They may have been something like student 'rags' (Translator).

similar festival was celebrated. This was the Lenaean Festival, of which we know little except that the Lenaea included a procession.

On the 11th, 12th and 13th of the month Anthesterion which roughly corresponds to our February, came the *Anthesteria,* a festival both joyous and funereal as was customary for most of the rustic ceremonies devoted to the cult of fertility. The first day was marked by 'the opening of the *pithoi,'* or wine-casks. Each vintner brought a *pithos* of wine to the sanctuary of Dionysus 'in the Marsh,' the oldest sanctuary in Athens, opened it, poured a libation and tasted the wine. This was a day of family rejoicings and drinking-bouts in which all the servants were associated.

The object of this opening of the *pithoi* was to raise the ban on the last vintage which could now be consumed without sacrilege. To consecrate the event, the second day, which was known as the day of 'Pitchers,' was devoted to a drinking contest at which the king himself presided. Each competitor provided himself with a pitcher of wine. At the signal of the trumpet, he had to swallow the contents as quickly as possible. The victor received a crown of foliage and a leather bottle full of wine.

On the same day the god made his solemn entry into the city. Dionysus, who was supposed to have come by sea, was borne on a 'naval chariot' at the head of the procession. The prow of this boat on wheels was formed by a pig's head, the stern rose in the form of a swan's neck. Accompanied perhaps by mummers, the god went to fetch the queen, who, in the historical period, was the wife of the king-archon. They then formed a kind of wedding procession which repaired to the old royal palace of the *Boucoleion,* and here was consummated the union of the god and the queen, a symbol and pledge of fertility.

Meanwhile, precautions were taken throughout the city to ward off the malignant influence of the souls of the dead who, that day, emerged from the depths of the earth. People decked themselves with hawthorn and smeared their doors with pitch; and all the sanctuaries were closed and surrounded with a rope, save only the temple of Dionysus in the Marsh.

The third day of the Anthesteria was devoted to the souls of the departed. For their benefit the citizens prepared a pudding of mixed grains, in earthenware saucepans—a pledge of abundance—which had to be consumed before nightfall. This was the day of 'Saucepans.' When it was over, one took leave of the infernal powers amid cries of: "Out go the Keres: the Anthesteria are over." [3]

A number of ceremonies of the same order, beneficent or purifying, gay or funereal, sometimes even tragic, were performed in similar circumstances and in many another city. We conjecture that variants of the Anthesteria were celebrated in the Ionian cities of Asia Minor. Memories

---

[3] For details of these ceremonies, see H. Jeanmaire, *Dionysos.* Paris, 1951, Ch. I.

of most of these rites have been but sparsely preserved in later texts. But the most widespread of them appear to have related to the practice of the scapegoat, which consisted in removing the sins, misfortunes or sufferings of the whole people by transferring them to a victim who was then expelled or sacrificed.

A few echoes of them have reached us. At Chaeronaea, for example, each head of a family, and also the chief magistrate in the Prytanaeum, practised "the expulsion of Hunger." A slave was beaten with rods and driven away amid cries of: "Begone, Hunger; enter, Health and Wealth!" On the sixth of the month Thargelion (May) in Athens, the people led out of the city two human victims, one wearing a collar of white figs, the other a collar of purple figs, and then stoned them. On the following day, after this rite of collective purification, an offering was made of the first fruits. At Abdera a citizen was excommunicated every year "in order that he alone should bear the burden of all the sins of the people." Six days later he was stoned by the whole population. There was also a very ancient custom still surviving in the sixth century before our era in the cities of Asia Minor: in order to banish plague or famine, they chose an ugly or deformed person, took him to an appropriate spot, made him eat dry figs, a barley loaf and cheese, and then, while the flut was being played, whipped him on the genital organs with branches of a forest tree. Finally he was burned on a pyre of wood cut from the forest and his ashes were then thrown into the sea.

These cruel and joyous festivals were essentially collective. If they were to be efficacious, the whole population had to take part, at least indirectly. It was a common belief in the archiac period that life was born of death.

FUNERALS

Hence the place and importance of funerals in family life. For the great families a funeral was the occasion for a public demonstration in which they displayed their wealth and power, and the extent of their clientèle.

The first and imperative duty of the living was to bury the dead according to the rites. Denial of sepulture was the most terrible punishment that could be inflicted on the dead: it was the supreme penalty reserved for traitors, for those guilty of sacrilege and often for suicides. Their ghosts were condemned to wander without respite; they might also become dangerous.

It has long been held, on the testimony of the Homeric poems themselves, that cremation was the funeral rite normally and even exclusively practised in the older Greek communities. Homer appears to have been acquainted with no other. In both the *Iliad* and the *Odyssey* the souls of the dead beg with anguish for cremation. The shade of Elpenor who, unknown to his companions, had broken his neck by falling from the terrace of Circe's house, because he had drunk too much wine, demands it imperiously of Odysseus when the latter visits the kingdom of the dead, that lies beyond the Ocean:

> Nay, burn me with mine armour, all I have,
> And heap a mound for me upon the shore
> Of the grey sea. . . .[4]

In the same way the soul of Patroclus, appearing to Achilles in a dream, begs him to hasten and give him his "due of fire."

Cremation alone, according to Homer, gives final rest to the souls of the departed by opening for them the doors of the house of Hades. The shade of Patroclus explains it in this way:

> Bury me soon as may be; let me pass
> The gate of Death: they keep me at a distance,
> The spectres and the wraiths of men outworn,
> And will not let me mix with them beyond
> The river, but I wander baffled through
> Hades' wide-gated house. Give me thy hand,
> I do entreat thee, since no more again
> Shall I come back from Hades, when ye once
> Have rendered me my due of fire.[5]

When the body has been burned, the soul finally leaves the world of the living which need have no more fear of him.

Homer thus appears to have been an exclusive partisan, almost an ardent apostle, of cremation. No doubt the cause of cremation was inspired by a conception of the after-life which was probably not the most widespread and popular; it therefore had to be defended. Hence Homer's proselytism.

Excavations have in fact revealed to us that in the early centuries of the first millenium before Christ, that is, in the age of Homeric civilization, cremation was far from being the exclusive or even the most frequent practice. The oldest tombs in the Dipylon cemetery at Athens were almost exclusively devoted to burial of the body. It was only by a gradual progress that the great Athenian families were converted to cremation, while inhumation continued to be widely practiced by others.

Homer gives us three detailed descriptions of funeral ceremonies; there are the funerals of Patroclus and Hector in Books XXIII and XXIV of the *Iliad,* and that of Achilles which is related by Agamemnon in the

---

[4] *Odyssey*, XI, vv. 74–5, p. 183.
[5] *Iliad*, XXIII, vv. 71–6, p. 508.

last book of the *Odyssey*. These narratives are magnificently illustrated by the paintings on the large sepulchral vases of the Dipylon.

The ceremony comprised three great episodes.

When the body had been washed, anointed and covered with a shroud, it was exposed on a litter or a ceremonial bed. Beside it now came and stood the singers—the relatives, male and female, of the dead man, his friends and intimates—and they in turn sang the chant of mourning, the ritual dirge, to which the whole company responded with sobs and groans. At Hector's funeral, Andromache commences the chant by taking the hero's head in her hands:

> . . . O my man,
> Thou art gone young from life, and leavest me
> A widow in thy house. . . .

Then Hecuba raises her voice:

> Hector, of all my sons the best beloved. . . .

Finally it is Helen's turn:

> . . . Hector, whom I loved the best
> Of all my husband's brothers. . . .[6]

The end of each couplet is followed by a long wail from the mourners.

The exposure of the body did not usually last long, but the time varied. In the classical period it was often limited by law. The shade of Patroclus asks for it to be short. Hector's body on the other hand was exposed for nine days, and Achilles' for seventeen. In this case the body had to be roughly embalmed. The kings of Sparta continued to be embalmed. A sacrifice was then offered to the dead. The blood of animals was poured from cups round the body, and the flesh was consumed in a copious repast.[7]

The second act was represented by the funeral procession. The body was carried to the place of burial on a four-wheeled carriage, accompanied by a sometimes splendid train of women-mourners on foot and men in chariots.

The supreme ceremony of burial was reserved for the close relatives of the departed, who, after dismissing the procession, proceeded alone to this duty. In the case of cremation, those nearest and dearest to the dead man themselves raised the pyre. The body was placed on the sum-

[6] *Iliad*, XXIV, pp. 564–5.
[7] *Iliad*, XXIII, vv. 29–34.

mit. Victims were then offered in sacrifice: their fat served to cover the corpse, while their bodies were laid round about, with jars of honey and oil. In addition to all this, Achilles sacrificed four mares on the pyre of Patroclus and two of the dead man's favourite dogs.[8] When the whole pyre had been consumed, wine was scattered over the ashes to extinguish them; then the bones were gathered together and after being wrapped in a double layer of fat were placed in an urn. This was wrapped in a cloth and set in a grave covered with large flagstones, Earth was piled up on it to form a "tomb," on which a 'stele' or vertical stone was sometimes planted.

When the burial was a matter of simple inhumation, the body was laid in a rectangular grave about a yard deep. Beside the dead man they placed, for his use or diversion, his weapons, his jewels and an assortment of vases and household utensils. Finally, on the flagstone that covered the grave, they sometimes set a large sepulchral urn, open at the bottom, as a means of transmitting to the departed the family offerings, such as libations of wine, oil, and honey. The funeral ceremony itself was often depicted on these painted vases.

On returning home, the members of the family purified themselves and partook of the funeral banquet. The soul of the dead man was supposed to be present at this, a fact which forbade anyone's saying a word that was not in his praise. On the third and again on the ninth day after the funeral, another repast was offered on the tomb to the dead man himself. This was the end of the period of mourning; in other words, it was held that from that moment the departed had finally taken his place in the world beyond.

FUNERAL GAMES AND PUBLIC GAMES

It is obvious that the public for whom the Homeric poems were written was extremely fond of games, athletic contests, chariot-races, and also of artistic competitions in singing, dancing and poetry.

The greater part of Book XXIII of the *Iliad,* which is one of the longest in the poem, is devoted to an extraordinarily vivid and picturesque description of the games given by Achilles on the occasion of Patroclus' funeral; while a long passage in Book VIII of the *Odyssey* shows us the public games, mingled with dance and song, that were celebrated in Phaeacia in presence of Odysseus.

The games given in honor of a hero's funeral are represented in the Homeric poems as a current practice: as witness what the shade of

---

[8] Not to speak of the twelve Trojan prisoners who were slain to appease the soul of Patroclus. (See Book XXIII. Trans. Marris, pp. 511, 512).

Agamemnon says to the shade of Achilles as they stand in the fields of pale asphodel:

> . . . Thou in thy day
> Hast seen the funeral games of many heroes,
> When young men gird themselves and make them ready
> To struggle for the prize, at some king's death;
> But at that sight thou wouldst have marvelled most;
> Such glorious prizes did the goddess offer,
> Thetis the silver-footed, in thy honour. . . .[9]

The games celebrated in honor of Achilles are not the only ones to be so described. The talkative old Nestor does not fail to recall his own triumphs at the games which, when he was a young man, had been held in honor of Amarynceus, king of the Epeians.[10] And the same book of the *Iliad* contains an allusion to the games celebrated at Thebes after the death of Oedipus.[11]

That the holding of these contests, which were not always exclusively athletic, persisted to a late period and even to the end of the Homeric age, among the great royal and aristocratic families, is proved by reference to Hesiod. He recalls how he once went to Chalcis to take part in the funeral games in honor of the valiant Amphidamas. The dead man's sons offered a great quantity of prizes, and Hesiod himself won a prize for his hymn, a two-handled tripod which, on his return home, he dedicated to the Muses of Helicon.[12]

These contests and the prizes that crowned them were simply a survival of old customs or rather very ancient institutions the meaning of which has long been lost. There was in fact a time when funeral games were not games, but veritable combats, fights for the succession which often had a tragic issue, and in which the competitors disputed among themselves the offices, honors and property of the departed; sometimes also his wife or daughter, pledges or vehicles of legitimacy. The ultimate victor was the elect of heaven. It was held that he owed his triumph less to skill, strength and intelligence than to the protection and assistance of the deity. And we find very clear traces of this conception not only in the ancient tradition relative to the games but also, naturally, in the Homeric texts.

Thus the chariot race, which was the main feature of the funeral games for Patroclus, was really only a contest between Apollo and Athena. The former who is protecting Eumelus, son of Admetus, causes the whip to fall from Diomed's hand at the most dramatic point in the race. Athena

---

[9] *Odyssey,* XXIV, vv. 87–9, p. 421.
[10] *Iliad,* XXIII, vv. 630 et seq.
[11] *Ibid.,* vv. 679–80.
[12] Hesiod, *Works and Days,* ed. Mair, p. 24.

restores the whip to her favorite and breaks the yoke of Eumelus' team which is hurled to the ground, opening a way for his rival. In the foot race Athena makes the son of Oileus slip in the dung of the sacrificed oxen, in order to assure Odysseus' victory. But in the contest with the bow it is Apollo's turn to secure the triumph of Meriones.

However that may be, it is evident that the funeral games described by Homer and Hesiod served then only to honor the memory of the dead and to permit his descendants to display their power, wealth and magnificence.

According to the legendary tradition, the public games and, specifically, those which became the great Panhellenic contests—the Olympic, the Isthmian, the Nemean and the Pythian—were in principle no other than funeral games held near the tomb of an ancient hero or tutelary genius, the tomb of Pelops at Olympia, of Melicertus at Corinth, of Opheltes at Nemea and of Pytho at Delphi. It seems difficult, however, to reconcile this identification with the regular renewal of these celebrations from generation to generation, and with their periodical character. Was it not the peculiar feature of funeral games that they were held by the family once for all? If in the first instance they had been a means of establishing the succession, they ceased to have any reason when it was once established.

But when this has been said, we must admit that the identification of public games with the funeral games of the family is not, in certain respects, entirely unjustified, and that it at least deserves attention.

The public games held at regular intervals were very probably designed to promote the renewal of those subterranean energies which perpetuated life and presided over its annual restoration. Now according to primitive notions this vital energy was normally incarnated in the king. He had therefore to be put to trial at fixed intervals. In a certain number of Greek cities the normal duration of a reign appears originally to have been limited to eight years. Homer tells us that Minos caused his power to be renewed every ninth year by Zeus.[13] In the historic period the ephors could suspend the powers of the kings of Sparta after they had reigned eight years. In primitive times the public games were doubtless only a means of periodically testing the vital energy of the reigning king—every eight years perhaps. If victorious, he commenced a new reign; if beaten he yielded up his place, and also his wife or daughter, to the victor.

The public games therefore, like those which followed a funeral, were also in principle designed to regulate a succession or inheritance: hence certain of their funereal aspects. The presidents at the Nemean games were dressed in mourning garb.

We have already remarked how, in our opinion, the games held in

---

[13] *Odyssey,* XIX, vv. 178–9.

Phaeacia at the time of Odysseus' return were doubtless simply an episode in a number of renewal rites. In these games the man who represents the spirit of the Tree, the incarnation of vegetable life—and this happens to be Odysseus—is victorious. It is even worth noting that his success is immediately followed by a song of Demodocus who, amid an accompaniment of dances, describes in a sprightly vein the union of Aphrodite and Ares. That this should be a coincidence is by no means certain. It was normal and frequent for a marriage in heaven to be evoked, and even celebrated, on the occasion of ceremonies of which the purpose was to honor the forces of generation and life, as witness the union of Dionysus with the queen at the festival of the Anthesteria in Athens.

In any event, what appears certain is that the poet who described the Phaeacian games in the *Odyssey,* and the games that followed the funeral of Patroclus in the *Iliad,* was familiar with the celebration of the great Panhellenic games, notably those at Olympia which were the most ancient. This is the only explanation for the place of honor given in the *Iliad* to the chariot race which was certainly not a normal contest in the family funeral games. This race is described with such minuteness and precision that the narrative can only have come from an *habitué* of the race-courses, and that he is perhaps even alluding to an historical event, namely the victory at Olympia in 648 B.C. of the team belonging to Myron of Sicyon, brother of the tyrant Orthagoras.[14]

After the parade of competitors and horses we first hear a number of recommendations which Nestor makes to his son Antilochus, a kind of lesson on the art of driving and, more especially, on the way of handling the team at the turning-post.

> . . . Drive close to it,
> And bear thy car and horses hard upon it,
> Throwing thy weight upon the well-laced car
> A little to their left; and then call on
> The off horse, voice and whip as well, and give him
> The rein, and let the near horse hug the post
> So tightly that the nave of thy stout wheel
> Appears to graze it; but beware of hitting
> The stone, for fear of smashing up the car
> And injuring the horses. . . .[15]

A judge is needed, to stand by the turning-post. Achilles appoints Phoenix. Then the signal for the start is given.

There follow in succession all the unexpected turns and incidents of a fine race: the breaking of the harness on Eumelus' team and his fall;

---

[14] Cf. *Les Poèmes homériques et l'Histoire grecque,* Vol. II, Ch. VIII.
[15] *Iliad,* XXIII, p. 518.

the jostling in a narrow passage between Menelaus and Antilochus who, by irregular and alarming procedure, compels his rival to yield him the passage; the cries and arguments between the betters, between Ajax and Idomeneus on the lawn near the finishing-post; and lastly, after the race, Menelaus' complaint against the unfair manoeuvre of Nestor's son. Things must have happened like this on the race course at Olympia; we must remember, too, that the chariot race was only the most spectacular and aristocratic of the contests.

Homer also mentions the boxing-match in which the combatants wore thongs of hide on their fists; the foot race; the fight in armour; throwing the discus; the archery contest; hurling the javelin; and also songs and dances.

In imagining the scene at Olympia, we can picture the crowd of pilgrims and other men—for married women were excluded on pain of death—who have flocked to the ancient sanctuary from every part of Hellas, under the protection of the sacred truce. Over the little plain swept by a singularly gentle and restful breeze, unique in Hellas, there reigns the atmosphere of a kermesse. People are eagerly awaiting victories that will confer lustre on the cities of the champions, and all amid the tumult of a fairground and place of pilgrimage.

It was a tireless and insatiable public, in any case, an admirable public for the bards who had come to seek glory and profit by reciting to the multitude their latest works, which had probably been enjoyed in the first instance by the courts of the nobility.

Perhaps, indeed, it was for this public that the *Iliad* and *Odyssey* were written.

J. P. V. D. BALSDON

Life and Leisure

A Roman was—once in practice, later in theory—liable to military service, in the class of "Iuniores," between the ages of seventeen and forty-six, and in that period, the prime of his life, he might be called a young man (*iuvenis* or *adolescens*) until he was well advanced in his thirties. He had ceased to be a boy (*puer*) and had become a *iuvenis* when he adopted the *toga virilis* at the age of fourteen. From forty-six to sixty came "the decline into old age" and at sixty, when liability to jury service ceased and a senator was excused attendance at the Senate, old age itself. Age clamped down on women earlier than on men; at the age of thirty-eight Julia, the wayward daughter of Augustus, could be said to be face to face with old age already. There was general agreement that life spent itself far too quickly. Trimalchio, "who kept a clock and a uniformed trumpeter in his dining room to remind him of time passing beyond recall," sentimentalized morbidly over a bottle of vintage wine: "it has a longer life than man." Preaching as a philosopher, Seneca urged men to realize before it was too late that life, as most people led it, was not life at all (in the sense of philosophical preoccupation with the problems of truth and reality) but a mere waste of time.

By upper-class standards public service was the noblest activity of man —the life of the barrister, the soldier, the administrator and the politician; for normally the senator's life embraced all those four activities. Rhetoric was a main constituent of his education and at an early age he put his learning into practice by pleading at the Bar. He climbed the ladder of a senatorial career, absent from Rome sometimes for considerable periods in which he served as an army officer or governed a province. If he committed no indiscretion, he was a life-member of the Senate—if he held the consulship, an important elder statesman from then onwards. In the Empire he might be one of the Emperor's privy counsellors.

This was not a career in which, except in the last centuries of the

J. P. V. D. Balsdon, "Life and Leisure," in *The Romans*, ed. J. P. V. D. Balsdon (New York: Basic Books, Inc, 1965), pp 270–81.

Republic, great fortunes were to be made. The senator therefore needed to be a wealthy man, in particular to own considerable landed property. To this he escaped when he could, particularly if he came of a good family, for the Roman aristocrat was a countryman at heart, interested in farming well, happy in the saddle, fond of hunting. He would have been shocked by the parvenu Sallust's description of farming and hunting as "occupations fit for a slave"; and other Romans no doubt were shocked too, for in the case of the farmer (and perhaps only of the farmer) the notion of work had a wide romantic fascination. Everyone liked to be reminded of Cincinnatus in the fifth century B.C., of how, when they sent for him to be dictator, they found him ploughing and how, once the business of saving Rome as dictator was accomplished, he returned happily to his farm. When Scipio Africanus found himself driven from public life, he worked on the land with his own hands.

If an aristocrat's means were not sufficient to support him in a life of public service, he might turn to business, banking, trading, tax-farming, the activities of the "Equestrian order." In this way distinguished families sometimes disappeared from politics for a generation or more and then, their wealth restored, they returned. There was nothing disgraceful about being a business man, as long as you were rich and successful enough, in which case you were likely to invest largely in land and to become one of the land-owning gentry. Equestrians, whether business men or rich country residents were fathers of senators often and sometimes sons, frequently close personal friends, Atticus of Cicero for instance.

A man who avoided or deserted "the sweat and toil" of a public career in favor of industrious seclusion—"a shady life"—could excuse himself and indeed (like Cicero and Sallust when, elbowed out of an influential position in public life, they became writers) found it desirable to excuse himself. If he became a writer, then he made it clear that he wrote as an educationalist, employing his seclusion to teach valuable lessons to his readers, particularly his young readers, a purpose which nobody disparaged. But if his retirement was the retirement of self-indulgence, like the later life of L. Lucullus, an obsession with fantastically expensive landscape gardening and extravagant fish ponds, he was a traitor to serious and responsible standards of living and won the contempt—however envious—of all but his like-minded friends. There was no secure happiness in such a life, as serious men like Lucretius, Horace and Seneca knew. One form of self-indulgence palled; so despair pursued another—

> The Senate is often in session all day long, at the time when the good-for-nothings are idling their time away taking exercise in the parks, out of sight in restaurants or wasting time gossiping with their friends.

Worse still—

> People set out on journeys with no particular objective in view. They
> wander down the coast. In a purposeless way they go by sea, they go by
> land, always wishing they were doing something else. "Let us go to
> Campania." "No, smart resorts are a bore. Rough country is the thing
> to see." "Let us go to Bruttium and see the ranches in Lucania." Once
> in the bush, they must find a nice resort; after the extensive tedium of
> these uncultivated districts, something civilized is needed for their cul-
> tured gaze to feed on. "Let us go to Taranto. People are always talking
> about its harbours and its splendid winter climate" . . . "No, let us go
> back to Rome." It seems a lifetime since they last heard the applause
> and din of the games. "It might be rather nice, too, to see somebody
> killed."
>
> (SENECA, *De Tranquillitate Animi,* 2,13).

Romans in public life, particularly if they wrote in their spare time,
worked hard. Meetings of the Senate started very early in the day and
might continue until dark. The same was true of the law courts. Emperors (at least, the good ones) perhaps worked hardest of all, up before daybreak and poring over their papers late at night. Such was
Vespasian's life. Marcus Aurelius even took official papers to study at
the Games, as Julius Caesar once had done. And business men did not
make their fortunes in idleness; when Trimalchio was establishing his
wealth, his life was not the fantasy of vulgar enjoyment which the *Satyri-
con* depicts.

Literature, alas, does not introduce us to the daily life of the shopkeeper or the artisan, whether in the city of Rome or in other towns,
men who took sufficient pride in their pursuits for them to be recorded
(often with illustrations) on their tombstones. And, worst of all, we
know little of the manner in which the proletariat earned its bread and
butter. These men were the dregs of Rome for Cicero—unless someone
else had used the expression, and cheap credit was to be won by de-
nouncing him in public. They cannot have supported themselves on "free
corn and the games," in Juvenal's contemptuous phrase. Nor can they
have lived by daily attendance at the morning levees of the affluent, as
Martial might be thought to indicate. Like the slaves and the freedmen,
a large number of them must have done an honest day's work.

There was no such thing as a "retiring age," except for noncommis-
sioned soldiers, who should have been below their middle forties when
they were discharged and, with their gratuities, started a new life as
farmers or shopkeepers or turned their hand in civilian life to the exercise of what had been their army trade. The freedman Trimalchio—
with an astrologer's assurance of thirty years four months and two days

life ahead—was evidently not far advanced into middle age when he realized that he was indecently rich, and retired from commerce and speculation to a life of colorful self-indulgence. Most business men were not so wise, if the satirists, epigrammatists and moralists are to be believed. Pursuit of wealth became an ingrained habit, impossible to arrest. The money-lender sighed enviously at the thought of a countryman's retirement—and continued with his money-lending. Men talked of retiring, but never retired—like the Emperor Augustus. Diocletian was in fact the only Emperor to retire (and enjoy growing cabbages), just as Celestine V was the only Pope. Yet a respected retirement was thought proper for a man who by his public service had earned it. But even in the retirement of old age he should not be self-indulgent like Lucullus, but respectably occupied, like Scipio Africanus, or like the elder Cato, who thought that the time had come to improve his Greek. Though we know more under the late Republic and Empire of politicians who found retirement of an unwanted kind in exile (or, in the Empire, through the withdrawal of imperial favor), we have descriptions of others who retired voluntarily and wore retirement well—Vestricius Spurinna, for instance, at the end of the first century A.D., with perhaps three consulships to his credit, whose active daily life at seventy-seven won the younger Pliny's admiration. It started with a three mile walk and included exercise with the medicine ball when he went to the baths.

The Roman day was a daylight day, its twelve hours being twelve hours of daylight; so that an hour at midsummer was, by our reckoning, thirty minutes longer than at midwinter. Water clocks must have required almost daily readjustment. Daylight marked the beginning of the first hour of day, darkness the conclusion of the twelfth. Midday was the conclusion of the sixth hour, the time at which people knocked off work. The first six hours of the day constituted a "good day's work."

The first two hours of the day were the time of the *salutatio* when in Rome clients jockeyed in discomfort, for the exiguous reward of a small sum of money or a ration of food, to call on their patrons, in a ceremony which was as undignified for the caller as it was tedious for the host. Once the client had received real benefits (good legal advice, perhaps, if he was in a difficulty), but in the Empire the ceremony had lost its usefulness, and the prevalence of this daily round by the hangers-on of society may be greatly exaggerated by the modern historian from the fact that it was evidently such an important part of the poet Martial's daily life and also of Juvenal's.

Breakfast, except for a glutton like the Emperor Vitellius, was an exiguous meal, as it is on the continent of Europe today. Lunch at midday was not a large meal either. After lunch in summer, but not for most people in winter, came the siesta, to be followed by exercise, mostly of a kind which the Romans adopted, under the general influence of Hellenism, from the Greeks in the second century B.C.—running, wrestling, discus and javelin throwing, boxing, gladiatorial-type exercises and strenuous ball games for the young, gentler ball games for the old. For youths under seventeen, especially if they belonged to the Youth Movement which Augustus had started, exercise was very strenuous indeed. This was taken, in cities, in the open spaces often attached to the public baths. After his exercise the young man might plunge into an open air pool just as in earlier and simpler days the young Roman, who had taken his exercise in the Campus Martius, plunged into the Tiber. But generally a man repaired to the baths (with a slave, if he was rich enough, to carry the bag containing his oil flask, his strigil and his towel, and to attend to his oiling, scraping and towelling in the baths themselves). He stripped and proceeded through the temperate room (the *tepidarium*) to the hot bath or sweat chamber, where oiling and strigilling did for him what soap does in a bath today, and then he went to the cold bath, returning thence to the *tepidarium* and the changing room, and might receive a second light oiling, to prevent him from catching a cold when he went out.

The great imperial baths in Rome contained art galleries of statuary, recreation and reading rooms, and had all the social adjuncts found by the eighteenth and early nineteenth centuries at Bath. These buildings—splendid even in their ruins—apart, baths varied in comfort and elegance, down to the lowest in the scale, which were thinly disguised brothels. There were one hundred and seventy baths (most of them charging for admission and run by private enterprise) in the city of Rome at the time of Augustus, more than nine hundred in the late period of the Empire; and a man had his favorite baths, just as today the Frenchman and Italian have their favorite cafés. Snacks were to be had in baths, and also drinks. We can well believe Seneca, who lodged over one, that they were often extremely noisy.

Women bathed in separate baths, often contiguous to the men's baths, so that the same hypocaust might be used to supply the heat; and sometimes they bathed in the men's baths at different hours. Mixed bathing, which probably flourished only in the lowest baths, was twice forbidden by Emperors, by Hadrian and by Alexander Severus.

The time was shouted aloud by slaves; and at the conclusion of the ninth hour (in the middle of the afternoon) it was time for dinner, the one substantial meal of the day.

In Rome, unlike earlier Greece, women and men dined together. Though in rich households of a certain kind the meal was often the gross orgy which modern imagination, stimulated by ancient satirists, likes to imagine, most families dined alone or with a few guests, and the meal was a three-course meal. The use of emetics, approved by doctors, was not always a mark of gluttony; for Julius Caesar, who ate and drank very little, had recourse to emetics. Reading aloud by a slave with a good voice often supplemented conversation. At parties there was sometimes prolonged drinking after dinner—or you went to another house for drinks; your head was wreathed with flowers, and entertainment was often provided by professionals (acrobats, perhaps, or dancing girls from Cadiz).

Life in early Rome was a countryman's life and the year was divided into eight-day periods, the eighth day being market day. On this day the farmer spruced himself up. He cut his nails and, in those primitive times, had a bath. He went to market, consulted his lawyer if necessary (for it was a day on which lawyers were available for consultation), and school-children had a holiday from school. In the public calendars the division of the year into eight-day periods was marked; they were not an exact division of the year either before or after Julius Caesar, because the year—before on 1st January, 45 B.C. Julius Caesar gave the Romans a 365-day year and the calendar which, with minor adjustments, we use today—was a year, with alternate insertions of an intercalary month, of 355, 377, 355, 378 days in a four-year cycle. The first day of each month was the Kalends, the 13th (in certain months the 15th) the Ides and the 5th (or 7th) the Nones.

Somewhere and at some time in the Hellenistic world the seven-day week (itself in the East a far earlier thing) came into existence in the form in which Latin Europe knows it today, with its successive planetary rulers, Saturn, the Sun, the Moon, Mars, Mercury, Jupiter and Venus. This seven-day week was known in Rome at the time of Augustus and its days were often called by their planetary names by the middle of the first century A.D. A graffito from Pompeii gives a date 6th (February, A.D. 60) as—

> In the consulship of Nero Caesar Augustus and Cossus Lentulus, eight days before the Ides of February, on Sunday, on the sixteenth day of the moon, market-day at Cumae, five days before market-day at Pompeii.

Saturn's day was the first day of the seven until in the third century Aurelian's exaltation of Sun-worship made Sunday the first day. Sunday was not a day of rest until the Empire's official conversion to Christianity.

The market day, then, had the regularity and importance which, outside great cities, it everywhere retains, but Roman life had no regular relaxation comparable with the modern weekend. Every day of the year had its individual public and private significance. A mark on the calendar showed whether it was a *dies fastus* (on which the law could take its full course) or *comitialis* (a day on which public meetings could be held) or whether it was neither. In private life there were unlucky days on which it was imprudent to start a journey, for instance, to announce an engagement or to get married. And nearly every day of the year was sacred to some divinity or other, many of them of limited significance—the primitive festivals, for instance, which being concerned with one critical moment or other in the farmer's year, had little meaning for the city-dweller. Others were colorful and important, like the Lupercalia on 15th March, when the half-naked priests ran about the streets of Rome striking women with leather thongs which were believed to engender fertility, and the Saturnalia, the seven days starting on 17th December, when the slaves enjoyed a short pretense of freedom. The Empire brought new festival days, small and great, some local (a benefactor's birthday, perhaps, remembered by the terms of his benefaction, with cakes and wine) others common to the whole Empire, like the Emperor's birthday or accession day. And, outside the fixed festivals (many of which were individual to particular cities) there were irregular festivities (triumphs and celebrations for imperial victories), and also the games. The most important games were held in April and early May (the Ludi Megalenses, Cereales and Florales, twenty-two days in all), in July (the Ludi Apollinares and, after 44 B.C., the games in honour of Caesar's Victory, nineteen days in all), in September (the fifteen, later sixteen, days of the Ludi Romani) and in November (the fourteen days of the Ludi Plebeii). The first days of the games were the occasion of theatrical performances, the last days were devoted to chariot racing. All these games and festivals, whether in Rome or the municipalities, were a responsibility of magistrates and a charge on their pockets. In the late Republic they were often given with reckless extravagance by the aediles at Rome, in the hope of a popularity which would be reflected in the voting when they proceeded to stand for higher office.

Gladiatorial exhibitions were at first no part of the regular games. Of Etruscan—perhaps in the circumstances of their first introduction to Rome, of Samnite and Campanian—origin, they were first celebrated in Rome in 264 B.C. as funeral games, and throughout the Republic the pretense was observed that they were given for this purpose. Julius Caesar's extravagant gladiatorial exhibition during his aedileship in 65 B.C. was ostensibly in memory of his father, who had died twenty years earlier and his exhibition in 46 B.C. was in part given in memory of his daughter, who had been dead for eight years. The scale of these immensely popular exhibitions increased inside and outside Rome during the Empire. Ten thousand men fought in eight different games given by Augustus. After the Dacian war, Trajan exhibited ten thousand fighters in a display lasting a hundred and twenty-three days.

Neither comedy (after Plautus and Terence) nor tragedy had any important history at Rome. Audiences only enjoyed mime and pantomime, and tolerated tragedy only if it was a spectacular riot. Chariot racing and gladiatorial fighting, on the other hand, appealed to all ranks of society, in Rome and in Italian and provincial towns; also the sight of rare wild beasts on display, performing animals and, more commonly, animals fighting one another (bulls fighting elephants, for example) or wild beast hunts, the hunters as well as the beasts having been brought from overseas. The immense interest taken in wild animals, and in the vast business of their hunting, trapping and transport is illustrated by sculptured reliefs and by mosaics from all over the Roman world, notably from Antioch, North Africa and Piazza Armerina in Sicily. This, like the training (mainly at Capua in Campania) and exhibition of gladiators, was a business in which there was a lot of money to be made. As for the chariot racing, great numbers of people in all ranks of society from Emperors like Commodus and Caracalla downwards, were circus-mad, passionate supporters of one or other of the Colors (White, Green, Red, Blue), idolizing charioteers (some of whom made great fortunes), and betting heavily on the races.

Whoever condemns the Romans for the coarse brutality of their spectacles must condemn large sections of society in modern civilized countries too, for tastes which are hardly more refined. It is a bold hazard that gladiatorial games, with the frequent sight of death, would not attract spectators today. Only in their tolerance of the spectacle of condemned prisoners mauled to death by animals (something which was even depicted in rich people's houses in North Africa) are the Romans an utterly unsympathetic people. Even public executions, which survived until not so long ago in Europe, were not so horrible. The throwing of men to the beasts was deplored even in Rome, as gladiatorial fighting and mania for horseracing was deplored, by sensitive persons like Cicero and Seneca, and of course by the Christian writers. Yet even Tertullian, when he instructed Christians to avoid the games and spectacles, offered them, for consolation, the ultimate prospect of a far more terrible carnage, on the day when the world came to its glorious end.

All over the Empire in theatres and amphitheatres people flocked to see the sort of innocent spectacle which survives in the modern circus: jesters, buffoons, gymnasts, conjurers, acrobats, tricksters, tight-rope walkers and trapeze artists, clowns, jugglers, performing monkeys, elephants walking the tight-rope. . . .

W. WARDE FOWLER

Holidays and Amusements

The Italian peoples, of all races, have always had a wonderful capacity for enjoying themselves out of doors. The Italian *festa* of to-day, usually, as in ancient times, linked to some religious festival, is a scene of gaiety, bright dresses, music, dancing, bonfires, races, and improvisation or mummery; and all that we know of the ancient rural festivals of Italy suggests that they were of much the same lively and genial character. . . .

The Latin word for a holiday was *feriae,* a term which belongs to the language of religious law. Strictly speaking, it means a day which the citizen has resigned, either wholly or in part, to the service of the gods.[1] As of old on the farm no work was to be done on such days, so in the city no public business could be transacted. Cicero, drawing up in antique language his idea of the ius divinum, writes thus of feriae: "Feriis iurgia amovento, easque in familiis, operibus patratis, habento": which he afterwards explains as meaning that the citizen must abstain from litigation, and the slave be excused from labor.[2] The idea then of a holiday was much the same as we find expressed in the Jewish Sabbath, and had its root also in religious observance. But Cicero, whether he is actually reproducing the words of an old law or inventing it for himself, was certainly not reflecting the custom of the city in his own day; no such rigid observance of a rule was possible in the capital of an Empire such as the Roman had become. . . .

As a matter of fact a double change had come about since the city and its dominion began to increase rapidly about the time of the Punic wars. First, many of the old festivals, sacred to deities whose vogue was on the wane, or who had no longer any meaning for a city population, as being deities of husbandry, were almost entirely neglected: even if the priests per-

W. Warde Fowler, *Social Life at Rome in the Age of Cicero* (New York: St. Martin's Press, 1965), pp. 285–88, 291–93, 301–4.

[1] Wissowa, *Religion und Kultus,* p. 366. "Feriae" came in time to be limited to public festivals, while "festus dies" covered all holidays.

[2] *de Legibus,* ii. 8. 19 : cp. 12. 29.

formed the prescribed rites, no one knew and no one cared,[3] and it may be doubted whether the State was at all scrupulous in adhering to the old sacred rules as to the hours on which business could be transacted on such days.[4] Second, certain festivals which retained their popularity had been extended from one day to three or more, in one or two cases, as we shall see, even to thirteen and fifteen days, in order to give time for an elaborate system of public amusement consisting of chariot-races and stage-plays, and known by the name of *ludi,* or, as at the winter Saturnalia, to enable all classes to enjoy themselves during the short days for seven mornings instead of one. Obviously this was a much more convenient and popular arrangement than to have your holidays scattered about over the whole year as single days; and it suited the rich and ambitious, who sought to obtain popular favor by shows and games on a grand scale, needing a succession of several days for complete exhibition. So the old religious word *feriae* becomes gradually supplanted, in the sense of a public holiday of amusement, by the word *ludi,* and came at last to mean, as it still does in Germany, the holidays of schoolboys.[5] . . . The oldest and most imposing of these were the Ludi Romani or Magni, lasting from September 5 to September 19 in Cicero's time. These had their origin in the return of a victorious army at the end of the season of war, when king or consul had to carry out the vows he had made when entering on his campaign. The usual form of the vow was to entertain the people on his return, in honor of Jupiter, and thus they were originally called ludi *votivi,* before they were incorporated as a regularly recurring festival. After they became regular and annual, any entertainment vowed by a general had to take place on other days; thus in the year 70 B.C. Pompey's triumphal ludi votivi immediately preceded the Ludi Romani of that year,[6] giving the people in all some thirty days of holiday. The centre-point, and original day, of the Ludi Romani was the Ides (13th) of September, which was also the day of the epulum Jovis,[7] and the dies natalis (dedication day) of the Capitoline temple of Jupiter; and the whole ceremonial was closely connected with that temple and its great deity. The triumphal procession passed along the Sacra via to the Capitol, and thence again to the Circus Maximus, where the ludi were held. The show must have been most im-

---

[3] Thus Ovid describes the rites performed by the Flamen Quirinalis at the old agricultural festival of the Robigalia (Robigus, deity of the mildew) as if it were a curious bit of old practice which most people knew nothing about.—*Fasti,* iv. 901 foll.

[4] Greenidge, *Legal Procedure in Cicero's time,* p. 457.

[5] It is the same word as our *fair.*

[6] Cic. *Verr.* I. 10. 31; where Cicero complains of the difficulties he experienced in conducting his case in consequence of the number of ludi from August to November in that year.

[7] *Roman Festivals,* p. 217 foll.

posing; first marched the boys and youths, on foot and on horseback, then the chariots and charioteers about to take part in the racing, with crowds of dancers and flute-players,[8] and lastly the images of the Capitoline deities themselves, carried on biers. All such shows and processions were dear to the Roman people, and this seems to have become a permanent feature of the Ludi Romani, whether or no an actual triumph was to be celebrated, and also of some other ludi, e.g. the Apollinares and the Megalenses.[9] Thus the idea was kept up that the greatness and prosperity of Rome were especially due to Jupiter Optimus Maximus, who, since the days of the Tarquinii, had looked down on his people from his temple on the Capitol.[10]

The Ludi Plebeii in November seem to have been a kind of plebeian duplicate of the Ludi Romani. As fully developed at the end of the Republic, they lasted from the 4th to the 17th; their center point and original day was the Ides (13th), on which, as on September 13, there was an opulum Jovis in the Capitol.[11] They are connected with the name of that Flaminius who built the circus Flaminius in the Campus Martius in 220 B.C., the champion of popular rights, killed soon afterwards at Trasimene; and it is probable that his object in erecting this new place of entertainment was to provide a convenient building free of aristocratic associations. But unfortunately we know very little of the history of these ludi.

If we may suppose that the Ludi Plebeii were instituted just before the second Punic war, it is interesting to note that three other great ludi were organised in the course of that war, no doubt with the object of keeping up the drooping spirits of the urban population. . . .

We can picture to ourselves the Circus Maximus filled with a dense crowd of some 150,000 people,[12] the senators in reserved places, and the consul or other magistrate presiding; the chariots; usually four in number, painted at this time either red or white, with their drivers in the same colors, and at the signal racing round a course of about sixteen hundred yards, divided into two halves by a *spina;* at the farther end of this the chariots had to turn sharply and always with a certain amount of danger, which gave the race its chief interest. Seven complete laps of this course constituted a *missus* or race,[13] and the number of races in a day varied from time to time, according to the season of the year and the equipment

[8] See the account in Dion. Hal. vii. 72, taken from Fabius Pictor.

[9] See Friedländer in Marquardt, *Staatsverwaltung,* iii. p. 508, note 3.

[10] For full accounts of this procession, and the whole question of the Ludi Romani, see Friedländer, *l.c.;* Wissowa, *Religion und Kultus,* p. 383 foll.; or the article "Triumphus" in the *Dict. of Antiquities,* ed. 2. All accounts owe much to Mommsen's essay in *Römische Forschungen,* ii. p. 42 foll.

[11] On the parallelism between the Ludi Plebeii and Romani see Mommsen, *Staatsrecht,* ii. p. 508, note 4.

[12] Dionys. Hal. iii. 68 gives this number for Augustus' time, and so far as we know Augustus had not enlarged the Circus.

[13] Gell. iii. 10. 16.

of the particular ludi. The rivalry between factions and colors, which became so famous later on and lasted throughout the period of the Empire, was only just beginning in Cicero's time. We hear hardly anything of such excitement in the literature of the period; we only know that there were already two rival colors, white and red, and Pliny tells us the strange story that one chariot-owner, a Caecina of Volaterrae, used to bring swallows into the city smeared with his color, which he let loose to fly home and so bear the news of a victory.[14] Human nature in big cities seems to demand some such artificial stimulus to excitement, and without it the racing must have been monotonous; but of betting and gambling we as yet hear nothing at all. Gradually, as vast sums of money were laid out by capitalists and even by senators upon the horses and drivers, the color-factions increased in numbers, and their rivalry came to occupy men's minds as completely as do now the chances of football teams in our own manufacturing towns.[15]

Exhibitions of gladiators did not as yet take place at ludi or on public festivals, but they may be mentioned here, because they were already becoming the favorite amusement of the common people; Cicero in the *pro Sestio* [16] speaks of them as "that kind of spectacle to which all sorts of people crowd in the greatest numbers, and in which the multitude takes the greatest delight." The consequence was, of course, that candidates for election to magistracies took every opportunity of giving them; and Cicero himself in his consulship inserted a clause in his *lex de ambitu* forbidding candidates to give such exhibitions within two years of the election.[17] They were given exclusively by private individuals up to 105 B.C., either in the Forum or in one or other circus: in that year there was an exhibition by the consuls, but there is some evidence that it was intended to instruct the soldiers in the better use of their weapons. This was a year in which the State was in sore need of efficient soldiers; Marius was at the same time introducing a new system of recruiting and of arming the soldier, and we are told that the consul Rutilius made use of the best gladiators that were to be found in the training-school (ludus) of a certain Scaurus, to teach the men a more skilful use of their weapons.[18] If gladiators could have been used only for a rational purpose like this, as skilful swordsmen and military instructors, the State might well have maintained some force

---

[14] Pliny, *N.H.* x. 71: he seems to be referring to an earlier time, and this Caecina may have been the friend of Cicero. In another passage of Pliny we hear of the red faction about the time of Sulla (vii. 186; Friedl. p. 517). Cp. Tertullian, *de Spectaculis*, 9.

[15] For a graphic picture of the scene in the Circus in Augustus' time see Ovid, *Ars Amatoria,* i. 135 foll.

[16] ch. 59.

[17] See Schol. Bob. on the *pro Sestio*, new Teubner ed., p. 105.

[18] Val. Max. ii. 3. 2. The conjecture as to the object of the exhibition by the consuls is that of Bücheler, in *Rhein. Mus.* 1883, p. 476 foll.

of them. But as it was they remained in private hands, and no limit could be put on the numbers so maintained. They became a permanent menace to the peace of society. Their frequent use in funeral games is a somewhat loathsome feature of the age. These funeral games were an old religious institution, occurring on the ninth day after the burial, and known as Ludi Novemdiales; they are familiar to every one from Virgil's skilful introduction of them, as a Roman equivalent for the Homeric games, in the fifth Aeneid, on the anniversary of the funeral of Anchises. Virgil has naturally omitted the gladiators; but long before his time it had become common to use the opportunity of the funeral of a relation to give munera for the purpose of gaining popularity.[19] A good example is that of young Curio, who in 53 B.C. ruined himself in this way. Cicero alludes to this in an interesting letter to Curio.[20] "You may reach the highest honors," he says, "more easily by your natural advantages of character, diligence, and fortune, than by gladiatorial exhibitions. The power of giving them stirs no feeling of admiration in any one: it is a question of means and not of character: and there is no one who is not by this time sick and tired of them." To Cicero's refined mind they were naturally repugnant; but young men like Curio, though they loved Cicero, were not wont to follow his wholesome advice.[21] . . .

[19] The example was set, according to Livy, *Epit.* 16, by a Junius Brutus at the beginning of the first Punic war.

[20] *ad Fam.* ii. 3.

[21] The origin of these bloody shows at funerals needs further investigation. It may be connected with a primitive and savage custom of sacrificing captives to the Manes of a chief, of which we have a reminiscence in the sacrifice of captives by Aeneas, in Virg. *Aen.* xi. 82.

MANORS AND MANNERS IN MEDIEVAL TIMES

part **II**

4. SERFS AND
THEIR MASTERS

The slow dissolution of the Roman Empire and the steady incursion of Germanic peoples into the Mediterranean world brought important social changes. It is arguable, however, that social elites were far more affected than the common people. True, the institution of slavery as it had been known in previous times was shaken along with the rest; but the confusion and conflict of early medieval Europe hastened the creation of serfdom. This was a protracted process of many centuries, and the conditions of manorial life were rarely identical from one plot of land to the next. Yet everywhere in Europe men labored in the fields, and everywhere their existence was narrowly circumscribed by custom, law, and religious practice.

Eileen Power has composed a classic account of a French peasant of the ninth century which is as charming as it is scrupulously documented. She gives a picture of daily life on an abbey estate near Paris: the physical setting, the toils and pleasures, the beliefs and superstitions of the serf. We also catch a glimpse of family life on the manor and of the many ways in which those two great abstractions, Church and State, actually impinged on the routine of ordinary people.

Friedrich Heer is directly concerned with the symbiotic relationship of lord and serf. While aristocrats set the tone of medieval life, their own means and manners were often crude. What distinguished them from their underlings was not so much great wealth and elegance but personal freedom. Heer documents the "unfreedom" of the peasants who were so often forced, in effect, to barter liberty for safety.

J. R. *Hale* rounds out this period of history and elaborates on a theme announced by Heer: the wide variations in manorial organization from locale to locale and from territory to territory. Increasingly, as he notes, the impact of town life was felt throughout medieval Europe. This did not suddenly transform the nature of serfdom, but it did begin to provide some individual peasants with an option which previously had not existed.

No three articles could perfectly convey the variegated history of serfdom in every corner of Europe, yet these are sufficient to put us on guard against facile assumptions. Above all it becomes clear that mankind's experience has not always been a steady advance in the goal of freedom.

EILEEN POWER

The Peasant Bodo

LIFE ON A COUNTRY ESTATE
IN THE TIME OF CHARLEMAGNE

Three slender things that best support the world: the slender stream of milk from the cow's dug into the pail; the slender blade of green corn upon the ground; the slender thread over the hand of a skilled woman.
Three sounds of increase: the lowing of a cow in milk; the din of a smithy; the swish of a plough.
—From *The Triads of Ireland* (9th century)

Economic history, as we know it, is the newest of all the branches of history. Up to the middle of the last century the chief interest of the historian and of the public alike lay in political and constitutional history, in political events, wars, dynasties, and in political institutions and their development. Substantially, therefore, history concerned itself with the ruling classes. "Let us now praise famous men," was the historian's motto. He forgot to add "and our fathers that begat us." He did not care to probe the obscure lives and activities of the great mass of humanity, upon whose slow toil was built up the prosperity of the world and who were the hidden foundation of the political and constitutional edifice reared by the famous

Eileen Power, *Medieval People* (New York: Barnes and Noble, 1963), pp. 1–23.

men he praised. To speak of ordinary people would have been beneath the dignity of history. Carlyle struck a significant note of revolt: "The thing I want to see," he said, "is not Red-book lists and Court Calendars and Parliamentary Registers, but the Life of Man in England: what men did, thought, suffered, enjoyed. . . . Mournful, in truth, it is to behold what the business called 'History' in these so enlightened and illuminated times still continues to be. Can you gather from it, read till your eyes go out, any dimmest shadow of an answer to that great question: How men lived and had their being; were it but economically, as, what wages they got and what they bought with these? Unhappy you cannot. . . . History, as it stands all bound up in gilt volumes, is but a shade more instructive than the wooden volumes of a back-gammon-board."

Carlyle was a voice crying in the wilderness. Today the new history, whose way he prepared, has come. The present age differs from the centuries before it in its vivid realization of that much-neglected person the man in the street; or (as it was more often in the earliest ages) the man with the hoe. Today the historian is interested in the social life of the past and not only in the wars and intrigues of princes. To the modern writer, the fourteenth century, for instance, is not merely the century of the Hundred Years' War and of the Black Prince and Edward III; more significantly it is for him the era of the slow decay of villeinage in England, a fact more epoch-making, in the long run, than the struggle over French provinces. We still praise famous men, for he would be a poor historian who could spare one of the great figures who have shed glory or romance upon the page of history; but we praise them with due recognition of the fact that not only great individuals, but people as a whole, unnamed and undistinguished masses of people, now sleeping in unknown graves, have also been concerned in the story. Our fathers that begat us have come to their own at last. As Acton put it, "The great historian now takes his meals in the kitchen."

This book is chiefly concerned with the kitchens of History, and the first which we shall visit is a country estate at the beginning of the ninth century. It so happens that we know a surprising amount about such an estate, partly because Charlemagne himself issued a set of orders instructing the Royal stewards how to manage his own lands, telling them everything it was necessary for them to know, down to the vegetables which they were to plant in the garden. But our chief source of knowledge is a wonderful estate book which Irminon, the Abbot of St. Germain des Prés near Paris, drew up so that the abbey might know exactly what lands belonged to it and who lived on those lands, very much as William I drew up an estate book of his whole kingdom and called it "Domesday Book." In this estate book is set down the name of every little estate (or *fisc* as it was called) belonging to the abbey, with a description of the land which was worked under its steward to its own profit, and the land which was held by tenants, and the names of those tenants and of their wives and of their children, and the exact services and rents, down to a plank and an egg, which they had to do for their land. We know today the name of almost every man, woman, and child who was living on those little *fiscs* in the time of Charlemagne, and a great deal about their daily lives.

Consider for a moment how the estate upon which they lived was organized. The lands of the Abbey of St. Germain were divided into a number of estates, called *fiscs*, each of a convenient size to be administered by a steward. On each of these *fiscs* the land was divided into seigniorial and tributary lands; the first administered by the monks through a steward or some other officer, and the second possessed by various tenants, who received and held them from the abbey. These tributary lands were divided into numbers of little farms, called manses, each occupied by one or more families. If you had paid a visit to the chief or seigniorial manse, which the monks kept in their own hands, you would have found a little house, with three or four rooms, probably built of stone, facing an inner court, and on one side of it you would have seen a special group of houses hedged round, where the women serfs belonging to the house lived and did their work; all round you would also have seen little wooden houses, where the household serfs lived, workrooms, a kitchen, a bakehouse, barns, stables, and other farm buildings, and round the whole a hedge carefully planted with trees, so as to make a kind of enclosure or court. Attached to this central manse was a considerable amount of land—ploughland, meadows, vineyards, orchards and almost all the woods or forests on the estate. Clearly a great deal of labor would be needed to cultivate all these lands. Some of that labor was provided by servile workers, who were attached to the chief manse and lived in the court. But these household serfs were not nearly enough to do all the work upon the monks' land, and far the greater part of it had to be done by services paid by the other landowners on the estate.

Beside the seigniorial manse, there were a number of little dependent manses. These belonged to men and women who were in various stages of freedom, except for the fact that all had to do work on the land of the chief manse. There is no need to trouble with the different classes, for in practice there was very little difference between them, and in a couple of centuries they were all merged into one common class of medieval villeins. The most important people were those called *coloni*, who were personally free (that is to say, counted as free men by the law), but bound to the soil, so that they could never leave their farms and were sold with the estate, if it were sold. Each of the dependent manses was held either by one family or by two or three families which clubbed together to do the work; it consisted of a house or houses, and farm buildings, like those of the chief manse, only poorer and made of wood, with ploughland and a meadow and perhaps a little piece of vineyard attached to it. In return for these holdings the owner or joint owners of every manse had to do work on the land of the chief manse for about three days in the week. The steward's chief business was to see that they did their work properly, and from every one he had the right to demand two kinds of labor. The first was *field work:* every year each man was bound to do a fixed amount of ploughing on the domain land (as it was called later on), and also to give what was called a *corvée,* that is to say, an unfixed amount of ploughing, which the steward could demand every week when it was needed; the distinction corresponds to the distinction between *week work* and *boon work* in the later Middle Ages. The second kind of labor which every owner of a farm had to do on the monks' land was called handwork, that is to say, he had to help repair buildings, or cut down trees, or gather fruit, or make ale, or carry loads—anything, in fact, which wanted doing and which the steward told him to do. It was by these services that the monks got their own seigniorial farm cultivated. On all the others days of the week these hard-worked tenants were free to cultivate their own little farms, and we may be sure that they put twice as much elbow grease into the business.

But their obligation did not end here, for not only had they to pay services, they also had to pay certain rents to the big house. There were no State taxes in those days, but every man had to pay an army due, which Charlemagne exacted from the abbey, and which the abbey exacted from its tenants; this took the form of an ox and a certain number of sheep, or the equivalent in money: "He pays to the host two shillings of silver" comes first on every freeman's list of obligations. The farmers also had to pay in return for any special privileges granted to them by the monks; they had to carry a load of wood to the big house, in return for being allowed to gather firewood in the woods, which were jealously preserved for the use of the abbey; they had to pay some hogsheads of wine for the right to pasture their pigs in the same precious woods; every third year they had to give up one of their sheep for the right to graze upon the fields of the chief manse, they had to pay a sort of poll-tax of four pence a head. In addition to these special rents every farmer had also to pay other rents in produce; every year he owed the big house three chickens and fifteen eggs and a large number of planks, to repair its buildings; often he had to give it a couple of pigs; sometimes corn, wine, honey, wax, soap, or oil. If the farmer were also an artisan and made things, he had to pay the produce of his craft; a smith would have to make lances for the abbey's contingent to the army, a carpenter had to make barrels and hoops and vine props, a wheelwright had to make a cart. Even the wives of the farmers were kept busy, if they happened to be serfs; for the servile women were obliged to spin cloth or to make a garment for the big house every year.

All these things were exacted and collected by the steward, whom they called *Villicus,* or *Major* (Mayor). He was a very hard-worked man, and when one reads the seventy separate and particular injunctions which Charlemagne addressed to his stewards one cannot help feeling sorry for him. He had to get all the right services out of the tenants, and tell them what to do each week and see that they did it; he had to be careful that they brought the right number of eggs and pigs up to the house, and did not foist off warped or badly planed planks upon him. He had to look after the household serfs too, and set them to work. He had to see about storing, or selling, or sending off to the monastery the produce of the estate and of the tenants' rents; and every year he had to present a full and detailed account of his stewardship to the abbot. He had a manse of his own, with services and rents due from it, and Charlemagne exhorted his stewards to be prompt in their payments, so as to set a good example. Probably his official duties left him very little time to work on his own farm, and he would have to put in a man to work it for him, as Charlemagne bade his stewards do. Often, however, he had subordinate officials called *deans* under him, and sometimes the work of receiving and looking after the stores in the big house was done by a special cellarer.

That, in a few words, is the way in which the monks of St. Germain and the other Frankish landowners of the time of Charlemagne managed their estates. Let us try, now, to look at those estates from a more human point of view and see what life was like to a farmer who lived upon them. The abbey possessed a little estate called Villaris, near Paris, in the place now occupied by the park of Saint Cloud. When we turn up the pages in the estate book dealing with Villaris, we find that there was a man called Bodo living there.[1] He had a wife called Ermentrude and three children called Wido and Gerbert and Hildegard; and he owned a little farm of arable and meadow land, with a few vines. And we know very nearly as much about Bodo's work as we know about that of a small-holder in France

---

[1] "Habet Bodo colonus et uxor ejus colona, nomine Ermentrudis, homines sancti Germani, habent secum infantes III.   Tenet mansum ingenuilem I, habentem de terre arabili bunuaria VIII et antsingas II, de vinea aripennos II, de prato aripennos VII.   Solvit ad hostem de argento solidos II, de vino in pascione modios II; ad tertium annum sundolas C; de sepe perticas III.   Arat ad hibernaticum perticas III, ad tramisem perticas II.   In unaquaque ebdomada corvadas II, manuoperam I. Pullos III, ova XV; et caropera ibi injungitur.   Et habet medietatem de farinarium, inde solvit de argento solidos II."   *Op. cit.,* II p. 78.   "Bodo a *colonus* and his wife Ermentrude a *colona,* tenants of Saint-Germain, have with them three children. He holds one free manse, containing eight *bunuaria* and two *antsinga* of arable land, two *aripenni* of vines and seven *aripenni* of meadow.   He pays two silver shillings to the army and two hogsheads of wine for the right to pasture his pigs in the woods.   Every third year he pays a hundred planks and three poles for fences.   He ploughs at the winter sowing four perches and at the spring sowing two perches. Every week he owes two labor services (*corvées*) and one handwork.   He pays three fowls and fifteen eggs, and carrying service when it is enjoined upon him. And he owns the half of a windmill, for which he pays two silver shillings."

today. Let us try and imagine a day in his life. On a fine spring morning towards the end of Charlemagne's reign Bodo gets up early, because it is his day to go and work on the monks' farm, and he does not dare to be late, for fear of the steward. To be sure, he has probably given the steward a present of eggs and vegetables the week before, to keep him in a good temper; but the monks will not allow their stewards to take big bribes (as is sometimes done on other estates), and Bodo knows that he will not be allowed to go late to work. It is his day to plough, so he takes his big ox with him and little Wido to run by its side with a goad, and he joins his friends from some of the farms near by, who are going to work at the big house too. They all assemble, some with horses and oxen, some with mattocks and hoes and spades and axes and scythes, and go off in gangs to work upon the fields and meadows and woods of the seigniorial manse, according as the steward orders them. The manse next door to Bodo is held by a group of families: Frambert and Ermoin and Ragenold, with their wives and children. Bodo bids them good morning as he passes. Frambert is going to make a fence round the wood, to prevent the rabbits from coming out and eating the young crops; Ermoin has been told to cart a great load of firewood up to the house; and Ragenold is mending a hole in the roof of a barn. Bodo goes whistling off in the cold with his oxen and his little boy; and it is no use to follow him farther, because he ploughs all day and eats his meal under a tree with the other ploughmen, and it is very monotonous.

Let us go back and see what Bodo's wife, Ermentrude, is doing. She is busy too; it is the day on which the chicken-rent is due—a fat pullet and five eggs in all. She leaves her second son, aged nine, to look after the baby Hildegard and calls on one of her neighbors, who has to go up to the big house too. The neighbor is a serf and she has to take the steward a piece of woollen cloth, which will be sent away to St. Germain to make a habit for a monk. Her husband is working all day in the lord's vineyards, for on this estate the serfs generally tend the vines, while the freemen do most of the ploughing. Ermentrude and the serf's wife go together up to the house. There all is busy. In the men's workshop are several clever workmen—a shoemaker, a carpenter, a blacksmith, and two silversmiths; there are not more, because the best artisans on the estates of St. Germain live by the walls of the abbey, so that they can work for the monks on the spot and save the labor of carriage. But there were always some craftsmen on every estate, either attached as serfs to the big house, or living on manses of their own, and good landowners tried to have as many clever craftsmen as possible. Charlemagne ordered his stewards each to have in his district "good workmen, namely, blacksmiths, goldsmiths, silversmiths, shoemakers, turners, carpenters, swordmakers, fishermen, foilers, soapmakers, men who know how to make beer, cider, perry and all other kinds of beverages, bakers to make pasty for our table, netmakers who know how to make nets for hunting, fishing and fowling, and others too many to be named." [2] And some of these workmen are to be found working for the monks in the estate of Villaris.

But Ermentrude does not stop at the men's workshop. She finds the steward, bobs her curtsy to him, and gives up her fowl and eggs, and then she hurries off to the women's part of the house, to gossip with the serfs there. The Franks used at this time to keep the women of their household in a separate quarter, where they did the work which was considered suitable for women, very much as the Greeks of antiquity used to do. If a Frankish noble had lived at the big house, his wife would have looked after their work, but as no one lived in the stone house at Villaris, the steward had to oversee the women. Their quarter consisted of a little group of houses, with a workroom, the whole surrounded by a thick hedge with a strong bolted gate, like a harem, so that no one could come in without leave. Their workrooms were comfortable places, warmed by stoves, and there Ermentrude (who, being a woman, was allowed to go in) found about a dozen servile women spinning and dyeing cloth and sewing garments. Every week the harassed steward brought them the raw materials for their work and took away what they made. Charlemagne gives his stewards several instructions about the women attached to his manses, and we may be sure that the monks of St. Germain did the same on their model estates. "For our women's work," says Charlemagne, "they are to give at the proper time the materials, that is linen, wool, woad, vermilion, madder, wool combs, teasels, soap, grease, vessels, and other objects which are necessary. And let our women's quarters be well looked after, furnished with houses and rooms with stoves and cellars, and let them be surrounded by good hedge, and let the doors be strong, so that the women can do our work properly." [3] Ermentrude, however, has to hurry away after her gossip, and so must we. She goes back to her own farm and sets to work in the little vineyard; then after an hour or two goes back to get the children's meal and to spend the rest of the day in weaving warm woollen clothes for them. All her friends are either working in the fields on their husband's farms or else looking after the poultry, or the vegetables, or sewing at home; for the women have to work just as hard as the men on a country farm. In Charlemagne's time (for instance) they did nearly all the sheep shearing. Then at last Bodo comes back for his supper, and as soon as the sun goes down they go to bed; for their handmade candle gives only a flicker of light, and they both have to be up early in the morning. De Quincey once pointed out, in his inimitable manner, how the ancients everywhere went to bed, "like good boys, from seven to nine o'clock."

[2] *De Villis*, c. 45.
[3] *Ibid.* cc. 43, 49.

"Man went to bed early in those ages simply because his worthy mother earth could not afford him candles. She, good old lady . . . would certainly have shuddered to hear of any of her nations asking for candles. 'Candles, indeed!' she would have said; 'who ever heard of such a thing? and with so much excellent daylight running to waste, as I have provided *gratis!* What will the wretches want next?' " [4] Something of the same situation prevailed even in Bodo's time.

This, then, is how Bodo and Ermentrude usually passed their working day. But, it may be complained, this is all very well. We know about the estates on which these peasants lived and about the rents which they had to pay, and the services which they had to do. But how did they feel and think and amuse themselves when they were not working? Rents and services are only outside things; an estate book only describes routine. It would be idle to try to picture the life of a university from a study of its lecture list, and it is equally idle to try and describe the life of Bodo from the estate book of his masters. It is no good taking your meals in the kitchen if you never talk to the servants. This is true, and to arrive at Bodo's thoughts and feelings and holiday amusements we must bid goodbye to Abbot Irminon's estate book, and peer into some very dark corners indeed; for though by the aid of Chaucer and Langland and a few Court Rolls it is possible to know a great deal about the feelings of a peasant six centuries later, material is scarce in the ninth century, and it is all the more necessary to remember the secret of the invisible ink.

Bodo certainly *had* plenty of feelings, and very strong ones. When he got up in the frost on a cold morning to drive the plough over the abbot's acres, when his own were calling out for work, he often shivered and shook the rime from his beard, and wished that the big house and all its land were at the bottom of the sea (which, as a matter of fact, he had never seen and could not imagine). Or else he wished he were the abbot's huntsman, hunting in the forest; or a monk of St. Germain, singing sweetly in the abbey church; or a merchant, taking bales of cloaks and girdles along the high road to Paris; anything, in fact, but a poor ploughman ploughing other people's land. An Anglo-Saxon writer has imagined a dialogue with him:

> "Well, ploughman, how do you do your work?" "Oh, sir, I work very hard. I go out in the dawning, driving the oxen to the field and I yoke them to the plough. Be the winter never so stark, I dare not stay at home for fear of my lord; but every day I must plough a full acre or more, after having yoked the oxen and fastened the share and coulter to the plough!" "Have you any mate?" "I have a boy, who drives the oxen with

[4] From "The Casuistry of Roman Meals," in *The Collected Writings of Thomas De Quincey,* ed. D. Masson (1897), VII, p. 13.

a goad, who is now hoarse from cold and shouting." (Poor little Wido!) "Well, well, it is very hard work?" "Yes, indeed it is very hard work." [5]

Nevertheless, hard as the work was, Bodo sang lustily to cheer himself and Wido; for is it not related that once, when a clerk was singing the "Allelulia" in the emperor's presence, Charles turned to one of the bishops, saying, "My clerk is singing very well," whereat the rude bishop replied, "Any clown in our countryside drones as well as that to his oxen at their ploughing"? [6] It is certain too that Bodo agreed with the names which the great Charles gave to the months of the year in his own Frankish tongue; for he called January "Winter-month," February "Mud-month," March "Spring-month," April "Easter-month," May "Joy-month," June "Plough-month," July "Hay-month," August "Harvest-month," September "Wind-month," October "Vintage-month," November "Autumn-month," and December "Holy-month." [7]

And Bodo was a superstitious creature. The Franks had been Christian now for many years, but Christian though they were, the peasant clung to old beliefs and superstitions. On the estates of the holy monks of St. Germain you would have found the country people saying charms which were hoary with age, parts of the lay sung by the Frankish ploughman over his bewitched land long before he marched southwards into the Roman Empire, or parts of the spell which the bee-master performed when he swarmed his bees on the shores of the Baltic Sea. Christianity has colored these charms, but it has not effaced their heathen origin; and because the tilling of the soil is the oldest and most unchanging of human occupations, old beliefs and superstitions cling to it and the old gods stalk up and down the brown furrows, when they have long vanished from houses and roads. So on Abbot Irminon's estates the peasant-farmers muttered charms over their sick cattle (and over their sick children too) and said incantations over the fields to make them fertile. If you had followed behind Bodo when he broke his first furrow you would have probably seen him take out of his jerkin a little cake, baked for him by Ermentrude out of different kinds of meal, and you would have seen him stoop and lay it under the furrow and sing:

> Earth, Earth, Earth! O Earth, our mother!
> May the All-Wielder, Ever-Lord grant thee
> Acres a-waxing, upwards a-growing,
> Pregnant with corn and plenteous in strength;
> Hosts of grain shafts and of glittering plants!

[5] Ælfric's *Colloquium* in *op. cit.* p. 95.
[6] The Monk of St. Gall's *Life* in *Early Lives of Charlemagne*, pp. 87–8.
[7] Einhard's *Life* in *op. cit.*, p. 45.

Of broad barley the blossoms,
And of white wheat ears waxing,
Of the whole land the harvest. . . .

Acre, full-fed, bring forth fodder for men!
Blossoming brightly, blessed become!
And the God who wrought with earth grant us gift of growing
That each of all the corns may come unto our need.[8]

Then he would drive his plough through the acre.

The Church wisely did not interfere with these old rites. It taught Bodo
to pray to the Ever-Lord instead of to Father Heaven, and to the Virgin
Mary instead of to Mother Earth, and with these changes let the old spell he
had learned from his ancestors serve him still. It taught him, for instance,
to call on Christ and Mary in his charm for bees. When Ermentrude heard
her bees swarming, she stood outside her cottage and said this little charm
over them:

Christ, there is a swarm of bees outside,
Fly hither, my little cattle,
In blest peace, in God's protection,
Come home safe and sound.
Sit down, sit down, bee,
St. Mary commanded thee.
Thou shalt not have leave,
Thou shalt not fly to the wood.
Thou shalt not escape me,
Nor go away from me.
Sit very still,
Wait God's will! [9]

And if Bodo on his way home saw one of his bees caught in a brier bush,
he immediately stood still and wished—as some people wish today when
they go under a ladder. It was the Church, too, which taught Bodo to add
"So be it, Lord," to the end of his charm against pain. Now, his ancestors
for generations behind him had believed that if you had a stitch in your
side, or a bad pain anywhere, it came from a worm in the marrow of your
bones, which was eating you up, and that the only way to get rid of that
worm was to put a knife, or an arrow-head, or some other piece of metal
to the sore place, and then wheedle the worm out on to the blade by saying

[8] Anglo-Saxon charms translated in Stopford Brook, *English Literature from the
Beginning to the Norman Conquest* (1899), p. 43.

[9] Old High German charm written in a tenth-century hand in a ninth-century
codex containing sermons of St. Augustine, now in the Vatican Library. Brawne,
Althochdeutsches Lesebuch (fifth edition, Halle, 1902), p. 83.

a charm. And this was the charm which Bodo's heathen ancestors had always said and which Bodo went on saying when little Wido had a pain: "Come out, worm, with nine little worms, out from the marrow into the bone, from the bone into the flesh, from the flesh into the skin, from the skin into this arrow." And then (in obedience to the Church) he added "So be it, Lord." [10] But sometimes it was not possible to read a Christian meaning into Bodo's doings. Sometimes he paid visits to some man who was thought to have a wizard's powers, or superstitiously reverenced some twisted tree, about which there hung old stories never quite forgotten. Then the Church was stern. When he went to confession the priest would ask him: "Have you consulted magicians and enchanters, have you made vows to trees and fountains, have you drunk any magic philtre?" [11] And he would have to confess what he did last time his cow was sick. But the Church was kind as well as stern. "When serfs come to you," we find one bishop telling his priests, "you must not give them as many fasts to perform as rich men. Put upon them only half the penance." [12] The Church knew well enough that Bodo could not drive his plough all day upon an empty stomach. The hunting, drinking, feasting Frankish nobles could afford to lose a meal.

It was from this stern and yet kind Church that Bodo got his holidays. For the Church made the pious emperor decree that on Sundays and saints' days no servile or other works should be done. Charlemagne's son repeated his decree in 827. It runs thus:

> We ordain according to the law of God and to the command of our father of blessed memory in his edicts, that no servile works shall be done on Sundays, neither shall men perform their rustic labors, tending vines, ploughing fields, reaping corn and mowing hay, setting up hedges or fencing woods, cutting trees, or working in quarries or building houses; nor shall they work in the garden, nor come to the law courts, nor follow the chase. But three carrying-services it is lawful to do on Sunday, to wit carrying for the army, carrying food, or carrying (if need be) the body of a lord to its grave. Item, women shall not do their textile works, nor cut out clothes, nor stitch them together with the needle, nor card wool, nor beat hemp, nor wash clothes in public, nor shear sheep: so that there may be rest on the Lord's day. But let them come together from all sides to Mass in the Church and praise God for all the good things He did for us on that day! [13]

[10] Another Old High German charm preserved in a tenth-century codex now at Vienna. Brawne, *op. cit.*, p. 164.

[11] From the ninth-century *Libellus de Ecclesiasticis Disciplinis*, art. 100, quoted in Ozanam, *La Civilisation Chrétienne chez les Francs* (1849), p. 312. The injunction, however, really refers to the recently conquered and still half-pagan Saxons.

[12] *Penitential* of Halitgart, Bishop of Cambrai, quoted *ibid*. p. 314.

[13] *Documents relatifs à l'Histoire de l'Industrie et du Commerce en France*, ed. G. Faigniez, t. I, pp. 51–2.

Unfortunately, however, Bodo and Ermentrude and their freinds were not content to go quietly to church on saints' days and quietly home again. They used to spend their holidays in dancing and singing and buffoonery, as country folk have always done until our own gloomier, more self-conscious age. They were very merry and not all refined, and the place they always chose for their dances was the churchyard; and unluckily the songs they sang as they danced in a ring were old pagan songs of their forefathers, left over from old Mayday festivities, which they could not forget, or ribald love-songs which the Church disliked. Over and over again we find the Church councils complaining that the peasants (and sometimes the priests too) were singing "wicked songs with a chorus of dancing women," or holding "ballads and dancings and evil and wanton songs and such-like lures of the devil"; [14] over and over again the bishops forbade these songs and dances; but in vain. In every country in Europe, right through the Middle Ages to the time of the Reformation, and after it, country folk continued to sing and dance in the churchyard. Two hundred years after Charlemagne's death there grew up the legend of the dancers of Kölbigk, who danced on Christmas Eve in the churchyard, in spite of the warning of the priest, and all got rooted to the spot for a year, till the Archbishop of Cologne released them. Some men say that they were not rooted standing to the spot, but that they had to go on dancing for the whole year; and that before they were released they had danced themselves waist-deep into the ground. People used to repeat the little Latin verse which they were singing:

> Equitabat Bovo per silvam frondosam
> Ducebat sibi Merswindem formosam.
> Quid stamus? Cur non imus? [15]

> Through the leafy forest, Bovo went a-riding
> And his pretty Merswind trotted on beside him—
> Why are we standing still? Why can't we go away?

Another later story still is told about a priest in Worcestershire, who was kept awake all night by the people dancing in his churchyard and singing a song with the refrain "Sweetheart have pity," so that he could not get it out of his head, and the next morning at Mass, instead of saying "Dominus

[14] See references in Chambers, *The Medieval Stage* (1913), I, pp. 161–3.

[15] For the famous legend of the dancers of Kölbigk, see Gaston Paris, *Les Danseurs Maudits, Légende Allemande du XI⁴ Siècle* (Paris 1900, reprinted from the *Journal des Savants,* Dec., 1899), which is a *conte rendu* of Schröder's study in *Zeitschrift für Kirchengeschichte* (1899). The poem occurs in a version of English origin, in which one of the dancers, Thierry, is cured of a perpetual trembling in all his limbs by a miracle of St. Edith at the nunnery of Wilton in 1065. See *loc. cit.,* pp. 10, 14.

vobiscum," he said "Sweetheart have pity," and there was a dreadful scandal which got into a chronicle.[16]

Sometimes our Bodo did not dance himself, but listened to the songs of wandering minstrels. The priests did not at all approve of these minstrels, who (they said) would certainly go to hell for singing profane secular songs, all about the great deeds of heathen heroes of the Frankish race, instead of Christian hymns. But Bodo loved them, and so did Bodo's betters; the Church councils had sometimes even to rebuke abbots and abbesses for listening to their songs. And the worst of it was that the great emperor himself, the good Charlemagne, loved them too. He would always listen to a minstrel, and his biographer, Einhard, tells us that "He wrote out the barbarous and ancient songs, in which the acts of the kings and their wars were sung, and committed them to memory"; [17] and one at least of those old sagas, which he liked men to write down, has been preserved on the cover of a Latin manuscript, where a monk scribbled it in his spare time. His son, Louis the Pious, was very different; he rejected the national poems, which he had learnt in his youth, and would not have them read or recited or taught; he would not allow minstrels to have justice in the law courts, and he forbade idle dances and songs and tales in public places on Sundays; but then he also dragged down his father's kingdom into disgrace and ruin. The minstrels repaid Charlemagne for his kindness to them. The gave him everlasting fame; for all through the Middle Ages the legend of Charlemagne grew, and he shares with our King Arthur the honor of being the hero of one of the greatest romance-cycles of the Middle Ages. Every different century clad him anew in its own dress and sang new lays about him. What the monkish chroniclers in their cells could never do for Charlemagne, these despised and accursed minstrels did for him: they gave him what is perhaps more desirable and more lasting than a place in history—they gave him a place in legend. It is not every emperor who rules in those realms of gold of which Keats spoke, as well as in the kingdoms of the world; and in the realms of gold Charlemagne reigns with King Arthur, and his peers joust with the Knights of the Round Table. Bodo, at any rate, benefited by Charles's love of minstrels, and it is probable that he heard in the lifetime of the emperor himself the first beginnings of those legends which afterwards clung to the name of Charlemagne. One can imagine him round-eyed in the churchyard, listening to fabulous stories of Charles's Iron March to Pavia, such as a gossiping old monk of St. Gall afterwards wrote down in his chronicle.[18]

---

[16] "Swete Lamman dhin are," in the original. The story is told by Giraldus Cambrensis in *Gemma Ecclesiastica*, pt. I, c. XLII. See *Selections from Giraldus Cambrensis*, ed. C. A. J. Skeel (S.P.C.K. *Texts for Students*, No. XI), p. 48.

[17] Einhard's *Life* in *op cit.* p. 45. See also *ibid.*, p. 168 (note).

[18] The Monk of St. Gall's *Life* in *op. cit.*, pp. 144–7.

It is likely enough that such legends were the nearest Bodo ever came to seeing the Emperor, of whom even the poor serfs who never followed him to court or camp were proud. But Charles was a great traveler: like all the monarchs of the early Middle Ages he spent the time, when he was not warring, in trekking round his kingdom, staying at one of his estates, until he and his household had literally eaten their way through it, and then passing on to another. And sometimes he varied the procedure by paying a visit to the estates of his bishops or nobles, who entertained him royally. It may be that one day he came on a visit to Bodo's masters and stopped at the big house on his way to Paris, and then Bodo saw him plain; for Charlemagne would come riding along the road in his jerkin of otter skin, and his plain blue cloak (Einhard tells us that he hated grand clothes and on ordinary days dressed like the common people); [19] and after him would come his three sons and his bodyguard, and then his five daughters. Einhard has also told us that

> He had such care of the upbringing of his sons and daughters that he never dined without them when he was at home and never travelled without them. His sons rode along with him and his daughters followed in the rear. Some of his guards, chosen for this very purpose, watched the end of the line of march where his daughters travelled. They were very beautiful and much beloved by their father, and, therefore, it is strange that he would give them in marriage to no one, either among his own people or of a foreign state. But up to his death he kept them all at home saying he could not forgo their society.[20]

Then, with luck, Bodo, quaking at the knees, might even behold a portent new to his experience, the emperor's elephant. Haroun El Raschid, the great Sultan of the "Arabian Nights" had sent it to Charles, and it accompanied him on all his progresses. Its name was "Abu-Lubabah," which is an Arabic word and means "the father of intelligence." * and it died a hero's death on an expedition against the Danes in 810. It is certain that ever afterwards Ermentrude quelled little Gerbert, when he was naughty, with the threat, "Abu-Lubabah will come with his long nose and carry you off." But Wido, being aged eight and a bread-winner, professed to have felt no fear on being confronted with the elephant; but admitted when pressed, that he greatly preferred Haroun El Raschid's other present to the emperor, the friendly dog, who answered to the name of "Becerillo." [21]

It would be a busy time for Bodo when all these great folk came, for everything would have to be cleaned before their arrival, the pastry cooks

---

* *Abu-Lubabah.*—It is remarkable that the name should have suffered no corruption in the chronicles.

[19] Einhard's *Life* in *op. cit.*, p. 39.

[20] *Ibid.*, p. 35.

[21] Beazley, *Dawn of Modern Geography* (1897), I, p. 325.

and sausage-makers summoned and a great feast prepared; and though the household serfs did most of the work, it is probable that he had to help. The gossipy old monk of St. Gall has given us some amusing pictures of the excitement when Charles suddenly paid a visit to his subjects:

There was a certain bishopric which lay full in Charles's path when he journeyed, and which indeed he could hardly avoid: and the bishop of this place, always anxious to give satisfaction, put everything that he had at Charles's disposal. But once the Emperor came quite unexpectedly and the bishop in great anxiety had to fly hither and thither like a swallow, and had not only the palaces and houses but also the courts and squares swept and cleaned: and then, tired and irritated, came to meet him. The most pious Charles noticed this, and after examining all the various details, he said to the bishop: "My kind host, you always have everything splendidly cleaned for my arrival." Then the bishop, as if divinely inspired, bowed his head and grasped the king's never-conquered right hand, and hiding this irritation, kissed it and said: "It is but right, my lord, that, wherever you come, all things should be thoroughly cleansed." Then Charles, of all kings the wisest, understanding the state of affairs said to him: "If I empty I can also fill." And he added: "You may have that estate which lies close to your bishopric, and all your successors may have it until the end of time." In the same journey, too, he came to a bishop who lived in a place through which he must needs pass. Now on that day, being the sixth day of the week, he was not willing to eat the flesh of beast or bird; and the bishop, being by reason of the nature of the place unable to procure fish upon the sudden, ordered some excellent cheese, rich and creamy, to be placed before him. And the most self-restrained Charles, with the readiness which he showed everywhere and on all occasions, spared the blushes of the bishop and required no better fare; but taking up his knife cut off the skin, which he thought unsavoury and fell to on the white of the cheese. Thereupon the bishop, who was standing near like a servant, drew closer and said: "Why do you do that, lord emperor? You are throwing away the very best part." Then Charles, who deceived no one, and did not believe that anyone would deceive him, on the persuasion of the bishop put a piece of the skin in his mouth, and slowly eat it and swallowed it like butter. Then approving of the advice of the bishop, he said: "Very true, my good host," and he added: "Be sure to send me every year to Aix two cartloads of just such cheeses." And the bishop was alarmed at the impossibility of the task and, fearful of losing both his rank and his office, he rejoined: "My lord, I can procure the cheeses, but I cannot tell which are of this quality and which of another. Much I fear lest I fall under your censure." Then Charles, from whose penetration and skill nothing could escape, however new or strange it might be, spoke thus to the bishop, who from childhood had known such cheeses and yet could not test them: "Cut them in two," he said, "then fasten together with a skewer those that you find to be of the right quality and keep them in your cellar for a time and then send them to me. The rest you may keep for yourself and your clergy and your family." This was done for two years, and the king ordered the present of cheeses to be taken in without remark: then in the third year the bishop brought in person his laboriously collected cheeses. But the most just Charles pitied his labour and anxiety and added to the bishopric an excellent estate whence he and his successors might provide themselves with corn and wine.[22]

We may feel sorry for the poor flustered bishop collecting his two cart-loads of cheeses; but it is possible that our real sympathy ought to go to Bodo, who probably had to pay an extra rent in cheeses to satisfy the emperor's taste, and got no excellent estate to recompense him.

A visit from the emperor, however, would be a rare event in his life, to be talked about for years and told to his grandchildren. But there was one other event, which happened annually, and which was certainly looked for with excitement by Bodo and his friends. For once a year the king's itinerant justices, the *Missi Dominici,* came round to hold their court and to see if the local counts had been doing justice. Two of them would come, a bishop and a count, and they would perhaps stay a night at the big house as guests of the abbot, and the next day they would go on to Paris, and there they would sit and do justice in the open square before the church, and from all the district round great men and small, nobles and freemen and *coloni,* would bring their grievances and demand redress. Bodo would go too, if anyone had injured or robbed him, and would make his complaint to the judges. But if he were canny he would not go to them empty-handed, trusting to justice alone. Charlemagne was very strict, but unless the *missi* were exceptionally honest and pious they would not be averse to taking bribes. Theodulf, Bishop of Orleans, who was one of the Emperor's *missi,* has left us a most entertaining Latin poem, in which he describes the attempts of the clergy and laymen, who flocked to his court, to buy justice.[23] Every one according to his means brought a present; the rich offered money, precious stones, fine materials, and Eastern carpets, arms, horses, antique vases of gold or silver chiselled with representations of the labors of Hercules. The poor brought skins of Cordova leather, tanned and untanned, excellent pieces of cloth and linen (poor Ermentrude must have worked hard for the month before the justices came!), boxes, and wax. "With this battering-ram," cries the shocked Bishop Theodulf, "they hope to break down the wall of my soul. But they would not have thought that they could shake *me,* if they had not so shaken other judges before." And indeed, if his picture be true, the royal justices must have been followed about by a regular caravan of carts and horses to carry their presents. Even Theodulf has to admit that, in order not to hurt people's feelings, he was obliged to accept certain unconsidered trifles in the shape

[22] The Monk of St. Gall's *Life* in *op. cit.,* pp. 78–9.
[23] See the description in Lavisse, *Hist. de France* II, pt. I, p. 321; also G. Monod, *Les mœurs judiciaires au VIII Siècle,* Revue Historique, t. XXXV (1887).

of eggs and bread and wine and chickens and little birds, "whose bodies" (he says, smacking his lips) "are small, but very good to eat." One seems to detect the anxious face of Bodo behind those eggs and little birds.

Another treat Bodo had which happened once a year; for regularly on the ninth of October there began the great fair of St. Denys, which went on for a whole month, outside the gate of Paris.[24] Then for a week before the fair little booths and sheds sprang up, with open fronts in which the merchants could display their wares, and the Abbey of St. Denys, which had the right to take a toll of all the merchants who came there to sell, saw to it that the fair was well enclosed with fences, and that all came in by the gates and paid their money, for wily merchants were sometimes known to burrow under fences or climb over them so as to avoid the toll. Then the streets of Paris were crowded with merchants bringing their goods, packed in carts and upon horses and oxen; and on the opening day all regular trade in Paris stopped for a month, and every Parisian shop-keeper was in a booth somewhere in the fair, exchanging the corn and wine and honey of the district for rarer goods from foreign parts. Bodo's abbey probably had a stall in the fair and sold some of those pieces of cloth woven by the serfs in the women's quarter, or cheeses and salted meat prepared on the estates, or wine paid in rent by Bodo and his fellow-farmers. Bodo would certainly take a holiday and go to the fair. In fact, the steward would probably have great difficulty in keeping his men at work during the month; Charlemagne had to give a special order to his stewards that they should "be careful that our men do properly the work which it is lawful to exact from them, and that they do not waste their time in running about to markets and fairs." Bodo and Ermentrude and the three children, all attired in their best, did not consider it waste of time to go to the fair even twice or three times. They pretended that they wanted to buy salt to salt down their winter meat, or some vermillion dye to color a frock for the baby. What they really wanted was to wander along the little rows of booths and look at all the strange things assembled there; for merchants came to St. Denys to sell their rich goods from the distant East to Bodo's betters, and wealthy Frankish nobles bargained their for purple and silken robes with orange borders, stamped leather jerkins, pea-cock's feathers, and the scarlet plumage of flamingos (which they called "phœnix skins"), scents and pearls and spices, almonds and raisins, and monkeys for their wives to play with.[25] Sometimes these merchants were

[24] See Faigniez, *op. cit.*, pp. 43–4.

[25] See the Monk of St. Gall's account of the finery of the Frankish nobles: "It was a holiday and they had just come from Pavia, whither the Venetians had carried all the wealth of the East from their territories beyond the sea,—others, I say, strutted in robes made of pheasant-skins and silk; or of the necks, backs and tails of peacocks in their first plumage. Some were decorated with purple and

Venetians, but more often they were Syrians or crafty Jews, and Bodo and his fellows laughed loudly over the story of how a Jewish merchant had tricked a certain bishop, who craved for all the latest novelties, by stuffing a mouse with spices and offering it for sale to him, saying that "he had brought this most precious never-before-seen animal from Judea," and refusing to take less than a whole measure of silver for it.[26] In exchange for their luxuries these merchants took away with them Frisian cloth, which was greatly esteemed, and corn and hunting dogs, and sometimes a piece of fine goldsmith's work, made in a monastic workshop. And Bodo would hear a hundred dialects and tongues, for men of Saxony and Frisia, Spain and Provence, Rouen and Lombardy, and perhaps an Englishman or two, jostled each other in the little streets; and from time to time there came also an Irish scholar with a manuscript to sell, and the strange, sweet songs of Ireland on his lips:

> A hedge of trees surrounds me,
> A blackbird's lay sings to me;
> Above my lined booklet
> The trilling birds chant to me.
>
> In a grey mantle from the top of bushes
> The cuckoo sings:
> Verily—may the Lord shield me!—
> Well do I write under the greenwood.[27]

Then there were always jugglers and tumblers, and men with performing bears, and minstrels to wheedle Bodo's few pence out of his pocket. And it would be a very tired and happy family that trundled home in the cart to bed. For it is not, after all, so dull in the kitchen, and when we have quite finished with the emperor, 'Charlemagne and all his peerage,' it is really worth while to spend a few moments with Bodo in his little manse. History is largely made up of Bodos.

---

lemon-coloured ribbons; some were wrapped round with blankets and some in ermine robes." *Op. cit.,* p. 149. The translation is a little loose: the "phœnix robes" of the original were more probably made out of the plumage, not of the pheasant but of the scarlet flamingo, as Hodgson thinks (*Early Hist. of Venice,* p. 155), or possibly silks woven or embroidered with figures of birds, as Heyd thinks (*Hist. du Commerce du Levant,* I, p. 111).

[26] The Monk of St. Gall's *Life* in *op. cit.,* pp. 81–2.

[27] This little poem was scribbled by an Irish scribe in the margin of a copy of Priscian in the monastery of St. Gall, in Switzerland, the same from which Charlemagne's highly imaginative biographer came. The original will be found in Stokes and Strachan, *Thesaurus Palæohibernicus* (1903) II, p. 290. It has often been translated and I quote the translation by Kuno Meyer, *Ancient Irish Poetry* (2nd ed., 1913), p. 99. The quotation from the *Triads of Ireland* at the head of this chapter is taken from Kuno Meyer also, *ibid.* pp. 102–3.

FOOTNOTE SOURCES

1. The Roll of the Abbot Irminon, an estate book of the Abbey of St. Germain des Prés, near Paris, written between 811 and 826. See *Polyptyque de l'Abbaye de Saint-Germain des Prés,* pub. Auguste Longnon, t. I, *Introduction;* t. II, *Texte* (Soc. de l'Hist. de Paris, 1886–95).

2. Charlemagne's capitulary, *De Villis,* instructions to his stewards on the management of his estates. See Guerard, *Explication du Capitulaire "de Villis"* (Acad. des Inscriptions et Belles-Lettres, *Mémoires,* t. XXI, 1857), pp. 165–309, containing the text, with a detailed commentary and a translation into French.

3. *Early Lives of Charlemagne,* ed. A. J. Grant (King's Classics, 1907). Contains the lives by Einhard and the Monk of St. Gall, on which see Halphen, cited below.

4. Various pieces of information about social life may be gleaned from the decrees of Church Councils, Old High German and Anglo-Saxon charms and poems, and Ælfric's *Colloquium,* extracts from which are translated in Bell's Eng. Hist. Source Books, *The Welding of the Race,* 449–1066, ed. J. E. W. Wallis (1913). For a general sketch of the period see Lavisse *Hist. de France,* t. II, and for an elaborate critical study of certain aspects of Charlemagne's reign (including the *Polyptychum*) see Halphen, *Etudes critiques sur l'Histoire de Charlemagne* (1921); also A. Dopsch, *Wirtschaftsentwicklung der Karolingerzeit, Vornehmlich in Deutschland,* 2 vols. (Weimar, 1912–13), which Halphen criticizes.

FRIEDRICH HEER

Aristocracy and Peasantry

Medieval Europe abounded in castles. Germany alone had ten thousand and more, most of them now vanished; all that a summer journey in the Rhineland and the south west now can show are a handful of ruins and a few nineteenth century restorations. Nevertheless, anyone journeying from Spain to the Dvina, from Calabria to Wales, will find castles rearing up again and again to dominate the open landscape. There they still stand, in desolate and uninhabited districts where the only visible forms of life are herdsmen and their flocks, with hawks circling the battlements, far from the traffic and comfortably distant even from the nearest small town: these were the strongholds of the European aristocracy.

The weight of aristocratic dominance was felt in Europe until well after the French Revolution; political and social structure, the Church, the general tenor of thought and feeling were all influenced by it. Over the centuries, consciously or unconsciously, the other classes of this older European society—the clergy, the bourgeoisie and the "common people" —adopted many of the outward characteristics of the aristocracy, who became their model, their standard, their ideal. Aristocratic values and ambitions were adopted alongside aristocratic manners and fashions of dress. Yet the aristocracy were the object of much contentious criticism and complaint; from the thirteenth century onwards their military value and their political importance were both called in question. Nevertheless, their opponents continued to be their principal imitators. In the eleventh and twelfth centuries, the reforming Papacy and its clerical supporters, although opposed to the excessively aristocratic control of the Church (as is shown by the Investiture Contest) nevertheless themselves first adopted and then strengthened the forms of this control. Noblemen who became bishops or who founded new Orders helped to implant aristocratic principles and forms of government deep within the structure and spiritual life of the Church. Again, in the twelth and thirteenth centuries the urban bourgeoisie, made prosperous and even rich by trade and industry, were

Friedrich Heer, *The Medieval World. Europe 1100–1350,* trans. Janet Sondheimer (London: Weidenfeld and Nicolson, 1961), pp. 14–16, 22–29.

127

rising to political power as the servants and legal protégés of monarchy. These "patricians" were critical of the aristocracy and hostile towards it. Yet they also imitated the aristocracy, and tried to gain admittance to the closed circle and to achieve equality of status. Even the unarmed peasantry, who usually had to suffer more from the unrelieved weight of aristocratic dominance, long remained tenaciously loyal to their lords, held to their allegiance by that combination of love and fear, *amor et timor,* which was so characteristic of the medieval relationship between lord and servant, between God and man.

The castles and strongholds of the aristocracy remind us of the reality of their power and superiority. Through the long warring centuries when men went defenseless and insecure, the "house," the lord's fortified dwelling, promised protection, security and peace to all whom it sheltered. From the ninth to the eleventh centuries, if not later, Europe was in many ways all too open. Attack came from the sea, in the Mediterranean from Saracens and Vikings, the latter usually in their swift, dragon-prowed, easily maneuvered longboats, manned by some sixteen pairs of oarsmen and with a full complement of perhaps sixty men. There were periods when the British Isles and the French coasts were being raided every year by Vikings and in the heart of the continent marauding Magyar armies met invading bands of Saracens. The name of Pontresina, near St. Moritz in Switzerland, is a memento of the stormy tenth century; it means *pons Saracenorum,* the "fortified Saracen bridge," the place where plundering expeditions halted on their way up from the Mediterranean.

It was recognized in theory that the Church and the monarchy were the principal powers and that they were bound by the nature of their office to ensure peace and security and to do justice; but at this period they were too weak, too torn by internal conflicts to fulfil their obligations. Thus more and more power passed into the hands of warriors invested by the monarchy and the Church with lands and rights of jurisdiction, who in return undertook to support their overlords and to protect the unarmed peasantry.

Their first concern, however, was self-protection. It is almost impossible for us to realize how primitive the great majority of these early medieval "castles" really were. Until about 1150 the fortified houses of the Anglo-Norman nobility were simple dwellings surrounded by a mound of earth and a wooden stockade. These were the motte and bailey castles: the motte was the mound and its stockade, the bailey an open court lying below and also stockaded. Both were protected, where possible, by yet another ditch filled with water, the moat. In the middle of the motte there was a wooden tower, the keep or *donjon,* which only became a genuine stronghold at a later date and in places where stone was readily available.

The stone castles of the French and German nobility usually had only a single communal room in which all activities took place.

In such straitened surroundings, where warmth, light and comfort were lacking, there was no way of creating an air of privacy. It is easy enough to understand why the life of the landed nobility was often so unrestrained, so filled with harshness, cruelty and brutality, even in later, more "chivalrous" periods. The barons' daily life was bare and uneventful, punctuated by war, hunting (a rehearsal for war), and feasting. Boys were trained to fight from the age of seven or eight, and their education in arms continued until they were twenty-one, although in some cases they started to fight as early as fifteen. The peasants of the surrounding countryside, bound to their lords by a great variety of ties, produced the sparse fare which was all that the undeveloped agriculture of the early medieval period could sustain. Hunting was a constant necessity, to make up for the lack of butcher's meat, and in England and Germany in the eleventh and twelfth centuries even the kings had to progress from one crown estate to another, from one bishop's palace to the next, to maintain themselves and their retinue. . . .

As has been said, the aristocracy lived off, and mostly on, the land; they lived off their peasants, who were bound to them by a great variety of formal ties. In England, at the time of the Norman Conquest, the great majority of peasants were in some degree unfree. This unfreedom should not be confused or identified with slavery, whether ancient or modern— although there were slaves in Europe until the seventeenth and eighteenth centuries, mostly Slavs captured as booty in Eastern Europe (because of their name medieval people thought of them as predestined slaves), or prisoners of war from the Eastern Mediterranean. The English villein, the French *vilain* and the German *Holde* were all bound to their lords by the specific obligation of rendering services and dues. The villein worked his lord's demesne and also had to pay something from the revenues of his own plot; he was required to be at his lord's service for manual and team-work, to build castles, roads and bridges. Everyone was under an obligation to take all his grain to the lord's mill to be ground, for which payment was naturally exacted. In addition to windmills (which probably originated in Persia), there were also water-mills; by the end of the eleventh century there were over five thousand of them in England, about as many as there were knights in the army of the English king. The mills, like the castles and the bonds of obligation, demonstrated the hold of the baronage over the countryside and its people. Most oppressive of all was the liability (in France) to pay *taille* or tallage, which was nothing but an arbitrary tax, levied by the seigneur as and when he found it "necessary"; it was taken both from free and from unfree peasants. None of these peasants were slaves, however; the monarchy and the Church offered them protection, chiefly because both institutions were concerned to safeguard the "good old law," which was the peasant's own law, the law he defended in the manorial courts. These, however, came under the lord's control; he appointed, or at any rate confirmed in office, the provost or reeve, who was the judge of the court, and who might be subjected to heavy pressure from the lord, or in his absence, the lord's bailiff or steward. But where a lord was very dependent on the goodwill and labor of his peasants, and was often absent, occupied in warfare or political affairs, the peasants had a chance to improve their position.

The origins of the unfreedom of the medieval peasant were various. In the Mediterranean lands it stemmed from the arrangements of late antiquity, when the peasants were bound to the soil by the state, in order to make sure of its taxes. For people in this situation the invasion of their lands by Germans, Saracens, Normans, Spaniards or Frenchmen meant only a change of masters, not of status: and the position of the Sicilians and south Italians is much the same today. In the Germanic North the pattern of development was different. During the stormy centuries of the early Middle Ages free peasants often "commended" themselves, more or less voluntarily, to a lord. Anyone who commended himself to his lord's protection was in return relieved of all military service, which the lord now performed for him through his knights; the peasant, for his part, became liable to pay rent on behalf of himself, his family and his landed property. As an example of what was happening, there is evidence from a particular district of the Salzburg region in the eighth century of the absorption of 237 small free peasant holdings into 50 greater estates, of which 21 belonged to the Church, 12 to the Dukes of Bavaria and 17 to other great lords. This alienation and amalgamation of free peasant properties was one of the most important and momentous developments in the social history of Europe, perhaps only comparable to the decline of independent small-scale manufacturers, tradesmen and *entrepreneurs* which started in the late nineteenth century and is still proceeding. Like their peasant predecessors, these independent middle-class industrialists and traders have "voluntarily" surrendered their businesses into the ownership or control of some larger industry, bank or combine, or even to the state, in which case the surrender has usually been even less "voluntary."

The unfree peasants of Western Europe, the serfs, were thus the descendants of the dependent peasantry of Carolingian times. Their name was a bequest from the slaves of antiquity (*serf* < *servus*); nevertheless they possessed certain rights in law. In addition to the property they held from their lords they might also have a free property of their own, an allod.

Their lord owed them protection and patronage, they owed him obedience and aid, in the form of personal services and payments. An annual payment of a small sum known as "head-money" set a symbolical seal on the bonds of their personal attachment. Tallage, an extraordinary tax, might be demanded from serfs, and also from those who were nominally free whenever a lord was in difficulties. Special payments had to be made by a serf marrying outside his lord's dependents, and by a serf's direct heirs when he died: this "death duty" entailed the surrender of the best head of cattle, or, in some districts, a share of the chattels.

In the twelfth century, apart from some tiny and much debated areas (debated, that is, among scholars), there were no longer any completely free peasants. The peasants described as "free" were nevertheless bound to a lord in a protective relationship of some kind, just like the rest. But the greater the lord (for example if he were the king or a great vassal, with a hundred and more estates), and the more remote his court, the freer was the peasant. Bound to the service of one or more lords, the rural population of Europe lived in varying degrees of dependence, unfreedom or serfdom, and the distinctions of grade were in practice as great as that between highly born vassals of the crown and "knights and noble squires" who had virtually nothing to call their own, or between highly educated wealthy prelates and village priests bound to the soil. Our vocabulary does not even possess the words necessary to distinguish clearly between the different groups, classes, and ranks of "free," "half-free," "unfree" and "dependent" peasants. And the actual situation was more confusing still, for in many places a "free" peasant might be more oppressed and much poorer than an "unfree" peasant living only a few miles away.

But, despite the gravitational downward pull of further oppression and the rapid increase in the numbers of serfs in some areas, some classes of peasants, and some individuals, were working themselves higher up the social scale. By the twelfth and thirteenth centuries the peasantry had become a factor kings and nobles had to reckon with, even to the point of calling on their help, as in France where peasant troops fought victoriously on the king's side against the "robber barons," the great feudatories.

Barons and kings were eager to increase their revenues and took in hand the clearance of forests and the improvement of land which had become marshy or arid through neglect. Peasants were urgently needed for this work of internal colonization and they were in good supply since the vicissitudes of medieval life, war, harsh masters, and their own *Wanderlust* were continually driving them from their homes. Those peasants who had, as it were, won their freedom by invitation, were known as *hospites;* they received a charter which promised them protection against unjust oppression, excessive dues, and arbitrary actions on the part of the landlord. Numerous new settlements (for example the *villes neuves* in northern France) originated in this way. To attract more settlers, the "recruiting officers" read the charters aloud at markets in other districts, like the North American railroad companies in the nineteenth century when they needed pioneers to colonize the empty lands of the West.

In twelfth and thirteenth century Germany one went not West but East. The kings of Poland, Bohemia and Hungary and the German princes were colonizing Brandenburg, Prussia, East Prussia and the Baltic lands as far as Riga. They all needed German peasants, and increasingly tended to look for them through agents known as *locatores*. The *locator* recruited the peasants, took care of them on their long journey, staked out the new territory, and put up an enclosed camp. In return for all this he was recognized as "provost" of the local court and given the monopoly of local amenities, such as the ale-house and the mill, and sometimes also of the sale of bread, meat and fish. His position was then made hereditary.

The medieval world, particularly the "open" world of the twelfth century, thus offered opportunities to at least a section of the rural population, particularly in the East and in Germany, the Netherlands, northern France and England. For example, during the thirteenth and fourteenth centuries more than twelve hundred new villages were founded in Silesia alone in rather less than 150 years. In Western Europe, however, the thirteenth century also saw the beginnings of stagnation in agriculture and of a corresponding deterioration in the peasants' position. Europe was already starting to turn in on itself, social and geographical boundaries were becoming more rigid.

This inevitably affected the peasants. Clearing of the waste land stopped; in fact some lords, eager for cash, were already converting arable into pasture, buying up and expropriating peasant farmers. In England and France this development was a cause of conflict between the king and the barons. During the thirteenth and fourteenth centuries English villeins were contesting their freedom in the royal courts. Feudal estates changed masters much more frequently than used to be realized—by marriage, death, sale, or confiscation. When property changed hands the peasant stood an equal chance of losing or gaining from the change. The manorial courts, which regulated the affairs of the peasantry, had not always kept a written record of their proceedings, so that it was often very difficult for a peasant whose lord claimed him as a villein to prove his freedom in court. From the thirteenth century onwards the English courts were filled with peasants' pleas about "distraint," that is, enforced services and payments demanded from them by old and new masters. But at the same time, some peasants were able to improve their position and many villeins succeeded in purchasing their freedom from their lords. In this they were sometimes assisted by the Church, or, in France, by the monarchy, since under the strict letter of the law an unfree peasant, who had no possessions of his own, could not buy his own freedom. The lords' growing need of money gave industrious and enterprising peasants an excellent means of bettering themselves. The "free" peasants who were under royal protection later merged with the burgesses to become the "Third Estate," sending their representatives directly to the Estates General, the representative body of the different estates. In southern France, which followed its own path of development and was only very slowly brought into line with the north during the thirteenth century, peasant and urban communities often acted side by side in a successful struggle to make their voices heard on political matters.

There is an interesting contrast in the attitudes towards their land of the French and English baronage, a contrast which had an important effect on political and social development. Anxious to avoid the trouble of farming them for themselves, the French seigneurs fell into the habit of transferring their estates to the peasants to work in return for money rents. In consequence, as the nobility became more and more involved in campaigning, court life, and even in intellectual pursuits, they drew further and further apart from the life of their peasants, until they were nothing but a remote and oppressive burden. In England, however, the baronage were taking an active interest in agriculture from early in the thirteenth century. The period between 1200 and 1340 has been justly described as the "great age of demesne farming," the great age of the development of baronial estates. Walter of Henley's small but very important manual *On Husbandry,* which describes the essentials of this demesne economy, is a characteristic product of it. The lord was keenly interested in improving the yield, made his peasants work harder, grew for the market and not simply for subsistence, and took advantage of the rising prices for agrarian products. With their venture into wool production, it could be said that the English nobility were among the first to turn agriculture into an industry. Peasants were bought out or expropriated to make room for sheep. In striking contrast to their continental counterparts, the English aristocracy carried on and extended this commercial tradition; and later their involvement in trade and industry was to link them with the bourgeoisie and also make them amenable to changing conditions, social, political, and intellectual.

Meanwhile, the peasants' activities were becoming more and more restricted. Even the forests belonged to the king or to some noble lord, to hunt there as they would, ruining whatever young crops were left in the neighboring fields after wild pigs, roebuck and red deer had had their fill. And it must not be forgotten that medieval peasants, like the medieval clergy, had a passion for the chase, although it could only be indulged by poaching. Arable land was also becoming scarcer, since some of it was being turned into pasture for sheep. There was nothing inherently objectionable about sheep. Rightly used, they were hard-working and service-able animals, providing dung to manure the ground, milk for cheese, skin for parchment and fleece for wool. But side by side with the peasants' sheep there were now the lord's sheep, no longer beasts of all trades but devoted only to the production of wool.

Development elsewhere in Europe was equally diverse during the later Middle Ages. In Italy, where city states were rapidly becoming estab-lished, the nobility lived in towns and became assimilated with the town bourgeoisie. Here man was an urban animal, life meant urban life and culture urban civilization. The peasants of the surrounding countryside had no share in all this. They lived on in their shacks or their wretched farmhouses and stables, sinking to the level of the late Roman *colonus*: nothing in their lord's village was theirs except the clothes they stood up in and their own families, and even these might be required by the lord for his own use. Alongside them were tenant-farmers, peasants who paid rent and dues and were free of lordship.

In Spain, the conquerors from the north who took the country from the Arabs managed to attract some "free" peasants as settlers. These Christian peasants found the countryside already populated by a rural proletariat, sunk in the depths of oppression and squalor, which had been there since late Roman times—their counterparts can be seen today all over the Mediterranean Arab world. The pastoral economy practiced by the aristocracy, and the disorder arising from the growing weakness of the monarchy in the five Christian kingdoms, all conspired to depress the status of the free peasants to the lowest level.

This levelling down, this paring away of rights to the minimum, was a characteristic feature also of Germany and of Eastern Europe towards the end of the Middle Ages. The German aristocracy, unhindered by the monarchy, which was engaged in critical struggles in Italy and with the Papacy (not to mention the German princes themselves), made every effort to reduce the "free" peasants, who had been subject only to certain exactly stipulated annual obligations, to the lower status of serfs and to the performance of increasingly arbitrary duties. This Germany contained the seeds of the "Land of Serfdom" described by Herder and Lessing in the eighteenth century, *terra oboedientiae*. There was a particularly marked deterioration in the legal and economic position, in fact in the whole standard of living, of the German peasants living in the northeast; here there was a substratum of old Prussian and Slavonic serfs to form the basis of a servile peasant community. This belt of serfdom extended over the lands east of the Elbe, Bohemia, Moravia, Poland and the Baltic region, all of them now largely in the power of the aristocracy. Over this whole region, where there were no royal courts to protect the peas-antry, the nobility appropriated all governmental rights for themselves and their estates became large-scale agrarian enterprises. The result for the peasants was that the late medieval and early modern periods saw the creation of a new, hereditary serfdom.

Even so, this European serfdom differed fundamentally from that of the Russian peasant. In Russia it was the state that was largely responsible for the evolution of serfdom; it was by government decree that the peasants were bound to the soil, the soil of the aristocracy and the monarchy. This state-serfdom (*gosudarstvennye krestjane*) had its roots in earlier forms of enslavement from the period of immigration and conquest by alien peoples. Slavonic tribes thus became subject tribes, owing tribute to their Alan, Gothic or Magyar lords. The Kievan state took over several such dependent groups and made them *smerdy,* that is, tributary serfs of the princes of Kiev. The Mongols, when they came, imposed fresh forms of servile obligation on these peoples, setting local agents over them to keep them to their duties. These agents, members of the Horde, were called *kalannye,* which means people bound to perform a special task or *kalan.* After the break-up of Mongol rule in western Russia (i.e. the Ukraine and White Russia) these serf communities acquired new masters, those in Galicia the King of Poland, those in other parts of the Ukraine the Grand Duke of Lithuania. The Grand Dukes of Moscow obtained from their Mongol overlords power over the servile communities in the rest of Russia. During the Mongol period even free Russian peasants, obliged to pay tribute to the Khan, were reduced to dependence on the nobility, the only class capable of meeting such an obligation, who thus came to regard the peasants as "theirs." It was at this period, when all peasants were obliged to pay tribute, that the Russian word for peasants first appears: *krestjane* (Christians), used originally of peasants on monastic estates in the fourteenth century, when the monastic landlords had assumed the responsibility of collecting the tribute from the rural population.

The later extension of serfdom in Russia and its establishment by law as a universal institution, between 1581 and 1649, falls outside our period. As late as the seventeenth century slavery and serfdom existed side by side; in the eighteenth century, however, the two merged into the new "body-serfdom" in which the peasant himself, instead of his land, was bound to the lord. . . .

JOHN R. HALE

Varieties of Rural Life

. . . The long medieval centuries had produced innumerable variations
in peasant tenure and services, from the right-less slave, through the serf,
able to catch the eye of the law of the land through the fence of his
lord's control, to the prosperous freeholder. The nature of the land produced its own variety; the rancorous independence of the Breton peasant,
walling off his thin-soiled patch from his neighbor, contrasting with the
broad open fields south of the Loire with their corporate triumph of
harvest-home. But some generalisation is possible. The essential social
difference was between those with a plough and animals to tow it, and the
majority who had only a spade or could contribute but one or two beasts
to fill a richer man's team. Illiteracy was the rule. Physical tiredness;
constant vigilance against incursions into strips or patches undefined by
hedges or fences; isolation; these factors produced the "peasant mentality"
and appeared to justify the stream of urban jest and abuse. Certainly they
produced a conservatism in agricultural practice and a tenacious bloody-
mindedness of which governments and would-be improving landlords had
to take account. With no privacy—the majority had one- or two-roomed
hovels which doubled as barn and stable—and few possessions, a table,
a chest (for storage and to sit on), an iron pot and a kneading trough,
with children who were set to scare birds as soon as they could toddle
and a wife who worked as hard as he, the peasant was unfitted to become involved with changes in the superstructure of the civilization of
which he was the foundation. The voice with which he speaks from the
written sources is violent, litigious, full of crude superstition. But this is
because we hear him most clearly when he is up against government or
being denounced from the pulpit. His endurance, his ability to work with
others, his urge to collect land and stock of his own: these can best be
seen in the land itself and the marks of his work in it, and for the rest we
must turn to the peasants of modern Europe, of, for example, Montenegro

John R. Hale, *Renaissance Europe: Individual and Society 1480–1520* (New
York: Harper & Row, Publishers, 1971), pp. 200–205.

or Sardinia or Ireland, to see how an ignorant conservatism can include generosity and humor.

A quick survey of Europe from west to east will show the regional variations against which these generalisations must be measured and how wide was the contrast between the reasonably prosperous peasantry of England and France and the declining status and living standards in Poland and Russia.

The variety in England was especially great. A gradually rising population meant that men with little or no land of their own, who relied on being employed by others, were meeting greater competition and being forced into reliance on charity. The same factor brought insecurity into the lives of the large number of cottagers, men who owned a house and a few acres of land but who looked to seasonal work for others to keep their families safely over the subsistence level. On the other hand, during the labor shortage after the Black Death significant numbers of peasants had bought or bargained their way into small farms of their own (or, if not absolutely their own in law, capable of being handed on without question to their heirs). The result was to increase the gap between the landless man and cottager and the smallholder who, while still working himself on the land, employed shepherds and laborers. Such a man might look forward to the time when his descendants could eschew labor with their hands and glide by the path to which no legal or universally recognised rules applied, but only local judgment and a reasonable prosperity, into the broad spectrum of the squirearchy or gentry; profits on farming were small and holdings could be built up only slowly, generation by generation.

In England the yeoman owed much to the comparative stability of his polity and the peace it brought to the countryside. Above all, he was indebted to the fact that the Hundred Years War had been fought on French soil. In France, though the proportion of independent small-holders was probably less, and the yeoman class did not have the "weight" that local opinion accorded them in England, there were large differences in the size of land holdings and, in spite of considerable vestiges of feudal and seigneurial law, possibly more freedom of action and security of tenure; for in their effort to reactivate estates devastated by war, landlords had made large concessions in order to tempt a tenantry back from dispersal and hiding. By the late fifteenth century there was still land waiting to be restored to productivity, and the *métayage* system, whereby rent was paid in produce in return for tools, seed and the use of the land, enabled men without capital to reclaim land and settle there securely, even though the profit to be made from a *métairie* was unlikely to lead to a rise in status. That our period—almost precisely our period—was one favorable to the French peasant who wished to buy land and increase his stock is suggested by figures collected by Mlle. Bezard. To buy a hectolitre of maslin (mixed wheat and rye) a laborer would have had to work for six days under Louis XI, two and a half under Charles VIII, two and three-quarters under Louis XII and eight under Francis I; to purchase a cow, twelve days under Charles VIII, forty-three under Francis I; to buy a hectare of land, forty-four under Louis XI, twenty-one under Charles VIII, one hundred and forty-six under Louis XII and nearly four hundred under Francis I.*

If the wealth of published material relating to English and French rural life makes generalisation hazardous, any conclusions about the position of the Spanish peasantry are temerarious for the opposite reason. A decree of the *cortes* held at Toledo in 1480 abolished servile tenure in Castile and feudal services were abolished for Catalonia in 1486 in return for a cash compensation. How far the peasantry actually benefited from these measures, in contrast to Aragon, where feudal relationships remained in force, it is impossible to say. There were enough prosperous peasant proprietors in Castile to be recognised as a social type in literature, but the possibility of a poor man's improving his status were severely inhibited by the massive support given by the government to the pasturage routes for the giant sheep flocks organised by the *Mesta*. In the peninsula as a whole it was further inhibited by the weight of seigneurial dues, state taxes and church tithes; for most peasants a life of desperate toil left their fortunes exactly as they had inherited them and provided no insurance against the indebtedness that followed a bad harvest. In Portugal rent, feudal dues and tithe could account for seventy percent of a peasant's produce.

Yet this was not, in Spain or Portugal, a time when peasant revolt, let alone peasant war was feared. King John of Denmark (1481–1513) could safely refer to the peasants as men born to servitude (a condition into which, in contrast to Sweden, they were declining in his reign). The French proverb "Jaques Bonhomme has a strong back and will bear anything" took the peasant's passivity for granted, as did the German "a peasant is just like an ox, only he has no horns"—though peasant wars were to break out in southern and central Germany in 1524–25 and were preceded by clandestine associations like the *Bundschuh* movement of 1502–1517. For its size and the heterogeneity of its institutions, Germany was, of all European countries, the one about which it is most dangerous to generalise, but the status and prosperity of the peasant (and therefore the range between poor and well-to-do) seems to have been highest in the southwest and to have dwindled towards the northeast. Speaking

---

* *La vie rurale dans le sud de la région Parisienne de 1450 à 1560* (Paris, 1929) 236–9.

of Alsace, Wimfeling wrote "I know peasants who spend as much at the marriage of their sons and daughters or the baptisms of their infants as would buy a small house and farm or vineyard." Moralists' evidence is always suspect; on the other hand, an ordinance issued in 1497 at Lindau forbad "the common peasant to wear cloth costing more than half a florin the yard, silk, velvet, pearls, gold, or slashed garments," evidence that the effects of the luxury trade routes through the Rhineland were not confined to the towns. Of greater concern to moralist and town council was the independence nurtured by the example of the neighbouring Swiss, who, by means of a largely peasant war, had not only thrown off the feudal dues which were still common (though no longer a badge of dependence) in southwest Germany but had created an independent community. It also reflects two crucial but at present immeasurable factors that bore on the position of the peasantry in western Europe as a whole: the mounting costs of bureaucratised administrations—state, civic and princely, which were passed on to the sector of society in which objection was least likely to be mobilised; and the professionalisation of war, which meant that landowners, denied profits from pay, loot and ransom, turned to the exploitation of their own properties. The *Junkers* of Prussia are a clear example of this second tendency; dormant feudal rights were reactivated in a movement to reduce peasant status to that of the numerous Slave bondmen whose labor was entirely at the disposal of their employers.

Clear, too, is the distinction between the ways in which magnates sought to secure enough labor on their estates east and west of the Elbe. Westwards, the tendency was to reduce, commute or abolish labor obligations, to rely on goodwill and voluntary contract rather than force. Eastwards, landlords intensified their demands for labor and their efforts to tie that labor to the land. This move to serfdom was backed by the governments of eastern Europe: urban life, always less vigorous than in the west, was in decline; rulers faced bankruptcy if they could not woo the financial, as well as the political support of the wide-acred class of noble or gentry landowners. In 1497 the Bohemian diet affirmed the servitude of peasants. In 1519 the service due for a peasant holding was declared by statute to be one day a week (in lieu of from one to six days a year) and was in practice considerably heavier; by a series of laws passed from 1496 to 1511 neither a peasant nor his sons could leave the land without his master's consent, and during the same period right of appeal from seigneurial justice was removed from all but church and crown lands. In 1514 all Hungarian peasants outside the royal free boroughs were condemned to "real and perpetual servitude" to their masters. The same debasement in status and freedom of action proceeded in Lithuania and Russia, with increased demands both for money dues and labor services and with a firmer tying of the peasant to the soil; by the Russian Code of 1497 a peasant could only leave his lord during the two weeks following St. George's day and only then after paying heavy fees for the privilege of being a free man for one twenty-sixth of the year.

A prime cause of this descent into serfdom was the declining importance of towns and of influential urban classes in eastern Europe. Noble resentment of the rival marketing activities of the towns, the high prices charged there for manufactured goods, the refuge they gave to runaway peasants and the consideration given them by rulers in need of cash subsidies; these factors led to a successful pressure on governments to reduce the independence and the commercial activity of the towns. And this pressure came at a time when the Hanseatic League, itself in decline and harassed in the Baltic by English and Dutch shipping, could no longer act as an example of urban energy in northeastern Europe, and when the westward overland trade routes virtually dried up when the Turks occupied the north coast of the Black Sea. In 1500 townsmen were excluded from representation in the Bohemian diet; they regained it in 1517, but the tendency was clear: nobles, with the support of government, confronted the peasants without the political and economic buffer of the towns.

5. WOMEN AND THEIR DUTIES

With very few exceptions the women of medieval Europe remained stylized figures: they were rarely allowed to become real people. For the most part this can be explained by a social ethos which assigned to men the roles of warrior and priest, the dominant idealized types of the time. If a woman was taught anything other than simple handicraft, she usually learned only to listen, to respond, to pray, to serve. To be sure there were important exceptions—one need only recall Eleanor of Aquitaine, the patroness of troubadours—but most medieval women, depending on their class, were left either on a pedestal or in the field.

Dorothy Margaret Stuart provides a vignette of daily life in Plantagenet England. She observes, paradoxically, that the only women who may have shared a rough equality with men were those at the bottom of the social scale, those who worked beside their peasant husbands from day to day. Education was available to the others only at home or, at best, in a convent school where learning was strictly by rote and the prime virtue was obedience. To care for her man and tend to her needlework—these were more often than not a woman's chief occupations.

J. R. Hale disabuses us of the notion that women fared any better as time elapsed. In some regards, he contends, their condition actually grew more restricted and he points to the importance of male bonding outside of the home, something which was denied to females. He also elaborates on certain striking aspects of sexuality in medieval times—birth control, chastity belts, and prostitution—which served the convenience of men rather than the emancipation of women.

141

Friedrich Heer confirms Hale's view, at least insofar as women of royal and aristocratic lineage were concerned. He finds the fourteenth century to be a distinctly "masculine era" in which a certain feminine mystique was created that only veiled the reality of woman's servitude to man. Chivalric ideal and common practice were far apart.

While some of the evidence indicates that women were not always and everywhere as helpless as the medieval stereotype would suggest, the general picture is nonetheless bleak. The extraordinary few were far from constituting a rule, and the theory of woman's dignity was hardly consonant with the social reality. The legacy of medieval Europe, in short, was singularly unpromising for the female of the species.

DOROTHY MARGARET STUART

The Medieval Woman

. . . The mind and the manners of the typical woman were what the will of man made them. His prejudices, his preferences, his misgivings, ruled her way of life. Education—even as it was then understood—liberty, enlightenment, were not for her. She might use her hands, but not her brain. And her plain duty was to be first beautiful as a maiden, secondly, meek as a wife, and then to be the mother of as many infants as the saints would vouchsafe to send. Only in two ways, neither of them very dignified or worthy, might she hope to wield any power over men in general or her husband in particular—either by coaxing or by scolding. She who had neither a fair face nor a sharp and tireless tongue stood little chance of getting her own way in great things or in small. This applies, of course, to the women of the middle and upper classes. Among the tillers of the soil there was probably a sort of rough equality, and a sort of uncouth but kindly comradeship between men and women in the toils, hardships, and rewards of their laborious existence. Indeed, in

Dorothy Margaret Stuart, *Men and Women of Platagenet England* (New York: Harcourt, Brace and Company, 1932), pp. 260–65, 274–75.

La Court de Baron the villein charged with stealing a perch from his lord's pond offered as an excuse that his wife had been in bed for a month, able neither to eat nor drink, and that it was to satisfy her sick craving for a perch that he went to the pond.

One result of the narrowness of the gently born woman's activities was to reduce the great majority of them to a sort of dead level. No doubt their individual characters were as sharply differentiated as are those of their descendants today; but they had no scope, no means of self-expression, and a medieval woman had to be either exceptionally holy or exceptionally sinful in order to make an abiding mark upon the page of history. At this distance they of whom we read in the old chronicles seem almost as stiff and lifeless as their images on their sepulchral brasses or their carved Purbeck tombs. Look at these slim-flanked, tight-waisted, blank-visaged ladies, with their folded hands and their heraldic gowns. Did rebellious hearts beat under those rigid kirtles? Did wild dreams haunt the heads under those horned and peaked headdresses? Was the Lady Aveline in truth *exactly* like the Lady Ysabel, even to the number of kinks in her hair and the number of pearls on her coif? Were the mouth and nose, the eyes and eyebrows, of the Lady Blaunche absolutely identical with those of the Lady Elianor? And what did they think about and talk about all the long day, those medieval ladies who look incapable of thought or speech? . . .

The education of the medieval girl, especially in the twelfth and thirteenth centuries, was even more meager than that of the medieval boy, but there is abundant evidence in the old romances that reading, and especially *reading aloud,* was among the most coveted accomplishments. The lady must be able not only to spell out the angular black-letter script in her breviary, and the motto dight on the shield of her lord; she must be ready to take her turn in reading from the books, few and curious, but none the less delightful, whence she and her sisters drew all their ideas about far lands, and other times, and the great legends of love and war. Very often while one damsel was reading aloud from the tales of Arthur's knights or of the siege of Troy the others would sit round busily plying their needles, pausing only to smile, or sigh, or exchange quick glances of horror or amusement, as the many-colored narrative unrolled itself. All women were skilled in needlecraft, and Langland urges his fair and nobly born contemporaries to use their "longe fingres smale" in fashioning vestments and hangings for churches. A knowledge of music was not uncommon. We read in royal household accounts of sums expended on the purchase and repair of various quaintly named instruments destined to be played by the "longe fingres smale" of queens and princesses; and Josyan, the much-suffering heroine of *Bevis of Hampton,* was certainly well versed in music. The pages of illuminated manuscripts are crowded with little feminine figures performing upon rebecks, fiddles, harps, and sackbuts, and portable organs with gaily gilt pipes.

From the early thirteenth-century romance of *Sir Guy of Warwick* we gather that a lady of high degree must have at least seven accomplishments, astronomy, ars-metrick, or prosody, geometry, sophistry, rhetoric, 'clergy,' or clerkly learning, and music, and that her instructors would probably be white-haired scholars from Toulouse.

> Gentil she was, and as demure
> As ger-fauk or falcon to lure
> That out of mewe were y-drawe,
> So fair was none in soothe sawe!
> She was thereto courteous, free and wise,
> And in the seven arts learnèd withouten miss.
> Her masters were thither come
> Out of Thoulouse, all and some,
> White and hoar all they were,
> Busy they were that maiden to lere,
> And her lered of astronomy,
> Of ars-metrick and of geometry;
> Of sophistry she was also witty,
> Of rhetorick and of other clergy,
> Lernèd she was in musick,
> Of clergy was her none like.

In earlier times reading was regarded as a more important and useful accomplishment than writing, but by the middle of the fifteenth century the women members of the Paston family in Norfolk could write with fluency and vigor, even if their spelling left much to be desired. Most of the larger nunneries received little girls as boarders, and when Henry VIII had abolished all the convents and monasteries, great and small, one of the grievances set forth by the leaders of the Pilgrimage of Grace was the lack of any place where young girls might be virtuously taught and trained, since the nuns had been scattered and brought to naught. Embroidery, church music, and reading would be the principal studies pursued by the pupils in these convent schools. There is a pretty little story told of two small girls who were fellow-pupils at a nunnery in Friesland. Between these two there was a keen rivalry as to who should acquit herself the better at her lessons. It happened that one of them fell ill, and, in her anxiety lest her friend should outstrip her, she begged that she might have speech with the prioress. When the prioress came the child said, "Good lady! do not let my companion learn any more till I am well again, and I shall pray my mother to give me sixpence, and I shall give it to you, if you will do as I ask; for I am afraid that while I lie sick she may pass me in learning, and I would not that she did so."

The pupils at these schools did not belong to the knightly and noble class only. The daughters of prosperous merchants and worthy citizens walked there two by two with the daughters of famous Anglo-Norman families. The wife of the Miller in Chaucer's Reeve's tale had been

> y-fostred in a nonnerye,

and for that reason gave herself airs, and was majestic and disdainful long after she had left the convent to be the bride of simple Symkin of Trumpington mill. In this same century it would appear that children of both sexes were sometimes taught together, for Sir John Froissart tells us that when he first went to school he found little girls there, "whose youth was as tender as his own," and strove to please them with garlands of violets, and gifts of pins, apples, pears, and rings of glass.

In the fifteenth century a very curious and instructive chain of verses was written for the benefit of those mothers who were confronted with the difficult task of bringing up girl-children. It is called *How the Good Wife taught her Daughter,* and it is crammed with excellent advice. Evidently the speaker belongs to the humbler ranks of life, for she warns her daughter that when she has been to the market to sell the 'borel,' or coarse cloth, that she has woven at home she should not afterward go and refresh herself at an alehouse, and also that she must not give way to envious feelings if she sees her neighbor's wife better clad then herself. Most interesting of all is the advice given to the damsel as to how she shall some day teach her *own* boys and girls:

> And if thi children been rebel,[1] and wole not [t]hem bowe,[2]
> If ony of [t]hem mys-dooth, nouther banne [3] [t]hem ne blowe,[4]
> But take a smert rodde,[5] and bete [t]hem in a rowe,
> Till thei crei mercy, and be of [t]her gilt aknowe.[6]

Ladies of high degree occupied themselves almost as much with spinning as did their humbler sisters, but in their case the cloth was used to make garments for their own households, and not sold in the market. They also cultivated medicinal herbs, and with them made potions, plasters, and ointments for the benefit of the sick. A knight who returned to his castle in a sad plight, owing to a tumble at a tournament or a mishap in the chase, would be promptly "doctored" by his lady, and dosed and anointed with strange compounds prepared by her own fair hands. It was

---

[1] Rebellious.
[2] Be obedient.
[3] Curse.
[4] Slap.
[5] A sharp stick.
[6] And acknowledge their guilt.

often unnecessary to send for a professional Doctour of Phisik, and sometimes, when the ladies of the patient's family had done their worst, it must have been hopeless. . . .

The position of woman in the Middle Ages was, indeed, a peculiar one. She was the butt of the most vehement and merciless satire, and at the same time the object of the most exaggerated homage and devotion. No young esquire, no bachelor knight, was thought worthy of the name who did not gasp himself green in the face for love of some fair lady; no satirical poet, monk, or layman was accounted a master of his craft unless he made of the image of womankind a sort of Aunt Sally at which to fling his wordy missiles. In Boccaccio, in Chaucer, in all the popular collections of stories in the fourteenth and fifteenth centuries, there is no more familiar or more abject figure than that of the henpecked and hoodwinked husband. Of the Wyf of Bathe's five husbands three, she says, were good, and two were bad; and she makes it clear that it was the good ones who found her most tyrannical and exacting:

> They were ful glad when I spak to [t]hem faire,
> For God it wot I chidde [t]hem spitously.[7]

And a nameless versemonger of the same century exclaimed unkindly:

> There were three wily, three wily there were,
> A fox and a fryer—and a womán.

JOHN R. HALE

Family and Personal Relationships

. . . As far as the individual was concerned the most important form of association was, of course, the family. The ties of kinship were strong even among those who names have some symbols of "individualism."

John R. Hale, *Renaissance Europe: Individual and Society 1480–1520* (New York: Harper & Row, Publisher, 1971), pp. 124–36.

[7] Bitterly, angrily.

Popes accepted the scandal of nepotism. Michelangelo, though elevated to the epithet "divine," cared restlessly for his unpromising brood of relatives. Dürer, who in his great engraving *Melancolia I* stressed the essential loneliness of the creative artist, wrote with detailed, thoughtful sadness of his mother's death. Family records, reminiscences of dead ancestors, commissions for portraits and busts, multiplied; so did the ordering of masses for the dead, the purchase of indulgences, the building of chantries. Books described the perfect household. Princes were proud not only of illustrious lineage but to be known as the fathers of their people. Though conservative churchmen still deplored the necessity of the married state, an increasing number of men saw the godly life as something to be achieved as easily within the context of the home as of the cloister. Respect for the familial *pietas* of ancient Rome coupled with distrust of monastic morals produced an idealisation of life in the family.

The solidarity of the family owed much to its being the center of, not a retreat from, production. In the country the entire family worked on the land and, in winter, shared their home with the animals for the sake of their warmth. The craftsman worked in his own house, as did the shopkeeper. Servants and apprentices lived as members of the family segregated from the ordinary life of the household only by their duties. Under the partnership agreements that were common among French peasants different families lived under the same roof, all their property, down to kitchen utensils, being held in common. A more conscious feeling for family unity led to the production of household scenes in illumination, painting and woodcut, sometimes as backgrounds for, say, the Birth of the Virgin, but frequently as straightforward genre scenes. Servants ministered to masters with little sense of social divisiveness. Wife and husband ministered to one another as a necessity that might be affectionate and respectful even if it was rarely self-sufficient from the points of view of passion and understanding. The father was expected to rule, though his authority might be under heavy siege, and the atmosphere was gregarious; desire for privacy was still tentative (even in wealthy families very few girls had, as had Carpaccio's St. Ursula, a bedroom of their own).

The functional solidarity of the home makes it difficult to judge the quality, the emotional tone of family life. A high death rate meant frequent remarriages; not only were marriages planned by kinsmen and thus lacking, at least in the initial stages, in romance, but the speed with which a new marriage partner was brought into the home suggests a certain emotional casualness. Three successive marriages were common. Again, in wealthy families it was customary to send children out to a wet-nurse for the first months and also (though infrequently in Italy) to send them to be educated by growing up in some great household, a 'finishing' that began at the age of seven or eight. That the family did not always care for its oldest members as a matter of course is suggested by contracts whereby an old person made over his property to his children in return for a guarantee of support, in sickness and health, as long as his life should last. And that the atmosphere of the family was not necessarily such as to keep children absorbed and law-abiding is shown by the tirades of preachers and satirists against juvenile delinquency, in which parents are blamed for not keeping an eye on their offspring and for allowing them to read trivial romances and to strike up undesirable acquaintances. Late marriage for men and a high death rate at thirty-five to forty possibly meant that many children were fatherless by the time they reached adolescence and that few would have a grandfather's eye upon them.

More common than comments on relations between the generations were those on relations between the sexes. It is probable that the status of women had, as a whole, declined. When men were absent at war, or for purposes of trade, the law had accepted that their wives were competent to run their estates and manage their businesses. With wars waged increasingly by mercenaries and trade conducted increasingly by agents, women had a less prominent role to play in affairs. In some trades— especially those which depended on female labor, ribbon-making, dress-making, embroidery—women were admitted to guild membership, but seldom to positions of authority. Shopkeepers' wives looked after customers as an extension of their domestic duties. There were women barbers in France, a few women money-changers in Germany, some women musicians have been recorded, and while women were generally excluded from religious drama they were admitted to minstrel groups and performed in *tableaux vivants* and moralities. When visiting Antwerp, Dürer bought a manuscript illuminated by an eighteen-year-old girl. "It is very wonderful that a woman can do so much,' he commented. What women were really capable of only appears in exceptional circumstances. Caterina Sforza defended Forli in the Romagna against Cesare Borgia with a bravery any man would have envied. Zoe Paleologus, wife of Ivan III, played an important part in the Italianising of Muscovite culture. The refinement of the courts of Ferrara, Mantua and Urbino undoubtedly owed much to the influence of a few highly educated women like Isabella d'Este and Elisabetta Gonzaga. Born to rule, or with the possibility of ruling, an Anne of Brittany or a Margaret of Austria could show herself the equal of men. By chance the shopkeeper's daughter Sigbrit, mother of Christian II of Norway's mistress, had an opportunity to show that a shrewd bourgeoise could run a state better than a feeble king; by chance a peasant girl, Maroula of Lemnos, showed that a woman could rally a wavering garrison and lead it in a successful counterattack against the Turks, an action for which she was offered a dowry and the pick of an officer husband by the Venetian state. Literature offered a few vivacious and independent-minded heroines but for most writers, women's place was firmly in the home, their interests restricted, as in Fernando de Rojas' portrait, to ' "What did you have for dinner?" and "Are you pregnant?" and "How many chicks have you got?" and "Take me to lunch at your house" and "Point your lover out to me" and "How long is it since you saw him?" and "How are you getting on with him?" and "What are your neighbors like?" and other things like that.' Vespasiano da Bisticci, the Florentine bookseller and biographer, would not even grant them this liberty. Women, he wrote, should follow these rules: "the first is that they bring up their children in the fear of God, and the second that they keep quiet in church, and I would add that they stop talking in other places as well, for they cause much mischief thereby." The same note was sounded in England; "there is nothing that doth so commend, advance, set forth, adorn, deck, trim and garnish a maid as silence," warned an anonymous English tract. Among the patrons of William Caxton's printing press was that vigorous woman Margaret Beaufort, Countess of Richmond and Derby and cofounder of Christ's and St. John's Colleges at Cambridge, but the printer described a more passive ideal when he wrote that "the women of this country be right wise, pleasant, humble, discreet, sober, chaste, obedient to their hus-bands, secret, steadfast, ever busy and never idle, temperate in speaking and virtuous in all their works, or at least should be so." A rare excep-tion, Cornelius Agrippa, wrote in 1509 a little treatise in praise of women, designed to catch the eye of Margaret of Austria. His contention was bold: that only masculine tyranny and lack of education prevented women from playing a role in the world equal to man's. But floundering for ar-guments to support his thesis he was forced to use such unconvincing ones as that "Eve" has more affinity than "Adam" with the ineffable name of God, JHVH, and that physically women were finished off more neatly than men. It is a failure of nerve that is easy to understand in an age when a scholar could scribble "becoming mad, he took a wife" against a colleague's name in the matriculation roll of the University of Vienna.

Save in court circles and some exceptional bourgeois households women were educated casually, if at all. The wealthier the family the earlier were marriages arranged in the interest of property and inheritance; thus the girls most likely to receive a good education were also those most likely to have it cut short. In law the Roman notion that 'in foemina minus est rationis' was gaining ground, leaving it open to judges to im-pose less severe penalties on women because they lacked the mental and moral force necessary to constitute wrongful intent in the full force of the term, and there is some indication that laws entitling widows to a proportion of their husbands' effects at his death were being set aside. Moreover, to judge from the (admittedly biased) evidence of sermons, parents showed less concern over a strict upbringing for girl children. Josse Clichthove, not by any means an alarmist preacher, took it for granted that his congregation would accept his picture of a society where the education of girls was neglected and where they were allowed a dangerous liberty to rove and mingle with bad company. There was thus a suspicion that once a girl had been 'bought' by a husband, she would have to be watched.

Though authority in the family, and in the determination of inheritance was legally vested in the male, his authority, according to satire, was seldom to be taken for granted. A favorite theme in popular art was the battle for the trousers, in which a man and wife wrestled for who was to wear them; victory (sometimes determined by a delighted demon) usually went to the termagant wife. Other woodcuts and engravings dwelt alarmingly on famous cases of men being dominated by women: Adam tempted by Eve, Samson shorn by Delilah, Holofernes decapitated by Judith, Aristotle bridled and driven by Campaspe. The henpecked husband was a stock character in the drama. In a farce by Cuvier, Jacquinot's mother-in-law reminds him that he "must obey his wife as a good husband should." She and her daughter pen a lengthy list of his obligations and force him to sign it. He is to get up first, light the fires, prepare the breakfast, wash the children's soiled clothes, in fact "come, go, run, trot, toiling away like Lucifer." The dénouement comes, much to the relief of husbands in the audience, when his wife falls into an enormous wash-tub and begs him to pull her out. "It's not on my list" is his answer to each plea, and he only rescues her in return for a promise that henceforward he will be master in his own house. This is caricature in humorous vein, but behind it is the fear of a darker form of domination, for this was a time when women were introduced into crucifixion plays gleefully forging the nails for the cross, and when a misericord could portray a woman heaving a man off to perdition with a rope round his genitals.

Fear of woman's sexuality appears to have been widespread. "Where, alas!" sighed the foremost student of the printed sermon literature of late fifteenth-century England, G. R. Owst, "where is our merry medieval England?" The church, of course, drew on a long tradition in which woman was identified with *luxuria* and described in terms of pathological disgust. But it was not only clerics who believed, with Michel Menot, that "luxuria etiam breves dies hominis facit." Etienne Champier, a doctor as well as a poet, warned the readers of his *Livre de Vraye Amour* that too much lovemaking led to gout, anaemia, dyspepsia and blindness, and he was doing no more than repeat a medical commonplace. Both clerics and doctors reflected a fear that had its roots in the darkness of folk terrors. It was expressed in that most popular of travel books, the *Travels* of Sir John Mandeville. He describes the inhabitants of an (imaginary) island "where the custom is such that the first night they be married, they make another man to lie by their wives for to have their maidenhead . . . For they of the country hold it so great a thing and so perilous for to have the maidenhead of a woman, that them seemeth that they that have first the maidenhead putteth him in adventure of his life . . . And I asked them the cause why that they held such custom: and they said me that of old time men had been dead for deflowering of maidens that had serpents in their bodies that stung men upon upon their yards, that they died anon." A similar story is told by the traveller Lodovico Varthema, and there is little doubt that the plot of Machiavelli's *Mandragola,* which hinges on the fact that a gulled husband believes that a drug his wife has taken will kill the first man who sleeps with her, refers, for all its comic implications, to an unacknowledged fear of woman as castrator. To this fear, and to the teaching of church and medicine we must add another factor. The bourgeois literature of the time harps on the theme of women devouring, pestering, exhausting their husbands. Girls and wives were not insulated from sex. Bedrooms were not private places (though domestic architecture was beginning to reflect a desire that they should be), language and gesture were bawdy and woman's sexual appetite openly acknowledged.*

At the poorer levels of society a natural sexual relationship between man and wife was complicated by economic circumstances. 'Little property and many children', as a Flemish proverb put it, "bring great distress to many a man." The church and, to a lesser extent, military service did provide opportunities for employment outside the local community, but the family was commonly preserved as a self-sufficient unit (even if only a marginally viable one) by a series of voluntary restraints. One was postponement of marriage itself, for poor men frequently until between thirty and thirty-five. A second was making love in ways that could not lead to conception—ways in which the clergy were briefed to inquire about in the confessional and which they sought to combat. A third was abortion, again condemned, and, indeed, punishable with death, but common. The last recourse was exposure, and here, at least in the towns, foundling institutions accepted, wet-nursed and put out discarded infants to foster-parents, a system supported by a fairly general lack of social, if not legal, prejudice against the bastard. Thanks to these restraints and the high incidence of death due to disease, the average household probably did not number more than the parents and two or three children, though as kin

---

* 'It is convenient that a man have one several place in his house to himself from cumbrance of women.' (William Hormon's Latin phrasebook of 1519). A similar work of the same date, John Stanbridge's *Vulgaria,* shows something of the tone of conversation. Boys learned the Latin for male and female genitals and for words like 'fart', 'stynke', 'shyte', and 'pysse', and for phrases like 'tourde in thy teethe' and 'he lay with a harlot at night.'

usually lived in the same district, if not in the same street, this figure may conceal some redistribution of children among childless or slightly better-off relatives. Even so, it is difficult not to suspect that the confessions in witch trials involved a hysterical shifting of responsibility for the fantasies and aberrations caused by a fear-haunted sex-life, as did, in all probability, the accusations of sexual interference laid by men, with the assistance of celibate inquisitors, against the night-hags.

The contrast between precept and appetite was not only deep but open. Almost all the practices forbidden by the clergy can be illustrated in popular art, in books or in public entertainments. It was a mortal sin to take pleasure in watching the couplings of animals. In 1514 a widely publicised animal entertainment was put on in the Piazza dei Signori in Florence. Particularly noted was the moment when a mare was sent in among some stallions. In the opinion of one observer, the pious diarist Luca Landucci, "this much displeased decent and well behaved people." But in the eyes of another diarist. Cambi, it "was the most marvellous entertainment for girls to behold." Erasmus, in his very widely read *Colloquies,* takes lesbianism for granted as a hazard for young nuns, and among the popular stories attributed to Priest Arlotto Mainardi was one of a peasant who confessed not only to stealing the priest's corn but to masturbation; the jovial absolution was 'take your beater out prominading as often as you like, but do not steal any more; leave other people's property alone, and above all give me my wheat back!' In art, themes like Potiphar's wife, Susanna and the Elders, Bathsheba, Lot and his daughters gave an opportunity for painters to display a directly sensual appreciation of the nude. In stone and wood carvings in churches, figures of *luxuria* strained the use of allegory into simple carnality and straightforward phallicism. In woodcuts and engravings the 'influence' of Venus was demonstrated by scenes of lovemaking, Folly and Death were shown presiding over brothel scenes in which the didactic convention was used as an excuse to celebrate the pleasures of sex in the same way that, in a playfully scholarly guise, patrons like Federigo Gonzaga and Alfonso d'Este could indulge a taste for mythological erotica with Ios and Danaes; coaxing, in the case of Alfonso, the genial *Feast of the Gods* from one of the greatest of all painters of religious subjects, Giovanni Bellini, and a broodingly sensual *Leda* from Michelangelo. When to this we add the jokes which Castiglione in his *Courtier* tells as suitable for mixed company, the sexual content of the French *chanson* and the Italian carnival song (lutes and song books were among the 'vanities' burned by Savonarola) we get a picture of the pleasure of sex, either completely open or employing, as in the case of Lorenzo de' Medici's 'Song of the fir cone sellers,' an easily-translated sexual imagery, but in any case flouting conventional Christian morality.

There was a clear confrontation. On the one hand a printed (Italian) anecdote like this: 'Because of his excessive addiction to lust, Febo dal Sarasino was gradually losing his eyesight. When he turned completely blind, he said "The Lord be praised; now I will be able to indulge all I want without fear of going blind"!' and, on the other, a sermon preached in Paris by Olivier Maillard in 1494 in which he asked "Are you here, printers of books? . . . O miserable booksellers, your own sins do not suffice you; you print vile sensual books, books on the art of love, and give occasion for sin in others; you will all go to the devil." Dürer, fervent draftsman of the Apocalypse, teased Willibald Pirckheimer about his taste for young men, and Pomponius Laetus brushed off criticism of his homosexuality with a reference to Socrates; yet preachers warned the Italians that disaster after disaster, from the French invasion of 1494 to the Venetian earthquake of 1511, was a punishment for sodomy. For many the black of conduct or daydream could apparently contrast with the white of Christian teaching without strain, men turning easily from sin to absolution, helped by a church which, realistically, was more lenient in court and confessional than in the pulpit. But it is clear that not all could accept this simple dualism, the tension perceptible in sexual obsession was too apparent. In the course of the French mystery play *The Vengeance and Destruction of Jerusalem,* Nero orders an operation to be performed on his mother so that he can see the precise place where he had been conceived. Chastity belts were made, and shown in art, even if they were not used. The tension inherent in the secular version of Christian morality worked out in the chivalrous romance—in which there was a revival of interest at this time—was shown by woodcuts spelling out the real object of the heroes' worship. The mingling of sexual and devotional imagery in the poetry of Skelton shows how that other etherealisation of feeling for women, the literature of Mariolatry, could be penetrated by imaginings of the grossest sort.

All this, of course, is evidence to be treated with great caution. The fashion (in some places) for low cut dresses and (mainly in Germany) for codpieces of aggressive cut and color tells us little: it is impossible to recapture the emotional effect of a past fashion. Similarly, we can draw no conclusion from the proliferation of the lifelike nude in art. Suggestiveness has little to do with realism. Besides, the nude could still draw on a tradition which associated it with shame or humility: it was in this guise that Memling painted Tommaso Portinari kneeling naked, his wife beside him, in the scales of judgement. We may doubt, however, if anyone took sex as neutrally as the Utopians, among whom it was lumped with the comparable off-hand pleasures of scratching and defecating.

Nor can there be any doubting the existence of true, sympathetic understanding between men and women. Nevertheless, Christian morality and the problems of voluntary birth control within the family had produced a state of mind in which women could readily be seen in terms of categories. There was the woman of romance, the ideal daydream partner of man's intellectual, fantasy-building self. There was woman as sexual recreation. And there was woman as wife, a stereotype of houseminding and child-rearing, too ignorant to be mentally intriguing, too familiar in background and too much the product of a largely businesslike negotiation to arouse curiosity. Trapped amid fears and cares the married man looked, in imagination or reality, outside the home for romance or for unworried lust. There is a long list of popular dirges (all written from the male point of view) with such titles as: *The Newly-wed's Complaint* and *The Shades of Marriage*. The French poet Coquillart described at bitter length how love flies out of the window as a wife becomes physically repulsive through childbearing and breast feeding. A German drawing symbolised marriage by depicting two trunks growing from one tree stump; they end in crossbars on which a nude man and a nude woman, both blindfold, are crucified. It is an attitude later summed up in Luther's rueful "Yes, one can love a girl. But one's wife—ach!"

In his *Courtier,* Baldassare Castiglione defended marriage unless there were great inequality in age or temperament, but talking of joking and banter between men and women he made one of his characters say that women "can taunt men for lack of chastity more freely than men can sting them; and this is because we ourselves have made a law, according to which a dissolute life is not a fault or degradation in us, whereas in women it is such utter disgrace and shame that a woman who has been slandered once, regardless of whether the charge is true or false, is disgraced for ever." In his obituary character sketch of Louis XI, Commines noted with amazement that he had remained faithful in his last years "considering that the queen (though an excellent princess in other respects) was not a person in whom a man could take any great delight." Antonio de Beatis wrote of the young Francis I that "although of such slight morals that he slips readily into the gardens of others and drinks the waters of many fountains, he treats his wife with much respect and honor." Johann Cuspinians's eulogy of the Emperor Maximilian stressed that "unlike other princes" he was always virtuous in his relations with women. This double standard of morality was not peculiar to princes, and that it was avenged is shown by prints in which the lover slips from the bedroom as the husband enters. The Utopians were anxious guardians of sexual morality. "The reason why they punish this offence so severely," More explained, "is their fore-knowledge that, unless persons are carefully restrained from promiscuous intercourse, few will contract the tie of marriage, in which a whole life must be spent with one companion, and all the troubles incidental to it must be patiently borne."

It is not surprising that prostitution flourished, government and, much more grudgingly, the church, seeing it as an essential safety valve. Recruitment was kept up by poverty, especially in times of dearth when families could only survive by prostituting their daughters. The demand was maintained by population figures that point to a considerable imbalance between the sexes, men being well in the majority. There were (unreliable) estimates of 6,800 for the prostitutes of Rome in 1490 and 11,000 for those of Venice in the early sixteenth century. Their regulation differed according to the views of the municipal authorities. Coquillart represents the streets of Paris haunted by a familiar figure: 'Woman who goes torchless by night. And murmurs to each "do you want me?" ' while in Nuremberg prostitutes, though protected by statutes of their own, were required to stay in state-licensed brothels. The introduction of syphilis made little difference to this open mindedness; caution, not panic, was the main reaction. It was indeed during this period that the prostitute came into her own. The substitution of the word "courtesan" for "sinner" reflects a growing tolerance for the profession as a whole, and in Italy, and especially in Rome, the prostitute catered for romantic companionship as well as lust. From the home, then, men looked out to guild or confraternity comradeship, to the consolations of less workaday love, and the satisfactions of friendship. In societies such as Florence, where it was common for girls to marry at about twenty and men in their late thirties, the imbalance encouraged homosexual relationships as well as prostitution. But in general, and apart from the routine companionship of business and administration and the strong feeling of solidarity among men as a whole vis-à-vis women, it was an age of strong and unaffectedly sentimental relationships between men. . . .

FRIEDRICH HEER

The Social Status of Women

. . . Some illustrations from French history will help to show the extent
to which woman's position declined. The Merovingian era had been dominated by forceful, not to say formidable, women; Brünhilde, although the
most memorable, was by no means unique. The mother of Charlemagne
and Hildegard, his third wife, were women of considerable influence, while
the Empress Judith, wife to Louis the Pious, his successor, was a stronger
and more effective character than her husband, a worthy namesake of the
great heroine of the Apocrypha. In the disorders of the succeeding centuries, when monarchy was weak and the baronage powerful, widows of
apparently superhuman strength frequently fought to preserve their children's inheritance intact from the depredations of vassals and neighbors.
Although a ninth century council held in the diocese of Nantes forbade
women to attend political assemblies, there is evidence that in the south of
France women took part in elections to the *commune,* the municipal government. From the eleventh century it seems that there was something like
equality between the sexes in this region. Still later, in 1308, we hear of
certain women in the Touraine who were apparently eligible to assist in
the election of deputies to the assembly of estates at Tours. The town
charter of Beaumont, which served as model for over five hundred small
towns in Champagne and eastern France, has a regulation requiring the
assent of the vendor's wife to any sale of goods or property.

There were still great ruling ladies in the France of the twelfth and thirteenth centuries. Eleanor of Aquitaine, the Empress Matilda and Blanche
of Castile at once spring to mind. This period opens with the elder Matilda,
wife of William the Conqueror, firmly in control of Normandy during her
husband's absences in England. Then there was Ermengarde, Countess of
Narbonne, who ruled her lands and her troops for fifty years and was the
leader of the French royalist party in the south of France in opposition to
the English—a nobly-born Joan of Arc. Ermengarde was married several
times, but her husbands took no part in the government. She fought nu-

Friedrich Heer, *The Medieval World: Europe 1100–1350,* trans. Janet Sondheimer
(London: Weidenfeld and Nicolson, 1961), pp. 261–66.

156

merous wars in defense of her territories, was a patron of troubadours and a protector of the Church, and had great renown as an arbiter and judge in difficult cases of feudal law.

At the time when Philip Augustus was engaged in unifying the country under the crown, large tracts of France were governed by women—Eleanor of Aquitaine, Alix of Vergy in Burgundy, and the Countesses Marie and Blanche in Champagne, where they fostered the growth of the trade fairs and of urban settlement. Flanders, the other great centre of economic activity in northwestern Europe and a much fought-over territory, was ruled by women for sixty-five years, first by Joanna and after her by her sister Margaret, who rehabilitated the country after its devastation by war. Margaret regarded herself as the vassal of the French King and of the German Emperor in her own person, and did all in her power to promote urban independence. She was the first ruler to adopt French as the official language of her chancery. This was in 1221; it was not used at Paris until some years later, in the time of Louis IX. The growth of the vernacular languages owed much to feminine influence, as is clear enough from religious and literary sources.

Blanche of Castile impressed her personality on every department of French life in the first half of the thirteenth century. Her political contribution as regent for her son, St Louis, has already been described. She also made a significant social contribution, as protector of the Jews and champion of the poor. St Louis was persuaded by his Franciscan advisers to adopt a most unhappy policy towards the Jews, and it was during his reign that the first burnings of the Talmud took place. When some Jews came to plead their cause at the royal court in Paris they found the Queen-Mother in charge; she treated them with far more wisdom and understanding than her son in his agony of mind had been able to show. Blanche appears as protector of the poor in an anecdote told by the chronicler of St Denis, who praises her for shielding them from the cruelty of affluent clerks: the cathedral chapter of Paris had imprisoned large numbers of tenants (both dependent and free) from the villages of Orly, Chatenai and other neighboring places because of their refusal to pay a special tax. The Queen came in person to open the doors of the prison and set free the men, women and children suffocating from the heat inside.

Blanche had a worthy successor in her daughter-in-law, Margaret of Provence, though the two had little liking for each other. A woman of great strength and courage and the mother of eleven children, Margaret made Philip, the heir to the throne, swear to remain subject to her advice until he was thirty years old.

The rise of France in the twelfth and thirteenth centuries thus owed something to the achievements of its great ladies. But then a masculine era set in; in 1317 an assembly of notables meeting in Paris under Philip

V declared that women were excluded from succession to the crown. The career of Joan of Arc at the close of the Middle Ages seems to promise a return to women's former political status and prestige. Almost at once, however, she was turned into a figure with largely supernatural associations and made the subject of legend. This was characteristic of the age: what had once been sober reality was now felt to be impracticable and improper.

We have already noted the considerable positive contribution made by noble and other women to Catharism. For the first time women had been admitted to a leading role in a religious society. Women were eligible to become Perfects and were authorized to preach and to dispense the *consolamentum*. A countess of Foix left her husband to become head of a feminine Albigensian community. The women and girls of Toulouse fought alongside their men against the masculine array of crusaders from the North led by Simon de Montfort, the epitome of brutal and ambitious manhood, who met his death under a hail of stones hurled at him by a band of women.

There had been women troubadours as well as women Perfects. Five songs have survived by the Countess Beatrix of Die, an open and unashamed expression of her love for Count Raimbaut of Orange. Other women troubadours included Beatrix's daughter Tiberga, Castellox, Clara of Anduse, Isabella of Malaspina and Marie of Ventadour. The celebrated poetess Marie de France says of herself, with proud and serene assurance, *'Marie ai nom, si sui de France.'* This simple statement, 'Marie is my name and I come from France,' finds its echo in the equally proud and unaffected avowal of Joan of Domrémy, who withstood the examination of some fifty crabbed theologians only to be broken by imprisonment: 'My name is Joan and I came to France from Domrémy.'

Around the year 1250 there were some five hundred nunneries in Germany, with a total population of between twenty-five and thirty thousand religious. Even so, it is evident that the Church had not succeeded in giving full scope to the religious energies of women. Hildegard of Bingen, who lived in the twelfth century, had already appreciated the seriousness of the situation. She held that the decadence of Church and society was chiefly caused by masculine weakness: women therefore must act where men had failed; this was the *tempus muliebre,* the era of woman. Since the clergy would not, it was left to women to go and preach against heretics and make missionary journeys up and down the Rhine and the Nahe. The Abbess Hildegard in fact had many masculine traits to her character and for a long time yet the life of the female religious would continue to be ordered along the lines laid down for men. The *Speculum Virginum,* for example, a handbook for nuns composed about 1100 and still extant in versions in Latin, Middle Low German and Swedish, has no section devoted to love, private prayer is not mentioned, nor is there any hint of concern for the soul of the individual nun. The spiritual regime prescribed is harsh and unyielding. No penance could be accepted from the fallen, though all the world knew how easy it was for young nuns to fall from grace, seduced as often as not by clerks.

Heterodox and heretical groups offered women much greater freedom and a wider field of activity. The Waldensians and Cathars, and other sects as well, encouraged women to preach and propagandize and to cultivate their own souls, both actively and passively. When these groups were suppressed—not before many women and girls had gone cheerfully to their deaths, serenely confident, inwardly set free—a number of passionately devout and spiritually awakened women sought refuge in Dominican and Franciscan convents and in Beguinages. But there they often found themselves in little better case, and their position became increasingly difficult during the thirteenth and fourteenth centuries. Men were reluctant to assume responsibility for the spiritual direction of women and evaded it wherever they could; the Church continued to distrust women who were spiritually restless, suspecting them all the time of heresy. For a brief space the omens were more propitious, when Meister Eckhart, Tauler and Suso were bringing their mysticism into the Dominican convents of Germany. They succeeded in absorbing and deflecting much of this restless yearning after personal communion with God, channelling it into forms of expression recognized by the Church; but this was a passing phase.

The increasing gloom and anxiety which spread over Europe in the later Middle Ages, when nations, churches and minorities drew further and further apart, to eye one another with mutual hostility and envy, is closely bound up with the failure to harness to the social and religious needs of the age that feminine spiritual energy which had burst forth so dramatically in the twelfth century. The embers were banked down, but they still smouldered. Cast spiritually and intellectually adrift, women were confronted with the closed ranks of a masculine society, governed by a thoroughly masculine theology and by a morality made by men for men. The other half of humanity came into the picture only when specifically feminine services were needed. Aquinas's ethical system related entirely to men. He speaks blandly of "making use of a necessary object, woman, who is needed to preserve the species or to provide food and drink." "Woman was created to be man's helpmeet, but her unique role is in conception . . . since for other purposes men would be better assisted by other men." True, some relaxation of this suspicious fear is evident in a few thirteenth century books of penitence and in some scholastic writers, but the great mass of homilectic literature is still pervaded with hatred and distrust: woman is portrayed as "sin," without qualification. The tradition is an ancient one, going back to Augustine and the early Fathers, above all to St Jerome, the patron saint of misogynists: "woman is the gate of the devil, the path of wickedness, the sting of the serpent, in a word a perilous object."

The inner schizophrenia of the waning Middle Ages is clearly shown up in the gulf between prevailing theories and social reality. Women, feared by monks and theologians and disdained as the least valuable of all human material, contributed largely by their labors to both urban and rural economic life. Women worked in the fields and sometimes, as among the Germans, were responsible for the entire agricultural routine. Townswomen were active in a wide variety of trades and industries. The women of Paris are known to have been engaged in more than a hundred different occupations. They worked as weavers, embroiderers and retailers; when their husbands died they carried on their businesses with resource and courage, proving themselves master craftsmen in their own right; they were teachers, doctors and merchants, capable of handling the large-scale affairs of foreign trade. In all these fields they acquitted themselves like men. The decline of the German towns in the late Middle Ages is bound up with the suppression of flourishing feminine industries and the replacement of skilled women by men, which created a large female proletariat. This class of distressed women was much augmented by the appalling growth of public prostitution and the moral collapse of Beguinism. We know the extent of the disproportion between men and women in some of the larger towns during the later Middle Ages: for every thousand men Nuremberg had 1,207 women, Basel 1,246 and Rostock 1,295. There was no suitable outlet for their great abilities and no satisfaction for their spiritual and intellectual yearnings.

The women who grew up in the courtly civilization of the twelfth century had learned to "sing and say," to use their minds and their imaginations, to conduct their lives and loves on a highly-civilized plane. In the later Middle Ages there are a few ecstatic figures, burning with a prophetic flame, who stand out sharply against the undifferentiated mass of oppressed women forced to accept life and men and misery as they found them: these were exceptional women by any standard, women such as Catherine of Siena, who threatened the Popes with dire penalties if they refused to return to Rome from Avignon. The Middle Ages had conspicuously failed to solve the problem of woman's place in society; it was left as a heavy mortgage on the future.

6. TOWNS AND THEIR DWELLERS

From civic records and other scattered sources scholars have been able to recreate the sights and sounds of medieval town life. Since most urban centers were little more than tiny villages by modern standards, with a population rarely exceeding a thousand souls, the life of the majority of town dwellers usually blended into the surrounding countryside. But some were true cities which by the fifteenth century had grown beyond 100,000 inhabitants. Our selections treat a cross-section of these: London, Paris, Florence, and a few of the more important communities in Germany.

Urban T. Holmes recounts the experiences of a twelfth-century youth by the name of Alexander Neckam as he travels from his village to discover the city of London. We are able to share the astonishment and alarm of a country boy at his first sight of densely crowded streets. We observe with him the buildings and houses, the hawkers and artisans, the lame and the blind, the drunks and the toughs, the cries and the smells of a new way of life. We are bound to conclude that medieval society was anything but static and that many urban problems which we regard as modern were well known to medieval people.

Letha Curtis Musgrave focuses on a characteristic creation of medieval townlife: the university. She is less concerned with what students studied than with how they lived, drawing her examples from Bologna, Oxford, and especially Paris. From the beginning, as we see, town-and-gown relationships were seldom exercises in sweet reason. The institution of student riots, albeit in a distinctly medieval setting, was already well established by the fourteenth century. The student of today is likely to find many of his problems already prefigured in the life of his earliest predecessors.

J. Lucas-Dubreton reconstructs the life of Florentine burghers in the late medieval period. He describes their habits of eating and drinking, and he gives a hilarious rendition of the basic rules of good breeding for the resident of Florence. He also examines the practice of medieval medicine, palmistry, and astrology—all subjects of fad and fashion in the towns of Italy—before closing with a fairly unappetizing account of Florentine funerals.

Fritz Rorig estimates that the German territories still contained few towns of any real consequence before the fifteenth century; yet the importance of civic tradition, he concludes, should not be neglected. He introduces us to a number of urban types: the merchant, the shopkeeper, the weaver, the worker, the Jew. Finally, he shows the economic and social importance of the medieval trade guilds and thereby locates one important source of future social conflicts.

Social organization in medieval times remained for the most part both personal and local. Apart from the over-arching structure of the Church, one finds little evidence in everyday life of large corporations and multi-territorial enterprises. Yet social forms and social concerns do display a remarkable similarity in many areas of Europe, and one might even identify several universal types known to all Europeans: the peasant, the village priest, the artisan, and the small merchant to name a few. If medieval society was rapidly changing after the twelfth century, many of its characteristic members were steadfast and not soon to disappear from the European scene.

URBAN TIGNET HOLMES JR.

Medieval London

In 1178 or thereabout, Alexander Neckam, a young clerk teaching in the grammar schools at Dunstable, Bedfords, decided to go to Paris to continue his own studies. The little town of Dunstable was a village in the Chilton Hills, thirty-four miles to the northwest of London, situated at the juncture of two Roman roads. . . .

As the road approached London the tillage lands seemed more prosperous and the traffic increased.[1] The site of London was low, lending itself to frequent flooding from the waters of the Thames. Only by building up an embankment was this avoided. Many springs and pools were in the vicinity. Two swift streams ran through London proper—the Walbrook and the Langbourn. As Alexander and his companions rode along, they were first made aware of their destination when Watling Street dipped a bit towards the Thames.[2] In the distance they caught their first glimpse of the big river and of the royal tower at Westminster, with its abbey church of St. Peter and clustering houses.[3] Alexander had been told there were interesting wall paintings in this royal tower, and he hoped someday to see

Urban Tignet Holmes, Jr., *Daily Living in the Twelfth Century: Based on the Observations of Alexander Neckam in London and Paris* (Madison: The University of Wisconsin Press, © 1952 by the Regents of the University of Wisconsin), pp. 18, 25–42.

[1] John Stow, *A Survey of London,* with Fitzstephen in the Appendix (London, 1908), p. 502. Hereafter referred to as F.S.

[2] This picturing of the relative location of sites and buildings is made from various sources. See note to London map, above. A solicitor of Gray's Inn, with whom I had the pleasure to talk recently, confirmed my opinion of the distances in Holborn. He has walked over these streets countless times. Fitzstephen says of the palace at Westminister: ". . . the royal palace rears its head, an incomparable structure, furnished with breastworks and bastions, situated in a populous suburb at a distance of two miles from the city" (p. 502). In 1184 the Templars abandoned their tower in Oldborne and moved down to the bank of the Thames.

[3] The earlier name for Westminster was Thornley. The abbey church, adjacent to the royal tower, was dedicated to St. Peter, but by the mid-twelfth century the designation "West minster," as contrasted with St. Paul's, the minster within the wall of London, was far more common. Cf. on all this *La vie d'Edouard le confesseur,* vv. 1499–1500 and *passim.*

them.[4] The Scotsman snorted a bit at this. He preferred to visit the palace of the English king at Woodstock, where during the reign of old King Henry there had been lions, leopards, and other strange beasts. Perhaps there were some still.[5] Then the road bent sharply to the left, and they were soon out of the forest, riding beside the Old Bourn, a little stream that appeared suddenly out of nowhere and flowed beside the road. Houses appeared, adjacent to pretty gardens. One house, on the right, was magnificent. Alexander, who had ridden there before, knew that it was the town house of the Bishop of Lincoln. Just a few paces farther along stood a large round tower of light-yellow stone, bleak and uninviting. There was much going and coming before its drawbridge gate. It was easy to tell from the dress of the inhabitants that this was the Temple, the stronghold of the Knights Templar. Many unsightly wooden buildings cluttered up the adjacent land. It was evident that the Templars had no room for expansion there. Someone said that the stone for their tower or donjon had been brought from Caen in Normandy.

A few more yards and the road prepared to drop down into a ravine. Our travelers gazed at a glorious sight which took the breath away from those who had not see it before. At the foot was a small river, the River of Wells, which flowed on into the Thames. Mill wheels were turning in it with a pleasant rumbling sound, and there were flocks of small boats gathered at each of the two bridges. One of these wooden bridges lay straight ahead, carrying Watling Street across the stream; the other was nearer the Thames and led across to Ludgate in the city's wall. The city lay at the crest of the opposite slope, several hundred yards beyond the ravine, but Old Bourn Hill was a little higher and our travelers got a sweeping view over the top of the massive wall into the teeming mass of chimneys and houses. The roar of many cries and jarring sounds now filled their ears. The guards on the *aleoir* or top of the wall, the throngs at the two gates, clamoring for admission through the narrow apertures—all were sights which held the travelers for a few minutes before they descended the slope to the bridge ahead, the stream of the Old Bourn rushing down the hill at their side. Alexander was not expecting to enter the city that night. He went up the road toward Newgate, but he took the lane to the left and skirted the wall to the open ground of Smithfield, the market site and

---

[4] Only one mural painting from twelfth-century England has survived. This is "The Ladder of the Salvation of the Soul and the Road to Heaven," recovered in the parish church of St. Peter and St. Paul at Chaldon (or Chalvedon) in Surrey, not far from Westminster. The background is in red and the figures are in lighter red, pink, yellow, and white. See *The Victorian History of the County of Surrey,* ed. H. E. Malden (London, 1902–12), IV, 191–93. There is a reference to the murals at Westminster in the accounts of Henry's grief over the rebellion of his sons in 1173–74.—Giraldus, VIII, 295.

[5] F.S., p. 45.

jousting ground. Here, close to the wall, were the buildings of the Augustinian priory of St. Bartholomew's, built by the minstrel Rahere, on the spot where a gallows had stood some fifty years before. Rahere had caused the whole of Smithfield to be drained, leaving only one large pond, which was named the "Horsepool" as it served to water the horses at the fair and during the games. The priory served as a hostelry for travelers, and an auxiliary building was employed as a nursing home for the sick. The four canonesses and eight canons who were engaged in this work served under a master. The canonesses followed the rule of St. Benedict, and the canons obeyed that of St. Augustine. Men and women were kept strictly separate.[6] Alexander was undoubtedly known personally to the Prior from previous visits. Much advice, solicited and unsolicited, would be given him to help him make speed on his journey across the water.

The open area of Smithfield stretched wide, away from the buildings of St. Bartholomew's.[7] The smooth field, no longer marshy, supported a horse fair every Friday, except on special feast days. Crowds from the city, including many barons, flocked there to see the display of horseflesh. At one end were tethered the colts, elsewhere the palfreys, in another spot the *destriers* (war horses), and, in a place not so well favored, the pack animals, or *somiers*. Various races were run on these occasions. Stable boys did the riding, needing no saddle or any other harness except a headstall. Horses were raced in threes or in pairs. Farm animals and farm supplies were also on sale at this market: plows, harrows, pigs, and cows. Oxen were on sale and so were mares intended for the carts and plows, often with foals trotting at their heels. Another class of merchants were offering furs, spices, swords, lances, and wines—all from distant climes. On afternoons, many of the clerics and young tradesmen would go out on this field to play ball. Each of the three schools flourishing in London would have its own ball, and the same was true of each guild of tradesmen. During Lent, on Sunday afternoons, the young men of the baronial class, and presumably some of the serjant class, would practice with lances and shields on that same area. The smaller boys had no iron heads on their lances. When the king was at Westminster or Bermondsey, the youths of the upper class went there, and Smithfield was left to the serjantry. All this sham fighting was done on horseback while relatives, also mounted, would stand by and watch. There was much prancing about and going in pursuit. During the summer, on the afternoon of holy days, there were field sports: jumping, stone throwing, javelin hurling, wrestling, and archery. On moonlight nights, groups of girls would hold caroles, or dancing, on this same smooth field. One might say there was never a dull moment there

[6] Sir W. Dugdale, *Monasticon Anglicanum*, 6 vols. (London, 1846), VI, 626–27.
[7] The description of Smithfield or "Smoothfield" continues from F.S., pp. 506–507. Jocelin describes the stalls in a market (p. 209).

after dinner. The Friday market was a very important place for gathering and exchanging news of the day.[8]

On the morning following his arrival, Alexander may well have walked into London in the company of a canon, or perhaps with a servant of the priory. To ride on horseback would have been more comfortable, but progress through the crowded streets would have been slower. Aldersgate was just a few yards away and was less frequented than Newgate. A murage tax had to be paid by one entering the city, but the fee was not high.

London, like every other important walled town, teemed with people. The walls were some eighteen feet high. The gates were fitted with double swinging-doors of heavy oak, reinforced with iron.[9] Inside the walls, the houses were mostly of wood. Here and there appeared more prosperous ones of stone. These were seldom constructed from regular, hewn blocks of stone. Like the country houses, they were more often made of irregular quartz stones and flints, bonded together by cement. Some of the wooden houses had tile facings; some houses were obviously made with a sort of mud or stucco daubed over a wattle framework or lath. Alexander remarked, at a later date, that foolish people were not content with the practical details of a house. They must have useless ornamental decoration. This comment was highly justified in his day, the Romanesque era. "Gingerbready" is the word that would have come to us if we had beheld what Alexander saw on his visit to London. Stone houses had saw-tooth ornamentations, and elaborate moldings with small lozenges in the intersections, and criss-cross effects. Wooden houses, vastly in the majority, had the same sort of thing executed less skillfully.[10] Exterior decorative paneling such as we are accustomed to associate with Tudor architecture was extremely common. Many of the wooden structures had a little roof lift before the entrance. The beams supporting this could be topped by a heavy ornamental capital, imitating the opening of a flower or the head of a strange bird or animal. Some wooden piers which extended from the ground to the main roofs had this same type of capital. There were occasional wooden balconies, displaying tile and crossbeam decorations. Around windows and doors the casements were embellished with curlicues,

[8] ". . . it is a common saying, 'From mill and from market, from smithy and from nunnery, men bring tidings.' "—*Ancrene Riwle,* ed. James Morton (London, 1853), pp. 88–91.

[9] Naturally we can only imagine the appearance of the wall of London. A city wall and gate are illustrated in a Cambridge MS, Trinity College R.17.1, dating about 1150. The gate is there flanked by two towers with three upper stories to each tower. The crenelated top of the gate is higher than the walk on the top of the wall. See Dorothy Hartley and Margaret M. Elliot, *Life and Work of the People of England* (New York, 1931), I, Plate 20e.

[10] The description of wooden houses is elaborated from Bayeux Tapestry, No. 48, in Eric MacLagan, *The Bayeux Tapestry* (London, 1945).

not unlike what we find three centuries later in stone-decorated Gothic. Stone houses often showed the typical Norman chimney stack, that is, a conical cap pierced with smoke holes, rising from a cornice enriched with zig-zag ornament.[11]

Nearly all the smaller houses were in solid rows, not detached, extending down the street. They housed tradesmen who manufactured their goods on their own front premises. The lower floor of such houses resembled a sort of booth with a low counter extending across the front. An opening in the counter gave passage in and out. This was the type of workshop used by knife-maker, baker, armorer, or other tradesman. To one side there was a small spiral stair which led up to the main dwelling room. The stair well was a little tower which could be placed inside or outside the principal walls of the building. In these rows of houses it was surely inside. Upstairs was the *salle,* or main room, with ornamental windows facing on the street. There the wife of the household reigned supreme— during business hours, anyway. . . . We should notice that the floors of both shop and *salle* were strewn with rushes, green in summer, dry in winter.[12] The houses of wood were smeared with paint—most commonly red, blue, and black—which had a pitch and linseed base and gave constant promise of fires. It was hoped that by providing stone walls, to the height of sixteen feet, between adjacent houses this menace would be reduced.[13]

---

[11] J. P. Bushe-Fox, *Old Sarum. Official Guide* (London, 1934), p. 12.

[12] I cannot give my exact references for his impression of the houses of the time. It is a conglomerate of personal impressions acquired over some years from visiting extant houses in England, France, and Italy, combined with a study of illustrations and reading in texts. Some details will be easily traced. Houses at Chartres show the ornamental windows on the principal floor. In *Aucassin et Nicolette,* ed. R. W. Linker (1948), there is mention of the small pillar of stone in the center of such a window: *le noua au piler de la fenestre* (§12).

[13] The Assizes of 1189 established certain housing ordinances. The text from which we are quoting is that given in Thomas Stapleton's *De antiquis legibus liber* (Camden Society, No. 34, London, 1846), pp. 206–11. The greater part of the city had been built of wood previous to the fire of 1135–36 which destroyed from the Bridge to St. Clement's Dane (p. 210). To encourage construction in stone the Assizes gave many privileges to the owner of a stone house, over his less affluent neighbor. If anyone should have a stone wall on his own land to the height of sixteen feet, his neighbor must make a drain and receive in it, on his land, the water shed from the stone wall and carry it across his land, unless it can be brought into the King's street, and nothing must be constructed by him on the aforesaid wall when he builds near it. If he does not build he must continue to receive the water shed from the stone wall, without damage to the owner of the wall (p. 208). A common stone wall cannot be altered without the consent of both parties. *Garde-robe* pits, not walled, must be dug five and a half feet away from the neighbor's boundary; if walled, the pit can be only two and a half feet. A window facing upon a neighbor's land can have its view cut off by subsequent building unless a specific agreement forbidding this has once been made. One who is building is forbidden to make a *pavimentum in vico regio ad nocimentum civitatis et vicini sui injuste* (p. 211).

The street through which Alexander walked after passing the guard at Aldersgate was some ten feet across. It was a main thoroughfare, but not a principal street of the city. It led to Newgate Street and St. Paul's churchyard. Alexander would surely have been aware that the marvelous cathedral of St. Paul's was still under construction. Its tower was not yet erected. The stone used, like that of the Temple, was being transported from Normandy. After going around the churchyard by another street, Alexander and his companion crossed the important thoroughfare that led to Ludgate and then found themselves in the purlieus of the two keeps, or donjons, which hugged the western wall of the city. These were the keep of MontFichet, and a larger one directly on the river, known as Castle Baynard.[14] These crenelated towers were badly crowded in by tradesmen's dwellings. Alexander tells a story—an old folk tale, to be sure—about a monkey which slept on the wall of such a tower, right above a poor shoe-maker's window. The monkey had a habit of creeping down and imitating the shoemaker, cutting up his leather. The shoemaker ran the blunt side of his knife across his own throat, thus inspiring the animal to imitate him and commit suicide with the sharp edge.[15]

Turning to the left, Alexander and his escort walked along Thames Street, busy with seamen. From this waterfront approach, alleys led in regular succession to the quays: Baynards' quay, St. Paul's quay, and then Queenhithe, which belonged to Queen Eleanor.[16] Queenhithe was a curved basin which cut in nearly as far as Thames Street itself. It was considered to be quite a sight to see, with its water gate that could be closed when required, and the many ships, having figureheads in the form of weird beasts, which were moored around its sides.[17] The two men moved around the Queen's dock and then, going farther on Thames Street, came to the Vintner's quay, where casks were piled in great profusion. They saw and heard the mill wheel over which the Walbrook passed as it rushed into the Thames. The next alley descended more than the rest, to Downgate, or Dowgate as it was called familiarly. This had been granted to the merchants of Rouen since 1151 and earlier; it was there that ships from Normandy liked to tie up. As none of the ships masters, or *gouverneurs,* was available at the moment, Alexander and his guide promised to return and strolled farther along the quays. They came to Coldharbor, and then to Oystergate, and St. Botolph's. At this last it was all they could do to

---

[14] "On the west are two castles strongly fortified. . . ." F.S., p. 502. Marie de France wrote of two such castles, side by side, divided only by a single curtain wall, in her *Laostic,* vv. 35–44.

[15] Thomas Wright (ed.), *Alexandri Neckam De naturis rerum . . . with the poem of the same author, De laudibus divinae sapiential* (Rollo Series, London, 1863), p. 209. Hereafter referred to as N.R.

[16] Stow lists these docks in F.S. Queenhithe is still in existence.

[17] The Bayeux Tapestry, Nos. 43–45, shows these weird figureheads on ships.

buck the tide of people. They nearly turned back at once. Out in the middle of the river at this point, workmen were beginning to pave over the arches of the new stone bridge. The old wooden bridge, recently repaired, was discharging its passengers there before the church.[18] Billingsgate was just beyond. Wace describes this in brief: "In London, his best city, King Belin made a marvelous gate on the water which bears the ships. The gate was . . . set with marvelous skill; . . . over the gate he placed a tower exceedingly wide and high." [19] It can be judged from this that there was a gatehouse at the entrance to the basin, perhaps similar to one at Queenhithe. Fitzstephen was under the impression that a continuous wall had once enclosed the city on the water front but had been broken down by the water.[20] This wall may have existed at one time, but it is possible that gatehouses of a later date, guarding the entry to the more prominent wharfing spaces, might have created this impression of a once existent wall. Fitzstephen remarks that were was a large cookshop, a wonderful place, situated on the quays.[21] Whether it was on the Queenhithe side of the bridge or on the Billingsgate side we cannot be sure. I should make a guess that it was located close to the Vintners' quay. It was frequented by everyone in town. Cooked food was cheaper there than food "on the hoof." Vessels loaded with salt and, above all, with fish were tied up on all sides. Some were moored out in the river and had to be approached in small boats. Fitzstephen says that many foreign vessels, from the Scandinavian area as well as from the Mediterranean, were there. These were doubtless to be seen on the seaward side of the bridge, at Billingsgate or at Galleygate, near the city wall. By mooring there it was not necessary for these heavy ships to lower their rigging and masts. For a vessel to go through the piles of the wooden London Bridge at that time it was necessary to unstep the mast and handle by oars.

In the words of Wace we will picture what Alexander could have seen at the quays below the bridge:

> There were the ships brought and the crews [*maisnees*] assembled. You would see many a ship made ready, ships touching each other, anchoring, drying out, and being floated, ships being repaired with pegs and nails, ropes being hauled, masts set up, gangplanks [*punz*] being thrust over the side, and ships loading. Lances were being straightened up and

[18] For the two bridges consult Stow in F.S., p. 23. Jehan Bodel has a few words on bridge building: *Faisoit alignier ses granz mairiens qarrez, Faire trox et mortaisses.—Saisnes,* ed. F. Michel (1839), II, 49–50. The bridge was all important: *A sun batel en va amont Dreit a Lundres, desuz le punt, Sa marchandise iloc descovre.—Tristan,* ed. J. Bédier (SATF, 1902–1905), vv. 2647–49.

[19] Wace, *Brut,* ed. Ivor Arnold (SATF, 1938–40), vv. 3207ff.

[20] F.S., p. 502. Thomas says: *Al pé del mur li curt Tamise. . . .—Tristan,* v. 2659; and further: *Par une posterne del mur qui desur la Tamise. . .* (vv. 2792–93).

[21] The cookshop is in F.S., p. 504.

horses were pulling. Knights and men-at-arms were going on board, and the one would call to the other, some remaining and some leaving.[22]

Those vessels that were going under the bridge often had six men at the oars, three on a side. The vessels which were carrying horses were larger and were called *uissiers*. They had doors (*uis*) which opened in the side planking, making it possible to walk horses up the gangplank to the deck.[23] There were small merchant vessels called *sentines,* manned by only two seamen. Alexander had heard tell of one such boat which was operated by the owner—and a dog! The dog, he said, pulled the required ropes while the master steered.[24] This we cannot believe, but it is an indication of a kind of small vessel which Alexander must have seen. It is not easy to imagine all the boats which could have been on the Thames that day. There was a heavier type of craft which is clearly depicted in a bas-relief on the Campanile at Pisa.[25] This has a platform or castle constructed at the stern, with an open crow's-nest style of railing. There is another such castle at the bow. The *gouverneur* at the steering oar stands on the short deck forward of, and below, the aftercastle. A seaman is depicted on the aftercastle platform, bending forward, adjusting the yard of the mainmast on which the one sail is furled. Towards the bow is a second mast, canted well forward. It was a yard, and a fore-and-aft sail which looks like a lateen sail. This is set and is probably being used to keep the heavy vessel in the wind. Most of the boats seen by Alexander were of the lighter type, having one sail and no high castles—the kind which is represented somewhat crudely in the Bayeux Tapestry, and which was used for coastal and channel freighting. These had a transverse deck over the stern where the master sat at the steering oar and supervised the men working the lines and sail. A windlass would be placed on this deck, similar to the type used in building construction. It was a wheel on a frame, with spokes set into the hub. By spinning these spokes the sailor could tighten or loosen any line that was fastened to the axle of the wheel.

At this point there were other things to be observed besides ships. The huge white Tower of London stood on the left, outside the wall of the town. The exit from the wall toward the Tower was made by way of the Postern Gate. The Tower had not yet been incorporated into the wall, as it was in 1190, nor was the wide town ditch in existence which King John later had dug around the circumference of the wall. There was a vineyard planted between the town wall and the Tower, and a mill was on the river-

---

[22] *Brut,* vv. 11191–204.

[23] V. Gay and H. Stein, *Glossaire archéologique du moyen âge et de la Renaissance* (Vol. I, Paris, 1897; Vol. II, Paris, 1928), under Huissier.

[24] *N.R.,* p. 141.

[25] U. Nebbia, *Navi d'Italia* (Milan, 1930), Plate. See also Bayeux Tapestry, Nos. 5–6.

bank just beyond.[26] As Alexander looked across the river, he became aware of the King's manor of Bermondsey. The manor lands extended from London Bridge as far as Rotherhithe. The fields were being tilled by villeins and bordars or cotters.[27] The road to Dover, considered to be a continuation of Watling Street, wound through these fields. The Cluniac monastery of Saint Savior was visible where the Dover road turned more sharply to the left.

Alexander's companion may have told him, as they looked over the reaches of the Thames, perhaps from the wooden bridge, about the water tourney which was held on the river during Holy Week. A tree was set up in the river, and young men would stand at the prow of small boats being rowed swiftly down the stream and aim with a lance at the target on the tree. If a lance was broken on the target, the boy was hailed as a victor. If he missed, he was tossed into the water and then picked up by another boat that stood by. For this occasion the bridge and the balconies of houses facing the Thames were crowded with people. Perhaps at this point Alexander and his companion may have turned to thoughts of sliding on wintry ice. On Mooresfield, at the north side of the wall, there was still a marsh. When this was frozen in winter, young men would strap the shinbones of horses to the soles of their feet and slide rapidly along, aided by a pole shod with iron. Often the more mischievous boys would strike at each other with the pole as they shot past. There were many accidents. Ordinary sliding on the ice was also quite common. Still another sport was to seat someone on a cake of ice and pull him along.[28]

Remembering his agreement to call again at Dowgate, Alexander now turned back toward the western end of the city.

There is no evidence, one way or the other, that Thames Street was paved, with an old Roman pavement, but it surely was. Otherwise the mud would have been inevitable and the waterfront could not have been approached to any advantage. This was no low quarter of town, despite the crowds of seamen. In summer these sailors wore nothing but *braies,* or wide underdrawers, and possibly a snood cap, tied under the chin. Their hair was often long enough to curl at the back of the neck. Doubtless they had the usual part in the middle, affected by all classes and both sexes. The average man in the twelfth century did not shave more than once a week, and a short, dark stubble was the common thing. Many seamen wore true beards. On cooler days the seaman wore a coarse *gonne,* or frock, which he pulled up at the waist, over a belt, when he was obliged to step into the water.[29]

---

[26] F.S., p. 43.
[27] Dugdale, V, 85–104.
[28] F.S., pp. 506, 508–509.
[29] Bayeux Tapestry, No. 4.

As we have said, this was not a low part of town. There was much wealth on display. In that time and age, wealth was shown by cloth heavy with gold and silver thread, brocades, and dark and cloudy gems, cut roughly into cabochon shape, which were encrusted on almost anything, from a helmet to the metal covering of a manuscript book. Silks and spices, which were imported at considerable effort and expense from the East, were another indication of *richesse*. When we consider that silks were transported by sea—sometimes by land—from China to India, from there to the Red Sea region by water, and finally down the Nile to the Mediterranean area, where they were picked up by Italian merchants, it is not hard to understand why their price advanced; and yet most well-to-do people had silken garments, and even silken sheets. Thames Street displayed much of this southern wealth, as well as the northern wealth of expensive furs.

There was something in the air of a medieval community such as London which we moderns are apt to forget. This thing was authority. There was unquestionably much mob violence and considerable injustice on all sides practiced everywhere daily. But even an outraged person felt awed by authority, whatever form it took. The *ribauz,* or good-for-nothings, were always on the edge of a crowd. They begged and plundered at the slightest provocation. They hung around outside the door of the banquet hall when a large feast was held. The king of England had three hundred bailiffs whose duty it was—though not all at one time—to keep these people back as food was moved from the kitchens to the hall, and to see that guests were not disturbed.[30] Frequently in twelfth-century romances a beautiful damsel is threatened with the awful fate of being turned over to the *ribauz.*[31] Nothing more horrible can be imagined. These people accompanied armies on their expeditions, helping in menial tasks and plundering what was left by the knights and other fighting men. And yet they were kept under control by authority. I imagine that the news that Walter Fitzrobert, lord of Baynard Castle, was coming down Thames Street would have caused such vagrants to scatter out of the way. In similar fashion the *gouverneur* of a seagoing vessel doubtless had a presence of authority as he moved along the quays. A twelfth-century mob could be unruly, but it was seldom completely lacking in discipline. Up the social ladder, the same observations could be made about the men-at-arms. The Count of Baynard, the Lord of MontFichet, the Constable of the Tower, and others of the King's immediate officers allowed their men a liberty which they could control if they wished. These men were bound by feudal oaths, or by villeinage. On the other hand, when the king was weak, as was Stephen,

[30] Gaimar, *Estorie des Engleis,* ed. Thomas Wright (London, 1850), vv. 5981–98. Similarly in *Ille et Galeron,* ed. Löseth (Paris 1890), vv. 4100–4102.
[31] As in the *Tristan* where Iseut receives such treatment from King Marc.

and again John, the serjants and knights of London must have been a plague to every merchant and every visitor. This is what Fitzstephen meant when he said that London was a fine city when it had a good governor.[32] Rebellion in twelfth-centry England and France meant attachment to another overlord; it did not mean becoming a law unto oneself, unless the rebel chanced to be placed very high. When a prominent noble came to town, crowds of people of all classes would flock around him on the streets, anxious to see his dress and his equipment.[33]

It was not unsafe for a man such as Alexander Neckam to walk along the quays in the year 1178. He was only a clerk, and the occasional *ribaut* or man-at-arms who was looking for trouble did not make himself objectionable to a stray cleric. These young men dressed in black were under the jurisdiction of the Church, which, in the person of her bishops, was capable of avenging any outrage that might be visited upon her children by a layman, or king's man. Knowing this quite well, the students and other younger clergy often took full advantage of their position within a town. They roamed in groups, heading for the ball field without the walls on the afternoon of a holy day, but sometimes just looking for sport at the expense of others. A precept of the time was "Be wise with the wise, but relax and play the fool when you are with fools." [34] The medieval man loved a good laugh. He got this most often in ways that we would consider impolite or cruel. Running off with signs and other objects that were not fastened down, pitching unoffending creatures into the water, baiting an animal, mocking a man who had been the victim of misfortune—these were everyday sources of amusement. The streets of London, or of any other medieval town, showed a high percentage of mutilated and diseased people. The one-armed, the one-legged, the blind, the half-witted, and the just plain drunk were numerous. These unfortunates could furnish much amusement as they moved about awkwardly. The mockery was not often deep, and I dare say the victim sometimes joined in.

In a town where there was no sewerage, with *garde-robe* pits or privies in the better houses only, it is to be expected that the natural functions were much in evidence. Walls were dirty, and unless there had been a recent rain, the roadway was smelly. The *odeur de merde* was never completely absent from anyone's nostrils. People were used to it; but we must not assume that nobody ever complained. There is a story told by Jacques de Vitry of a man whose job it was to clean out *garde-robe* pits. He did

---

[32] F.S., p. 503.

[33] Such was certainly the case in the thirteenth century. Crowds gathered around the Earl of Gloucester in London, and the Earl of Oxford was greeted in the same way in Boulogne. See *Blonde d'Oxford,* vv. 2458ff., 5484ff. Those who have received Ille's charity crowd about him as he passes through the streets.—*Ille et Galeron,* vv. 3788–99.

[34] Scheludko in *Archivum Romanicum,* XI, 278.

not mind this odor in which he worked all day, but his nostrils were badly
offended by the smell of a snuffed candle.[35] The fastidious and very clean
persons were rather few in the twelfth century, but they existed. In all
ages, except perhaps in prehistoric ones, there have been three kinds of
people: the fastidious, the nonfastidious, and those—greatest in number—
who are neither one nor the other but conform more or less to circumstances. Today the fastidious are vastly in the majority in those levels of
society which most university people frequent. In the twelfth century the
proportions were different.

Alexander Neckam belonged to the majority group of his era and accepted smells and "sights" as a part of the daily scene. This time he paused
to gaze at the Langbourn as it carried its share of filth into the Thames,
but he made no comment other than that it was not so impressive a stream
as its neighbor the Walbrook. At Dowgate, Alexander found a Norman
shipmaster, or *eschipre,* who was free to talk with him. He was discouraged
from taking ship in London. Such a vessel would require at least four or
five days to get out of the Thames River and turn south into the Channel.
There could be still longer delay then, while waiting for a wind. This
compared most unfavorably with the short time at sea required to go from
Dover to the nearest Picard port. The Seine itself was a tricky, tidal river
which demanded that everyone on board should be a good sailor.[36] Shifting sandbanks meant poling off by all hands; the swift tides required sleep-
less vigilance and demanded that the ship be firmly anchored when the tide
ebbed. All these disadvantages made the Seine a poor route for passenger
service. Alexander was advised to follow one of the quick shuttle routes
to Paris: two days by mule or palfrey to Dover, and then across to Calais,
Wissant, or Boulogne. With a good wind a boat could make Wissant in
nine hours, or Boulogne in thirteen. There then remained a four-day
journey to Paris if the traveler landed at Boulogne. The stops en route
were Hesdin, Corbie, and Clermont. One could take his own palfrey or
mule across the Channel, but it would be more advantageous to buy a
mount at the port in Picardy and sell it in Paris.

As Alexander and his companion moved back through the crowded
streets, they may well have thought of the two afflictions which plagued this
fair town of London—drunkenness and fires. Evidence of the drunkenness
was plainly visible. On every crooked street within range of Alexander's
eyes, there was one or more houses showing evidence of fire. In most cases
the gutted dwelling was of wood and the adjacent structures were also
charred and marked. Repair work was slow, as it is apt to be in a civilization where people are not too finicky. If the upstairs should burn, one

[35] *Die Exempla des Jakob von Vitry,* ed. Joseph Greven (SMLT, 1914), No. 97.
[36] We are projecting into the past, present conditions of navigation on the Seine
River. See George Millor, *Isabel and the Sea* (New York, 1948).

could live for a while in the cellar. There was no organized fire fighting. Interested neighbors and passers-by rushed to the water supply with buckets and other containers. Adjacent houses might be pulled down if the conflagration was severe.

The city was filled with street cries from dawn to dusk: some announcing the sale of wine in the taverns, others advertising apples, pears, plums, and quinces, peddled from baskets. The soap-and-needle sellers were among the noisiest.[37]

Turning left into Newgate Street, our travelers could have heard the collegiate church of St. Martin's-le-Grand, on their right, ringing the canonical hour, and listened as the peal was taken up by the bells of other churches, which were obliged to take their cue from St. Martin's-le-Grand.[38] The ringing occurred at Prime (approximately six in the morning), Terce, Sext, None, Vespers, Compline, Matins, and Lauds, all of which were a vague three hours apart—vague because a kind of daylight-saving time was observed. In summer the daylight intervals were longer, and the night hours were shorter; in winter the reverse was true.

Although the twelfth-century Londoner worked from dawn to dusk, he did not work at all on holy days. We should not grow too sentimental, therefore, over the long hours of labor that were required. There were a number of holy days in the course of an average month. Men of the baronial class spent much time hanging about the houses of the higher royal officials, such as the king's chancellor. When Thomas Becket held that office, he used to strew fresh reeds and grasses on his floors each day so that the crowds of court seekers would be able to sit on clean floors.[39] All the writers of the time, from Giraldus to Marie de France, are insistent that this court life was degrading. A roomful of barons must have presented a colorful sight, with much of the appearance of a menagerie.[40] Barons carried about with them hawks, falcons, pet monkeys, and parrots.

[37] "A poon [*sic*] peddler, who carries nothing but soap and needles, shouteth and calleth out clamorously what he beareth, and a rich mercer goeth along quite silently." *Ancrene Riwle*, pp. 152–53.

[38] It was in 37 Edward III (1363) that the bells of Our Lady at Bow were substituted.

[39] Herbert de Boseham, *Materials for the History of Archbishop Thomas Becket* (Rolls Series), III, 20–21.

[40] *N.R.*, p. 213. The knights made up a smaller proportion of the population than is commonly believed. Poole estimates a maximum of seven thousand knights in England at this time, out of a total population of three million.—*Obligations of Society*, p. 36. The knight had two principal duties: war service (usually forty days every August and September), and garrison or ward duty. These could be commuted by payment of scutage, a fine. Knights on garrison duty had the work of police officers, sometimes that of detectives.—*Obligations of Society*, pp. 38–39, 40, 55. In the *Quatre fils Aymon*, ed. F. Castets (Montpellier, 1909), v. 9854, and elsewhere, exaggerated numbers are given. This is typical of the *chansons de geste*.

Dogs were always present, gnawing bones, spoiling the rushes, and getting in the way. Alexander remarks that an occasional wolf was tamed and kept as a dog, although these animals were apt to return to their wild state as they grew older.

Newgate was an impressive place with its royal serjants on guard, and its bailiffs collecting taxes and local customs. There was perhaps an uneasy stir about the place, for it shared with the Tower of London employment as a king's prison.[41] Malefactors were not detained very long before they received "justice." [42] Common offenders were herded into a single room of the gatehouse, where they diced and made merry in other ways. Serious offenders, including political ones, might be lowered into holes resembling wells, where there was almost no light. In one of these foul-smelling holes, which were sometimes damp and wet, the prisoner lay wondering what fate would be his. Food was lowered to him: a jug of water, hard moldy bread, and perhaps a piece of bad meat. He dreaded the possibility of meeting with toads, snakes, and other creeping things, of which the medieval man was very much afraid.[43] The East Gate at Exeter, Devonshire, was connected with the castle, and possibly with the cathedral, by an underground passage entered by an opening outside the wall. We wonder whether such a subterranean system was ever employed in London.[44] . . .

---

[41] Margery Bassett in *Speculum,* XVIII (1943), 234, argues *ex silentio* that Newgate was not used as a prison before 1188. The jail at Ludgate (later the Fleet) was in existence in 1189.—F.S., p. 348. I am inclined to believe that both these gates were used for prisoners for some years previous. The Tower of London also was an ordinary prison. Richard d'Amble was retained there in irons.—F.S., p. 11.

[42] The tendency was growing to take an amercement or fine in the place of physical punishment. Poole, pp. 81, 104, 106. This was imposed after the accused had thrown himself on the king's mercy.

[43] *Boz i ot et culovres, don ert esmaiés.—Floovant,* ed. Guessard and Michelant (1859), v. 845; *Prise d'Orange,* ed. Katz (1947), vv. 1230–31.

[44] E. P. Leigh, *Historic Exeter* (n.d.), pp. 35–37. In the *Prise d'Orange* there is a *bove,* or underground tunnel, extending from the tower to the river Rhone (vv. 1173 ff.). There is a *bove* in the *Quatre fils Aymon,* vv. 13751 ff.

LETHA CURTIS MUSGRAVE

Medieval University Life

When Oxford draws knife,
England's soon at strife

As the old rhyme indicates, university riots are nothing new. In medieval times internecine disputes often spread far beyond the student community; and frequently the scholars banded together in bloody battles against the townspeople. In fact, "town and gown" riots were an important factor in the gradual development of the early universities. Far from being formally founded, with rights and limitations clearly defined, these institutions grew up haphazard. During the revival of learning known as "the Renaissance of the Twelfth Century," which introduced Arabian arithmetic, texts of Roman law, and the works of ancient philosophers into Western Europe, groups of students gathered, usually at the site of a cathedral school, to hear lectures on the new subjects. For convenience and safety, the students and their teachers soon began to organize into unions, or guilds, called *universitates;* and it was purely by accident that the term came later to mean an accredited seat of higher learning.

At Bologna, the chief center for the study of Roman law, the guilds exercised a degree of power that modern students might consider enviable. The Cismontane University—men from Italy—and the Transmontane University—men from outside Italy—acting together through two groups of deputies headed by a rector, made strict rules for their teachers, even limiting them to one day's absence when they got married. If a master failed to attract more than five listeners to a lecture, he was obliged to pay a fine; and other Southern European universities, such as the great medical schools at Salerno and Naples, used Bologna as a pattern.

At Paris, on the other hand, the model for most universities in Northern Europe, a strong guild of masters governed. As an institution, Paris developed directly from the cathedral school of Notre-Dame, which was renowned for its great teacher and theologian, Peter Abelard. Largely

Letha Curtis Musgrave, "Medieval University Life," *History Today,* 22, no. 2 (February 1972): 120–27.

through Abelard's eminence, Paris became the center for the study of theology. It was also an important center for the study of the liberal arts, which were prerequisites for law and medicine, as well as for theology. Thus, although they ranged in age from fifteen to sixty, most of the Paris students were younger than those at Bologna or Salerno. Moreover, the theological interest tended to emphasize authority. Hence, the masters, rather than the students, made the rules. The students, however, had their own organizations. Upon arrival at the school of their choice, they were assigned to a "nation," supposedly on the basis of their homeland, although the divisions were rather artificial, and often led to controversy. At Paris, there were four nations—France, Normandy, Picardy, and England. They chose the rector; and, as each had a key to the fourfold lock of the money-chest, and representatives from all four must be present when the chest was opened, it is scarcely surprising that disputes were numerous.

Quarrels between the two Oxford nations, established in 1252, the Northernmen and Southernmen, were apt to be particularly savage; and, as the couplet quoted above shows, they often spread beyond the confines of the university. One of these fights, which took place in the fourteenth century, and was described by Adam of Usk, ringleader of the southern faction, as "a grave misfortune . . . whence arose broils, quarrels and oft-times loss of life," lasted two whole years. In the first year, the Northernmen were driven away from the University; but they managed to stage a comeback, and indicted many Southernmen for causing a felonious riot. Although he was finally acquitted, Adam had been much alarmed. "From that day forth," he wrote, "I feared the king . . . and I put hooks into my jaws."

Far more important than brawls of this kind were the "town and gown" riots, in which students, usually supported by the university authorities, united against the townsmen to obtain greater privileges. The theoretical right of the town to exercise control over the university was never denied; the problem in dispute was just how far the town's right extended, and in what manner it should be exercised. Economic problems also played a part—especially the vital question of what constituted reasonable rents; for the earliest university students had to find lodgings in the town.

Thus the aims of the bellicose medieval student bore little resemblance to those of the twentieth-century rioter, who is usually protesting against the policies pursued by the university administration. No less different are medieval and modern tactics. Whereas present-day students often attempt to enforce their demands by occupying and barricading university buildings, at a medieval university they had no such buildings to invade; and the rioters fought their battles in the streets or local taverns. The fact that they had no buildings of their own, however, gave the early universities an important tactical advantage in their struggles with the townspeople—they could threaten to migrate en masse to another city if their demands were not met.

This was a formidable economic weapon; for the university personnel, including the barbers, copyists, bookbinders and others who served the students, and would move away with them, usually exceeded the townsfolk in number. Some universities owed their beginnings to migrations; Cambridge University, for example, was founded after the battle of 1209 (which we shall be describing later), by indignant emigrés from Oxford. A migration to Padua forced the city fathers of Bologna to grant students a number of civil rights, including the all-important right to strike, or migrate, if they could get satisfaction by no other means.

The earliest recorded "town and gown" riot led to the first known charter of privileges, which was granted by Philip Augustus to the University of Paris in 1200. Besides formally recognizing many existing rights, it allowed students to be tried in ecclesiastical courts, rather than in the much more severe lay courts. A more important struggle occurred in 1229, when a few students, out for a walk, decided to stop for some "good, sweet wine." A dispute over the bill passed from words "to the pulling of ears and tearing of hair." The innkeeper called upon his neighbors to help him drive the students out; but they returned next day with reinforcements. Thus the quarrel grew, until the Queen Regent, Blanche of Castile, sent in troops and several students were killed. "Spouting scurrilous poems" about the alleged relations between Blanche and her adviser, the Papal Legate, a large body of masters and students departed for Toulouse, Orleans and elsewhere.

When the remaining masters had threatened to close the university for six years, Pope Gregory IX intervened, and granted the "Magna Carta" of Paris. This document, issued in 1231, recognized the university's right to regulate dress, lectures, funerals and prices of lodgings—above all, its right to migrate if demands were not met; and these privileges were included in grants to new universities for the next two hundred years. But the charter did not satisfy everyone. The Chancellor complained of too much organization and university business, saying that in the old days, when each master taught himself, there was "more zeal for study."

At Oxford, we first hear of a conflict between students and townspeople in the year 1209. Two or three students were then hanged after a pitched battle in which a townsman had been killed, perhaps accidentally, by a rioting scholar. Five years later, the University obtained from the Papal Legate a document that required townsmen who had taken part in the hanging to do penance by marching in procession, barefoot, to the victims' unconsecrated graves, and thence to the cemetery, where the dead were given proper burial. Practical privileges, in the form of rent refunds, a ten-year rent ceiling, and lower food prices were also obtained by the

University. Yet, until as late as 1533, when an attemtp was made to force a college election with clubs and swords, Oxford life was often violent; and, according to the nineteenth-century historian, Hastings Rashdall,[1] more blood has been shed in Oxford High Street than upon many a battle-field. Masters often encouraged students to commit crimes, like the professor charged with persuading his students to kill a priest who had offended him, or the proctor who, in 1526, "sate uppon a blocke in the streete afore the shoppe of one Robert Jermyns, a barber, havinge a pole axe in his hand, a black cloake on his backe, and a hatt on his head," and organized a riot in which many townsmen were "stricken downe and sore beaten."

A large percentage of entries on the Oxford coroners' rolls deal with riot-deaths. Indeed, of the twenty-nine coroners' inquests held between 1297 and 1322, twelve were concerned with murders committed by scholars, many of which seem to have been countenanced by the University. Such offences frequently went unpunished. After a riot between Northernmen and Southernmen in 1314, of thirty-nine students known to have committed manslaughter, only seven were apprehended, the others having claimed "privilege of the clergy," fled to sanctuary—thereby incurring banishment—or escaped altogether. Robert of Bridlington, for example, who sat in the window of Gutter Hall and shot an arrow through Henry of Holy Isle, survived for many years, only to lose his life at last in yet another town and gown affray.

Like the Paris riot of 1229, the most famous Oxford town and gown battle, on St Scholastica's Day, February 10th, 1354, grew out of a tavern dispute. In addition to killing and wounding several students, the townsmen scalped their fallen adversaries, removing the skin from some of the university chaplains' heads down to the tonsure. The university sought venegance through the King, who went so far as to grant it control over the market and a certain amount of jurisdiction over the city itself. The Bishop of Lincoln also placed the townsmen under interdict, which was removed only on condition that the mayor and bailiffs and "three-score of the chiefest Burghers" should "personally appear" in St Mary's Church every St Scholastica's Day to attend a mass for the souls of the slain. Each of these functionaries was to offer one penny at the altar, of which forty pence would be distributed to forty poor university scholars—a custom that survived until the nineteenth century.

This struggle is typical of the many riots in which the university managed to gain support both from the Church and from the secular government. After a riot, university officials would appeal to the King, who nearly always solved the dispute, as he had done after the St Scholastica's Day

---

[1] 1858–1924; author of *Universities of Europe in the Middle Ages,* 1895.

battle, by giving the head of the university increased power. If he hesitated, the university could usually rely on support from the Pope, as in the Paris riot of 1229. The limits of town control were largely established both through the riots themselves and through agreements—or, more often, the papal decrees and/or royal grants—that followed them; and thus the universities acquired an independence that helped to make them what they are today.

Yet, oddly enough, the independence they gained had little to do with our modern ideas of freedom. In the Middle Ages, truth was expounded, not sought. It was revealed by authority, not discovered by research, which must be free if it is to be objective. So long as the masters, therefore, stayed within the accepted bounds of dogma, they were allowed to teach pretty much as they pleased. In the climate of their time, they did not feel cramped by the rule of authority, as twentieth-century professors would; and the students they taught willingly accepted the curriculum. Although there were intermittent disputes over the teaching of Aristotle, his works had been reconciled with the Christian faith and become a fixed part of the curriculum by the middle of the thirteenth century. In Paris, during the course of that century only one case is recorded of a teacher being imprisoned for propagating theological errors; and only one other was deprived of the right to teach because of his heretical notions. Thus, in general, the masters taught as they wished. Even if they were accused of heresy, they could usually save themselves by falling back on a convenient doctrine of the time—that what was true in philosophy might be false in theology, and vice versa.

A glance at what was included in the medieval curriculum makes it plain that, apart from questions of theological heresy, there was little chance of controversy over subject-matter. The university course began with the Seven Liberal Arts—the *Trivium* and the *Quadrivium*. The *Trivium* included grammer, usually studied in verse form through Alexander de Villa Dei's *Doctrinale;* rhetoric, the art of letter writing; and dialectic, mainly the study of Aristotle's philosophy and logic. The *Quadrivium* included arithmetic; geometry, which comprised Euclid plus some geography, music, which included notation, singing and the numerical relations of sound; and astronomy, which was little more than astrology. After completing the Liberal Arts, usually at Paris, the student who wished to do graduate work in law would journey to Bologna, to absorb the laws of the Roman Emperor Justinian through an elaborate series of commentaries known as the Glosses. For medicine he might remain at Paris for six more years, to study the works of Hippocrates and Galen, his only laboratory work being the dissection of pigs. If he was more daring, he would go to Italy, where he could learn anatomy by dissecting human cadavers.

For theology, the highest study of all, he would remain at Paris, using as his primary textbook—not the Bible, but Peter Lombard's *Four Books of Sentences,* a series of questions answered by the authority of the Scriptures and the Fathers of the Church. These included such moot points as how many angels could dance at once on the point of a needle, and whether glorified souls spent the next world in the empyrean or in the crystalline heaven—as well as a number of other problems that had a more direct bearing upon human life.

For the privilege of following this rather limited curriculum, most students of the Middle Ages were prepared to go through dreadful hardships. Getting to the chosen school was, in the first place, far from simple. Unless the scholar was a nobleman, he had usually to make the journey on foot, finding free lodging at monasteries. Wearing a coarse tunic, laden only with his wax tablets and a stylus at his girdle, a packet of bread and herbs and salt on his back, he had little to fear from the robbers that infested the roads. But, if he were rich, he might travel by coach with an armed retinue to protect him, his clothing and books, his precious letter of introduction and album in which his professors and fellow students would later sign their names and write mottoes.

When he arrived at his university, he suffered mild persecution from upper classmen. He was called "yellowbeak," "cock of the walk," or "greenie." He might be bullied by being dressed in an oxhide, complete with horns, then springled with earth and made to pass a mock examination, or go through more strenuous antics to rid himself of his beastly nature. The newcomer soon discovered that he had better hasten to brush up his Latin; for all university men were required to converse in that language. Student dictionaries and conversation manuals came to his rescue, providing models of proper discourse for all situations— quarrelling with his roommate; borrowing money; falling in love and recovering; visiting the jugglers in the marketplace; getting into trouble for breaking rules; and even inviting his masters to a banquet, preceded by a free bath, upon the occasion of receiving his degree. To make sure his manners would be acceptable, he might also consult a manual of etiquette, which instructed him to wash his hands in the morning and his face, too, if he had the time; to eat with only three fingers; not to pick his teeth with his knife; and not to gnaw bones but to throw them on the floor.

Once he was settled at the university, his life was not altogether pleasant. Rising at four or five o'clock, he descended a narrow staircase and washed at a common trough in the courtyard. First, he attended mass. Then, usually without breakfast, he made his way through the dark streets to a square, a cloister or sometimes a stable, where he sat on a bundle of straw, listening to lectures until ten or eleven o'clock. After a meagre meal, he returned to school for the "meridian disputations," and spent the afternoon hearing repetitions of lectures. If he were lucky enough to have access to any of the few available manuscripts, he might study the next day's lessons—unless he decided to drink.

For drinking was the chief amusement of most of the students. Everything—the arrival of a new master, the end of examinations, even the funeral of a classmate—might be the excuse for a drinking bout. Among the heaviest drinkers were the wandering students called the Goliards (after Golias, the twelfth-century "Archpoet," who drifted from school to school, sometimes carrying for show only, huge wide-margined, red-bound books. Although they did little studying, they sang songs and wrote poetry, including a large number of ribald or romantic drinking songs. Gambling, too, was so prevalent that, in 1274, the Paris masters had to forbid students to shake dice on an altar in Notre-Dame while mass was being celebrated. Covered baskets of wafers were frequent stakes at dice; the winning students hung their baskets from their windows.

At Oxford and Cambridge colleges, the student had an especially strict routine. Besides "noxious, inordinate, unlawful and unhonest sports"— which included chess—the rules prohibited "light and idle talk," dancing, and musical instruments. The student had only two meals a day, and in his room did without heat and light. At dinner, an upper classman read from the Bible or from a book of martyrology. For one hour after this edifying meal, conversation and walking were permitted. In cold weather, the walk was almost a run, for it was the only means of warming the feet before one went to bed. Yet, despite this Spartan routine and the frequent disturbances to which they were exposed, many students worked hard, and even enjoyed their university career—like Richard Wyck, the thirteenth-century Bishop of Chichester, who felt that "in all his days, he had never after led so pleasant and delectable a life." Though poverty stricken, he even gave up the chance to go home and marry a rich and beautiful girl, saying that a young man "may always get a wife, but science once lost can never be recovered." Wyck must have been as conscientious as the many students who did their best to obey the six rules for study set forth by Robert de Sorbon, the Paris lecturer, active during the later thirteenth century, for whom the Sorbonne was originally named. According to Sorbon, the student should:

1. Consecrate a fixed hour to each study . . .
2. Fix the attention upon what is read, and do not pass over it lightly.
3. Extract from the daily reading . . . some truth, and grave it upon the memory with special care.
4. Write out a résumé, for words which are not confined to writing fly away like dust before the wind.

5. Discuss the matter with fellow students . . .
6. Pray. . . .

If he followed these rules reasonably well, and managed to avoid being killed in a riot—or, like one Bolognese scholar, being attacked with a cutlass in the classroom—the medieval student, at the end of his course, could hope to receive a bachelor's degree. He might go on for a licentiate and a master's degree, which in many places would both entitle him to noble rank and enable him to teach at a university. To obtain it, he had either to bribe his masters or pass a difficult examination, promising not to knife the examiner should he fail. As part of the test, he had to teach a sample lesson to a "shrewd boy," with the aid of a rod and a palmer —for inflicting corporal punishment on the palms. If he wielded these vigorously enough, he qualified as a future teacher and, provided he had the means, could then celebrate with a banquet.

Not many could. A constant need for money is one problem that medieval and modern university students have in common. A six-hundred-year-old version of a familiar letter runs as follows: "I crave your kindness, my respected father, devoutly, so that fatherly reverence may consider it worthy to give me some money with which I can now manage in school until the Feast of St Michael." Often the medieval scholar was able to supplement his father's contribution by copying manuscripts or carrying holy water. But abject poverty was the rule, except among the sons of noblemen; and many students were forced to maintain their existence by begging. We read of a trio of friends who were so poor that they had only two tunics among them. One wore a tunic and their single bonnet to lectures, while the others remained in their miserable room, one wearing the other tunic and the third staying in bed.

To alleviate the students' poverty, as well as to provide better discipline, the collegiate system developed. Bolognese students first organized residential halls as early as the twelfth century; and their plan rapidly spread to Paris and Oxford. During the second half of the thirteenth century, philanthropists, troubled by the plight of poor scholars, founded special hostels for their benefit. The universities gradually assumed control of all these residences, which were called "colleges," and required students to take up residence there. Originally the colleges were only dormitories; later, students were instructed under the college roof by the masters in charge. A few students, however, managed to avoid living in the colleges and continued to lodge in the towns. Known as "chamber deacons," they were responsible for a good percentage of the violence and marauding attributed to the student body. An Oxford statute of 1410 complained that the chamber deacons "sleep all day, and at night roam about taverns and houses of ill fame for opportunity of robbery and homicide;" and, in 1413, King Henry V banished the Irish deacons, hoping to bring greater tranquillity to his realm.

The crimes that chamber deacons committed led to the passing of laws that made it a more serious offence to be abroad after curfew than to shoot an arrow at a proctor with intent to wound him. Yet, although plenty of idlers, like the Goliards and the chamber deacons, must always have swelled the university ranks, during the Middle Ages, just as today, no doubt the typical university student had a genuine love of learning. Like Chaucer's Oxford scholar, "gladly wolde he lerne, and gladly teche." For, had there not been many such students, the medieval universities could not have exerted so wide an influence both on their own time and on future ages.

JEAN LUCAS-DUBRETON

Home Life In Florence

The Florentine was a home-bird because he was economical. He considered it "harmful, costly, annoying and inconvenient to change houses," and, as far as possible, he tried not to sink to the level of a lodger; but to have his own house in a respectable quarter so that his wife should make only honorable acquaintances. He did not like separating his family because to live under the same roof appeared to him to have solid advantages, if only because it economized lighting and heating.

Like most Italians, he was neither a drunkard nor a glutton; but, though the excesses of the Swiss and the Germans disgusted him, he was not averse to good cheer.

The first family meal was taken between nine and ten in the morning, the second before nightfall. In the days of "modesty and sobriety" these meals had been of the simplest. Husband and wife ate from the same dish and drank from the same cup, the menu being mainly composed of bread, "herbs," jam and fruit. Meat was eaten only on Sundays, and when a pig was slaughtered, one gave black-pudding to one's neighbor, who

Jean Lucas-Dubreton, *Daily Life in Florence in the Time of the Medici* (New York: The Macmillan Company, 1961), pp. 115–23.

was angry if one forgot to. The fare became more delicate as the years went by. Boiled kid or peacock might now be served, followed by colored jellies in the shape of little men or animals. This Florentine invention was made of almond-milk and other ingredients, colored with saffron, or *zafferano* as it was called, and sometimes even scented. Pastry came in only with the sixteenth century.

For a burgher or merchant—it was the same thing in Florence—entertaining was an obligation. It meant business-customers as well as friends. Here, according to an expert adviser, were the requisites for a pleasant dinner-party: the guests should not be less than three, or more than nine, because, if more are invited, they will be too many to listen to each other or hold consecutive conversation—which may be profitable—and because asides spoil the pleasure and create confusion. One should therefore invite a reasonable number of people, sociable and on good terms with each other; they should be entertained in a pleasant room, at a convenient hour, and the service should be faultless. The guests should be neither babblers nor of taciturn disposition, but moderate talkers. The topics of conversation should not be subtle, uncertain or hard to understand, but gay, amusing and useful. One must not forget to be practical.

The table is set facing the garden-door which lets in the fresh air. The host has a ewer of water passed round so that the company may wash their hands. They then take their places, ladies alternating with gentlemen. Slices of melon are served, then a *berlingozzo,* which is a cake made of flour, eggs and sugar. This is followed by boiled capon, fat and in perfect condition, prime quality sausages and veal, a good stew, roast chicken,[1] or else thrushes, pigeons or pheasants, and sometimes trout, "to appease the voluptuous and so fit the mind to cope with the things of this world. Something must be allowed to the weakness of the flesh."

This was a rich man's menu for festive occasions. There would be music for merriment: the kettle-drum, played with two sticks, or the jew's harp, an iron band bent double and fitted with a steel tongue to serve as a spring. It was held between the teeth, and the tongue vibrated as you pushed it with your finger. While this was going on, the servant would be running backwards and forwards from the kitchen and grumbling about her mistress: "She works hard talking, and I walking, and I have only two legs and down-at-heel shoes."

These Florentine banquets were, by the way, matched by the meals

---

[1] Did all the guests take all these courses? Probably not, but we do not know. If however (another query) the Florentines were still on the two-meal-a-day régime, this would make a great difference to their capacity. (Translator)

usually eaten in France, at least in the sixteenth century, if we are to believe the economist Jean Bodin, whose strictures are violent: "People are not satisfied, at an ordinary dinner, to have three dishes; boiled meat, roast meat and fruit. They must have meats prepared in five or six different ways, with so many sauces, mincemeats, pastries and every kind of hotch-potch and other fancy dish, that there is great intemperance."

But Florence was ahead of France in the use of that instrument which the Latinists designated as a *fuscina* and we call a fork. It was considered vulgar to dip one's fingers in the gravy; one should pick up the food one wants either with a knife or a fork.[2]

The average Florentine, of course, dined less expensively than the rich merchant. He would begin with a salad, followed perhaps by a small pigeon, goat's milk cheese and fruit. He was very fond of *fegatelli,* a sort of liver sausage. But his basic diet was already *pasta,* which he prepared in various ways, while the preachers railed at his self-indulgence. "You are great gourmands," cried one of them. "It's not enough for you to eat fried *pasta,* but you must flavor it with garlic. When you eat *ravioli,* it's not enough for you to boil them in the pan and eat them with the broth, but you must then fry them in another pan, together with cheese."

Wine, too, had its votaries, and everyone sang the praises of Vernaccia, Trebbiàno, etc. "Drunk in moderation, it nourishes the body, improves the blood, hastens digestion, calms the intellect, makes the heart joyful, enlivens the spirits, expels wind, increases the warmth of the body, fattens convalescents, rouses the appetite, purifies the blood, removes obstructions, distributes nourishment in the right places, gives color and health to the cheeks," and so on. It was the object of a cult. Luigi Pulci writes in the *Morgante Maggiore*: "I believe no more in black than in white, but I believe in boiled or roasted capon, and I also believe in butter and beer. . . .[3] But above all I have faith in good wine and deem that he who believes in it is saved."

Drunkards and gluttons were not however in favor. To have a good time but without swilling and gormandizing—that was the rule for most people, and they practised a delicate epicureanism. An English protonotary apostolic, who was staying in Florence and had been accustomed like his fellow-countrymen to spending four hours at table, was amazed by Florentine sobriety and ended by conforming to it.

There was no lack of inns and taverns in the city, and one of them, the Tavern of the Snail, near the Mercato Vecchio, was famous. Better-

---

[2] The fork, like so many of the amenities of civilization, was invented in Italy. It does not appear to have been much in vogue in England before the end of the seventeenth century. (Translator)

[3] 'Cervisia,' to be exact. It was the kind of beer the Romans made.

class citizens did not usually frequent them; but if a merchant's wife and children had left for the country, he would take his meals there—unless friends had invited him out—and return home only at bedtime.

The rules of courtesy and good manners are set out by a talented writer, Giovanni della Casa,[4] in the *Galateo,* a sort of manual which shows how Florentines behaved—or should behave.

When you are eating, do not masticate noisily [5] "or crouch gluttonously over the food without raising your face, as if you were blowing a trumpet. Don't hiccup. That is not eating but devouring; and then too you soil your hands and even your elbows, and dirty the cloth."

Avoid rubbing your teeth with your napkin, or, worse still, with your fingers. Do not scratch yourself, or spit, or at least only do it "reservedly." "I have heard," remarks Della Casa, "that there are nations so polite that they never spit; and we might well refrain from spitting. . . . Inviting people to drink repeatedly is not one of our habits and we describe it by means of a foreign word: *"fare brindisi,"* a reprehensible custom which one should not adopt. I thank Heaven that, among the scourges that have come from beyond the Alps (a reference to Germany and France), this one, which is the worst, has not gained a footing here; I mean, to consider it amusing and even estimable to get drunk."

In no circumstances should you bend over the glass of wine or the plate, where someone else is going to drink or eat, in order to take a sniff. And do not offer your neighbor a pear or other fruit which you have already bitten.

On rising from table, do not stick your toothpick in the back of your mouth, which makes you look like a bird carrying a twig to its nest; and do not wear your toothpick in your collar—a strange accoutrement for a gentleman. After blowing your nose, do not look into your handkerchief as if pearls or rubies had been deposited in it; and do not drum with your fingers on the table or wave your legs about. This shows little consideration for other people.

If you wish to speak with someone, do not go so close to him as to be breathing in his face. One does not always like to smell other people's breath. And do not nudge people with your elbow, and repeat: "Isn't that true? And what do *you* think? And Messer So-and-So?"

Avoid expressing yourself affectedly, "with the point of the fork"—

[4] Della Casa was born in the Mugello; he published the *Galateo* in 1558. He is famous also for his sonnets, of which the form influenced Milton. (Translator)

[5] A Frenchman observed in this connexion: 'The Germans keep their mouths shut when masticating, and consider any other way unsightly. The French on the contrary half open their mouths and consider the German way unsightly. The Italians go about it very gently, the French rather more briskly, and they consider the Italian way too refined' (cf. A. Lefranc, *La Vie quotidienne au temps de la Renaissance,* p. 150).

favellar in punto della forchetta. Do not for ever be talking about your wife, or the children, or the nurse; and refrain from long descriptions of your dreams, as though they were wonderful or important.

To lavish advice on those who have not asked for it is equivalent to saying that you are wiser than they, and that they are incompetent. This can only be done between close friends. And the same applies to counsels of health. To say with the gravity of a physician: "You ought to take *this* electuary, or *that* kind of pill," is like trying to clean another man's field when one's own is full of thorns and nettles.

In conversation, generally, do not be so anxious to hold the ball that you snatch it from your neighbor, "as one often sees a hen in a farmyard snatching a straw out of the beak of another." And if you want to make the company laugh, refrain from twisting your mouth, rolling your eyes, puffing out your cheeks or making other grimaces. "The goddess Pallas amused herself for a time by playing on the bagpipes. She became an expert player. But one day, being thus occupied at the edge of a pool, she happened to see her image in the water and was so much ashamed that she threw away the instrument." Imitate Pallas, and shun ridicule. . . . And stop making noises with your mouth to express surprise or contempt.

A few instructions now as to how one should appear in public. Do not be seen wearing your nightcap, or put on your garters in front of other people. Do not leave your office with your pen above your ear, or holding a handkerchief between your teeth. Do not put a leg on the table; avoid spitting on your fingers.

Your dress should be neither so pretty nor so elaborate as to make people remark that you are wearing Ganymede's hose and Cupid's doublet. If your legs are too fat or too lean, or slightly twisted, do not order from your tailor hose in gaudy colors or of a conspicuous cut, which would simply invite attention to your defects.

Observe the code of the *Galateo* and you will be an accomplished man of the world.

Well-informed though he was, the Florentine did not refrain from consulting palmists and having his hand read. It has in fact been established that the hand is the organ of every part of the body and that the natural disposition of the individual is revealed in its lines and contours. Why are there four lines in the hand? Because we have four principal organs: the heart, the liver and the brain, which counts for two. The palmist Bartolomeo Cocles says so. A short hand is the sign of a person subject to "cold humors"; a long hand with short, stiff fingers denotes a phlegmatic individual, without much courage; a long hand with a broad palm warns us that the person will be mischievous, even a knave and a thief. As to a woman, if her hand is short but her fingers excessively long, she will be "in peril of child-birth."

Palmistry was of course no antidote for sickness. What then of the physician? He belonged to the fifth of the major "arts," the art of drugs and groceries, which included the *speziale,* or apothecary, with whom the physician sometimes lodged. He had formerly been a man of modest appearance, in spite of his tall hat trimmed with fillets. He had worn a long fur gown, so shabby and threadbare that "a furrier could not have guessed what animal had provided the skin." In these days, however, he dressed with studied elegance, wearing a long and capacious robe, trimmed with squirrel-fur and bands of scarlet, heavily begemmed rings, and gilded spurs, like a knight's. Following the example of Pier Leoni, Lorenzo's doctor, he had abandoned Arabic medicine in favor of Greek. Educated until recently in the medical school of Salerno, he practised astrology as much as medicine, and was now acquiring a reputation abroad, especially in France.

In 1479 sixty-six doctors are recorded as practicing in Florence. They mainly prescribed simples, cabbage for example, which they regarded as a panacea. But in spite of his noble appearance, the physician was not taken very seriously, hardly more than the pedant. Years before this, Petrarch had described doctors as ignorant "spectators of maladies and sick persons." The facetious Poggio addressed them as follows:

> You visit the patient, inspect his water and excrement with attentive eye and puckered brow as if his malady required the most important attention. Then you feel his pulse, where you recognise the forces of nature. Next you consult your colleagues and after much discussion agree as to the remedies, as you call them. If by chance the beverage you prescribe has been effective, you never cease from extolling the cure; if it has done harm, you blame the patient.

Machiavelli is said to have died from taking too many pills containing aloes and cardamom, which a doctor had prescribed for him.

In cases where the patient entered one of the city's numerous hospitals, he found a high degree of comfort: abundant food, choice wine, competent nurses, and great cleanliness in his room and bed.

When a Florentine died—or "entered the great sea," as dying was called—the Signoria regulated the procedure. The body was to be simply dressed in white muslin lined with taffeta, with a plain cap on the head. In burying a woman, no ring was to be left on her fingers, unless it had little value. With a man, no armour was to be buried, no doublet, penon, flag or shield. The body rested on a common palliasse.

At the interment, two candles were permitted, or two torches containing at most thirty pounds of wax between them, or else four small torches. Candles or torches were to be extinguished immediately after the ceremony and returned to the dealer, the *speziale* in this instance, who was not allowed to sell candles weighing more than fifteen pounds, including the paper and candle-end. It was unreasonable to provide lighting for the dead, a useless display; and those who infringed the law were liable to a fine. This went into the *opera,* the fund for church-building and repairs.

The body was followed to the grave by mourners garbed in black; but this funeral attire was only loosely stitched "so as not to spoil the material which would later serve to make clothes." The wages of those who "announced" deaths and of the undertaker's men—the *beccamorti*—were fixed at a maximum of eight soldi. The widow was not to receive from the heirs either a gown, or petticoat, or girdle, or headdress, but simply a skirt and a cloak lined with taffeta. Two courses only might be served at the funeral dinner.

The interment took place at the charnel-house, or in the case of important persons, in the church. In Paris it was not until the middle of the sixteenth century that, on the occasion of an epidemic, the famous Dr. Fernel and a colleague, having heard of the fetid smell that hung over the Cemetery of the Innocents, recorded the fact that "in dangerous times the houses near the said cemetery have always been the first to catch the contagion and have remained infected longer than other houses in the city." But this warning remained a dead letter.

In Florence, however, as early as the fifteenth century, Bishop Narcissus, who was of Catalan origin and who had observed how crowded the Florentine churches were with sepulchres, gave the following warning: "The House of God, being clean and pure, should not be sullied with the presence of corpses. It is the monks who have introduced this custom. The primitive Church not only did not permit the burial in church of those who are now buried there, but even raised objections to the interment of holy men." And Narcissus cited the reply which a Pope had made when asked by some prelate for permission to inter the bodies of two martyrs in his church: "Place them at the entrance, but not elsewhere."

The Florentines unfortunately remained deaf to the words of this foreigner who was so concerned for the purity of a holy place and, perhaps without realizing it, for public health.

FRITZ RORIG

Urban Types In Germany

. . . The difference in population of medieval towns indicates the various degrees of activity and the various functions of individual towns. Not all so-called towns, not even those which may, legally, have been a town in the sense that this or that little place may have had "urban rights" bestowed upon it by some lord, can be included in an exposition whose aim is to elucidate the essential elements that made the medieval town into one of the most important impulses in world history. Nowadays we have freed ourselves from the notion that the medieval map of Germany was dotted with about 3,000 towns, each of which had the same aim— namely, as the central point of a minute territorial economic area, to lead as self-contained a life as the old manor farm of the local seigneur had once led. By far the greater part of these 3,000 "towns"—about 2,800 —had populations of less than 1,000; in other words, there is no question of their being considered as truly urban economies, least of all as self-contained ones, because there was really no possibility that within these tiny little populations there would be room enough for all the trades necessary to the self-sufficiency of a town, however modest. A further 150 "towns," roughly speaking, also very modest even by medieval standards, had populations of between 1,000 and 2,000. Only the remaining ones, about fifty of them, were towns of any real importance within the German economy, over half of which, with populations of less than 10,000, formed the German medium-sized towns. Finally there was a group of about fifteen large German towns whose populations were in excess of 10,000. Cologne was the largest with more than 30,000 inhabitants; the second largest was Lübeck with no more than 25,000 around 1400. Apart from these only Strasbourg, Nuremberg, Gdansk and perhaps Ulm would have reached and exceeded 20,000 in the fifteenth century. Towns of the rank of Frankfurt am Main, Wroclaw, Zürich and Augsburg grew from 10,000 to 18,000 in the course of the fifteenth century; in 1493 the population of Erfurt amounted to about 18,500. If the population of

Fritz Rorig, *The Medieval Town* (Los Angeles: The University of California Press, 1967), pp. 111–21, 146–56.

Leipzig is calculated at around 4,000 in 1474, then this is the clearest possible indication of the huge increase which this town experienced since then, mainly as an ancillary member of the Nuremberg trading system.

Similar conditions obtained in the northern European towns outside Germany. Of English towns only London had more than 10,000 inhabitants, and this certainly by a considerable amount; it already had 30-40,000 in the fourteenth century. An even higher incidence of population in a capital is certainly known to have obtained in Paris. This town, as the royal residence, as an episcopal see and as the seat of the famous university, exercised at the height of the Middle Ages a power of attraction such as did no other town north of the Alps. Among the Flemish towns Bruges appears, at least at the time of its greatest prosperity, to have had the largest population within its walls. It is somewhat surprising that Ypres had only a little more than 10,000 inhabitants; admittedly this was in 1412, when the Flemish weaving towns were already in decline and the weavers' suburbs depopulated. Ypres, but also particularly Ghent, would have had far greater numbers in the fourteenth century. Figures far in excess of the German towns were to be found particularly in Italy. Florence is supposed to have had 100,000 inhabitants around 1340; its decline from that time on is well known. Milan is said to have had 85,000 inhabitants towards the end of the fifteenth century. In the sixteenth century the respective populations of Venice, Naples and Palermo are all believed to have exceeded 100,000.

But nothing would be more mistaken than to underestimate a medieval German town of 20,000 people in terms of the function that it fulfilled in the Middle Ages simply because in modern times a town of this size is not usually very important. Within the framework of the whole, a German town of around that number of inhabitants in 1400 fulfilled a political, economic and cultural function of which many a present-day town of several hundred thousands would be envious. Even if one evaluates Aeneas Sylvius Piccolomini's account of German towns, particularly Cologne, Strasbourg and Nuremberg, in the middle of the fifteenth century as conscious exaggeration—nevertheless he was not the only foreigner to emphasise the outstanding importance of German towns; Cologne, particularly, was a match for any other town of Europe. Machiavelli even saw in the German town the heart of Germany's strength.

Certainly this urban population was subject to a terrible danger which could reduce its numbers very considerably. This was the scourge of the plague—the Black Death—which particularly in the middle of the fourteenth century held its slow but ineluctable victory procession throughout the countries of Europe, of which the best propagators were the flagellants, driving the terrible disease before them. The towns, with their populations squeezed within their walls, had the largest sacrifices to make. It is assumed that the population of Florence was reduced by a third in the terrible mass death of 1348. It was the lowest classes, the weavers, who were the most thoroughly depleted; a renewed outbreak of the plague hit the town in 1374. Western Europe was no less badly hit; England is thought to have lost up to half her population. Germany, too, hit by the first wave of the plague in 1349–50, suffered greatly. According to an entry in the citizens' book of Bremen, 6,966 known and named persons were carried off by it in the town.

The medieval town knew better how to defend itself against famine than against the plague. In this connection a careful policy of stock-piling on the part of the town council served as a precaution against times of corn shortage and war; and above all they saw to it that stocks of food stored either by the town or privately under municipal control did not perish. In cases of regional corn shortage in a region a foreign trade correspondingly intervened. The Flemish towns were dependent on regular corn imports from the Baltic as early as the thirteenth century; inland towns such as Görlitz were regularly supplied with corn from the east.

A continual and heavy restriction on increase in population was the unfavorable formation of the natural class structure in the urban popula-tion. Certainly many children were born. But the infant mortality rate was perhaps even more remarkable than the number of births. Of the twenty-one children of Konrad Paumgartner, a Nuremberg councillor and merchant who died in 1464, only five sons continued the line and four daughters married. Nevertheless shortly before his death Konrad Paum-gartner saw seventy-four grandchildren and forty great-grandchildren growing up around him. The Rorach family of Frankfurt saw sixty-five children come into the world between the end of the fourteenth and the end of the sixteenth centuries who lived; but only eighteen of them out-lived their fathers, and only twelve married! High infant mortality rates were certainly common to both the town and the countryside; but in the towns there was the additional ominous problem of the third or fourth generation, particularly in the most distinguished families. One can ob-serve again and again how the grandchildren of economically outstanding fathers grew weak in business sense, preferring to live on fixed invest-ments and died without leaving an heir. One can see just as frequently a branch of an old merchant family living an aristocratic-lord-of-the-manor life in the country and blossoming for generations, long after the original family in the town had died out. People in the towns were quite well aware of this disastrous process. When in 1548 a senior minister in Rostock dedicated a work to the Lübeck patrician Kinrich Castorp he wrote in the dedication:

Among all the families of Lübeck there are not three or four in which there is a living member of the fourth generation. It makes you angry, said Moses, that we thus perish, and raging that we must thus disappear. May the Lord promise and give to you, the fourth successor of your house, and to your father's and your mother's families everything which is good through Christ, temporally and eternally.

In spite of these good wishes, however, the house of Castorp died out with the man of the dedication. It was a consequence of this unfavorable condition for natural succession that the towns so encouraged the move from the country to the towns—we may remember the saying, "Town air brings freedom"—an encouragement strongly opposed by the lords of the countryside.

Even the ratio of the sexes was not a happy one. Notwithstanding the fact that an unusually high proportion of women died in childbirth, they were still more numerous than men in the urban population. In towns like Nuremberg, Basel and Rostock in the fifteenth century, for every 1,000 men there were respectively 1,207, 1,246 and 1,295 women. The greater dangers run by the armed merchants of the town, their frequently immoderate way of life, perhaps also their higher mortality in epidemics have been seen as the causes of this unequal proportion of the sexes by K. Bücher. In the light of this it is understandable that the laws of Lübeck allowed the same legal position to women in their business affairs as it did to men as early as the thirteenth century; and indeed how it came about that women could be members of workers' guilds. In far and away the largest proportion of such cases it was a question of widows; many a young journeyman was only able to become master in his trade by marrying his mistress. Such marriages were the breeding-ground for the much disparaged "shrew," a problem which has often been illustrated by medieval art with extreme bluntness. The frequent marriages of widows diminished for many unmarried women their chances of marriage, already slight enough on account of the preponderance of women.

There was also the fact that in a town like Lübeck at least three or four hundred men could not be considered for marriage on account of their being secular priests or regular clergy. In these circumstances nunneries became social institutions of great importance. Again and again in medieval merchants' wills one meets with stipulations that if the young growing daughters of the testator do not succeed in finding a husband they must buy their way into a nunnery with a certain sum of money. Marriage or the veil was the only solution in the most distinguished families. The upper class of Lübeck considered not only the St John's Nunnery of Lübeck but a whole series of nunneries in Mecklenburg and Holstein,

Rehna, Neukloster, Zarrentin and Preetz among them—as places where their unmarried daughters would be looked after, and endowed them richly with earthly goods. The *Klosterfahrt,* or ceremony of admission, was celebrated with great pomp; no greater proof of this fact is needed than the frequent attempts to limit the amounts spent even here. For women of lower class, hospitals offered a refuge and a living. Even more important, and highly characteristic of town life in the fourteenth and fifteenth centuries, were the Beguine houses, which looked after the un-married women of the middle and lower strata of the population. There is without doubt a connection between the proponderance of women and the distribution of Beguine houses, which were most patronised in the Nether-lands, but which were to be seen in German towns everywhere, most numerous in the Rhenish towns and least so in the colonial regions. The inmates of a convent—often less than ten and never more than fifty—led a communal life, but the life of a lay community and not the *vita religiosa* of the nuns. Between 1250 and 1350 about one hundred Beguine houses, which together had room for at least one thousand women, are said to have been founded in Cologne. The Beguine houses in Strasbourg had room for about six hundred sisters. In Lübeck there were only five convents with about one hundred sisters; but on the whole there was room here for six hundred women in institutions which had come into being for single women. But as much as reasons of care and attention were emphasised as being responsible for the large number of Beguine convents, neverthe-less, as places in which a strongly religious life was led, they had great importance in the development of medieval piety. Their societies were also full of the search for Christian perfection which brought convents here and there into conflict with the official church authorities. In most cases, however, these sisters fitted into the life of the church and town without difficulty, living off the income of the endowments and also per-forming works of various kinds. On the other hand it did occur later on that the rich foundations of the convents led to an unhealthy idleness amongst the inmates, which occasionally brought them into disrepute.

The Jews, who led a special existence by religion and by law deserve a special note. It was not as though there were Jews in every town; the chronicler remarks of Lübeck—a town which was highly self-conscious as a place of commerce: "There are no Jews in Lübeck; there is no need for them either." He was right; for even without Jews such things as money-lending and usury, mortgages and foreclosures were everyday things in Lübeck; in the same way Florentine banks were created by Italian entrepreneurs, and Italian, Hanseatic and English merchants of the fourteenth century carried on money businesses of considerable size for the English crown. The good and bad results of a commercial enterprise directed towards personal gain also affected towns which had nothing whatever to do with Jews. All this in spite of ecclesiastical prohibition of usury—a prohibition which, like so many, is to be taken rather as evidence that in fact things happened quite differently from the way in which the prohibitors, in this case the ecclesiastical moral theorists, supposed and demanded. Quite unabashed, the council of Constance forbade its townsmen to take more than eleven percent on the money they lent. Moreover, the behavior of the church itself was most strangely at variance with the demands of its moral theoreticians. On the other hand it is wrong to imagine that the Jews were restricted to money-lending. Like the Christians, they, too, combined trade in goods with money-lending—in the early centuries they were pioneers in foreign trade. Certainly in the later Middle Ages they concentrated on money-changing and banking, and particularly pawnbroking. Lords of the manor, knights and towns found themselves among the debtors of Jewish money-lenders; but also did a whole lot of small people—cobblers, tailors and sadlers. If the hatred of Jews in many towns reached special intensity in the fourteenth century, then this is connected with the fact that the small people, too, saw in them the burdensome, and certainly also frequently usurious creditor. To this, moreover, was added the religious contrast which divided Jews from Christians far more sharply than did the economic contrast, which in any case was to some extent artificially engendered by the church.

The first wave of persecution of the Jews in Western Europe was bound up with the crusading atmosphere, the second with the advance of the Black Death in the fourteenth century. It was at the beginning of 1348, when the plague was raging in a town of Provence, that in May of that year the first Jews were burnt. From there the rumor that the Jews had poisoned the wells of the town buzzed through the land, even throughout South, West and Central Germany. In most cases the Jews had already met their fate before the plague even hit the town, as in Strasbourg, where the chronicler confesses that money was the sole reason for the killing of the Jews. If they had been poor and the lords had not been indebted to them, they would not have been burnt. If the picture given of the burning of the Jews in Strasbourg is correct—apart from the certainly exaggerated total given of Jews burnt (two thousand)—then it becomes clear that religious hate was stronger than racial antipathy. If a Strasbourg Jew consented to be baptised he stayed alive; many small children are said to have been taken from the burning pyre and baptised against their parents' wishes. Frederick I's Jews' Charter of 1157 had already forbidden the baptism of secretly stolen Jewish children. Subsequent rulers were not able to withstand the temptation to exploit their rights of protection of the Jews ruthlessly for their own enrichment. However it would be wrong to assume that persecution of the Jews was the rule; decades of peace and lawfulness were suddenly interrupted by catastrophes. In the large towns it was in fact the circles of council and merchant families which energetically protected the Jews at least from arrest without trial, mob law and the like in the interests of law and order within the town until far into the fourteenth century. The worsening of the Jews' position in the towns is reflected also in the circumstances of their living quarters and the property they owned. The real obligation to live in a spatially enclosed Jewish settlement within the town, which was locked up at night—the ghetto—only set in towards the end of the thirteenth century. After the persecution of the Jews in the fourteenth century, remote streets and corners were set apart for them. . . .

The merchant, following a tradition which went back to earliest times, was an itinerant foreign trader; he was not a local middleman who only supplied what was absolutely necessary in raw materials and goods that could not be manufactured in the town, in order to keep the town's own economy going. It was quite a different story with the worker. His field was not the world, but primarily the market of his own town. The goods the merchant procured from foreign parts aroused the suspicion and ill-will of the manual worker. In his view he could have satisfied local needs just as well with his own goods; but that was his view, not that of the buying public. This is the reason why quality goods which came from outside, and of which the local shopkeeper and worker had no specialised knowledge, were generally retailed by the same wholesale traders who procured the goods. We may remember the "cutting rights" of the valuable Flemish materials held by the leading men of the wholesale and foreign trade in the German towns which lasted until a circle of local retailers having specialised knowledge, and devoting itself to the retailing of Flemish cloths, was formed, which allowed the wholesale traders progressively to renounce their "cutting rights." This happened in Lübeck in the fourteenth century. We may also remember such a large-scale business as that of Antonius Koberger the publisher, with his agents in Paris and Lyons, who at the same time systematically sent out men who had been specially schooled in the job of retailing the published works. Finally there were those Nuremberg merchants in the Hansa who also retailed their richly varied collection of Italian silks, their valuable silver and golden ornaments decorated with jewels, and found a receptive market for them. But one can also understand the troubled complaint of the Lübeck shopkeepers to their council about 1400 that a Nuremberg merchant in Lübeck sold twenty times as much as any other, and as much in one day as a Lübecker did in a year!

If the shopkeeper was the sworn enemy of free trade for foreign merchants in his own town, and would have liked to see their wholesale selling limited, things were different for the workers—or at least more complicated. For it was not only the local market which determined the selling conditions for medieval urban trades. Certainly the provision trades—bakers and butchers—had their circle of customers in the town itself. But even the shoemakers also worked for export, as for instance those of Lübeck worked for the Norwegian market. This was even more true of the metal-working trades of towns like Nuremberg whose products in this field had a good and widespread reputation. The textile trade was least concerned with the home market—particularly in those places whose products had a world-wide reputation, such as the Flemish towns or Florence. The linen and fustian weavers in the small South German towns near Lake Constance, and the linen weavers in Saxon and Lusatian towns also worked for consumers they did not know, who might be hundreds of miles away. However, it was not the worker's job actually to supply the goods to the consumers, but that of commerce. The framework of the relation between worker and merchant was a system of credit which could often bring about the complete dependence of the worker on the merchant, as was the case in Flemish towns and in Florence. It was as no more than a reaction against such grave abuses—in cases where the weavers' enmity towards the merchant upper class in the large weaving towns was especially strong—that the most bloody conflicts ensued, even though the economic interests of these same groups of workers were related not to the urban but to the world market. Relationships were better where the merchant with capital did not make contracts with individual workers but with a whole union, where it was thus a question of collective contracts. The first instance known of such a contract was in 1424—between the Lübeck amber-turners and a group of merchants for the selling of the greatest part of their production; Venice, Nuremberg, Frankfurt am Main and Cologne were the projected selling areas. The manual worker was really best off if he was himself in a position to carry on outside sales. But this was only possible for a few workers who produced quite valuable wares. Goldsmiths from Cologne, Augsburg and Nuremberg went in great numbers to the Frankfurt fair, where they found their best buyers in the international wholesale trade which was there to buy in bulk. But the trade of goldsmith counted as the most elevated trade in any case; it was no coincidence that many members of this trade transferred to the merchant upper class. Nor that the only surviving business book of a medieval manual worker belonged to a goldsmith. This was Stefan Maignow, who died in 1500, a man who failed to attain the degree of importance and artistic skill possessed by his colleagues in Nuremberg, Augsburg and Cologne, but who had numerous customers among the noble families in the region of Constance who bought eagerly from him, even if they were not quite so keen on paying up.

Shopkeepers and those workers who, unlike the weavers, were economically independent and mainly interested in the local market were, with their xenophobic tendencies, the real eulogists of the urban economy. Their aim was to assure all the advantages of the local market for local people and to organise foreigners' selling in such a way that local trade should not be at any disadvantage on account of it—the foreign merchant, if they had their way, would only have been permitted to sell wholesale. In this way he was robbed of a large number of potential customers in the town; moreover, on account of the prohibition on business with foreigners, he was eventually dependent on unions and shopkeepers as his only customers. They were, therefore, exceptionally favored. Yet the simple fact that trade dominated the economic, social and even political aspects of the more important medieval towns meant that such aims remained unrealised, or were only tolerated and partially achieved later on. Even the economically independent worker was himself in all ways dependent on the merchants, and on the merchant-dominated council. A Lübeck master-baker baked his bread in a bakery belonging to one or other of the old families, sold it in the booths by St Mary's church, which were at the disposal of the council, and lived in a house for which, as a rule, he paid a percentage to a distinguished merchant, or for which, as in Cologne, he only paid rent. Although the individual worker was of no consequence by comparison with the ruling families, the organised association of the workers of any particular trade was.

For this reason alone the development of the guild is one of the most important problems in the history of the German town; it is highly improbable in view of the element of necessary compromise and the variety of individual development that in Germany, or in Europe, it was solved by equal bargaining by the three parties involved—the lord of the town, its council and the workers themselves. In the towns of Flanders and Brabant, where a thorough-going sovereign power soon gained influence on working conditions alongside the patrician council, several attempts at a solution were made within a small area. Nevertheless, for Germany, the following characteristics of the development may claim a certain validity. To begin with it was the lord of the town who, aided by his supporters within the town, exercised what was frequently a very effective ruling power over the trades; the best examples of this are the regulations of the older town laws of the lord of Strasbourg. Very soon, as early as the twelfth century, the developing merchant councils exercised similar functions, above all the control of the provision trades and the market. Limitations as to the number of members in a particular trade resulted less from the efforts of the workers themselves than from the official power of the authorities. This was due either to the fact that a fixed number of trading concessions were officially granted to the members of a trade when the town was founded—as happened in Strehlen,

Silesia, in 1292, where thirty-four butchers' stalls, thirty-two bread stalls and thirty cobblers' stalls were set up with the express condition that this number was not to be exceeded—or to the fact that the town council wished to limit the numbers in a particular trade for other reasons such as control, or even punishment. In Lübeck in the fourteenth century the council reduced the number of needle-makers to fourteen and the butchers from one hundred to fifty because of their part in disturbances. In the earliest documents which determine the relations between the government and the traders, it was an important fact that the authorities disposed of and supervised everything concerning the trades. Nevertheless as soon as the members of a trade claimed and received the right to belong to a group recognised by the authorities, wide opportunities were opened up for their initiative and effort by means of which they could build up their groups in a way both useful and advantageous to the members. The occasional limits on the number of members of a trade by the authorities at the same time gave very valuable economic privileges to the lucky ones who were left in; only those authorised could practise a trade. This also meant compulsory membership of a guild—and without membership no-one could ply his trade. Only the authorities could grant this right; they also decided whether and how far the guild might exercise its own jurisdiction over offenses against the constitution of the guild or its regulations.

The guild could only retain its charter if it gave the authorities no excuse to intervene. If the interests of the buying townspeople were damaged through the exploitation of the guild's preferential position the guild might be dissolved, as the bakers and butchers of Erfurt found in 1264. In such cases the council at the very least would appoint free masters. On account of this ever-present threat, but also certainly on account of a feeling of duty towards the honor of the trade, the older guild ordinances in particular lay great stress on their obligation to protect the customer. Again and again, whether in Basel or Berlin, in Regensburg or Soest, concern for the quality of the goods is particularly stressed as being the main purpose of the guilds, in guild documents of the thirteenth century. They were also concerned that a good product should be sold at a fair price. In order to achieve both these aims, the process of production was supervised from the buying of the raw materials to the selling of the goods. A careful training of the future master as a journeyman and assistant, and the preparation of the masterpiece as proof of sufficient ability also worked in the same direction. Of course the training and its termination could be wilfully interfered with (as sometimes occurred later on) in order to make acceptance more difficult and in order to keep out new competitors. This leads us to consider those measures taken by the guilds in the interests of their members. Here, in guild circles, there actually existed that spirit which it would be a mistake to look for in the whole economic life of the town—the striving after a burgher livelihood. "Trades were introduced so that everyone could earn his daily bread from them" runs the so-called *Reformatio Sigismundi* of 1438. The aim was not a general levelling of incomes, but, where possible, to do so within a particular trade. On this account every member was supposed as far as possible to have the same working conditions in buying raw materials, working hours, number of assistants and shops. And because of this any attempt to advertise, or to tempt customers away from another man, was strictly forbidden in the guilds.

However, not all the provisions of the guild regulations were entirely effective. In spite of all the regulations there were rich workers and poor workers. Where the guild and its inclinations most prevailed it was not to the advantage of the town. The case of Freiburg im Breisgau is effective warning against overestimating the guild economy—for this, and not urban economy, is what it should be called, since the urban economy in reality remained far more influenced by commerce and economic aims opposed to guild interests. Here, where once distinguished merchants had labored to establish the town, the old foreign trade connections of the town were cut in pieces after the victory of the guilds around 1470 ("with great rapidity and with results that were carried too far") and the town strove after economic self-sufficiency. Along with trade the formation of capital was depressed. It all came down to the regulation of competition amongst the workers by themselves; each worker became an official suspiciously obeserving the other. Whoever lived in the town had to be organised in some way. It was only carrying the policy to its logical conclusion when the town itself was "closed" in the same way that the guilds had been "closed"—that is by having their membership restricted—the entry of foreigners into the town was made more difficult by increasing the guild and civic taxes. The result was that the old town of Freiburg which in 1385 had between 9,000 and 9,500 inhabitants decreased in size until in 1500 it had about 5,700; the number of houses diminished by a third, houses were turned into gardens and in the years between 1494 and 1520 between one-seventh and one-eighth of the entire housing came under the hammer! Even in some of the most important trading towns, such as Basel or Cologne the guilds' economic aims gained ground towards the end of the Middle Ages. In 1521 a series of reforms took place in Basel, likewise at the expense of commerce which made all foreign competition with local products impossible. In Cologne too, though to a lesser degree, concessions were made to the guilds' economic program—in every case visibly harming the economic importance of the towns. But Nuremberg—the healthiest of late medieval towns—knew how to suppress the influence of the guilds on its economy. It was not an "urban economy" but a free-trade economy that Nuremberg had to thank for its dominant position. And nobody fared better than the trades themselves in the process. The merchant-appointed council pressed for the highest quality in craft products, but at the same time, by virture of its commercial efforts, it guaranteed for them more of a world market than a local one.

In economic matters, the supposed harmony of the medieval town was broken by sharp differences between the commercial and the working classes. Obviously this contrast was reflected in the political field; the guildsmen could only achieve practical realization of their economic ideal if they shared in membership of the council, or occupied all of it themselves. The conflicts between guilds and patriciate often began in political terms—the guilds formed the core of the resistance to the actual or alleged financial mismanagement of the council. The story of the Flemish towns has shown with what bitterness these conflicts were fought out; here, too, the inseparability of political, economic and social aims within the opposing classes is clear. The conflicts also took a particularly acute form in German towns which had a large number of weavers—Cologne and Brunswick for example. Almost everywhere in the south-western towns in the thirteenth and fourteenth centuries the guilds gained some degree of a share in the government of the town. Sometimes they were directly represented by councillors on a council which had previously been the exclusive preserve of the leading families; at other times there were two councils in existence at the same time, the old and the new; in which case the constitution provided that the new council should be consulted on certain questions concerning the town. It also happened that the previous council was completely abolished so that the guilds formed the group from which the new council was to be elected. This occurred in Cologne in 1396, when twenty-two political guilds or *Gaffeln* were formed for election to the council. In each of these one of the commercial guilds was the main guild with which the others were associated. The first group was known as the weavers guild, along with related trades; it had the largest number of councillors to elect—four. The remaining twenty-one groups elected thirty-two between them. A further forty-four representatives of the groups were to be called in on the more important matters. All the inhabitants of the town who were not members of a guild—which included also the merchants and leading families—had to associate themselves with one of the groups. Radical as this change of constitution appears, it turned out in practice to be less so. Actually it was still the merchants and not the workers who ruled in Cologne after 1396—although they were prepared to make all kinds of concessions to the lower classes.

This was true of most of the larger trading towns in the fifteenth century. In a town like Lübeck, where the constitutional demands of the workers and those merchants who did not belong to the select families were not met, and where it became clear, at the beginning of the fifteenth century, that the workers simply could not do without the leading families' centuries-long experience in foreign politics, the leading class went an extraordinarily long way towards meeting the economic wishes of the workers and shopkeepers. In German towns the weaver proletariat did not have anything like the importance it did in Flanders, and independent master-craftsmen, often of sound economic standing, stood alongside the patriciate; even so a *rapprochement* was all the more possible because towards the end of the fifteenth century the upper section of guild-masters, which also had a share in the municipal offices, was terrified by the growing ill-will amongst the depressed population. Journeymen who could not manage to become masters, day-laborers and people who had to earn their bread without the protection of a guild played a dangerous role in this. Their fury was directed both against the patriciate and the guild-masters who ruled alongside them. Resentment over increasing burdens imposed on the small man by the monied classes through indirect taxation already mingled with the simple hate borne by the have-nots towards the haves. The council of Erfurt fled before this hate in 1509; in 1513 seven Cologne councillors ended up on the scaffold. Strasbourg, after dramatic struggles and endless compromises between the upper class and the guilds, had arrived in 1482 at a permanent constitutional reform of finely calculated equilibrium, and with its cautious financial politics and the goodwill of all groups participating in its apparently democratic, but in fact oligarchic constitution, appeared to the leading spirits of around 1500 like an oasis in the desert. In the famous words of Erasmus, he believed he could see here a monarchy without a tyrant, an aristocracy without factions, a democracy without uproar, wealth without luxury and happiness without presumption. . . .

INERTIA AND MOTION IN EARLY MODERN TIMES

part **III**

7. THE PEASANT GRINDS ON

As we advance in time it is crucial to retain some perspective and to recall that Europe remained an overwhelmingly rural society right through the eighteenth century. Agriculture was still the principal occupation of most people, and even those who might be classified as nonpeasants found that the quality of their lives depended in large measure on the success or failure of seasonal crops. One important fact began to emerge, however, which suggests a long-range theme in European social history. In England and the western portions of the mainland, methods of cultivation and patterns of landholding were changing to the extent that the entire notion of feudalism became of dubious applicability to the lands west of the Elbe River. In central and eastern Europe, on the other hand, the serf status of the peasantry was if anything retrenched. By the time of the French Revolution, therefore, it had already become more appropriate to conceive of an evolving social and economic dichotomy between West and East than to dwell on the longstanding ideological division between a Catholic South and a Protestant North. Thus it is not surprising that the political and industrial revolutions which began in the late eighteenth century were to have a more immediate impact in Western Europe where the process of social transformation was less hindered.

C. B. A. *Behrens* examines Western Europe, particularly France, from the age of Louis XIV to the French Revolution. She portrays a society in which there still existed no industrial cushion against the calamity of poor harvests. The European population was periodically stalked by the twin monsters of war and poor harvest, and plagued by their greedy off-

207

springs: conscription, taxation and starvation. This is hardly an idyllic picture of country life, nor is it intended to be. Poverty was the primary fact of life. The volatility of the peasants, or at least their latent hostility toward the privileged, is consequently not difficult to grasp.

W. H. Bruford looks to the German lands where the first intimations of change were to be detected in the western sections. Although Prussia and Austria were not without their enlightened administrators in the eighteenth century, the practical results for the rural laborer were seldom commensurate with the visions of reform. In large areas serfdom remained very much intact, whatever the variations of nomenclature, and farming was often as primitive as ever. For peasants under these circumstances, life literally remained a struggle for survival.

Jerome Blum considers the deteriorating condition of the Russian peasantry. Millions of people were constantly being pressed down into a serfdom barely distinguishable from the most wretched slavery. When freed from legal or moral restraints, masters were left to buy and sell their human property at will—in a manner much like the American slave market of the same era. At the complete mercy of his lord, the serf was thus subject to the extremes of kindness and cruelty, his personal fate being entirely dependent on the whims of his social superior.

These readings confirm the impression that change, not stagnation, produces the stinging indignities and frustrations which may lead to revolt. In this case the implications are clear. European society was unconsciously preparing itself for a long season of turmoil which would begin in the West and, taking different forms, would eventually spread eastward.

C. B. A. BEHRENS

Rural Labor In the West

THE PEASANT PROBLEM

In every country in Europe in the eighteenth century, the vast majority of people earned their living from the land. In France the category commonly described as peasants—that is, everyone who was not a nobleman, a cleric, or engaged full-time in some occupation other than agriculture— must have included by 1789 some twenty-two or more million souls out of a total population reckoned at twenty-six million.

The civilization on which the eighteenth century prided itself was the prerogative of only a very small minority, even in France, where the educated were more numerous than in most other countries. For the vast majority, life was a continual, and often a losing, battle to wring a bare livelihood from the soil. The calculations of governments and of private individuals revolved round the harvest. In France in the eighteenth century, the Contrôle Général (the department responsible for financial and economic affairs) issued every year to each of four hundred local officials a form divided into columns—one for wheat, one for rye, one for oats, etc.—with instructions to note the amounts that were harvested in the current year and that remained over from the previous harvest. In the words of Professor Labrousse: "the problem of grain dominated all the other problems." [1]

Bad harvests, though the substantial landowners and merchants benefited from the rising prices, meant shortage if not starvation for most people, in town and country alike; for most people, in France as in the greater part of the rest of Europe, either owned no land, or owned an amount insufficient to support a family, or worked land belonging to other people on terms that, for the most part, barely sufficed to meet their needs even when times were good.

The price of bread (and of wine in the wine-growing areas) was always

C. B. A. Behrens, *The Ancien Régime* (New York: Harcourt, Brace, and World, Inc., 1967), pp. 25–42.

[1] C. E. Labrousse, *La Crise de l'Economie Française* (Paris 1943), vol. I, p. 15.

the determining factor in the economy. As it rose in times of scarcity it diminished the amount that the poor could spend on other things. Consequently, agricultural calamities had repercussions on the urban and rural industries, which gave employment in the towns and supplemented that in the countryside, and whose products the majority in town and country could only afford when the price of bread was low or moderate.

Bad harvests also had repercussions on the government's revenues, since the yield of the taxes fell, and on its projects for moving about and provisioning its armies. In addition, they created administrative difficulties, since people who are starving have various ways of making themselves a nuisance to the authorities. Throughout the greater part of Europe in the eighteenth century peasant revolts were endemic. In some of the countries of central and eastern Europe—in Bohemia in 1772, in Russia during the Pugachev revolt of the following year—there were times when they reached the proportions of civil war. They had done so in France in the reign of Louis XIV, but this did not happen again until the spring of 1789, partly, no doubt, because there was no general famine, but partly also, it has been suggested, because the royal administration became more efficient. Scarcity nevertheless remained common, and hunger the fear and experience of most people. In bad times in France the unemployed and starving would band together and roam the countryside in search of food. They would attack the wagons carrying the grain to market and break into the barns where it was stored. Illiterate and brutalized by misery, the victims of irrational fears and superstitions which, if the strong hand of authority were removed, could set whole districts on the march against the scapegoats of the moment, they were always a potential menace to law, order and property, even in France where, if Ségur may be believed (and the facts seem to support him), they were normally more docile, and less hostile to the landlords, than in the serf-owning countries of Prussia, Russia and the Habsburg dominions.

In these circumstances, no government could be indifferent to the fate of the peasants, and none, the French government included, in principle ever was. Self-interest and Christian morality alike preached the same lesson: that the peasant had to be helped as far as possible in times of natural calamity; that he had to be protected against exploitation by the landlords; that he should not be subjected to unduly heavy taxation; above all, that the government should rigidly control the grain trade and maintain buffer stocks, in order to mitigate the effects of bad harvests and their attendant troubles.

Between the ideals of the paternalistic monarchies and the treatment the peasant received in practice, however, there was always a large gap, since the monarchs continually found themselves forced or tempted into pursuing policies contrary to the peasants' interests, and were unable or unwilling to prevent their officials and other classes of the population from doing the same. Until the days of the Enlightenment, and indeed often after-wards, the absolute monarchs were given to the pursuit of glory by means of war and conspicuous consumption. Louis XIV built great palaces, kept a splendid court, and—at vastly greater expense—maintained an army that, at its peak, is said to have numbered a million men, of whom one-third were mercenaries but who still had to be paid and fed. This was a larger army than the French ever raised again before the present century, and in Louis' long period of personal rule, which lasted for fifty-five years, war, after the first seven, was almost continuous. The enormous cost of his military operations inevitably fell, for the greater part, on the bulk of the population which consisted of peasants.

In the reign of Louis XIV, the peasant thus paid heavily for the glory of his king and country, and he continued to do so throughout the eigh-teenth century. Apart, however, from the prestige of belonging to a great nation (which there is no reason to suppose he appreciated), the sums of which he was mulcted brought him in no return, even in the long run, since they contributed nothing to the productivity of the land from which he lived and did much to diminish his own incentive to increase it.

Since the days of Colbert, the French government, like most other gov-ernments, had always been aware that its war potential turned on the sums it could raise in taxes and that these, in their turn, were largely dependent on the amount of wealth to be taxed. The way to increase a nation's wealth, however, had seemed to be to increase its shipping and foreign trade, particularly the colonial trades, and its industries as a means to trade. The example of the Dutch had greatly fostered this point of view. In the seventeenth century they had achieved a degree of power inter-nationally that was wholly disproportionate to their numbers—in 1700 their population was only about two million—and they owed this to their wealth, which had enabled them to maintain a large army of mercenaries and the greatest navy and merchant fleet in the world. Their wealth, however, had been built up principally on their fishing, their merchant ships and their trade. By the time of Louis XIV's death, the British were supplanting the Dutch as the largest shipowning and naval power, and their experience seemed to point the same moral, which was reinforced by the experience of private individuals. Great fortunes did not come from the profits of agriculture. When they were not accumulated from the perquisites of office or the manipulation of the royal revenues, they came principally from commerce, in particular the expanding commerce with the colonies. The spectacular successes achieved by these means inspired successive French governments with the conviction that commerce and colonies were essential to national greatness. As Choiseul, then Louis XV's minister, said in 1759, France could no longer be considered a first-class power because the British in that year had destroyed the French navy, conquered the French colonies and driven French merchant ships off the seas. These facts, Choiseul concluded, showed that the rank of a first-class power could belong only to a nation that "possessed the empire of the sea." [2]

While, therefore, the French government was not indifferent to the fate of the peasants, it nevertheless always subordinated the needs of agriculture, in the short term, to the needs of war, and in the long term, to the needs of trade and industry as it understood them. Colbert had recruited skilled workers from other countries by means of tax concessions and other benefits. In his day and on various occasions afterwards, the French government had sunk large sums in founding, developing and maintaining its colonies (tasks which in Britain were left to private enterprise), as well as in providing for their defense. It gave subsidies to merchants and manufacturers, whom it also virtually exempted from direct taxation, because, as in other countries until the turn of the eighteenth century (England included), the administration was incapable of assessing, even approximately, incomes derived from any source except land, and the arbitrary taxation of commercial wealth, it was feared, might kill the goose that laid the golden eggs. The government recouped itself by imposing heavy taxes on the sale of articles of general consumption, particularly wine and salt, and by laying the burden of direct taxes on the land.

The royal taxes hung like a millstone round the peasant's neck (and also, contrary to what is generally believed, round the necks of most noble landowners). The proportion of the peasant's means of livelihood that was taken from him in direct taxes varied so greatly from one part of France to another, and from one category of peasants to another, that no general estimate of it is possible. It is nevertheless significant that Turgot, when he was *Intendant* in the Limousin, attempted to estimate it in 1766 in relation to the peasant proprietors in two districts for which he could find sufficient data, and concluded—as a result of several different methods of calculation, all of which he claimed yielded comparable results—that these proprietors were paying from 50 to 60 percent of the gross value of their produce in direct taxation (that is, the value of the produce before deduction had been made for seed, which Professor Labrousse estimates required in general from a quarter to a fifth of the harvest). Turgot was a meticulous writer, and on this occasion was engaged in an official correspondence, with every reason to be accurate. His estimate is likely to be as good as any. Its purpose was to prove that the province for which he was responsible was much more heavily taxed than some others in the more prosperous regions of northwestern France—the so-called *pays de grande culture,* where the land was mainly let to tenant-farmers. He did not, however, believe that taxation was generally much lighter in the re-

[2] Quoted in Z. E. Rashed, *The Peace of Paris, 1763* (Liverpool 1951), p. 105.

maining four-sevenths of France where, as in the Limousin, share-cropping prevailed.

No peasant was exempt from the direct taxes unless, being wholly destitute, he had nothing to give, and their destructive effects were greatly increased by the ways in which they were assessed and collected. In France, as in most other absolute monarchies, it was impossible to induce the monarchs to relate their projects to their resources. For this reason, and because of the administrative difficulties, the direct taxes were never adjusted to the capacity of the tax-payers. The principal direct tax, the *Taille,* which fell only on the peasants, was imposed as a lump sum on the provinces (apart from certain provinces with special privileges), and was then divided up among the parishes where the responsibility for paying it was collective. If the collectors failed to raise the stipulated sums, or absconded with the money, the richest inhabitants had to make good the difference, until Turgot caused the law to be amended in 1775. Not surprisingly, this destructive provision, as Turgot described it, gave every peasant of substance the incentive to leave the village for the town. It was rare, Tocqueville said, to find more than one generation of rich peasants in the villages.

Whether the royal taxes were heavier in the eighteenth century than they had been in the reign of Louis XIV is a question which people at the time and later often debated. Tocqueville believed that they were, because new taxes, or analogous impositions such as the *corvée* (that is, forced labor without payment on the roads), were continually added to the existing ones. No attempt has been made to assemble the data which might make a judgement possible. Because of a combination of causes, however, among which one must give taxation an important place, the French did not invest capital in the modernization of their agriculture as the English did. The English had begun in the seventeenth century to embark on those agricultural improvements which were to astonish the world in the 1760s— the enclosures; the experiments with new crops and new implements; above all, "the *combination* of animal and arable husbandry," [3] which on the one hand made more manure available, thus increasing the yield of the land and diminishing the need to leave it fallow, and on the other hand, by means of root crops and better pasture, made it possible to improve the quality and augment the number of animals.

The prerequisite of these achievements, however, was the abolition of the communal system of agriculture and of the so-called *servitudes collectives* (the obligation on all landlords to plant the same crops and sow and harvest at the same time), in favor of individual ownership. The individual's strips of land, scattered over the open fields, had to be consolidated

[3] Charles Wilson, *England's Apprenticeship* (London 1965), p. 143.

and enclosed. In France in the eighteenth century, for reasons that must be discussed later, it proved impossible to make significant headway with this task. What was known as *vaine pâture,* the right of all the inhabitants of the village, the *seigneur* included, to pasture their beasts on the common fields after the harvest, precluded the enclosures which were the prerequisite of the new agriculture. Most of France, in consequence, continued to remain imprisoned in what was known to French agronomists in the eighteenth century as the "infernal circle" of the fallow land. Because so large an amount of land was always fallow, as much as possible of the rest had to be put under grain. This meant a shortage of pasture and, in turn, a shortage of animals. A shortage of animals, however, meant a shortage of manure; and the shortage of manure made the fallow seem imperative.

This state of affairs condemned the bulk of even the nobility to poverty by the English standards of the time. It would be contrary to common sense to assume that (apart from the small number of people with very large estates or access to sources of wealth other than agriculture) the noble landowners could have dissociated their fortunes from the fortunes of the cultivators of the land. Towards the end of the Ancien Régime this indeed became a platitude in enlightened circles. In Turgot's words, "When the post-horse falls down from exhaustion, the rider falls also, though the horse is more to be pitied." [4]

It is commonly implied by French historians that the privileged orders were principally to blame for the peasants' condition, and that the taxes imposed on peasants by the church and the nobility were as great as, if not greater than, those imposed by the state. Proverbially it is the last straw that breaks the camel's back, and in this sense the impression may be justified. It is hardly so in any other. The church took its *dîme,* or tithe, levying it on the gross product of the harvest on all land, whether belonging to peasant, bourgeois or nobleman. It seemed a heavy imposition, but it was not usually as much as a tenth and thus lighter than in England. The *seigneurs* took their feudal dues. These, however, were as much a consequence as a cause of the general poverty.

When the National Assembly put an end to these dues on 4 August 1789 it declared that in so doing it had "totally abolished the feudal régime." In fact, as is generally agreed, by that time the relations of peasant and *seigneur* were in many respects no longer feudal, however feudalism is understood. In France in the eighteeth century, the *seigneur,* or lord of the manor, did not, as in central and eastern Europe, work his land himself with serf labor. As in England, he let out all except what he needed for his own use to tenants with whom he concluded a commercial

---

[4] Turgot, *Oeuvres,* ed. Schelle (Paris 1913–23), vol. V, p. 168.

bargain, though these tenants, unlike the English, were for the greater part not tenant-farmers but *métayers* or share-croppers. His feudal dues were rights which the law allowed him, in accordance with the principle of *nulle terre sans seigneur,* over land which was to this extent dependent on him—in his *mouvance,* as it was called at the time—but which was not in any other respect his property.

In the terminology of the eighteenth century, which has continued in use ever since, it was land which the peasant was said to "own," and in total it is generally thought to have accounted by 1789 for about 35 percent of the cultivated land of France (some 20 percent of the rest being owned by the nobility, some 30 percent by the bourgeoisie on the outskirts of the towns, and most of what remained by the church). These so-called peasant proprietors, being very numerous, owned plots usually too small to support a family, so that they were forced to supplement their means of livelihood in other ways: for example, by share-cropping. Indeed, the plots were often so small that the term proprietor, when applied to their possessors, must seem a mockery. It was, nevertheless, the current term, and was justified in the sense that the peasant so described could not be evicted from his land, and could sell, bequeath or mortgage it as he saw fit. He was, however, subjected, as for that matter the *seigneur* was himself (for ownership in the modern sense was unknown in the countryside), to the *servitudes collectives* and to feudal dues.

The dues which the peasant proprietor paid to the *seigneur* were in part analogous to a money rent, which was generally very small. Sometimes, though much more rarely, they included payments in kind, which could be heavy. Usually they imposed on the peasant obligations such as to grind his corn in the *seigneur's* mill, to bake his bread in the *seigneur's* oven, to allow the *seigneur* special grazing rights and rights to hunt over his land.

It was obligations of this kind that were principally objected to. They were a constant source of damage, annoyance and frustration, and increasingly resented, as many *seigneurs* (though what proportion of the total we do not know) took to leasing them out to agents who had an interest in enforcing the letter of the law and an eye to claims that had been allowed to lapse.

It was, nevertheless, continually pointed out that the *seigneurs* did not derive a material benefit from their dues at all proportionate to the harm or the bitterness they caused. This was the theme of a famous work, written by a certain Boncerf, and called *Les inconvénients des droits féodaux,* which was published in 1776. Boncerf maintained that the mediocre sums which the dues on an average brought in were eaten up by the costs of enforcing them, of keeping the records, and of financing the interminable lawsuits to which they gave rise, which descended from father to son, and which, as he said, "devour the *seigneurs,* the vassals and the land." There seems no reason to doubt that, in general, this was true. On the rare occasions when the profits of commercial agriculture were large enough to drive the point home, there were landowners who saw the sense in Boncerf's thesis and allowed their dues to lapse. Public opinion among the *seigneurs,* however, in general remained in favor of them because, as is usual in poor agrarian societies, tradition, prestige and power over other human beings were valued more highly than material progress.

To be a *seigneur* was a great thing, and the dues were a symbol of authority. So it had always seemed to the rich bourgeois, who, for generations before the Revolution, had bought *seigneuries* for this reason, and also because their possession, after a lapse of time, conferred a prescriptive right of entry into the nobility. So it seemed, too, to the established aristocrats. Money was not everything, as Chateaubriand's father thought, in common with the rest of his class. Coming from a distinguished but impoverished family, he rehabilitated the family fortunes by entering the shipping business. He had a share in various merchant ships that plied between France and the West Indies during the War of the Austrian Succession and the Seven Years War, when most of such ships were driven off the seas. In these circumstances, freight rates could rise to astronomical heights and M. de Chateaubriand evidently benefited from them. He appears to have been a person of considerable business skill. Nevertheless, when he bought back the family estates, as his son tells us in his *Memoires d'Outre-tombe,* his proud and authoritarian temperament found its greatest satisfaction in the meticulous exaction of his dues.

When Arthur Young, in his travels, once met a peasant woman, whom he discovered to be twenty-eight years old though she had the appearance of sixty or seventy, she exclaimed to him: "Les tailles et les droits nous écrasent." [5] This cry has echoed down the centuries, repeated by one generation of historians after another, who have usually assumed, as the peasant woman doubtless did herself, that the state of affairs which provoked it was due to some peculiar degree of wickedness in the nobility and the high officials of the church. Tocqueville, a repentant aristocrat, whose indictment of the Ancien Régime has formed the basis of most later attacks on it, nevertheless knew better. Selfishness, he said, was a vice as old as the world and no more characteristic of one form of society than another, though it manifested itself in different societies in different ways. Comparing the society of pre-Revolutionary France with that of America at the beginning of the nineteenth century, he noted how strong had been the sense of family and kinship in France, and the ties of personal loyalty. These, he believed, could elicit a degree of individual self-sacrifice rarely found in the new societies. On the other hand, he noted how weak in the

[5] Young, *op. cit.,* p. 173.

old societies had been the sense of duty to the community and of obligation to one's neighbor.

The peasants had occasion to know this, nothwithstanding the communal organization of agriculture, which was naturally, in a society so organized, used by the strong to oppress the weak. At every level of social life, the people with the greatest wealth and influence framed, twisted or evaded the law to their own advantage. The mass of the peasantry was far from being the only victim of these circumstances, though it suffered most; nor, apart from the state, were the church and the nobility its only oppressors. The record of the bourgeois, who owned many *seigneuries* and farmed the dues in many others, was no better and is often said to have been worse. That of the small class of rich peasants was in some ways worst of all.

The village, like every other group, had its hierarchy. In the more prosperous districts there grew up a class of substantial tenant-farmers, comparable to those in England; but even over the greater part of the country, where the system of share-cropping prevailed, the villages had their *coqs de village*. These were well-to-do peasants, possessing carts and oxen, and enough land to feed their families. They could sometimes even save enough to buy themselves an office in the neighboring town, which served their children as a stepping stone for the ascent of the social ladder. In his analysis of the members of the Paris Parlement in the eighteenth century, Professor Bluche tells us that it was not uncommon for peasant families to climb into the nobility in three generations. No class, however, drove harsher bargains than these successful peasants, or showed more skill and effrontery in cheating and intimidating the tax-collectors; and the burdens they evaded, unlike those of the nobility which was separately assessed, fell directly and immediately on their neighbors because of the collective responsibility for the *Taille*.

In the poverty-stricken societies of eighteenth-century Europe, it seemed a law of nature, as Quesnay, the founder of the school of Physiocrats, said, that "A man can only acquire wealth by means of the wealth he already possesses." [6] Those who started destitute were more than likely to remain so. Money and education conferred advantages that grew in a geometrical progression, while the poor and ignorant were pushed to the wall. Tocqueville said of the mass of the peasantry that civilization seemed to turn against them alone. They were the predestined victims of a royal policy directed to the pursuit of objects other than agriculture; of a conservatism, of which admittedly they were themselves the principal exponents, that blocked the road to change; and of an administration in which, notwithstanding the paternalistic ideals, educated officials of goodwill were too

[6] *François Quesnay et la Physiocratie* (Institut National d'Études Démographiques, Paris 1958), vol. II, p. 537.

few, and other officials too ignorant, poorly paid and open to bribery and intimidation, to protect the weak against the strong.

It had always been so, and as a result the misery of the peasants had generally been accepted as part of the natural order of things. As one eighteenth-century writer expressed it: "The habit of suffering they have contracted has killed in them the knowledge that they suffer. It is a kind of ignorance of their misery, and if they know that they are unhappy they know it more or less as we know that we must die. Here is an admirable arrangement of nature; if she causes men to be born in misery she gives them the disposition that makes them able to endure it and even to forget it." [7] . . .

WALTER H. BRUFORD

Country Life In Germany

THE AGRARIAN ECONOMY

. . . The peasant, it will be seen, besides being dependent on the vagaries of the weather and exposed more than any other class to the ravages of war, was less of a free agent than the average townsman, being more closely bound by the routine of the little society into which he was born. On the other hand he was seldom in danger of actual starvation, as a "free" townsman might be, and although he had to work hard, he never experienced the still more unhappy situation of being out of work. Naturally his personal dependence was looked upon as a great evil by the liberals of the Aufklärung, while agricultural reformers criticized the inefficiency of forced and therefore scamped labor. We meet with many reflections in literature of the movement for the freeing of the serfs. In the strict legal sense there were no actual "serfs" (Leibeigene) in Germany like those of the early Middle Ages and of classical antiquity. The feudal dues and

W. H. Bruford, *Germany in the Eighteenth Century: The Social Background of the Literary Revival,* 1st ed.: 1935 (New York: Cambridge University Press, 1965), pp. 111–24.

[7] Quoted in Robert Mauzi, *L'idée du Bonheur au XVIIIᵉ Siècle* (Paris 1960), p. 156.

services still exacted were a burden on the *land,* not on the *person* of the peasant, and had mostly been commuted for money. Most of the restrictions on their freedom had had their origin not in medieval serfdom but in later developments, particularly in the "Gutsherrschaft," of the lands east of the Elbe. But even if the peasants were at worst only what Knapp has called "erbuntertänig" (hereditarily subject) it was natural that the reformers should use the familiar word serfdom for a relationship which in practice was very little better than slavery. The movement for the freeing of the serfs made little progress in Germany until the nineteenth century.

It was only from the prince of the territory that the peasant could hope for relief. He did not always look to him in vain, for in Prussia and Austria the state needed a flourishing peasantry, to provide healthy recruits for the growing armies, and billets in their houses and barns for the soldiers. Actuated in the main by these motives the Prussian and Austrian rulers endeavored by a number of ordinances to prevent the confiscation of peasants' land (Bauernlegung), but they were not so successful, or perhaps so desirous of success, when they joined in the attempts at the abolition of serfdom that began to be made in Germany in this century. The demesne peasants were freed in Prussia in 1798 and the following years, but the rest did not obtain their freedom until between 1808 and 1816, and then only at the cost of concessions that made the landowners' position even better than before. In Austria, in spite of Joseph II's humane attempts, the peasants were not freed till 1848, but other German-speaking territories were not so backward. In the north and west, where conditions were better to begin with, it was only a small step to release the peasant from feudal dues and give him an independent holding, yet here too it needed the impetus of the French Revolution to induce the peasants to assert their claims.

To pass now from the legal to the technical aspect of country life, we may note that there are two extreme types of agricultural system, the primitive or self-sufficing one and the modern capitalistic type, in which the agricultural unit, a larger and more highly organized one than before, produces mainly for export, and is consequently obliged to purchase many of the commodities it requires, instead of producing them itself. In eighteenth-century Germany the former type prevailed almost exclusively, and it continued to do so till quite the middle of the nineteenth century. The main aim was, both on small holdings and on large estates, to grow what the owners and their families and dependents themselves needed for their upkeep. Any surplus there might be would be sold in whatever market was available, but commercial considerations were not paramount.

There were of course exceptions to this rule, conditions naturally varying considerably over so large an area. Three zones may be distinguished, one of small independent holdings in the southwest, one of dairy farms in Hanover and Schleswig-Holstein, and one of large estates in the colonized east. Of these the dairy farms, under Dutch supervision, early became dependent on trade owing to their specialized nature, but the small farmers of the southwest were for the most part content if they could feed themselves. Even the large estates of the east only exported a small proportion of their produce. Sombart estimates [1] . . . that the annual export of corn from Danzig in this century was only about as much as could be grown on one hundred thousand acres, or half one Prussian "Kreis"; yet Danzig was the main port for the whole of the eastern corn land. The agricultural population consumed about two-thirds of their total production even in 1850; out of the remaining third came not only the amount exported, but also the supplies of the towns. The smaller towns very often needed little from outside, for they grew a large proportion of their food themselves, and in the larger towns too (in Frankfort, for instance—see *Dichtung und Wahrheit!*) the citizens had large gardens and vineyards outside the gates, while some kept cattle or pigs on the common and in the woods. There had been edicts since the fifteenth and sixteenth centuries forbidding citizens to allow their pigs to run about the streets at all hours of the day and night, but pig sties were to be seen in front of the houses in Berlin till nearly the end of the seventeenth century,[2] and small places like Weimar still had their "town herdsman" at the end of the eighteenth century.

When we know that the claims made on the productivity of the land were so modest, we do not expect to find very advanced methods of cultivation in practice, nor indeed had the methods in vogue in Germany at this time progressed very far beyond the standard of the Middle Ages. In this respect, however, Germany differed little from the rest of Europe. England only began to introduce rational methods on a large scale, following Holland's example, in the second half of the eighteenth century. We know from Arthur Young's writings that a large proportion of the English land under tillage lay in open fields, the same rotation being used on all soils alike. These village farms were run by associations of agricultural partners who occupied intermixed strips, and cultivated the whole under common rules of cropping, or "field constraint." The obstinate conservatism of the farmers added to the inherent defects of this system. "In 1768 turnips and clover were still unknown in many parts of the country; and their full use only appreciated in the eastern counties." "Turnips remained, at the close of the eighteenth century, an alien crop in many counties." "In Middlesex, in 1796, it was no uncommon sight to see ploughs drawn

[1] Werner Sombart, *Die deutsche Volkswirtschaft im 19. Jahrhundert* (5th ed., Berlin, 1921), II, 630.

[2] K. Biedermann, *Deutschland im 18. Jahrhundert* (Leipzig, 1854–80), I, 366.

by six horses, with three men in attendance." "Traditional methods were treasured with jealous care as agricultural heirlooms." [3]

The reforms initiated in England by Young did not spread to Germany till well into the nineteenth century. Cultivation remained extensive instead of becoming intensive; deep ploughing was held to be not merely unimportant—it was generally left to the most incompetent laborers or even children—but harmful and unnatural. The open-field system (Dreifelderwirtschaft) with an unvarying succession of spring-sown corn (barley and oats), autumn-sown corn (wheat and rye) and fallow, was all but universal. Only gardens, where vegetables, fruit and fodder were grown, were exempt from "Flurzwang" or field constraint, the community routine of cultivation. Age-old tradition, unaided by theoretical knowledge, determined all the methods employed, and there was no room for individual experiments, for the "natural" methods handed down from antiquity had a greater sanctity in the country than even the traditional arts of the craftsmen in the towns. To attempt with impious hand to improve on nature, in the manner of manuring the soil, for instance, was a crime against God, said an old steward in Bohemia in the early nineteenth century. Conservatism so deeply rooted could only be overcome by interference from high quarters: "Your burgher or peasant will do nothing unless he is paid for it or kicked into it," said the officials of those days.[4]

Agriculture proceeded therefore in a vicious circle. The open-field system with its large and neglected permanent pasture provided insufficient fodder, so that the cattle were often so weak in spring that they had to be dragged on sledges to their grazing ground; shortage of cattle involved lack of manure, without which an improvement of the yield was impossible. It is not surprising then that J. C. Schubart (1734–87), who in the latter half of the century made great efforts to extend in northern, southeastern and central Germany the cultivation for fodder of clover, that had been grown in the Spanish Netherlands for centuries, was hailed as one of the greatest benefactors of the century, and ennobled by the emperor, Joseph II, with the title of "Edler von dem Kleefelde." The effects of this revolution were slow to make themselves felt, for throughout the century the productivity of the land remained on the whole extremely low. In Silesia for instance between 1770 and 1780 wheat gave an average crop of 5.6 fold, and rye of 5.2 fold, while in England in Young's time wheat and rye already produced a 10-fold crop, bad as methods were, and other crops were twice as good as the Silesian ones.[5]

[3] Lord Ernle (R. E. Prothero), *English Farming Past and Present,* 2nd ed. pp. 202–3.
[4] Biedermann, I, 168.
[5] Sombart, *op. cit.*

In parts of northern Germany and in Austria sheep-rearing was carried on for the export of wool and was considerably improved in this century by the Spanish government's consenting at last to the export of merino sheep. These sheep-farms, and the dairy-farms on Swiss and Dutch models, that produced cheese and later butter beyond home needs, were the most advanced types of farming to be found in Germany then, though in proportion to the rest they were of small account. Before the end of the century attempts were made at the reform of other branches of agriculture, particularly by the above-mentioned clover-Schubart, and by an admirer of Young, Albrecht Thaer (1752–1828), who did much to spread the "Norfolk System" of rotation in Germany. By this the years of corn-growing were interrupted by the growth of other crops to allow the soil to recover and to supply fodder. With more fodder the stock of cattle could be increased and the land could be more adequately manured. But what was principally lacking was a theoretical understanding of the processes involved, and only the first steps had been made in this direction by Priestley, Lavoisier and others in the last two decades of the century.

The vigorous efforts made by the rulers of Prussia, by some lesser princes (like Karl August) and by a number of individual landowners—for the national importance of agriculture was obvious to all—were not attended by proportionate results. The most useful accomplishment of the Prussian government in this direction was the establishment in the thinly populated eastern districts of religious refugees from France and Holland (from 1685 onwards), and later of emigrants from the southern states like the Palatinate and Württemberg, where agricultural practice was relatively good. It was with the same intention and by the promise of similar privileges that the Russian government attracted South German settlers to the Volga basin, where their descendants still form separate communities today. Frederick the Great continued in this respect the policy of the Great Elector and his own father. Frederick William had also gained new land for cultivation by extensive draining operations in the Havel valley, had deepened rivers and improved roads to facilitate the export of produce, and made many efforts to improve methods. Frederick the Great similarly carried out a big drainage scheme in the Oder and Warthe marsh, an area of three hundred thousand acres. In the matter of methods perhaps his best work was the encouragement of the cultivation of the potato. It was not until the 70s that potatoes were grown in fields, and we hear that severe measures were needed to overcome the apathy and prejudice of the peasants. It was commonly believed for many years that eating potatoes gave rise to scrofula, rickets, consumption, gout and all sorts of diseases. Nettelbeck tells us in his memoirs that when Frederick sent the first cartload of them to Kolberg in 1744, after a famine, so that citizens might try the crop in their gardens, they could make nothing of them. "The things have no smell and no taste," they said, "and not even dogs will eat them (raw!). What is the use of them to us?" But next year a gendarme, a Swabian by birth, was sent with the load to show people how to grow and use them. In the south the potato was better known, though only as a garden plant. Perhaps the greatest single difference between the usual diet of all classes in 1700 and in 1800 was that in 1700 the potato was almost unknown and in 1800 indispensable. For the peasantry the chief consequence was that absolute famine came to be a thing of the past. If the corn crops failed they had potatoes to fall back on, and in time the potato was a more important staple article of diet than bread.

THE PEASANT

The everyday life and thought of the country dwellers were such as one might expect, given the fundamental conditions of their life outlined above. There were naturally great differences between family and family, both amongst the nobility and the peasantry, according to the economic position and inherited privileges of each. As in France, there were some families of noble extraction whose standard of life was no higher than a peasant's, and there were free peasants here and there, particularly in the south, who were little lords in everything but name.

The average peasant and his family, as we have seen, had never much more than was necessary to keep body and soul together. There could be no question of luxuries in their life. It was necessary for them to buy from the towns only what could not possibly be dispensed with, a few spices perhaps and metal ware. For the rest they depended on what they themselves or their neighbors could grow in their fields and gardens and make with their own hands. Houses and furniture and the clothing of both men and women were the work of members of the household, assisted occasionally perhaps by a neighbor, or more rarely by a traveling craftsman. The following description of English and rural life at this period could be applied in almost every detail to German conditions:

> The inhabitants had little need of communication with their immediate neighbours, still less with the outside world. The fields and the livestock provided the necessary food and clothing. Whatever wood might be required for building, fences or fuel, was provided on the wastes. Each village had its mill, generally the property of the lord of the manor; almost every house had its oven and brewing kettle. Women spun wool into coarse cloth; men tanned their own leather. Wealth only existed in its simplest forms, and natural divisions of employment were not made, because only the rudest implements of production were now used. The rough tools required for the cultivation of the soil, and the rude household utensils needed for the comfort of daily life, were made at home. In the long winter evenings farmers, their sons, and their servants carved

the wooden spoons, the platters, and the beechen bowls; fitted and rivetted the bottoms into the horn mugs, or closed, in coarse fashion, the holes in the leather jugs. They plaited the wicker baskets; fitted handles to the scythes, rakes and other tools; cut the staves, and fixed the thongs for the flails; made the willow or ashen teeth for rakes and harrows, and hardened them in the fire; fashioned ox yokes and forks, racks and rack-staves; twisted willows into scythe cradles, or into the traces and other harness gear. Travelling carpenters, smiths and tinkers visited farmhouses and remoter villages at rare intervals to perform those parts of the work which needed their professional skill. But every village of any size found employment for such trades as those of the smith and the carpenter. Meanwhile the women plaited the straw for the neck-collars, stitched and stuffed sheepskin bags for the cart saddle, wove the stirrups and halters from hemp or straw, peeled the rushes for and made the candles. Spinning wheels, distaffs, needles were never idle. Coarse, home-made cloth and linen supplied all wants. The very names of spinster, webster, shepster, litster, brewster, and baxter, show that women span, wove, cut out and dyed cloth, as well as brewed and baked for the household.[6]

In the matter of clothing the villagers were almost beyond the reach of fashion. They used their clothes until they were worn out. Styles of dress did, of course, change over long periods. The great variety of peasant costumes worn as best clothes on special occasions all embodied features of the town dress of much earlier periods, perhaps of the sixteenth century or earlier.[7] The peasantry had at some time or other adopted modified versions of town fashions, but these had become stereotyped, because the conditions necessary for quick changes of fashion, above all a surplus of means and variety of stimulus, were not present in the country. It was the same with many other features of their material civilization and even of what higher culture they possessed, as has been pointed out by Hans Naumann and those who like him believe in the "Sinken des Kulturguts." [8] But the opponents of this theory are no doubt right in claiming a considerable degree of creativeness for the peasant. It was by no means all the features of his culture that had been passively received by him from "higher" social classes. Many of the most important went back to a time when there were no other classes—the form of the peasant house and of the chief agricultural implements, as well as innumerable customs and beliefs owed little or nothing to either knighthood or bourgeoisie, for they were older than both. And though admittedly strongly attached to tradition, the peasant was no more incapable than any other man of modifying what he borrowed to serve his own purposes, and of having occasionally good ideas of his own.

What prevented rapid change was the strength of community feeling in

[6] *Social England,* ed. Traill, V, 101 (article by R. E. Prothero).
[7] See K. Spiess, *Die Deutschen Volkstrachten,* Leipzig, 1911.
[8] See H. Naumann, *Grundzüge der deutschen Volkskunde,* Leipzig, 1922.

the village, and institutions like the three-field system, with its rules of common cropping, which both expressed and fostered this feeling. It is now fashionable in Germany to praise the traditionalism of the peasant, by a reaction against the views expressed when the individualistic middle class led public opinion. For the townsman from the Renaissance age onwards, however, the countryman was "der dumme Bauer." He was held to be coarse, stupid, dishonest, drunken and quarrelsome, and it was not until the time of the Romantics, after hints from Rousseau and the "Sturm und Drang," that it was discovered that the countryman was in his own way a completely civilized person who was even superior to the townsman in much that was now held to be important in life.

In reading eighteenth-century descriptions of peasant life the change of attitude, by which our present-day views have been affected, must be kept in mind. It was not the townsman's feeling of superiority, however, that inspired the following description of the peasant's life by a man revered by Goethe in his youth, J. M. von Loen:

> The peasant is brought up in complete ignorance like a mere animal. He is plagued continually with feudal services, running messages, beating up game, digging trenches and the like. From morning till night he must be digging the fields, whether scorched by the sun or numbed by the cold. At night he lies in the field and becomes little better than a beast of the fields, to keep the beasts from stealing his seed, and what he saves from their jaws is taken soon afterwards by a harsh official for arrears of rent and taxes. The countryman today is the most wretched of all creatures. The peasants are slaves and their men are hardly to be distinguished from the cattle they tend. The traveler comes to villages where children run about half-naked and call to every passer by for alms. Their parents have scarcely a rag on their backs. A few lean cows have to till their fields and give milk as well. Their barns are empty and their cottages threaten to collapse in a heap any moment. They themselves look neglected and wretched; one would have more pity for them, if their wild and brutish appearance did not seem to justify their hard lot.[9]

These general impressions are confirmed by such different writers as Laukhard, *Der reisende Franzose,* Nicolai, Knigge and Crabb Robinson. The references to the peasantry by Crabb Robinson in his *Letters* are particularly interesting because he is able to compare German with English conditions. The condition of the peasantry varied greatly in the provinces he visited. He was never in the eastern and northern states, where the lot of the peasantry was hardest. Of those he saw, the peasantry of the Catholic ecclesiastical states like Bamberg and Würzburg seemed the best placed. Even where the material prosperity of the peasant was equal to that of the

[9] J. M. v. Loen, *Freye Gedanken vom Hof,* 3rd ed. Frankfort and Leipzig, 1768, p. 28.

English villager, he seemed to Crabb Robinson to be more subservient, owing to the feudal burdens he still bore, and it seemed wrong to him that so much field work should be left to women. Howitt, writing forty years later, but before the Industrial Revolution had seriously affected Germany, was inclined to minimize the hardness of the German peasants' lot because he was so pleased to find that the majority of them owned the land they cultivated, whereas the average villager in England was a laborer dependent on a master. Howitt too was only familiar with the south and the Rhineland, where it is true that the peasant proprietor preponderated, and where he had, by this time, commuted his services for money payments. His picture would not have been so favorable if based on conditions in Mecklenburg or Prussia. He was struck by the patient laboriousness of the German peasants, men and women, and by the economy they practiced, collecting as they did every scrap that could be used for fodder, manure or firewood. These habits he explained as the result of their working for themselves and not for a master. Aesthetically, however, he preferred the English countryside, with its variety of large and small estates, manor-houses and cottages, and the neatnes and cleanliness of even the smallest homesteads. The rarity of gentlemen's seats in the country was a point noted by all English travelers—it was due to the attraction of the nobility to the courts. The cottages were less spick and span than in England because the women worked so much more in the fields, and perhaps also because there was no Hall near by to set a higher standard in these matters.

The chief civilizing influences in the village were the minister and the schoolmaster. The power of the minister was so largely a matter of personality, whatever the sect he represented might be, that no brief general statements can be made about it. . . . The power of the village schoolmaster can be more usefully discussed at this point. Generally speaking, it was very slight indeed, for though, in an age that believed so passionately in education, country people were not neglected by the reformers, most of their proposals remained on paper. In Prussia, for instance, the most advanced of the German states in this respect, the village schools seem to have remained wretched in most cases until after the end of the century. From official reports of an inspection made in 1802 and 1803 in Cleve, a Prussian province where conditions were favorable, it appears that Frederick the Great's admirable General-Landschul-Reglement of 1763 had remained a dead letter. Theoretically, attendance at school for six hours a day was compulsory for all children between the ages of five or six and thirteen. For the poor no fee was charged. The qualifications necessary for a teacher were defined, classes were to be duly graded and uniform textbooks to be used. But at their inspection it was found that forty-three teachers out of sixty-seven were incompetent. Hardly any had attended the training school set up for Cleve in 1784, they had usually been ap-

pointed without being examined and once in office they had neither the
leisure nor the books they required to improve themselves. They were so
wretchedly paid that all had some other occupation. Many were organists
or vergers or both, some were tailors or exercised some other craft, some
sold brandy or collected tolls. The school buildings, where regular buildings existed, were almost always in bad repair. Often a room had to be
hired for the purpose in a house, and sometimes the teacher slept in the
school room. There were often no separate classes. Each child came up
book in hand and said its lesson. The curriculum was extremely narrow,
reading, writing and perhaps a little arithmetic, and a good deal of religion. Little was read beyond the Bible and catechism. Attendance was
extremely irregular. In summer the schools were empty.[10] If these were
the conditions in an enlightened state, it can be imagined what they were
like in the average small state. But in the second half of the century a considerable number of peasants could at least read and write, as is indicated
by the large sales of the calendars and so forth that were written for them.

JEROME BLUM

Serfdom In Russia

. . . During the years in which millions of free peasants were forced
to become serfs the nature of serfdom grew ever more oppressive. By the
last part of the eighteenth century the Russian serf was scarcely distinguishable from a chattel slave. That was able to happen because the state
withdrew almost entirely from supervision and interference in the relationship between lord and peasant, and thereby allowed the serfowners to gain
nearly unlimited powers over the people they owned.

The deterioration in the status of the seignioral peasantry had been going on since the fifteenth century. But the concessions to the dvorianstvo

Jerome Blum, *Lord and Peasant in Russia from the Ninth to the Nineteenth
Century* (Princeton, N.J.: Princeton University Press, 1971), pp. 422–23, 424–25,
433–36, 437–39, 440–41.

[10] W. Meiners, "Landschulen und Landschullehrer im Herzogtum Cleve vor hun-
dert Jahren," in *Archiv für Kulturgeschichte*, III, 1905.

made by Peter I and his successors up to the accession of Paul in 1796, gave a great new impetus to the decline in the position of the peasants. Peter, who needed a large and steady supply of men and money to carry out his grandiose schemes, introduced more efficient systems of taxation and conscription, and made the serfowners responsible for their successful operation. To make it easier for them to perform these duties he allowed them to have new rights over their serfs, and gave legal sanction to powers they had preempted. The rulers after Peter followed his precedent, so that seignioral authority continued to grow. In the last part of the century the increase in prices and the rise in the standard of living of the nobles, made it harder for them to make ends meet. Inevitably, they took advantage of their favored position in the state to demand still greater controls over their peasants, in order to be able to extract greater quantities of goods and services from them. . . .

In a ukase of 15 April 1721 Peter stated that it had been, and still was, customary in Russia for peasants and domestics to be sold "like cattle," and for families to be split up in these transactions. With obvious censure (but complete inaccuracy) Peter stated that there was nothing like this in the whole world, and commanded the practice to cease.[1] Yet in earlier decrees he had not only given recognition to the sale of human beings, but had encouraged it by allowing persons subject to military draft to buy substitutes.[2] In fact, in the very ukase in which he condemned the trade in serfs, he went on to say that if it was impossible to stop it the serfs should be sold only in cases of need, and then by family rather than by individual. He repeated these pious sentiments three years later in another decree. But the sales went on, and families continued to be broken up, without reproof from the government.

The trade in peasants reached its peak—as did so many of the cruelest aspects of Russian serfdom—during the reign of Catherine II. To give that self-proclaimed disciple of Voltaire her due, she did try to do something about this. In 1771 she decided that the spectacle of human beings on the block should be banned, and ordered that the serfs of bankrupt seigniors could not be sold at public auction. Her prohibition was disregarded, and so in 1792 she amended the law to allow these sales—but forbad the use of the hammer by the auctioneer! She also took measures to cut down on the commerce in recruit substitutes. This traffic always boomed whenever the army issued its draft calls. In 1766 Catherine decreed that men suitable for military service could not be sold during the recruiting period, or for the three months that preceded it. This law, too, was generally evaded.[3]

---

[1] *PSZ*, VI, no. 3770, p. 377.
[2] Engelmann, *Die Leibeigenschaft*, p. 104.
[3] Semevskii, *Krest'iane*, I, 148–49, 151.

The sale of peasants without land had been illegal in the White Russian provinces when they had been part of Poland. After their annexation by Russia the landlords there began to follow the example of their peers in the rest of the empire, and a lively business in humans grew up. The terms of the annexation, however, had guaranteed the maintenance of the existing laws, so the legality of the trade was brought into question. The Senate, after deliberating on the problem, solemnly informed Catherine in 1775 that "the proprietors of White Russia as subjects of Your Majesty must enjoy the same rights that the Russian nobility enjoy, and therefore they cannot be deprived of the right to sell their peasants without land." [4] In Lifland the provincial diet in 1765 ordered the imposition of heavy fines on serfowners who sold peasants without land. This measure, inspired apparently not by humanitarianism but by the desire to keep peasants within Lifland, proved unsuccessful, and in 1804 new legislation was adopted to end the practice.[5] In 1798 Paul, overruling a recommendation of the Senate, declared the sale of serfs without land in Little Russia illegal and ordered it to cease. Yet fifty years later the seigniors there were reported to be evading the law, and selling recruit substitutes to buyers in the Central Industrial region.[6] . . .

I

The increase in the judicial and police powers of the serfowners had as its corollary an increase in their control over the private lives of their peasants. The marriages of their serfs were a matter of especial concern to the seigniors. They preferred to have their peasants wed one another and produce more serfs for the master, rather than have their female serfs marry a man who did not belong to them. If one of their women did want to marry someone outside her master's property, the law required her to get his consent. He could refuse to give it except in the event the girl wanted to marry a soldier (Peter I had ordered this exception). Some proprietors demanded a fee for their permission. Often the amount they asked varied with the wealth of the applicant, and on occasion it amounted to hundreds and even thousands of rubles. Thus, two rich serfs of Ivanovo had to pay Count Sheremetev seven thousand and nine thousand rubles each for his consent.[7]

The law did not require serfs of the same master to get his permission if they wanted to marry. But this was a universal custom, and some

---

[4] Engelmann, *Die Leibeigenschaft*, pp. 143–44.

[5] Semevskii, *Krest'iane*, I, 158.

[6] *PSZ*, XXV, no. 18706, 16 October 1798, pp. 419–20; Samarin, *Sochineniia*, II, 409.

[7] Schepetov, *Krepostnoe pravo*, p. 78; Berlin, *Russkaia burzhuaziia*, p. 87.

lords charged a small fee for their consent. Often, too, serfowners who felt that their peasants' obligations to them included producing children and thereby adding to their master's assets, ordered two of his serfs to wed one another without regard to the couple's own wishes. Peter I had forbidden this practice in 1724, but serfowners paid no heed to the ban. Serfs tried to defend themselves against these unwelcome matches by standing together as sponsors at a christening, for church law prohibited a marriage between godparents. This stratagem had its obvious limitation; infants in need of baptism were not always available to a man and woman who had just been told to get married. But farsighted peasants who had always felt distaste for one another could use it, and so foil their master's wish if he should later decide to pair them off.

Another matter that interested seigniors was the real and personal property held by their peasants. This had long been considered as belonging ultimately to the master. Usually serfowners allowed their peasants to keep their property, and to take it with them when they were sold to another master. The law did not allow serfs to buy real property until a few years before the emancipation, but, as was pointed out earlier, many lords permitted their peasants to buy land and even serfs in the lord's name. But the lord always had the right to take anything he wanted from his serf's property without paying for it. Sometimes that happened. A group of serfs who belonged to Count Panin pooled their savings and bought a piece of land near Riga to raise vegetables. They made the purchase, of course, in Panin's name. A little while later Panin, inspired no doubt by patriotic ardor, gave the land to the state for a new railroad line. The serfs who had paid for the land received nothing. A wealthy serf owned by Count Sheremetev left 150,000 rubles in bank deposits when he died. His children, who had bought their freedom from the Count, tried to get the money as the heirs of their father, but the court awarded it to Sheremetev on the ground that he had owned the dead man and therefore owned his property.[8]

II

In return for its grant to the serfowners of nearly complete powers, the government did charge them with certain responsibilities for the well-being of their serfs. But the nature and extent of these obligations were far from commensurate with the privileges allowed the seigniors, while the ease with which they were avoided gives testimony to the government's lack of interest in the lot of the common people.

[8] Kulischer, "Die kapitalistischen Unternehmer," p. 352n; Turgenev, *La Russie,* II, 129.

The only provisions in the Code of 1649 concerned with welfare dealt with slaves and not serfs. The slaveowner was ordered to feed his thralls in time of famine. If he failed to do this, and his slaves had to seek alms, they were to be taken from him. When a captured runaway slave was returned, his owner had to pledge that he would not punish the fugitive by maiming or killing him, or starving him to death.[9] These pitifully inadequate ordinances provided the foundation for the legislation of the next two hundred years on the duties the proprietor owed his serfs.

In 1719 Peter ordered that if a serfowner's conduct worked undue hardships upon his peasants his land and serfs were to be placed under the guardianship of his kinsmen until he mended his ways. If he failed to reform he was to be sent to a monastery and put under ecclesiastical censure. Peter justified this law not by any reference to the need to protect peasants from cruelties and injustices they might suffer from their masters. Instead he pointed out that mistreated serfs were likely to run away, thereby depopulating properties and so reducing the government's tax revenues.[10] Empress Anna in 1734 enjoined private proprietors, and also the managers of lands owned by the crown, to care for their peasants during famines and see to it that they did not become beggars. This command was repeated a number of times in succeeding years, and seigniors were threatened with punishment for noncompliance. In 1775 Catherine II instructed provincial officials to be on the watch for lords who cruelly mistreated their serfs, or who lived so lavishly that they brought ruin to themselves and their peasants. She also tried to make it more difficult for nobles to free serfs when they became too old to work. These unfortunates were turned out of their holdings to fend for themselves. Catherine did not abolish nor even question the right of the seignior to do this, but she ordered that the serfs had to give their consent to be emancipated, and she made the lord responsible for the taxes of the freed peasants until the next revision was made. Her successor, Paul, issued a series of decrees ordering the construction of bins in every village to store food for emergencies, and instructed the serfowners to see to it that their peasants kept these granaries stocked.[11] . . .

The inadequacies of the legislation and the government's lack of interest in protecting the serfs did not mean, of course, that every serfowner mistreated his peasants. Many, and probably most of them, moved by economic considerations and by fellow-feeling, looked after their people. They did not need the goad of law and the threat of punishment to

9 *Ulozhenie,* Chapter XX, sec. 41, 42, 92.
10 Semevskii, *Krest'iane,* I, 316; Miller, *Essai,* pp. 268n.
11 Engelmann, *Die Leibeigenschaft,* p. 141; Dodge, *Abolitionist sentiment,* p. 127.

feed their serfs when crops failed, or to take care of their aged and in-
capacitated serfs at their own expense.[12] Nonetheless, the nearly unlimited control the seignior had over his people, the fact that the serfs
had no legal way to protect themselves against his excesses, and perhaps
most important, the absence of social disapproval among the serfowner's
peers if he did mistreat his peasants, opened the door to callousness, and
often to brutality. Foreigners were shocked when they listened to people
of fashion and prominence chat about whippings they had meted out to
their serfs, or heard a noble at his club preen himself before an apprecia-
tive audience because he had sentenced three of his serfs to nearly triple
the legally allowed number of strokes with the cane.[13]

The serf lived always at the mercy of the whims, appetites, and temper
of his owner. Women, and especially those who served in the master's
house, could not defend themselves against a lustful seignior. Some proprietors kept harems of slave girls, and there were even seigniors (and
in some cases stewards) who practiced *ius primae noctis,* though this had
never been an established principle of Russian seignioral law. Captious
or finical seigniors had a serf whipped because he upset a saltceller—a
serious offense because it was believed to foretell the coming of some
misfortune—or because he made the soup too salty, or had not roasted
the chicken to his master's taste. General Kropotkin lost his temper
because he thought his serfs were stealing from him, became still angrier
when he discovered he was mistaken, and vented his rage by having a
serf beaten with one hundred blows of a birch rod. Ivan Turgenev's
mother sent two of her serfs to Siberia because they neglected to bow to
her when she passed by while they were working.[14]

The helplessness of the serfs proved too great a temptation for those
proprietors in whose natures sadism lay close to the surface. These people inflicted frightful cruelties upon their peasants.[15] One of the most
infamous cases was that of Daria Saltykov who in 1756 inherited six
hundred serfs from her husband. In seven years she tortured scores of them
to death for petty or imagined offenses. Her conduct became so notorious
that the authorities decided they had to do something. So in 1762 they began an investigation. It lasted for six years. Finally, she was stripped of
her noble rank, pilloried for one hour in Moscow, and then sentenced to
spend the rest of her life in confinement in a convent. In contrast to her
mild punishment, the serfs who at her command had aided in the torturing

---

[12] Cf. Le Play, *Les ouvriers,* II, 58; Haxthausen, *Die ländliche Verfassung,* pp.
121–22; Semevskii, *Krest'iane,* I, 238–40; Grekov, "Tambovskoe imenie," pp. 513–14.

[13] Passenans, *La Russie,* II, 124–30; Bernhardi, *Aus dem Leben,* II, 69.

[14] Kulischer, "Die Leibeigenschaft," p. 9; Passenans, *La Russie,* II, 120–23;
Kropotkin, *Memoirs,* pp. 49–51; Yarmolinsky, *Turgenev,* p. 13.

[15] Cf. Semevskii, *Krest'iane,* I, ch. VII.

of her victims were beaten with the knout and then condemned for life to hard labor in Siberia.

Daria Saltykov and the people like her were psychopaths. But thoughtless and unconscious cruelty was omnipresent. A story told by Peter Kropotkin about his father is a revealing, and at the same time wryly amusing, illustration of the inhumanity inherent in a society where men owned their fellow humans. The elder Kropotkin, as he emerges from his son's memoirs, is a familiar figure to readers of the great nineteenth century Russian novels—the bumbling, pompous, bigoted, self-indulgent landlord. He had been decorated for gallantry in 1828 during the war with the Turks and was inordinately proud of this honor. When his children asked him to tell them about it, he explained that he had been billeted in a Turkish village when fire broke out. His bodyserf, Frol, rushed into the flames to have a child trapped in a burning house. Kropotkin's commanding officer saw this and was so impressed that he awarded the Cross of St. Anne for bravery on the spot—to Kropotkin. The children, of course, pointed out that Frol had saved the child and so deserved the decoration, whereupon their father, nettled by their obtuseness, exclaimed, "What of that? Was he not my man? It is all the same."[16] . . .

The peasants themselves had no legal way of calling official attention to injustices inflicted upon them by their masters. The code of 1649 had not outlawed the right of serfs to present petitions of complaint against their lords, but had declared that no credence was to be placed in them unless they contained proof of treason by the person against whom the complaint was lodged.[17] Despite this rule it had been customary for serfs to send petitions to their sovereigns, and especially to tsaritsas, presumably because women were thought to be more tenderhearted (a serious error in judgment so far as Russian empresses were concerned). Then Catherine II, after a tour in which she had been besieged with petitions, decided that this nuisance must cease. In a ukase of 22 August 1767 she decreed that henceforth it would be a criminal act for serfs to present petitions against their masters. Those who violated this law were to be beaten with the knout and sent to forced labor in Siberia.[18] Serfs could still denounce their owner if they presented evidence that he was treasonous, or plotting an attempt on the life of the tsar, or evading taxes by not having serfs entered on the assessment lists.[19] These exceptions were of small moment. Catherine's decree had stripped the serfs of the only

---

[16] Kropotkin, *Memoirs,* pp. 10–11.
[17] *Ulozhenie,* Chapter II, sect. 13.
[18] *PSZ,* XXVIII, no. 12966, pp. 334–36. Later legislation mildened these penalties.
[19] *SZ,* 1857, IX, sect. 1036.

legal weapon they had to protect themselves against the wilfulness of their masters.

Early in the nineteenth century a Frenchman who had lived in Russia for many years, wrote that the serfowner's domination over his peasants was greater than that of any sovereign in the world. He pointed out that the authority of a crowned despot was limited by law, custom, and public opinion, but in Russia these forces supported and furthered the prerogatives of the seigniors.[20] He was scarcely exaggerating. For, as Empress Catherine II herself explained in a letter to her friend Denis Diderot, Russian serfowners were "free to do in their estates whatever seemed best to them, except to give the death penalty which is prohibited to them." [21] She could have added that the death penalty, too, was meted out by serfowners under the guise of ordering a serf to be whipped. If enough blows were given the victim died, but that of course was not the master's fault.

[20] Passenans, *La Russie,* I, 86–87.
[21] Quoted in Schkaff, *La question,* p. 58.

8. GROWING TOWNS
AND QUIET VILLAGES

Even before the onset of industrialism, town life in Western Europe was beginning to develop a style and a tenor of its own. But with their poorly developed network of roadways and their uncomfortable vehicles, Europeans still moved inland at a pace no faster than a walking man or a horsedrawn carriage. Communication between one region and another was dreadfully slow with the result that most towns were obliged to survive on their own resources and those of the surrounding countryside. Nevertheless, commerce and trade were assuming an importance only hinted at in earlier centuries. Above all the towns served as a marketplace; yet even those outside of the main cities were becoming complex social organisms in their own right. The shopkeepers, tradesmen, and merchants who thrived there were fully conscious of their nonrural way of life. Historians can now describe this gradual growth of civic tradition and identify some of the urban social types who were other than transient or relocated peasants.

J. Crofts reminds us of the sheer physical obstacles which had to be surmounted in order to construct a primary system of roadways. Without these arteries of communication it was literally every horseman for himself. Construction of viable highways capable of supporting heavily loaded wagons was halting and erratic. All-weather streets in the towns were usually so few as to be a curiosity rather than a convenience. Still, the roadmap of Europe was being slowly redrawn.

Roger Hart illustrates how imperceptible this change actually was, even in England, to the majority of villagers. Most people preferred to leave the hazards and discomforts of travel to entrepreneurial types whose business it was to move from place to place. Rural village life meanwhile continued in a more accustomed routine of labor and leisure, an existence more often glorified by romantic poets than carefully investigated by social historians. Hart reconstructs the eating and drinking habits of Englishmen in the eighteenth century, an age in which the pub, the pint of gin, and the poorhouse became national institutions.

W. H. Lewis draws some distinctions between England and France and he demonstrates that, within France (as elsewhere on the Continent), legal and social conditions varied greatly from town to town. Here we encounter the first meaningful use of the term "bourgeois." We are also able to trace the origins of municipal government as it developed under the somewhat reluctant and never financially disinterested aegis of monarchy. Finally, by accompanying Lewis on a walking tour of late seventeenth-century Paris, we can gain some sense of the mixture of revulsion and admiration which the large town must have given its citizens and visitors.

It would be overwrought to find in these developments a great social mutation. What we perceive here, rather, is an embryonic stage of change. Except in isolated instances, the pace of life by the end of the eighteenth century had not been altered for most Europeans since medieval times. But clearly there was already a movement, a stirring, which the dramatic political events after 1789 were to accelerate.

JOHN CROFTS

The Roads

The Tudor governments had made some effort to deal with the problem of the roads, and the system of repair by statute labor under parish overseers, set up by the Acts of 1555 and 1563, worked well enough in remote country places to survive until the nineteenth century. What

John Crofts, *Packhorse, Waggon and Post: Land Carriage and Communications under the Tudors and Stuarts* (Toronto: University of Toronto Press, 1967), pp. 16–21.

they had failed and perhaps without the help of Dutch engineers could not have attempted to do, was to establish any standard or prescribe any technique of road-making; and this was a fatal omission. It is clear from the methods of repair usually adopted that a road was hardly regarded as a structure at all. It was commonly thought of as a strip of land upon which no member of the community had the right to sow his peas, or stack his manure, or dig his marl. It is true that over-thrifty individuals frequently tried to use it in this way; but public opinion was against them for the simple reason that once a highway was blocked the King's lieges had a statutory right to make their way over the land adjoining to their destination.[1] This right was well understood by the public of the seventeenth century, and was exercised so freely as to constitute a serious menace to agriculture. A gentleman like Sergeant Hoskins, contemplating a journey by coach in 1627, would order his servants as a matter of course "to study the coach-way; where to break hedges, and how to avoid deep and dangerous ways";[2] and Justice Ellwood's coachman "seeing a nearer and easier way than the common road through a cornfield, and that it was wide enough to run without damaging the corn," turned into the cornfield without hesitation.[3] In winter especially, when a highway had become in parts impassable the traffic was compelled to use "driftways on trespass through the neighboring enclosures," with the result that the original line of the road was sometimes forgotten and superseded. "Travellers begge passage through another's grounds in winter" says Thomas Adams in a sermon of 1630, "for avoydance of the Miry wayes, and so long use it on sufference that at last they plead it by Prescription, and hold it by Custome." The problem was particularly grievous in the close-farming districts of the southeast, where the hedges and banks, by confining the traffic to one track, had brought the roads into such an abominable state that they could be used as a potent argument against the enclosure system. Fitzherbert tries to meet the objection by suggesting that fenced-in lanes should be used only where the ground is stony and dry, and that where it is soft "at every hedge that goeth overthwart the highway, there to make a gate. . . . And then hath every man the whole close to ride, carry or go in as they had before."[4] Wherever possible the traffic trampled out a wide verge of land "thrown in, as it were, for an overplus to the highway." In Sussex especially Defoe says he had seen "the road, sixty to a hundred yards broad, lie from side to side all poached with cattle, the land of no manner benefit, and yet no going with a horse but at

[1] See C. H. Hartman. *The Story of the Roads,* 1927, p. 46.
[2] *Memoir of Colonel John Birch* (Camd. Soc.), p. 186.
[3] *History of the Life of Thomas Ellwood,* ed. C. Crump, 1900, p. 6.
[4] *Surveyenge,* Ch. XL.

every step up to the shoulders, full of sloughs and holes and covered with standing water." [5]

In the open-farming districts the traveler was free to pick his way to a much greater extent, but the result often was that the line of the road evaporated in an abstract right of way. This year the approach to the village might be straight forward across the fallow; but next year the fallow (following the usual rotation) might have been ploughed in long strips separated by balks or furrow leys, and the traveler might have to make a wide detour to reach his destination. A witness before the Star Chamber in the reign of James I testified that "sometymes when the common feilds of Ladbrooke (in Warwickshire) lay open, the passengers . . . did in their jornies . . . passe and goe over the said comon feilds now and then upon one furrow ley and sometymes uppon another furrow ley as they would, but they did notwithstanding usually keepe neare one place." He said that "passengers doe the like in other common fields," but nevertheless gave it as his opinion "that there is and may be a high and comon way through such places." [6] No doubt he was right, but it was evidently difficult in such districts even for the local farmers to say exactly where the road lay, and for the stranger it must often have been impossible. "Travellers know no highwaies in the common fields" complains an agriculturist of the period, and much land was "spoiled and trampled down in all wide roads where coaches and carts take liberty to choose for their best advantage." The tendency of the traffic to "fan out" wherever possible was particularly noticeable over heaths and commons. Arthur Young, writing in 1760, could remember the time when carriages approaching Norwich from the south "would sometimes be a mile abreast of each other in pursuit of the best track." Carriers crossing Salisbury Plain in 1689 were "about two miles apart" when they were caught in a blizzard. Travelers to Brigg in Lincolnshire were guided by a land lighthouse; and those benighted on their way to Barton on Humber listened for the tolling of a bell. [7]

Evidently then, it was to the interest of the agricultural community that a thoroughfare, where it existed, should be kept clear. Nobody expected it to be good going. Indeed it seems to have been generally accepted in some districts that the worst possible way between two given points was along the common road. But as long as it was free from certifiable obstructions, and not demonstrably an impassable slough, it enabled Tom Touchy to take the law of any man who trespassed on the land adjoining. And to many a remote and stagnant and self-supporting village this was its sole value. The inhabitants did not use it themselves.

[5] Defoe. *Essay on Projects,* 1697.
[6] *Star Chamber Proc.:* James I, 68, file 3.
[7] Prothero. *The Pioneers and Progress of English Farming,* 1888, pp. 44, 56.

They did not want to go anywhere. They were sometimes quite ignorant even of the name of a parish six miles father along the road.[8] As far as they were concerned it was simply a strip abandoned to the stranger-public in return for their undisturbed occupation of the fields on either side.

Regarded in this light, the road was not likely to make any serious call upon their energy or invention, and the statutory repairs to it were usually undertaken in a purely agricultural spirit. The commonest method was simply to plough up the two edges of the track, throwing the earth inwards, and then level the surface with a harrow. A refinjment consisted in filling up the ruts with stones or brushwood. Sometimes the whole surface was covered with gravel or broken stones; but this must have meant a good deal of heavy carting, and can only have been possible where carts were easily available. In general the process consisted in filling up the worst holes with something solid, and throwing back upon the surface the mud and gravel that the year's traffic had displaced.

Now as long as it had nothing more serious to bear in winter than packhorse traffic, even a road of this kind might remain passable;[9] for packhorse trains, by picking their way and avoiding the tracks of their predecessors, distributed the gross weight that the road had to take pretty evenly over its surface. But once a gang of maltsters' carts or clothiers' wagons had ploughed its way down such a road in wet weather, the deep ruts, widened by frost and surface-water, soon engulfed any surface dressing that might have been used upon it, and in a low-lying stretch converted the whole road into one protracted slough, in which pack-horses were certain to be bogged and foot passengers might even be drowned.[10] When this stage was reached the highway ceased to be passable except by wagons with teams powerful enough to drag them through "on their bellies," and the small farmers, dairywomen and huxters who had been in the habit of taking their wares to market on horseback by that route, were compelled either to set up wagons for themselves, or to become the clients of those who possessed them. It is to this breakdown of the roads that we may probably attribute the appearance of those "long wagons" carrying "passengers and commodities" which Stow mentions under the year 1564. Nobody traveled by them who could possibly avoid it: even Verney's housemaids felt entitled to demand pad-nags, "the very name of a wagon was soe offensive to them." They are a sign that the growing commercial traffic had brought some of the main roads into such a condition that they were no longer fit for the private traveler, and could

---

[8] *H. M. Com.* Clements, p. 222; and compare *Diary of Celia Fiennes*, ed. Griffiths, p. 81

[9] W. Marshall. *Rural Economy of the Midland Counties*, 1796, I, 43. See Note 04.

[10] *Diary of Ralph Thoresby*, 1830, I, 295; and see Kemp's *Nine Days Wonder*, 1600, for the slough near Chelmsford which he tried to jump.

be safely navigated only by professional wagoners with very powerful teams.

To give precise dates for a process which was in its nature gradual and cumulative is impossible, but this appearance of a wheeled passenger traffic in 1564 may perhaps be taken to mark the moment when the demands made upon the Elizabethan roads had become definitely greater than they could bear without a properly metalled surface, and when therefore the skilled services of professional carriers had become practically indispensable. Until road-surfaces could be strengthened, as they were at last by the Turnpike Acts from 1663 onwards, the progress could only be from bad to worse. The palliatives tried from time to time by the Stuart governments were quite ineffective, and in some cases certainly aggravated the evils they were supposed to cure. The proclamation of 1618, for instance, which forbade the use of heavy wagons altogether, and limited the load of a cart to one ton, was, for lack of machinery to ensure that the weight restriction was observed, positively mischievous. It simply tempted the carrier to load upon two wheels what ought to have been carried on four, and trust that the paucity of weighing machines would enable him to get by with it. A great deal could be done with English carts. The Duke of Württemberg was much struck by their size and capacity, and says that they would carry nearly as much as a wagon.[11] If so, they must have been, as the carriers themselves argued, far more destructive to an unmetalled road.

Another and later expedient was to encourage the use of broad wheels, in the hope that they would prevent or mitigate the formation of ruts. A proclamation of 1662 prescribed four inches as the minimum breadth for cart and wagon wheels; but it had to be withdrawn. The ruts already existed; and every wagoner knew that until they could be filled in, a narrow wheel traveled best and took the least out of his team. Hence while theorists continued to advocate the use of broad wheels, the practical wainwright (if we may judge by seventeenth-century illustrations) took pains to make them as narrow as possible. Not that he expected his handiwork to solve the traffic problem altogether. The moment was sure to come when even with the narrowest wheels a wagon would stick fast. But he provided for this contingency by equipping the narrow rim with iron boltheads or cogs, which protruded about an inch and gave a purchase in a difficult place when the wagoner had to put his shoulder to the wheel.[12] Granted the conditions there can be no doubt that these "shod" wheels were a thoroughly practical invention from the wagoner's point of view.

---

[11] *England as seen by Foreigners*, ed. Rye, p. 14.

[12] "Divers great nailes of iron were there found such as are used in the wheels of shod carts, being each of them as big as a man's finger, and a quarter of a yard long, the heads two inches over." (*Stow's Survey of London*, 1598, Ed. Morley, p. 184.)

But meanwhile the narrow rims cut the ruts deeper where the ground was soft, and the iron cogs smashed and tore it up where it happened to be hard: so much so that towns, such as Bristol and Bury St Edmunds, which were trying to get their streets pitched, were obliged to prohibit the use of these "shod" carts within the city boundaries.[13] They remained the bane of English traffic until the eighteenth century, when the Turnpike companies taxed them out of existence.

The effect of this growing traffic problem was to maintain and even to intensify the social and intellectual contrast between London and the provinces. The spirit of national unity fostered by Elizabeth's government and the successful contest with Spain had found a focus and a rallying point in the life of the capital. Here the spectacle of English wealth and English power, English law and English genius, might be seen not in dim vision or hopeful outline but as a thing achieved, solid and incontrovertible. Here were the beginnings of a social sense that ignored the old class distinctions, and of an intellectual freemasonry that drew together under the same starry heaven of wit the nobly born exquisite and the bricklayer's son. But this dazzling scene was becoming the more inaccessible the brighter it shone. A widening circle of mud and misery, caused by those very activities that gave the city its wealth and prestige, tended to insulate the capital from the life and thought of the country as a whole. A hundred miles from London they were still living in the fifteenth century; two hundred miles away they were hardly out of the fourteenth. While Ben Jonson was refining upon points of scholarship at the Devil Tavern Sir Thomas Metcalfe of Wensleydale was laying siege to Raydall House with forty armed retainers; blazing away at the windows as though the War of the Roses was still in full swing;[14] and while fashionable congregations listened to the theological subtleties of a Sanderson or a Jeremy Taylor, an old man at Cartmel Fell was assuring his minister that he had indeed "heard of that man you speak of (Jesus Christ) once at a play at Kendall, called Corpus Christi play, where there was a man on a tree, and blood ran down."[15]

To bridge this enormous gulf many things were needed besides better roads—better education, an effective journalism and a more regular system of communications. Meanwhile the carrier did what he could. For more than a century he was the community's sole champion against its inveterate enemies, the wind and the rain. While the citizen took his evening pipe, and the tired farmer dozed by his fire, the carrier's gangs were still splashing thigh-deep through Mimm's Wash, or unpinning the wheels

[13] *H. M. Com. Bury St Edmund's*, p. 141; Latimer, *Annals of Bristol* (seventeenth century), p. 58.
[14] *Journal of Nicholas Assheton*, 1617–18 (Chetham Soc.).
[15] *Life of John Shaw* (Surtees Soc., 1875), p. 138.

of their wagons to haul them one by one out of Dunchurch Lane; or their clanging pack-trains were vanishing into the wintry heights of the Pennines, there to plod on, hour after hour, along tracks known only to the curlews, until at last their bells would be heard again on Hartside, bringing news from London down the long zigzag path into Melmerby and the Valley of the Lune.

For most country dwellers the carrier was the only regular means of contact with the outside world, and the recurring freshets of news that he brought stirred the sleeping pool of local opinion like the return of the tide, enabling its inhabitants to glow momentarily with a sense of the open sea. He was also, no less, the channel of rumor, and must often have done something to foment that extraordinary propensity to groundless panic which seems to have afflicted most country places in the seventeenth century. "To tell news after the carrier" had become a proverbial way of describing a futile undertaking. The carrier had told all there was, and sometimes a good deal more. "Simondshall news" was what they called it in Gloucestershire.

> The clothiers, horsecarriers and wainmen of this hundred who weekly frequent London, knowinge by ancient custome that the first question, after welcome home from London, is 'What newes at London?' doe usually gull us with feigned inventions, devised by them upon those downes; which wee either then suspecting upon the report, or after findinge false, wee cry out 'Simondsall newes'. A generall speach betweene every cobler's teeth.[16]

But this was peace-time fooling. At moments of crisis when the public was terrified by rumors of a hideous Popish Plot, or of a disbanded Irish army storming across the country and burning folk in their beds, the arrival of the London carrier on his usual day, reporting all quiet on the road, must have had a steadying effect. If the carrier could keep his day, things could not be so bad; and thus his stubborn figure, plodding along the roads which most of them would never travel, and through regions which they hardly knew by name, became the symbol and almost the assurance of an immutable order. . . .

[16] J. Smyth. *Lives of the Berkeleys,* III, 30.

ROGER HART

The Village

With few and bad roads, the villages of eighteenth-century England were self-contained and inbred. A village had to be able to clothe and feed itself, provide work for all, and look after its old and sick. Conditions had hardly changed since Shakespeare's day. Village women made the cloths—spinning, weaving and sewing. They also baked the bread from locally grown corn, brewed the beer, salted meat for winter and sometimes helped in the fields. The men made nearly all their own equipment, for examples axes, shears, knives, saws, spades, hoes, wagons and carts, hurdles for the sheep-pens, woven baskets. They dug stone and chalk for building cottages and barns. Wages, where paid at all, were very low, perhaps 6s. or 7s. a week; most village workers received payment in kind, shelter, corn, milk, sometimes fish, rarely meat, wool. They were at least more or less immune from the wild fluctuations in the price of bread and other products which hit eighteenth-century townspeople so hard. Every village had one or two craftsmen for special jobs, such as a blacksmith, potter, joiner, weaver, maltster or tanner, depending on local needs and resources. Buying and selling with other villages or towns in the same county was rare. Work was hard—up at dawn and to bed at sundown. Children had to help as soon as they were strong enough to hold a broom or carry timber.

Relaxations and pleasures were few, perhaps fishing, snaring rabbits, a little poaching. A visit to the market or fair in a distant town would be an experience of a lifetime.

Those villagers who farmed three or four acres of their own in the common fields could afford a little more independence of the local squire. Those squires who wanted to make improvements to the property by enclosures often complained about it. One wrote, "If you offer them work, they will tell you that they must go to look up their sheep, cut furzes, get their cow out of the pound or, perhaps, say that they must take their horse to be shod that he may carry them to the horse race or a cricket

Roger Hart, *English Life in the Eighteenth Century* (New York: G. P. Putnam's Sons, 1970), pp. 24–32.

match." In his book *Horse-Houghing Husbandry* (1731), the great agriculturalist Jethro Tull agreed: "The deflection of [workmen] is such that few gentlemen can keep their lands in their own hands but let them for a little to tenants who can bear to be insulted, assaulted, kicked, cuffed and Bridewelled with more patience than gentlemen are provided with. . . . It were more easy to teach the beasts of the field than to drive the ploughman out of the way."

Rural housing, if such it can be called, was very primitive. Villagers lived in hovels made of stones piled up and covered with thatch or brushwood, or of cheap local materials, such as "mud and stud" in clay districts, or wood on the edge of the great forests such as Wychwood, Wyre, Sherwood, Rockingham, Knaresborough and elsewhere (many of which have since disappeared). The structures were barely weatherproof, and few have survived from Johnson's time into the present century. Brick cottages were unknown until the next century. Cottages were tiny, perhaps one living room and one bedroom for the entire family. Ceilings were low; the windows were small and without glass, the floor beaten earth, perhaps covered with straw.

Yet to many contemporaries, the English village sometimes seemed set in a Garden of Eden. In *The Deserted Village,* Goldsmith wrote:

> How often have I loitered o'er thy green,
> Where humble happiness endeared each scene!
> How often have I paused on every charm,
> The sheltered cot, the cultivated farm,
> The never-failing brook, the busy mill,
> The decent church that topped the neigbr'ng hill,
> The hawthorn bush, with seats beneath the shade,
> For talking age and whispering lovers made.

But this was a particularly rosy view. What does seem clear, however, is that the English village compared extremely well with villages on the Continent in the same period. The young Comte de la Rochefoucauld wrote on his visit to Norfolk in 1784, "As always, I admired the way in which in all these little villages the houses are clean and have an appearance of cosiness in which ours in France are lacking. There is some indefinable quality about the arrangement of these houses which makes them appear better than they actually are."

THE FAMILY AT HOME

Breakfast for most people consisted of just tea and rolls, or bread and butter; sometimes toast would be eaten in winter. Foreigners were surprised at this dish. C. P. Moritz wrote in 1782: "The slices of bread and butter given to you with tea are as thin as poppy leaves, but there is a way of roasting slices of buttered bread before the fire which is incomparable. One slice after another is taken and held to the fire with a fork until the butter is melted, then the following one will be always laid upon it so that the butter soaks through the whole pile of slices. This is called *toast*."

People did not usually breakfast until the day had already begun; many rose at six but did not breakfast until ten. Fashionable people often took their breakfast so late that they were able to make calls beforehand; and in Bath and other spas and resorts the whole business of bathing and "taking the waters" usually took place before breakfast. In the first part of the century, breakfast parties were popular. We know from the *Gentleman's Magazine* that public breakfast parties were held at such places as Ranelagh, or Ruchholt near Stratford, or Marylebone Gardens, or Cox's at Dulwich. Bubb Dodington (1691–1772) the diarist, recorded a private breakfast party in his *Diary:* "The Princess of Wales and Lady Augusta attended by Lady Middlesex and Mr. Breton did Mrs. Dodington and me the honor of breakfasting with us. After breakfast, we walked all round my gardens: we came in, and they went into all the rooms . . . it was near three o'clock."

Dodington was not the only person to breakfast so late in the day. Fashionable people thought of the morning as lasting until dinner-time, say two or three in the afternoon. C. P. Moritz wrote in 1782 that "it was usual to walk out in a sort of *negligée* or morning dress, your hair not dressed, but merely rolled up in rollers, and in a frock and boots."

Dinner was the chief meal of the day, eaten at two or three o'clock in the afternoon, although the rich often did not sit down until four or five. The Swiss visitor César de Saussure, who was in England between 1725 and 1730, wrote "an Englishman's table is remarkably clean, the linen is very white, the plate shines brightly, and knives and forks are changed surprisingly often, that is to say, every time a plate is removed. When everybody has done eating, the table is cleared, the cloth even being removed, and a bottle of wine with a glass for each guest is placed on the table." At this point, the ladies retired, leaving the men to propose toasts— a long and solemn ceremony—and smoke clay pipes of tobacco.

C. P. Moritz complained bitterly about the poor standard of English dinners: "An English dinner . . . generally consists of a piece of half-boiled or half-roasted meat; and a few cabbage leaves boiled in plain water; on which they pour a sauce made of flour and butter." English coffee, he called "a prodigious quantity of brown water." The wheat bread, the butter, and Cheshire cheese, however earned praise. The middle classes were heavy beef- and mutton-eaters, although some people ate fish; and oysters became a delicacy. Parson Woodforde leaves an account of a dinner which included a leg of mutton with caper sauce, a pig's face, a neck of pork roasted with gooseberries, and plum pudding. Delicacies included "potatoes in shells," cold tongue, partridge, roast swan ("good eating with sweet sauce"), Parmesan cheese, orange and apple puddings, syllabubs and jellies.

Supper was the last meal of the day, and included the same sort of dishes that were eaten at dinner. In 1726, César de Saussure noticed that "supper is not considered a necessary meal," but by the end of the century, this had changed, and people liked "a late and great dinner" (Johnson). Ordinary people had their supper at eight or nine o'clock, at the end of a long day's work, but the rich often ate supper in the small hours, after a dance or party. Horace Walpole commented in 1777, "The present folly is late hours. . . . Lord Derby's cook lately gave him warning: the man owned he liked his place [job] but said he should be killed by dressing suppers at three in the morning."

The diet of the poor was very plain. At the start of the century, coarse rye and barley bread was eaten a good deal, although the purer bread made from wheat became more widely available later on. Former luxuries such as tea and sugar now came within the means of many people, causing Arthur Young to refer disapprovingly to the "growth of luxury among the poor." Young took a note of some average prices of food during his tour of 1771: bread 1¼ *d.* a pound, butter 6*d.* a pound, butcher's meat 3*d.* a pound, cheese 3*d.* a pound. These items had to be purchased from wages which were probably only 6*s.* to 8*s.* a week.

Daily life in the eighteenth century was an almost nonstop round of work, and more work. Ordinary people rose at 5 A.M. or 6 A.M. and usually worked through until 8 P.M. or 9 P.M. Those families who were self-employed, and paid piece-work, naturally tended to work long hours to scrape money together; those who were employed by others had to work these hours, or be sacked for "idleness." There was no escape from this routine for children. They were set to work by their parents as soon as they could do anything useful. In towns, very young children might be made to run errands, wash floors, help carry and give other domestic help. In the countryside, they scared birds from the crop fields, picked stones from the soil in readiness for tilling, combed wool and collected rushes for dipping in tallow. Daily life was extremely hard, and children had to play as much a part as the old, sick and destitute in the struggle for existence. There was no idea that children occupied any special place in the home or in society; there were no schools for them to go to, no idea of "education." They were regarded more or less as small adults, and everyone hoped they would grow up as quickly as possible to do their share of work, to learn a useful trade, or perhaps go to sea, as many did, at the age of twelve or less.

Many people felt that the treatment of children was a disgrace to society and encouraged them to become lawless or idle. One man who decided something should be done was Jonas Hanway, who with the help of Sir John Fielding, and others, founded the Marine Society, which trained poor boys for the sea. He also spoke out against the cruelties of chimney-sweep boys, before the time of Bennet and Shaftesbury. But his main self-appointed task was to rescue pauper children. Having studied poor-houses and foundling hospitals abroad, he became a Governor of the Foundling Hospital in London, and helped bring about the Acts of 1761 and 1767. The Act of 1761 obliged parishes to keep registers of their infant poor. The 1767 Act ("the Hanway Act") made parishes send their pauper children under the age of six into the country to be looked after, at not less than 2*s*. 6*d*. a week. But many parishes had little interest in really helping, and Hanway himself sadly commented, "the apprenticeship of some parish children is as great a scene of inhumanity as the suffering of others to die in infancy."

Marriage in those days was a binding contract for life, always performed by a priest, often at the instructions of the parents. Divorce was extremely rare and difficult to obtain, since it required an Act of Parliament in each case. Bigamy, desertion and other marital offenses were probably more common then than now, partly because women had very few rights they could legally enforce against bad husbands, and partly because of the lack of law enforcement. Yet there are more complaints from the husbands than the wives. Johnson thought, "Our marriage service is too refined. It is calculated only for the best kind of marriages; whereas, we should have a form for matches of convenience, of which there are many." He agreed with Boswell, "that there was no absolute necessity for having the marriage ceremony performed by a regular clergyman, for this was not commanded in scripture."

Boswell wrote a little "epigrammatick song" which Garrick had had set to music, bewailing the fate of husbands:

A Matrimonial Thought

In the blithe days of honeymoon,
With Kate's allurements smitten,
I lov'd her late, I lov'd her soon,
And call'd her dearest kitten.

But now my kitten's grown a cat,
And cross like other wives,
O! by my soul, my honest Mat,
I fear she has nine lives!

Later, Boswell "mentioned to him a dispute between a friend of mine and his lady, concerning conjugal infidelity, which my friend had maintained was by no means so bad in the husband as in the wife. Johnson: 'Your friend was in the right, Sir. Between a man and his Maker it is a different question: but between a man and his wife, a husband's infidelity is nothing. They are connected by children, by fortune, by serious considerations of community. Wise married women don't trouble themselves about infidelity in their husbands.' "

GIN DRINKERS

The first half of the century saw more gin drunk by the people of Britain than at any other time. Gin was not expensive—certainly more within the means of the ordinary person then than now. The order of the day was, "Drunk for 1*d*. dead drunk for 2*d.,* straw for nothing"; the amount consumed was enormous. Henry Fielding wrote in 1751 after two years as a London magistrate, "Gin . . . is the principal sustenance (if it may so be called) of more than a hundred thousand people in this metropolis. Many of these Wretches there are, who swallow Pints of this Poison within the Twenty Four Hours: the Dreadfull Effects of which I have the Misfortune every Day to see, and to smell too," he added. The root of the trouble lay in the last part of the seventeenth century; home manufacturers had been encouraged by the Government in making English spirits from corn, to discourage imports. Alehouses had to be licensed by the magistrates, but the sale of gin went unchecked. In London alone there were perhaps eight thousand places where gin was openly sold, apart from alehouses: stalls and barrows, chandlers and tobacconists were some.

Both drinkers and manufacturers opposed reform; in fact, a £20 retail license fixed in 1720, and a 2*s*. per gallon duty were lifted in 1733, when wheat-growers protested to Parliament that sales had slumped. But three years later, Parliament returned to the attack, fixing a new license fee of £50, and a tax of 20*s*. per gallon. In those days, it amounted to virtual prohibition; but due to evasion of payments, violence against informers, and difficulties of administration, Parliament in 1743 again reduced all these charges, though from now on the distillers could not sell their own liquor direct to the public, but had to wholesale it to licensed retailers paying a 20*s*. license. But outside London, the towns were still very anxious about the effects of gin in increasing lawlessness and idleness, and after Bristol, Salisbury, Rochester, Manchester and Norwich petitioned Parliament a new Act was passed (1751) which stopped the worst excesses. After 1751, the situation began to improve although gin still continued to be as popular a drink as tea is today.

DOWN AND OUT

Parishes, of which England had fifteen thousand, were responsible for looking after their own poor (as well as for their sick, aged and orphans). The Government did not concern itself. Most parishes only contained a few hundred people, and so had small resources. Most relied upon the services of an overseer, appointed by the local magistrates. The poor could apply to the parish for "relief," and the overseer then had to decide whether to give them a few pence from the rates and send them on their way; try to find them work; or threaten them with trouble if they didn't find work themselves. Most people of the time agreed with Daniel Defoe, who said that a "pauper given employment was a vagabond given a favor." So it was, that the ratepayers used the parish workhouses as a way of driving idle beggars to find work for themselves.

Under the Poor Law Act of 1722, parishes were allowed to build their own workhouses, and to put their poor to work. Many parishes turned their poor over to a road-builder or other contractor in exchange for a hire fee; a parish would sometimes let a road-builder put a whole work-house under marching orders. The parish purse would be protected, the contractor would get workmen—and the poor would probably suffer. As the Quaker John Scott wrote in 1773, "By means of this statute, the pa-rochial managers are impowered to establish a set of petty tyrants as their substitutes, who, farming the poor at a certain price, accumulate dishonest wealth, by abridging them of reasonable food, and imposing on them unreasonable [toil]." The workhouse was often feared as a "House of Terror." As well as the workhouse, there was the poor-house, virtually a doss-house. Crabbe paints a pathetic poor-house scene in *The Village* (1783):

> Theirs is yon House that holds the Parish-Poor,
> Whose walls of mud scarce bear the broken door;
> There, where the putrid vap'rs, flagging, play,
> There Children dwell who know no parents' care;
> Parents who know no children's love, dwell there!
> Heart-broken matrons on their joyless bed,
> Forsaken Wives, and Mothers never wed;
> Dejected widows with unheeded tears,
> And crippled age with more than childhood fears;
> The Lame, the Blind, and, far the happiest they!–
> The moping Idiot and the Madman gay.

Henry Fielding in 1753, in his report on the Poor Law, said, "they starve and freeze and rot among themselves." But Dr. Johnson's complacent views were more typical of people of the time. Boswell described their talk on the subject: "He [Dr. Johnson] said, 'the poor in England were better provided for, than at any other country of the same extent . . . Where a great proportion of the people,' said he, 'are suffered to languish in helpless misery, that must be ill-policed [governed] . . . a decent provision for the poor is the true test of civilization.' " In 1750, about £700,000 of parish rates went to the relief of the poor. The middle classes who paid it felt it was a heavy and annoying burden.

Fielding wrote three years later, "Every man who hath any property must feel the weight of that tax which is levied for the use of the poor; and every man of any understanding must see how absurdly it is applied. So very useless, indeed, is this heavy tax, and so wretched its disposition, that it is a question whether the poor or the rich are more dissatisfied . . . since the plunder of the one serves so little to the real advantage of the other; for while a million yearly is raised among the former, many of the latter are starved; many more languish in want and misery; of the rest, many are found begging or pilfering in the streets today, and tomorrow are locked up in gaols and bridewells."

A further attempt at reform was made in 1782, with the passing of Gilbert's Act (Thomas Gilbert, M.P., 1720–98). From now on, the workhouse was to be reserved for the helpless, such as the old, the sick, orphans and unmarried mothers; the able-bodied poor were now exposed to the harsh Vagrancy Laws, under which vagabonds, "unlicensed pedlars" and others faced merciless prison sentences. Towards the end of the century, between three thousand and four thousand vagrants a year were sent to houses of correction; but needless to say, as many more were driven to crime. By 1800 there were over four thosuand workhouses and poorhouses in the country.

W. H. LEWIS

The Town

The latent hostility, or at least divergence of interests, between town and country, probably as old as civilization itself, is rooted in the basic fact that the countryman produces while the townsman consumes. No nation has yet evolved a policy that satisfies both classes, and the France of Louis XIV was less fitted to solve the problem than most. For the encumbering vestiges of feudalism which hampared seventeenth-century France at every turn engendered a friction between the country noble and the town *bourgeois,* which appears scarcely to have existed in the contemporary England. To the English squire the neighboring town was the social and commercial headquarters of the countryside, whilst to the French noble, it was a portion of his *seigneurie* which had enfranchised itself from his yoke, obtained many financial privileges, and was growing steadily richer while he grew poorer and more insignificant. He hated and despised a *bourgeois,* whilst the *bourgeois,* increasing in wealth and importance, asked himself why he should put up with the intolerable insolence of the beggarly squireen. A time came quite early on when a noble who attempted to cane a *bourgeois* in the street would find himself rabbled and hooted out of the town; the noble's only possible retort was to wash his hands of the town and seek the company of his own caste in the fields. In inflicting on himself this voluntary banishment from the town and exclusion from municipal office, the noble made a grave strategic error; had he, like his ancestors, solicited election as mayor or alderman, had the noble and the *bourgeois* realized that they had common interests, the centralizing policy of Richelieu and the later Bourbons would have encountered an obstacle which might very possibly have modified the whole course of seventeenth-century history. Here and there a noble may have had a glimmering of such an idea, or at least had an instinct which prompted him to keep a finger in the town pie; Maréchal d'Estrades, for instance, was perpetual Mayor of Bordeaux; the Duc de Grammont, hereditary Mayor of Bayonne; and the Duc de Villeroi had a preponderant influence in the affairs of the City of Lyons. But,

W. H. Lewis, *The Splendid Century* (New York: William Morrow and Company, Inc., 1954), pp. 160–68, 172–76.

broadly speaking, the nobles withdrew from the towns, creating a vacuum which was promptly filled by the Crown. Henceforward, the towns were the King's proteges, his chief counterpoise against the nobility, and within the towns grew up a municipal aristocracy to replace the self-exiled nobles. And the towns, though they were far from being democracies, and were under the royal protection, tended to become centers of resistance to arbitrary power, and indeed retained a remarkable degree of independence, even under Louis XIV; the town of Provins, for instance, in 1682 rejected an edict of the Council of State on the ground that it was contrary to the liberties of the province: and the edict was withdrawn.

On the whole, we may say that a well-to-do *bourgeois* of one of Louis XIV's *bonnes villes* was the most comfortably situated man of any estate in the realm, but the fact that the constitutions and problems of no two towns are the same makes generalization very difficult. And indeed conditions of life were often different in different quarters of the same town. Surrounding the town was the *banlieue,* often a considerable area of country; if you lived in one of the thirty-five villages of the *banlieue* of Rouen, you enjoyed the privileges of that city. But not one of the villages of the *banlieue* of Bordeaux enjoyed any municipal privileges at all. Inside the towns themselves the *faubourgs* would often pay the *Taille,* whilst the old municipal area in the center of the town would be exempt; sometimes one *faubourg* would pay *Taille* while another would not. But even the least-favored *faubourg* of the most oppressive town offered a better way of life to the ambitious commoner than did the countryside, and the drift to the towns was as serious a problem to Louis XIV's government as it is to many modern ones.

To become a townsman was by no means easy, for not only did the Crown seek to stay this drift to the city, but the cities themselves kept a sharp eye on intruders who seemed likely, in our language, to "come on the bread line"; as early as 1646 the central government had decreed that any peasant settling in a town must pay *Taille* in his last place of residence for the next ten years, while most of the towns demanded a financial guarantee from the intending settler. For instance, the municipality of Rethel in 1682 refused to allow anyone to take up residence in the town who could not pay a five-franc *Taille.* At Boulogne there was a domiciliary fee of twelve francs, and at Gray in 1698 there was a scale of domiciliary fees ranging from eight to seventeen francs according to the trade of the applicant. On the other hand, a man whose services would be valuable to the town was usually given free domiciliary rights, and was sometimes even offered a salary to settle.

The attitude of the *corps de ville* towards the admission of religious orders within the walls was a cautious one, for the establishment of a new religious house raised all sorts of municipal problems. Would the parish priest's income fall off? Would the revenue of the other houses of religious decline? If the order was a mendicant one, what would be the effect on the town charities? Teaching orders were, however, welcome, and so too were the popular Capuchins, for a curious reason. Fire brigades did not exist before 1699, and, somehow or other, the Capuchins had become expert firefighters; in emergencies, in which the modern Londoner dials "fire," the seventeenth-century householder sent for the Capuchins. Finally, all towns fought hard, but generally unsuccessfully, to prevent the Jesuits settling in their midst.

Domiciliary rights, be it noted, did not make the settler a *bourgeois.* For at this time the word *"bourgeois"* did not mean inhabitant of a *bourg,* and still less was it a derogatory adjective applicable to a political theory distasteful to the speaker. Qualifications were required to become a *bourgeois,* and we may perhaps think of him as a man on whom has been conferred the Freedom of the City. The domiciled man had civil rights, the *bourgeois* had both civil and municipal rights; to become a *bourgeois,* a qualifying period of residence was always required, varying from between five and ten years. At Paris, a *bourgeois* forfeited his rank if he failed to spend seven months each year in the city. In nearly all towns an oath of allegiance to the city was demanded from the new *bourgeois,* and everywhere a sharp lookout was kept for the bogus *bourgeois;* it was much easier in old France to become a sham nobleman than a sham *bourgeois.*

The *bourgeois* no doubt valued his municipal rights, which generally included that of trial by a special tribunal, but the privilege which was naturally treasured above all others was that the rank gave exemption from the hated and oppressive *Taille.* Amongst many other privileges we notice that the *bourgeoisie* often had collective hunting rights in the *banlieue,* and that at Paris, every *bourgeois* had a right to own a tax free farm, providing that it employed two carts.

The only man not noticeably less well off in the town than in the country was the parish priest, and that for a variety of reasons. First, many towns took the view that as he owed allegiance to an external authority, he was not eligible to become a *bourgeois;* the nature of town life rendered the bond between priest and flock weaker than in the country; and he had of course no agricultural *Dîme,* while only the oldest of the town parishes were endowed. Consequently, he had to look either to the civic authorities or to his parishioners for his stipend, generally to the latter; and whoever paid him insensibly acquired a right of interfering in parish matters which was unknown in the country, and whose extent can be clearly seen in an edict of 1675, which lays it down that the churchwardens, ex-churchwardens, and the incumbent, form the committee charged with the conduct of the parish. At Gray in 1697 it is the magistrates, one notices, and not the parish priest, who draw up the tariff of fees for burials and marriages.

But if there is an almost congregational air about a city parish of the period, the parish priest seems generally to have been popular, unlike the monks and the higher clergy. For if the town was a bishopric, the bishop, too, had his troubles; frequently he or the Chapter would hold the *seigneurie* of the town, which involved him in endless quarrels with the municipality, to say nothing of the clash between seigneurial and municipal justice. But the bishop, on the other hand, held a trump card, in that he could usually appeal to the King via the royal confessor and Mme. de Maintenon, whilst the municipality could only invoke the dangerous aid of the Intendant. Dangerous because, whilst he was always ready to support his town against the local aristocracy, the Parlement, and the provincial estates, he was an adept at fishing in troubled waters. By playing off the military against the municipality, the *seigneur* against the magistrates, he sooner or later produced a situation in which all concerned awoke to find that whilst they had been quarrelling, the Intendant had become the town dictator.

Municipal government under Louis XIV shows the same lack of uniformity which characterizes every aspect of life, and which makes it difficult to arrive at a picture which shall be even approximately true for the whole country. Office by election, purchase, and royal nomination, government by assemblies of the *bourgeoisie,* government by elective assembly, wide differences in the composition of elective and elected bodies meet us at every turn; and all that emerges clearly from the confusion is an overall picture of the Crown struggling for *de facto* control of the towns, with the towns fighting, on the whole successfully, for local self-government. In no case is there a formal absolute control of a town by the central government, and in every case there is a clear recognition of the elective principle within the town.

Let us look into the typical pattern in outline.

The townspeople fell into three broad divisions: an aristocracy consisting of the officers of justice, financiers, holders of Crown offices, and members of the Parlement if there was one: the merchants, with whom this aristocracy was often at loggerheads: and the artisans, who, by and large, sided with the merchants. The two latter classes were subdivided into trade groups, each forming as it were little republics, self-governing within the city state; thus at Paris the merchants formed seven *corps,* drapers, grocers, silk-merchants, furriers, hatmakers, and wine merchants, all under the general control of the provost of the merchants, who was the senior city magistrate.

The artisan class was split into *corporations,* very roughly corresponding to trade unions, and the member, called a *compagnon,* held a recognized legal status. He was forbidden to form any combination outside his *corporation,* though in fact he was often a member of some secret trade guild as well. It should be noted that while the artisan, the member of a *corporation,* was the social inferior of the tradesman, it not infrequently happened that the artisan was the richer man of the two. In addition to the normal advantages of trades guilds, both *corps* and *corporations* had the benefit of a recognized business court, that of the *Juges-Consuls,* elected by themselves, and empowered to judge all trades disputes. The *corporations* were, of course, more numerous than the *corps,* and in Paris, by 1673, there were sixty of the former to seven of the latter. Organization was a mania in Louis XIV's France, and to live in a town made membership of a *corps* or a *corporation* inevitable. One would have thought that at least the unemployed *rentier* would have been exempt; but not a bit of it. If you were in that happy position, you were automatically a member of the *corps of bourgeois* "living nobly," and liable to be elected to office, under the usual penalties in case of noncompliance. Even prison did not enfranchise you from guild membership; at Troyes in 1643 we find the prisoners, with the approval and indeed encouragement of their keepers, forming themselves into a *corporation,* with a formally elected provost, sub-provost, and lieutenant to undertake the proper conduct of their affairs. For each *corps* and *corporation* had, of course, its elected officers, as sumptuously robed as its finances would permit, its patron saint, its annual feast, and its communal Mass. Office-bearing in either, and indeed membership, put the individual to considerable expense. But the system was cherished as clothing the common man in a little brief authority and dignity; "you would have enjoyed," writes Racine from Uzès in 1661, "seeing the carpenter, Gaillard, in his red robe." We need hardly add that, this being old France, the various *corps* and *corporations* spent a great deal of their time in quarrelling with each other over matters of precedence, and that some *corps* and *corporations* had been at law with each other for over two hundred years; and naturally, where trades overlapped, as in the case of the bakers and the pastry cooks, there was endless friction and litigation. The aristocracy of the town quarrelled as energetically as did their inferiors, generally in defense of their beloved precedence, and frequently in public.

A ceremony which had begun with a pompous procession and a distribution of largesse to the *canaille,* might easily end, as did one in Lyons in 1679, when the provost of the merchants was knocked down with a halbert in the cathedral whilst trying to pass in front of the senior magistrate.

Entry to a *corporation* was by apprenticeship, followed by a practical examination, and the payment of certain dues to the guild chest. The members of the *corps* and *corporations* normally formed the municipal roll of voters, and by their votes the municipal government was elected. The sovereignty of the city had formerly resided in the general assembly, but as towns grew in size and business became more complex, an elective assembly took its place. Furthermore, the old general assembly, being a source of tumult and disorder, was looked upon unfavorably by the central government, which did all in its power to abolish it, and usually succeeded in doing so. By the middle of the century the usual, but by no means invariable, government of a French town, was by mayor, aldermen, and city councillors, the latter being partly *ex officio* and partly elected; thus at Abbeville in 1714 all ex-mayors were councillors, and in some towns so were all the law officers of the city. The authority of these officers, whether elected or *ex officio,* was collective only, and no authority rested in the hands of individual members.

These town governments, curious islands of democracy in the sea of French absolutism, had the defects of their qualities, the chief one being that the *corporations* or working-classes had the weight of numbers on their side, and thus generally secured a majority on the council. Not only were the artisan councillors accused of accepting bribes from their fellow-citizens, but their ignorance and stubbornness often gave rise to situations which gave the central government a plausible excuse for interfering in the affairs of the town. Colbert, for instance, complains to the King in 1670 that of the twenty-four Aldermen of Niort, not one is a merchant, and reinforces his case against the elective system by pointing out that at Condom in 1664, criminals condemned to death had been elected to the town council.

The number and functions of the municipal body, the *corps de ville,* varied as widely as did the manner of its election; but it is impossible to go into the matter in any detail, as may be realized when we discover that Paris, for instance, had more than three thousand officials, ranging from the provost of the merchants down to the controller of oranges. Even the mayorial system was not made compulsory until 1692. But the broad general pattern throughout is a mayor and aldermen, supported by a city council, and including under various names, a certain number of indispensable officers. First, the *Procureur du Roi,* officially described as "the counterpoise to the Mayor," the guardian of tradition and precedent, whose duty it was to oppose the council in the interests of the populace, and who acts as officer of the Crown when the council sits in a judicial capacity. Next in seniority comes the *Greffier* or town clerk, a permanent official whose functions tended to become hereditary, and whose permanence made him the most important of municipal statesmen; he was the man who knew all the ins and outs of the *Hôtel de Ville,* and without consulting whom, no one dare act, not even the all-powerful Intendant. The duties of the *Treasurer* and the *Overseer of Public Works* require no explanation, and with the innumerable juniors we need not concern ourselves.

Louis XIV, by temperament and policy, disliked the whole idea of municipal government, and would gladly have substituted for it control of all urban business by the Intendant. But this would have been too ticklish a matter, especially in the *Midi,* the most municipally minded portion of his kingdom, and the part in which royal infiltration was most strenuously resisted. He found himself reduced to a policy of nibbling, coupled with bluff in the case of weak municipalities; he could and did use his immense prestige to influence the municipal elections, and sometimes went so far as to advise troublesome voters to try a change of air during election week. But on the whole, the municipalities struggled successfully against both his threats and his blandishments; we notice, for instance, that in the Dijon elections of 1659, the King's candidate for the mayoralty polled 318 votes out of a total of 1,420.

It was not until the 'nineties that Louis, taking advantage of sundry municipal scandals, appeared to open a direct frontal attack on the liberties of the towns. His edict, after a fatherly preamble on his desire to secure for his good towns that enlightened government which can only be ensured by having substantial citizens for municipal officers, goes on to make the leading posts permanent, and purchasable. But Louis was in fact not seeking to destroy the elective system in the towns, he was trying to raise money: and the towns reacted to the edict in the way he had guessed they would. In almost every case the towns repurchased the right of election from the Crown, thus retaining municipal independence; things went on just as before, and the hard-pressed controller-general in Paris was the richer by a handsome windfall. Henceforward, the intervention of the Crown in municipal matters is limited to the blackmailing of the city fathers by the creation of new officers which they had to buy up to retain their liberty. . . .

Municipal government was least successful in that department of its duty whose efficiency we now take for granted, namely, public hygiene and sanitation. And Paris was perhaps the dirtiest city in France. Paris mud left an indelible stain on all it touched, and from whatever direction you approached the capital, Paris mud could be smelt two miles outside the gates. Only those who have traveled on foot through a Chinese town can form any accurate idea of a Paris street, and the resemblance between the two must have been remarkable. In Paris, the stroller would find the same narrow thoroughfare, carpeted in filth, with the central gutter, or rather succession of stagnant pools, choked with dung, entrails, litter of all kinds: the droves of foraging pigs and poultry, the dark open-fronted cavernous shops, each with its trade sign suspended on a gallows and almost touching that of the shop on the other side of the street: the mounds of human excrement and kitchen rubbish outside the doors, awaiting the arrival of the municipal cart to transport it out of the city, where it will be seized upon for manure by the suburban market gardener: the well-to-do in sedan chairs, whose bearers may at any moment deposit the chair in a midden for greater ease whilst expostulating with a clumsy carter. It was not until I first entered a Chinese city that I suddenly understood why Louis XIV's Parisians always wore scented gloves in the streets.

For this state of affairs the municipality was not entirely to blame. Paris contained several large *seigneuries,* each with full seigneurial rights, and within whose bounds the city was powerless to interfere; worse still, the Parisian *seigneurs* were not as a rule individuals, but religious orders, chapters, *commanderies* and the like, and such bodies are notoriously hard to move. Furthermore, all Parisians offered a stubborn passive resistance to all sanitary regulations, and as the middle of the street invariably formed the boundary between competing jurisdictions, any uniform policy of street cleansing was an impossibility, even had the inhabitants desired it, which they didn't. As early as 1644 it had been enacted that all latrines in the city must be emptied by the municipal scavengers before six in summer and before seven in winter, but with the usual result; the edict was reluctantly obeyed for a few days, then tacitly ignored, and as late as 1697 all household filth was still being disposed of by being flung out of the windows. In 1666 a further law was passed making the provision of sanitary accommodation compulsory in every Paris house; but several years later the city was found to have many tenements housing twenty to twenty-five families, with no sanitary arrangements whatever. In fact, generally speaking, no notice was taken of police regulations in Paris, or in any other city in the kingdom. Some little improvement is however noticeable after La Reynie became lieutenant of police in 1667, and especially after he persuaded Louis to clip the wings of the *seigneuries* in 1674. If La Reynie did not succeed in cleansing the street, he at least made them cleanable by paving them, with the result that heavy rain swept away the worst of the dirt instead of turning an evil smelling mud lane into an impassable bog. An attempt too was made to get builders to conform to a municipal specification for new constructions. But right up to the end of the reign and beyond it, complaints from a not oversensitive generation about the filth and stench of Paris are frequent and vigorous.

That such a street loving age could have tolerated this state of affairs speaks volumes for its insensibility; for to see the stir, to reap the harvest of a quiet eye, to stroll and gossip, was the chief amusement of the *canaille* and the lesser *bourgeoisie.* The true Parisian loved his dirty streets, and was never happier than when showing them off to a stranger. Let us play country cousin to Berthaud, and under his guidance explore this vanished Paris, going with him first to the Pont Neuf, which offers the appearance of a demented fairground, with more than its noise; the bridge is the rendezvous of *charlatans, passe volants,* quack ointment sellers, toothdrawers street singers, pimps, cutpurses, cloak-snatchers, conjurors, booksellers, and all, with the exception of the pimps, cutpurses, and cloak-snatchers, yelling, "Come, buy, buy, buy," at the full pitch of their lungs. Equally vociferous are the proprietors of the shooting galleries which line the bridge, who offer you three shots a penny, with the certainty of your winning a magnificent prize. The prize is your choice from an old box filled with battered books, dirty rosettes, nutcrackers, tobacco boxes, flutes, broken masks, seedy hats, and a quantity of other miscellaneous rubbish. A very little of the Pont Neuf goes a long way, and we cross the river, which here serves the triple purpose of open sewer, town drinking-water supply, and the washerwomen's place of business; though by the way, the washing of clothes in the Seine at Paris has been strictly prohibited since 1667. But nobody takes any notice of the edict. Here we are at the palace; not the King's palace of the Louvre, for the word "palace" has not yet acquired its modern meaning; the King's residences are *châteaux,* whilst palaces are law courts. The palace is a favorite strolling place, dirty and ill-smelling, even by Parisian standards, but probably no more disgusting than the Louvre, where visitors relieve themselves not only in the courtyards, but on the balconies, and staircases, and behind the doors.

Complaints of its condition were common as late as 1670, and when in the 'eighties the Court moved out to Versailles, one of the things that most surprised visitors about the new residence was that the King there insisted on the same degree of decency and cleanliness which was to be found in a private house. We find the gallery of the law courts full of little shops, and here is the place where the bookbuyer hunts for bargains, undaunted by the fact that the bookseller, like all other tradesmen, sells her wares by personal canvas, and issues a deafening catalogue of the less salable works while we turn over her stock—*Cassandra,* Arnauld's works, Bellerose, Molière, Montaigne, Rabelais, "Come buy, come buy!" Next door to her a girl is shouting her handkerchiefs and lace, pin boxes, and scissors, and from farther down the gallery come lusty praises of the next stall-keeper's Polish knives, English leather jerkins, and felt hats for wet weather, "as worn in Turkey"; while a rival tries to shout him down with his chant of collars and shirts.

Inside the hall of the palace the turmoil is nearly as great; here a lackey is caning a gingerbread seller, there we are shocked to see a man performing an operation which is not usually conducted in such publicity; not that the publicity shocks us, it is the fact that the man is in full view of a statue of the King. The room is full of attorneys of the lowest standing, and their ragtag and bobtail clientele brief them with a noisy repetitiveness and a wealth of gesticulation against which they are apparently hardened by long practice. The combined bar and restaurant of the palace is open to the public, and here we should have enjoyed our pint of wine, had we been able to shake off our hostess, who is infected with the general mania of shouting her wares, and plagues us unceasingly to order various singularly unattractive dishes; so gulping off our drink we emerge into the street to find ourselves in the middle of a fracas. Traffic, foot, horse, and wheeled, has stopped to take sides in the quarrel between that great lady's coachman and a carter, who has locked his wheel in that of the coach. Both drivers have dismounted to do themselves more justice, and the cloak-snatchers are turning the diversion to account, when a squad of archers puts an end to the entanglement with an impartial distribution of *coups de bâton,* during which we take refuge in a shop. We emerge when the storm is over, and a minute later find ourselves passing the police headquarters, the *Châtelet;* here it behooves us to be both swift and unobtrusive, for the place swarms with archers and attorney's clerks, who have a playful habit of identifying the passer-by as some badly wanted criminal and holding him to ransom. We omit the Place de La Grève from our sightseeing trip, for we have unfortunately hit upon a day when there is nothing to be seen there; had it been yesterday or tomorrow, we could have had the pleasure of watching a batch of women being flogged and branded, or a selection of rascals turned off on the gallows—dancing on air as we call it. For this, too, is one of the sights of Paris. Dr. Patin, writing to the father of his pupil, Noel Falconnet, tells him that the boy has been working so well that tomorrow he is taking him as a treat to see a man broken on the wheel. Forcing our way through a mob of itinerant image sellers, picture sellers, piemen, begging friars, led captains, and loafers, we arrive at the Cemetery of the Innocents where the professional letter-writers sit on the flat tombstones awaiting customers. That young footman has been snared by a pretty face at a window, and is commissioning a declaration of love in as high-flown a style as the writer thinks consistent with a fee of ten sous; the cook-maid in earnest colloquy with that other writer wants to *shoe the mule* as it is called, or in other words seeks his assistance in the preparation of a set of fraudulent housekeeping books; while the squint-eyed fellow in the shabby black suit wants help in drawing up a really taking circular advertising his infallible cure for syphilis.

From the cemetery we make our way to the thieves' market, a dirty, neglected street where the cloak-snatchers take their plunder to be dyed, altered, and sold, and where sometimes one can pick up a bargain. Here, as elsewhere, sales are made by patter, but the fences have a technique of their own. Commonly the dealer in stolen clothes poses as a retired soldier who has had some wonderful strokes of luck in looting; finger over lips he takes us in to the darkest recess of the shop and produces a tarnished cloak, which he took off the Grandee of Spain he shot at Rocroi, wishes he had never brought it home, for its extreme richness makes it difficult to dispose of, even at a sacrificial figure. Or, gentlemen, here is something very special; this pistol I had from a man who had it from the lackey who stole it from M. de Turenne; the actual pistol of the immortal Turenne, just think of that! But we don't think of it, and leaving the shop amidst a shower of curses, we set out for the fish market, the *Halles*.

It would be interesting to discover the connection between fish selling and bad language, which is evidently not peculiar to England; for it is clear from contemporary accounts that "the language of the *Halles*" can be best translated by the single word "billingsgate." Berthaud gives us a sample of a quarrel between two rival fishwives, conducted with a creditable pungency on both sides, but with a freedom of personal criticism and simile which unfits it for reproduction, even in a footnote. A formidable body, these ladies of the *Halles,* and, rather surprisingly, much addicted to hero-worship.

When the Duc de Beaufort was thought to have been taken prisoner by the Turks in 1669, they guaranteed a sum for his ransom that worked out at about seven louis d'or per head for the whole of their guild.

Their present favorite is Monseigneur, who sneaks into Paris as often as he thinks it safe to do so, and is in consequence very popular in the city; last time he was ill, a deputation of the corporation of fishwives went out to Versailles in cabs, were admitted to his sickroom, kissed him, promised to have Masses said for him, and after dining at Monseigneur's expense, was sent back to Paris at his charge. A periodical saunter round the *Halles* is essential to the Parisian man about town who wants to keep up-to-date, for in addition to displaying that animation which is so dear to his heart, the *Halles* is the grand manufactory of the type of story which in modern London is supposed to emanate from the Stock Exchange.

We have now exhausted the free entertainment afforded by the capital, unless you are adventurous enough to go home through the Rue de La Huchette, but most prudent visitors decline this item on hearing that its only interest lies in the fact that it is the residential quarter for the cutpurses and cloak-snatchers.

Court, country, town, which of them would we have disliked least? On the whole one is inclined to think the town.

9. PEOPLE IN PUBLIC AND IN PRIVATE

Privacy has always been a luxury and thus the possession only of the happy few. Common people were seldom left to their own devices whether at work, in their domicile, in their religious practice, or at play. Not only was everyday life to an extraordinary degree communal in conception and practice, there simply was no interior space to which to withdraw. It is a mistake to believe that only modern city dwellers have a sense of being crowded. Except for monks and hermits, in fact, the notion of "getting away from it all" seems to have been conspicuously absent during most of European history. The following essays illustrate this point as they examine forms of amusement, sexual practices, and family life in the seventeenth and eighteenth centuries.

Lilly C. Stone shows the importance that organized games and sports held for all strata of society. These were not the great spectacles of antiquity or modernity; rather they took the form of fairs, festivals, and public contests. As in medieval times, the Church often provided the occasion for a public gathering, even though clergymen were wont to condemn many innocent and some not so innocent pastimes. Not too much had changed in this regard, it seems, since Bodo's time. We may be surprised to learn how many forms of entertainment in which we engage today were commonplace centuries ago. These include both the sports in which common people could participate (archery, bowling, cricket, handball, soccer, fishing), and those reserved mostly for the upper classes (tennis, golf, fencing, card-playing, horse-racing). As a formalized ritual, of course, hunting was also a pleasure strictly for the well-to-do. The one universal sport was gambling; only the amount of the wagers varied.

Edward MacLysaght is aware that the tendentious nature of his sources requires the utmost caution in generalizing about the state of morality. He focuses on manners and morals in Ireland—marriage, divorce, prostitution, premarital sex, drunkenness—and finds a not unfamiliar blend of prudery and promiscuity. Perhaps the key word in his account is "unscreened"; however properly or improperly people conducted themselves, usually their behavior was of necessity in public view.

Philippe Aries traces the evolution of the family. The pattern of home life, he contends, was set by the higher orders of society and eventually imitated by the poor. Before the eighteenth century even the wealthy were accustomed to severe crowding indoors. Only gradually were separate rooms set aside for special purposes. Until then all the normal functions of life were performed in a single space within four walls. It is interesting to note how the precision of our vocabulary has increased as time proceeded and people developed the means and taste for privacy. We are reminded that the nuclear family is a relatively modern invention, one which the majority of mankind could not begin to adopt until very recent times.

Modernization is a relative concept for two reasons; first, because social change has been so various in time, place, and class; and secondly, because there is no fixed point toward which society is converging. No sooner do new social patterns appear than they are being altered in ways complex and unanticipated. If a sharper distinction between the private and public sectors of social discourse is a sign of modernity, it is scarcely one which has gone unchallenged. The recurrent complaints about the atomization of modern life, in fact, suggest the contrary. Innovation often seems, on closer examination, to be no more than a reversion to earlier social forms in a different combination. The truism remains true: change is the only constant.

LILLY C. STONE

Amusements and Sports

Although sports and pastimes in Shakespeare's Age were far less highly organized than they are today, human nature was much the same, and Englishmen enjoyed many of the activities that still have a place in their recreations. To have an understanding of the social life and customs of a nation, a knowledge of its recreations is essential. The way a people spend their moments of leisure provides a clue to their personalities and qualities of character.

During the years when the Tudors and early Stuarts governed England, roads were poor, travel was difficult and sometimes dangerous, and ordinary folk usually did not go far beyond their parish limits for pleasure. Furthermore, life was hard for the ordinary citizen, and few had time for much leisure. Consequently, both time and opportunity were lacking for organized sports that could attract widespread attendance like a modern football match or modern horse racing. To working men and apprentices many sports were forbidden by statute except on such specified holidays as Christmas, but the laws were not always rigidly enforced.

Despite difficulties and handicaps, however, people of all classes enjoyed a variety of simple sports and amusements. If the Elizabethans had to work long hours at hard tasks, they nevertheless found time for play and gaiety. Fairs, festivals, and church wakes provided opportunities to villagers for many amusements. Everyone could look forward to the local fair, at which vendors of a variety of wares spread out their goods for sale. To the fairs came gleemen, jugglers, tumblers, acrobats, and animal trainers with their beasts: a dancing bear, monkeys, an exotic camel, and an "educated" horse. Traveling showmen also brought freaks, as in the "sideshow" at carnivals today, and sleight-of-hand artists were common. After the buying and selling were over, visitors to the fair, adults and children alike, joined in the activities. Women might dance for a prize, and

Lilly C. Stone, *English Sports and Recreations* (Charlottesville, Va.: University Press of Virginia, 1971), pp. 429–35, 445–55. Published for the Folger Shakespeare Library.

264

the men engaged in foot races, bowling matches, wrestling, and other similar competitions. One of the most curious events, at which stout young men sought to show their worth and endurance, was the sport of shin kicking. Before this event the participants rubbed both their boots and shins with blue vitriol to harden them. At the close of the day many a young countryman must have been sore and sorry.

Festivals celebrated special occasions, such as the end of the harvest, sheepshearing, and the beginning of spring. Church wakes were held on a saint's day or the day of dedication of the church. A wake began with the vigil at the church and a service; then followed feasting, drinking, and contests of skill and strength like those at fairs. Originally these celebrations were held in the churchyard, but as the activities became more and more secular the churchyard was abandoned or forbidden. Many of the festivals stemmed from pagan rites, and the church thought to remove the taint of heathenism somewhat by acknowledging and modifying them. With the rise of the Puritans, however, objections grew louder, especially to such celebrations as church ales. On these occasions the churchwardens provided a quantity of malt, some from the church stock and the rest from parishioners. The malt was brewed into beer and ale and then sold to raise money for the church. This practice was condemned vociferously by Philip Stubbes, who complained in his *Anatomy of Abuses* (1583) of a situation in which profit to the church increased in proportion to the consumption of beer and the drunkenness that followed.

Pious Philip Stubbes also spoke out against the revelry that took place on May Day. On the eve of this holiday, or in the early morning hours of the day itself, people were accustomed to go into the forests to gather boughs and branches as decorations for their homes. A Maypole would be cut and drawn into the village by oxen. Each ox had flowers tied to its horns and the pole was decorated with herbs, flowers, and ribbons. When the pole was erected, the dancing began. The morris dance was traditional on May Day with a fiddler, Maid Marian, and ten men dressed with horns and bells. Maid Marian was queen of the May and mistress of the archery games. In later years Robin Hood was introduced, probably as king of the May. Upon such levity Stubbes frowned, but he deplored most of the fact that the young men and girls "run gadding over night to the woods, groves, hills, and mountains" and there spend the night "in pleasant pastimes." He declared on "good authority" (one wonders if his own) that of a hundred maids going out scarcely a third returned in the state of virginity.

Archery occupied an important place in the May-Day activities, for it was virtually the national sport. Laws discouraged other physical exercises so that men would not be diverted from the practice of archery.

From the time of Edward III when the value of the longbow was effectively demonstrated, it was thought wise to have all the men of England ready as trained archers in case of war. By the beginning of the seventeenth century the usefulness of archery in war was declining. As R. Barret says in *The Theory and Practice of Modern Wars* (1598) "they [archers] may serve to some sorts of service, but to no such effect as any of the fiery weapons," but the victories of the longbow at Crécy, Poitiers, and Agincourt were not quickly forgotten, and every man was expected to own a longbow and to practice regularly. Shooting contests were held to stimulate interest, and even chudchwardens' accounts sometimes include expenses for making archery butts. Butts were mounds of earth, banked with turf. Against this mound was placed a white disk for a target. Shooting at these taught accuracy. To learn to "keep a length" the archers practiced "prick" or "clout" shooting, which meant shooting at a target eighteen inches in diameter, stuffed with straw. This mark was placed at a distance of 160 to 240 yards. "Roving" was to shoot in the open, at no mark, and at unknown distances.

Archery was praised as good for all men, great or poor. Gervase Markham in *The Art of Archery* (1634), dedicated to Charles I, calls it an honest and wholesome sport, and much earlier, in *Toxophilus* (1545), Roger Ascham referred to archery as "the most honest pastime of all" and a cure of evil gaming. Ascham, who was at one time tutor to Elizabeth I, felt that a genuine effort should be made to teach archery because, truth to tell, the interest in archery was waning. He felt that many disobeyed the royal laws for lack of knowledge of how to shoot. Christina Hole suggests in *English Sports and Pastimes* that enthusiasm died out because laws commanded the practice of archery instead of leaving it to the pleasure of sportsmen.

An act passed in 1541 in the reign of Henry VIII shows us to what extent the government favored archery. After declaring that all able men under sixty must own a longbow and practice shooting, the act continues with a list of activities which are banned: "That no manner of person or persons . . . shall for his or their gain . . . keep . . . or maintain, any common house, alley, or place of bowling, quoiting, cloish, kayles, half-bowl, tennis, dicing, table, or carding, or any other manner of game prohibited by any statute heretofore made, or any unlawful new game now invented or made, or any other new unlawful game hereafter to be invented, found, had or made. . . ."

In spite of this act gaming houses were kept open, and the various sports flourished. Bowling was probably the most popular. Robert Crowley, printer and Puritan preacher as well as poet, testifies that bowling was not suppressed. In his *One and Thirty Epigrams* (1550), appeared this poem on bowling:

> Two sorts of alleys
> In London I find;
> The one against the law,
> And the other against kind.
> The first is where bowling
> Forbidden, men use,
> And wasting their goods,
> Do their labor refuse.
> But in London (alas!)
> Some men are devilishly
> Suffered to profess it
> As an art to live by. . . .

Two types of bowling were popular then as now. The favorite was played on bowling greens. Bowling in alleys, similar to the modern game, was also common. Bowling greens were often included as part of the gardens in the estates of the gentry, but bowling was not a sport for the rich alone. Besides having alleys in the supposedly illegal gaming houses, men also played at bowls in the open country, according to Gervase Markham's description in *Country Contentments* (1615): "There is another recreation . . . that is, bowling, in which a man shall find great art in choosing out his ground and preventing the winding, hanging, and many turning advantages of the same, whether it be in open wild places or in close alleys; and in this sport the choosing of the bowl is the greatest cunning; your flat bowls being the best for alleys, your round biased bowls for open grounds of advantage, and your round bowls like a ball for greenswards that are plain and level." Charles Cotton, who in the later seventeenth century wrote *The Complete Gamester* (1674), "borrowed" this passage from Markham. Cotton, however, does add a caution against gambling at a bowling match. In his advice on learning the game he states that "practice must be your best tutor . . . ; and that I shall say, have a care you are not in the first place rooked out of your money." Cotton's comments on the weird postures assumed by bowlers as the bowl is rolling down the alley, and the cries to go further or stop shorter, suggest that a bowler of the sixteenth century would not feel out of place in a twentieth-century bowling alley.

Many of the bowling terms, such as "rub," "jack," or "kiss," can be found in Shakespeare, and it appears probable that he was a knowledgeable bowler. A "rub" is anything that diverts the ball from its course (as in Hamlet's soliloquy: "Ay, there's the rub"); a "jack" (also "master" or "mistress") is a small bowl placed as a mark at which to aim; and a "kiss" occurs when one bowl touches another (as in *Cymbeline*, II.i.: "Was there ever man had such luck! When I kissed the jack, upon an up-cast to be hit away!").

Kayles, cloish, and loggats were all closely allied to bowling. In the game of kayles there were six or more pins set up in a straight row. Instead of bowling a ball at the pins, the object was to knock the pins down by throwing a stick at them. Cloish also consisted of setting pins in a row, but a bowl was used to knock them down. In loggats, a game popular with boys and country folk, bones were substituted for the pins, and another bone was thrown at them. Shakespeare has a reference to this sport in the grave-digging scene where Hamlet comments: "Did these bones cost no more the breeding but to play at loggats with 'em?"

Men and boys of the sixteenth century, like their counterparts in other ages, enjoyed various forms of ball games. The variety of games played with balls was great, but often the same game appeared in different sections of the country under different names. As early as 1598 one finds a reference to cricket being played fifty years before. Cricket perhaps was an outgrowth of stoolball and clubball. In playing stoolball, a bowler tried to hit a stool with a ball. One player tried to defend the stool with his hand. In some localities a bat was used. In this game, however, there were no runs. Another game with overtones of cricket was trapball. A ball was placed in a spoon-shaped piece of wood. When the spoon was hit, the ball would rise and was hit into the field. Opponents tried to catch the ball, or to bowl the ball in to hit the trap.

Handball is probably the oldest form of ball game. Many games were derived from it, including fives and a form of tennis. Fives was played against a wall or church tower. This led to complaints from ministers against the delinquent boys who not only did not attend church but disturbed the service by playing ball against the church walls! Rules apparently differed in various geographical areas, as at Eton, where the buttresses from the wall formed two additional sides, and the game called "Eton Fives" developed.

Football was not unknown to the Elizabethan age, but it is hardly recognizable as the game we know today. The main similarity is that a ball, usually a bladder filled with air and encased in leather, was used, and the object was to get the ball across a goal line. What happened in between was nothing short of chaos or, as Sir Thomas Elyot says in *The Book Named the Governor* (1531), "nothing but beastly fury and extreme violence." There were few if any rules, and each team could have an unlimited number of players. Often there were interparish contests, in which case much of the parish might be commandeered for the playing field, as one set of players tried to kick the ball into the opposing parish. On other occasions an open field or common was used. If the game was a parish affair, it was usually played on a holiday or feast day. At Chester a game was always played at Shrovetide, and legend has it that it commemorated the kicking about of the head of a captured Dane. Often it was a contest between two special groups of people, such as married men and bachelors. At Inverness, Scotland, an annual game was played between the married and the single women—and it is reported that the married women usually won!

Football was another sport prohibited by law to the working man as early as 1349 and as late as Elizabeth's reign. James I in *Basilicon Doron* (1599), a book of instructions for his son, forbids the prince to play football because he thought it "meeter for laming than making able the users thereof." Philip Stubbes gives us a vivid description in his *Anatomy of Abuses* of what happens during a game which he considers a "bloody and murdering practice."

> For doth not everyone lie in wait for his adversary, seeking to overthrow him and to pick him on his nose, though it be upon hard stones, in ditch or dale, in valley or hill . . . he careth not so he have him down . . . so that by this means, sometimes their necks are broken, sometimes their backs . . . legs . . . arms. . . .
>
> . . . They have the sleights to meet one betwixt two, to dash him against the heart with their elbows, to hit him under the shortribs with their gripped fists, and with their knees to catch him upon the hip and to pick him on his neck, with a hundred such murdering devices. . . .

Such a commentary suggests that Stubbes himself had been involved at least once in a friendly game of football. . . .

Fishing was as popular with Tudor Englishmen as it is with men of the atomic age. These fishermen of old had just as much trouble catching fish as men of all centuries, although modern editors of Elizabethan fishing treatises contend that fish have grown craftier over the years. Methods and equipment were somewhat different then. Although fishing rods could be bought at the haberdasher's, the various books on the subject describe the rod and line with such care that it is evident that many Elizabethans were given to making their own. Rods were of three types, according to Markham's *Pleasures of Princes* (1614): of two pieces, the lower being nine to ten feet and the upper about a yard long; of one whole piece, which meant a short rod good only for narrow streams; of many pieces, usually made of cane, that fit into one another. The line was made of horsehair with threads of silk intertwined. Some years later Robert Venables in *The Experienced Angler* (1662) preferred a line of either horsehair or silk, but not a mixture.

Until the middle of the seventeenth century fishermen had no reels. Since the line was attached to a loop at the end of the rod, it was not possible to play the trout until it tired. Even when reels did appear, they were used more for salmon than for trout.

Elizabethan fishermen did not favor fishing upstream with a dry fly. Upstream angling was first mentioned by Venables and then with disapproval. He believed that in casting upstream one's line was more likely to hit the water before the fly, or at least the line would be visible, and in either case the fish would be frightened away—all of which argues the inexpertness of Venables as a fly-caster or the poor quality of the equipment then available.

Various baits were used, and Venables suggests that once a week a fisherman, if he had a special fishing spot, should cast in all sort of food, such as corn boiled soft, grain dipped in blood, or worms. Then the fish would be less suspicious of bait. Live baits consisted of such delicacies as red worms, maggots, flies, grasshoppers, hornets, wasps, and snails. Dried wasps, clotted blood of sheep, corn, seed, cheese, berries, cherries, or pastes were used as dead bait. For those who preferred fly-fishing, books told how to make one's own flies. According to Izaak Walton's classic, *The Compleat Angler,* "if he hit to make his fly right, and have the luck to hit, also, where there is store of trouts, a dark day, and a right wind, he will catch such store of them as will encourage him to grow more and more in love with the art of fly-making." This implies a big "if," but all writers on fishing stress the virtues a fisherman must have, the foremost being patience. As Markham writes: "Then he must be exceeding patient and neither vex nor excruciate himself with losses or mischances, as in losing the prey when it is almost in the hand, or by breaking his tools."

One unusual form of fishing was "tickling," in which a fisherman cautiously ran his arm under a bank until he touched a trout and then slowly tickled it until he was in a position to seize it.

Fishing was a sport sufficiently in favor to receive the blessing of university authorities in a day when sports had only a small place in university life. Sir Simonds D'Ewes mentions in a diary kept at Cambridge that angling was one of the pleasures that he enjoyed. D'Ewes also mentions a few other sports which served "as antidotes to disastrous diseases" and of course did not interfere with studies, unlike the experience of Sir Andrew Aguecheek in *Twelfth Night,* who laments: "I would I had bestowed that time in the tongues that I have in fencing, dancing, and bearbaiting."

Sports in which the students participated in their leisure time included tennis, shovegroat (shuffleboard), cards, bowling, jumping, and running. They seem to agree with Robert Crowley's idea of how a scholar should amuse himself.

> To fish, to fowl, to hunt, to hawk,
> Or on an instrument to play;
> And some whiles to commune and talk,
> No man is able to gainsay.
> To shoot, to bowl, or cast the bar,

To play tennis, or toss the ball
Or to run base, like men of war,
Shall hurt thy study nought at all.
For all these things to recreate,
The mind, if thou canst hold the mean.

Scottish universities, somewhat more advanced than those below the border, included sports and exercises as a part of the official curriculum. On certain days the students were taken to the fields for organized exercises, and the University of Edinburgh had a tennis court on its grounds. James Melville, whose memoirs dating from the late sixteenth century were published in 1842, states that at school he was taught archery, golf, fencing, running, leaping, and wrestling, and at the University of St. Andrews he played golf and engaged in archery.

Golf was a great recreation in Scotland from early times, though it did not thrive in England until the Stuart kings popularized it there. The treasurer's records in the reign of James IV of Scotland included expenses for golf equipment:

1503, Feb. 3. Item to the King to play at the golf with the
   Earl of Bothwell   xlii s
1503, Feb. 4. Item to golf clubs and balls to the King   ix s
1503, Feb. 22. Item, xii golf balls to the king   iiii s
1506, Item the 28th day of July for ii golf clubs to the King   ii s

Golf balls at this time were stuffed with feathers and covered with leather.

Tennis was played in both England and Scotland as well as on the continent. In fact, it developed from the French *jeu de paume* or "palm play." In its early stages in the Middle Ages the palm of the hand was used instead of a racket. The hand was gloved, and later strings were stretched between the fingers of the glove. The next step was a crude racket with a handle. For a long time both the hand and the racket were used, but the racket had become sufficiently popular by Chaucer's day to be mentioned in his *Troilus and Criseyde*. The racket was oblong and strung diagonally with only a few strings.

The common people played some form of open-air tennis, but the game was largely the court tennis variety, played in an enclosed court. Because of the expense it was confined for the most part to the gentry and nobility, who could afford to build their own courts. Some public courts, however, were operated by the proprietors of gaming houses. . . .

In a country of inclement weather indoor games were bound to be popular. Furthermore, even the most active could not always be running, leaping, or hitting balls, and there are always those who have no desire to engage in active sports. For moments of less activity there were cards and table games. The origin of card games dates far back in history. Cardplaying had spread over Europe before it crossed the Channel into England. By the fifteenth century card games were common in England, and Edward IV in 1463 forbade the importation of playing cards to protect local cardmakers. By 1496 cardplaying was added to the list of activities forbidden the laboring classes. Henry VII's law read that servants and apprentices could play at cards only during the Christmas holiday, and then only in their master's house. In 1628 a charter was granted the London Company of Makers of Playing Cards.

It is uncertain whether English cards were derived more from French or Spanish cards. They appear to have taken the names of their suits and the symbols from both. The Spanish suits were *espadas* (swords), *copas* (cups), *dineros* (coins), and *bastos* (clubs). In France the suits were *piques* (spears), *coeurs* (hearts), *carreaux* (squares or lozenges), and *trefles* (trefoils). The face cards on French cards were named after various emperors, queens, or famous knights. The knaves appeared in various dress, including armor, depending on the current events of a particular period. Samuel Rowlands in 1612, in his *Knave of Hearts,* indicated that the English jacks were dressed in the costume of Chaucer's time.

> We are abused in a great degree;
> For, there's no knaves so wronged as are we
> By those that chiefly should be our part-takers:
> And thus it is my masters, you cardmakers.
> All other knaves are at their own free will,
> To brave it out, and follow fashion still
> In any cut, according to the time:
> But we poor knaves (I know not for what crime)
> Are kept in piebald suits which we have worn
> Hundred of years; this hardly can be borne.
> The idle-headed French devised us first,
> Who of all fashion-mongers is the worst.

Cardplaying, as well as dicing, was condemned by many. Some claimed it to be an invention of the Devil, and because the cards were named, they described cardplaying as a form of idolatry. John Northbrooke in his *Treatise wherein Dicing, Dancing . . . Are Reproved,* published about 1577, felt that cardplaying was not so evil as dicing because there was less trust in chance. But since cardplaying furnished small training for the mind, he saw little good in it. According to him, cheating was prevalent, "either by pricking of a card, or pinching of it, cutting at the nick; either by a bum-card [i.e., a raised or marked card for cheating] finely, under, over, or in the middle, &c. and what not to deceive?" Although moralists condemned cardplaying and rogues cheated, the various games remained extremely popular through the years. Primero was played by Elizabeth I. It was a game at which two or three could play. In this the ace of spades was the best card, as it was always trump in "ombre," which succeeded "primero." Three players could participate in ombre, each receiving nine cards apiece. Trumps were named by the first player. James I liked "maw," which later became known as "five cards." In this game the five of trumps was the best card, the ace of hearts next, then the ace of trumps, and the knave. The ace of diamonds was the worst card unless diamonds were trumps. Two people could play this game—each receiving five cards. "Ruff" and "honor" required four players. Twelve cards apiece were dealt out, leaving four cards in the stack. The top card was turned up and its suit was named as trumps. The player with the ace of trumps could get the stack pile and discard four other cards. As in poker, the player bet on his hand in "post and pair." A poker face and a good bluff often won the game regardless of the cards held.

Dicing was popular and was more condemned even than cardplaying. Thomas Elyot's *Book Named the Governor* has little good to say of this form of play. "And I suppose there is not a more plain figure of idleness than playing at dice. For besides that therein is no manner of exercise of the body or mind, they which do play thereat must seem to have no portion of wit or cunning, if they will be called fair players." John Northbrooke's treatise against dicing objects to it for similar reasons. To him only play which exercises the mind or body is permissible. He cites various laws against dicing but says that royalty sets a bad example, and certainly Henry VIII was an enthusiastic gambler. Nicholas Faret, giving instruction to young gentlemen in *The Honest Man,* indicated that they should know games at hazard, but they should not be gamblers, for as he says, "There are none but great princes (whose condition can never be miserable) which may abandon themselves boldly unto it [gambling]."

The most popular dice game was called hazard. In this game the thrower calls a number between five and nine before throwing. If he throws the number called or a number with a fixed correspondence to it, he "throws a nick" and wins. If he throws two aces or a deuce and ace he "throws out" and losses. If neither, he throws until the first number thrown (the chance) comes up and he wins, or the number first called (the main) comes up, in which case he loses.

Gambling took another form in betting, particularly on horse races. Public races were established by James I, and one of the famous races was the "Bell Course" race which had for a prize a silver bell.

There were other indoor games less harmful to the moral well-being of the participant. Among these was backgammon, called "tables" in Tudor times, probably because the board consisted of two tables hinged together. The ancient game of chess has been a favorite with contemplative men throughout the ages, though James I felt that, far from relaxing a person, chess filled his head with troubles. In England chess assumed its modern shape by Elizabeth's time, a little later than in Europe. Similar to chess was the philosopher's game in which the board was in the form of a parallelogram with squares marked. Instead of chessmen, the counters used had number on them. Each player had twenty-four counters, of which one was a king. The object was to take the opponent's king and make a triumph.

Shovelboard was played on a long table. The flat weights were shoved down the table to reach certain points. This is essentially the same as the shovelboard (or shuffleboard) played on board ship except for the use of the table.

Billiards in its modern form is not too different from the game known to the Elizabethans. The table was covered with a fine green cloth and had six pockets. One difference was that sixteenth-century players used a small ivory arch called a port which stood where the pyramid spot stands now; they also used an ivory peg called a king at the other end of the table. The players had two balls with which they tried to pass the port first and then gently to touch the king.

In the evening, for those men who preferred to pit their skill against the flashing eyes and nimble feet of a pretty girl, the music would sound and the dance would begin—either a "basse" dance in which the dancer's feet did not leave the ground or the "haute" dance which required hops, leaps, kicks, or stamps. A dance could be a dignified movement or a lively form of exercise. The pavan and allemande were stately dances, whereas the galliard and volta or lavolta were more lively. In many of the dances, as in the basse dance and the pavan, the man and woman danced side by side. The courante (sometimes spelled "coranto") presented another form, in which three couples in a straight line faced the onlookers, then each other, and finally turned around again to face the audience.

Dancing, however, was not approved by all. John Northbrooke described dancing as one of the evils of the world. In his diatribe he called this amusement "the vilest vice of all" and then went on to say that "truly it cannot easily be said what mischiefs the sight and hearing do receive hereby . . . ; they dance with disordinant gestures, and with monstrous thumping of the feet, to pleasant sounds, to wanton songs, to dishonest verses."

All sports did not require active participation. One of the favorite pastimes for all was a bearbaiting match or a cockfight. Cockfighting was an old sport. In the early days boys took a cock to their schoolmasters on Shrove Tuesday. Before the masters could claim the cocks, the boys were allowed to fight them in the yard. Or else they engaged in another pastime called cockthrowing, which involved throwing sticks and stones at the cock until it was killed.

The first cockpit was not built until the time of Henry VIII. He liked the sport so much that he added a cockpit to his palace at Whitehall. Drury Lane (or the old Phoenix) Theatre began as a cockpit. Philip Stubbes tells us that houses were erected for the purpose of cockfighting, that flags and pennants would fly on the day of a fight, and that proclamations were sent to announce the coming event.

Bearbaitings were often announced by a parade with the bearward leading the bears through the street, probably accompanied by music and jesters. As early as 1526 Paris Garden in Southwark became a popular resort for bearbaiting and bullbaiting. There the bear or bull was chained to a stake and four or six mastiff dogs were turned loose. As one dog was killed another was set upon the bear. The sight of tearing flesh and spilling blood accompanied by the yelps of the dogs and the growls of the bear evidently gave the crowds great pleasure, for the events were largely attended. Robert Crowley in *One and Thirty Epigrams* gives us a good picture of the event.

> What folly is this, to keep with danger,
> A great mastiff dog and a foul ugly bear?
> And to this only end, to see them two fight,
> With terrible tearing, a full ugly sight.
> And yet me think those men be most fools of all
> Whose store of money is but very small,
> And yet every Sunday they will surely spend
> One penny or two the bearward's living to mend.
> At Paris Garden each Sunday a man shall not fail
> To find two or three hundreds for the bearward's vail.
> One halfpenny a piece they use for to give.
> When some have no more in their purse, I believe.

These brutal sports were favored by royalty, aristocrats, and the lower classes alike. Cockfighting was highly favored by James I, and Elizabeth entertained the French and Danish ambassadors on two different occasions by attending a bearbaiting. The Puritans and the city aldermen objected to this sport, not for humane reasons but because of the disorderliness of the crowds who attended. Bearbaitings were usually held on Sunday, a fact that increased the disfavor of the Puritans. The city aldermen were opposed to any large gathering, for the plague was a bitter enemy and spread easily in crowded areas. It was not until many years later, when the conditions of life improved for many people, that these sports came to be looked upon as brutal. But in the sixteenth and seventeenth centuries, when it was a common experience to see hangings, beheadings, and victims burned at the stake, the sight of dogs and bears tearing at one another must have been only a mild form of amusement.

EDWARD MACLYSAGHT

Marriage and Morals

Morals, according to the definition of the Oxford Dictionary, are "habits of life in regard to right and wrong conduct; also *spec.* sexual conduct." In modern parlance the word has come to be used almost exclusively in its restricted sense, but in heading this chapter "Morals" I do not wish to convey that it will deal exclusively with sexual morals, though, writing as I am of the second half of the seventeenth century, it is only to be expected that such evils as perjury, official corruption and even drunkenness will occupy less space than matters coming under the head of the Sixth Commandment.[1]

At that period in the upper classes family alliances were often concluded by the marriage of quite young children. After the ceremony the bride and bridegroom were forthwith taken back to their respective nurseries or schoolrooms to await an age more fitting to matrimony. Marriage in its full sense was common at seventeen and eighteen, and sometimes the parties were brought together at a much earlier age than that. Thus Mr. Berry, in his article on the Jephson family of Mallow, states that the grandmother of William Jephson, who himself was married at twelve years old in 1686, was a bride at twelve and had her first child—his father—at fifteen.[2] This practice was common in England and on the Continent also; it was equally in vogue at the beginning of the century, as is well illustrated by the matrimonial history of the Boyle family,[3] and did not die out till after the time of Queen Anne. In all classes, except the very poor, marriages were usually arranged by the

Edward MacLysaght, *Irish Life in the Seventeenth Century: After Cromwell* (New York: Barnes and Noble, 1969), pp. 47–49, 58–63, 66–71, 74–75.

[1] The Sixth Commandment in the Catholic Church is the Seventh in the Protestant.
[2] Jnl. of Cork Hist. and Arch. Soc., 1906, p. 3, et seq.
[3] See Townshend, *Life and Letters of the Great Earl of Cork,* passim.

parents.[4] In such a system, where love cannot enter into marriage except occasionally by chance, and where the most which can be hoped for is that common interests and associations may in time engender mutual respect and possibly affection, marital infidelity might well be expected to be very usual, not perhaps among unimaginative rustics of low intelligence, but with a quick-witted and lively people like the Irish. It is well known, of course, that during the eighteenth and nineteenth centuries Ireland was freer of sexual irregularity than any other country in the world though not necessarily therefore an island of saints. In the seventeenth century there was unquestionably a greater laxity of morals in this respect, but at no time was the excessive license associated with the Restoration period in England to be found in Ireland. The upper classes who, it must be remembered, were by this time predominately Protestant in religion and more or less English in blood, if they regarded mistresses almost as much as a matter of course as wives, did not indulge in that promiscuity which is the real test of depravity. The ordinary men and women of the country, though they certainly had no very high sense of morality, sexual or otherwise, were on the whole a very decent sort of people, for in weighing evidence on this point, even more than on other subjects, we shall have to take the statements of all our witnesses, except the most reliable, with a good many grains of salt. . . .

The ease with which divorces were obtained was one of the public scandals adversely commented on by writers in the sixteenth, and early seventeenth, century, though stated by Keating in his Díonbhrollach to be exaggerated. They were by now altogether less frequent but, if we are to believe the Protestant Archbishops of Armagh and Dublin, were still "decreed by Popish priests resident in Ireland."[5] Dr. Lynch admits the existence of some unnatural vices, the introduction of which into Ireland he attributes to the English soldiery, saying that he himself was ignorant of their very names before he went abroad as a young man.[6] There is no reason to believe that they were at all general in Ireland in his time, any more than the vices retailed for the delectation of readers of the sensational Sunday press are really typical of the countries from which they emanate. Certain laws in force in England against some of these were among the Acts proposed for Ireland in 1611,[7] and in this connection we may note, on the authority of the revised edition of Cowel's Law Dictionary,[8] that a well-known unnatural vice was, with perjury, an offense

---

[4] Cf. documents *re* marriage of Charles Carthy and Ellen MacGillycuddy in 1672. MacGillycuddy Papers, folios 75 and 76.

[5] C. S. P. Ireland, 1663/65, p. 360.

[6] See *Cambrensis Eversus,* Chapters IX and XII.

[7] *Carew Papers,* Vol. VI, p. 163.

[8] Published 1708. This crime was the object of legislation in Ireland in the reign of Charles I. See House of Commons Journal.

exempted from the general pardon at the Restoration. Writing in 1698, Henri Mission remarks: "The English say both the word and the thing came to them from Italy and are strangers to England. Indeed they love the fair sex too well to fall into such an abomination. In England as well as almost all other countries, it is a crime punishable with death." [9]

There was, of course, no sensational press, Sunday or periodical, in the seventeenth century, but the State Papers contain quite a number of examples of crimes which would have delighted the editors of the Yellow Press, notably one in which the chief actors finished by unsuccessfully attempting to poison their jailer and eventually paid the penalty, the man being hanged, drawn and quartered and the woman burned presumably alive.[10] Burning alive was a punishment still inflicted, even a hundred years later: thus the notorious Darky Kelly, the proprietor of a Dublin brothel, was tried for murder in 1764 and publicly burnt on Stephen's Green.[11]

Under the Brehon Law incontinency was officially regarded as a misdemeanor. While not actually an offense against the State under English law in Ireland, when free from any element of compulsion, illicit sexual intercourse was subject to penalties which could be imposed by the ecclesiastical authorities, and the courts of the Protestant churches have left many records of sentences involving either excommunications or public humiliation.[12] The latter usually consisted of standing for the greater part of a day in the public place of repentance, in some parishes this ordeal having to be undergone Sunday after Sunday for months, when the guilty person did not show proper signs of contrition.[13]

Prostitutes were to be found in the towns, as probably they have been in all countries and in most ages. Barnaby Rich, writing in 1610 after forty-seven years in Ireland, describing himself as an enemy to Popery but not to Ireland—"let them understand that I love Ireland"—noted that there were in Dublin a number of idle, lazy housewives called tavern keepers, most of them well-known harlots, and remarks that it is rare

[9] *Memoirs and Observations* (English edn., London, 1719), p. 20.

[10] C. S. P. Ireland, 1666/69, p. 358.

[11] Gilbert, *History of Dublin*, Vol. I, p. 94. See also Appendix B. Dunton's Fourth Letter.

[12] Dwyer, *History of the Diocese of Killaloe*, pp. 350–66. For survival of public penance well into the eighteenth century, see *Alexander the Coppersmith*, p. 96.

Though not, of course, a member of the Established Church, the famous Quaker, William Edmundson, was excommunicated in 1682 for his persistent refusal to pay tithes. This penalty was accompanied by a sentence of imprisonment. Wight, *Hist. of People Called Quakers in Ireland*, 1653 to 1700. 4th ed., 1811, p. 135. See also Edmundson's *Journal*, Dublin, 1715. For Quakers see Chapter IX.

[13] See Session Book of Templepatrick Presbyterian Church, Co. Antrim, 1646. Printed Jnl. of R.S.A.I., Vol. LXXXI, pp. 164, 165: also Gilbert, *History of Dublin*, Vol. I, p. 213 and p. 255.

to find one of the innumerable taverns without a strumpet.[14] In 1644 le Gouz visited Limerick, and remarked: "In this city there are great numbers of profligate women, which I would not have believed on account of the climate." John Stevens, a Catholic like le Gouz, who also saw Ireland more or less under war conditions (1689), is very severe in his comments: "The women were so suitable to the times that they rather enticed men to lewdness than carried the least face of modesty, in so much that in every corner of the town might be said to be a public stew. In fine, Dublin seemed to be a seminary of vice, and an academy of luxury, or rather a sink of corruption and living emblem of Sodom."[15] By way of comment on this we may notice the opinion of Mr. Justice Clodpole in 1668, that Dublin was but the lesser Sodom but pure of Irish (i.e., it was not, in his opinion, an Irish town).[16] John Dunton, again, never tires of the subject of sexual looseness in Dublin, but this righteous hypocrite's obvious preference for a pornographic tit-bit to the dull truth detracts greatly from his value as a witness, notwithstanding his undoubtedly keen powers of observation. Nor were the institutions complained of, or enjoyed by our authorities according to their several characters and natures, entirely confined to the largest towns. In Bandon, for instance, one of the presentments of the Grand Jury of the County Cork in 1699 was against "Eliz. Dennis for being a whore and keeping a common bawdy house."[17]

In considering the general question of sexual morality we must keep in mind not only the difference which already existed between rural and urban life, and the difference between class and class, but also the fact that there were two fairly distinct races in Ireland, one constituting a powerful minority upheld by outside power, the other comprising the vast majority, but already descending towards that submergence which was completed a couple of generations later.

The two works known as *The Irish Hudibras* both purport to describe the native Irish in rural surroundings. Both were written by Englishmen, or at least by men of English blood: James Farewell is extremely coarse, but, beyond a reference to venereal disease, he has nothing to say against the morals of the ordinary people. His countrywoman is no doubt a rather revolting figure, but apparently virtuous enough, and it is only the "poor kitchen wench" who is ravished by tories, and unwillingly at that. William Moffet, writing later of the same time,

[14] *New Description of Ireland.* Introduction, and pp. 70–71.
[15] *Journal* (ed. Murray), p. 93.
[16] *Carte Papers,* Vol. I, p. 123. Quoted Prendergast, *Cromwellian Settlement,* p. 297.
[17] MS. T.C.D. N.3. 20.

is more explicit. The scurrilous abuse indulged in by his women during their dispute as to which of them belonged to the best family could hardly be equalled in Billingsgate: they accuse each other of indiscriminate relations with grooms and soldiers even after marriage, and one admits permarital indiscretions, but as she married the man afterwards she counts her wanton years no disgrace. "I was," she says, as a *coup-de-grace:*

> I was 'tis true for debt in jail
> But ne'er got living by my tail.

According to the same author it was their country way to "tumble together without screen from view." The fact that Moffet's book went into several editions is by no means a proof of the truth of the picture he paints, but it does indicate the existence of a market in England, in those days as well as today, for both pornographic literature and anti-Irish propaganda.

There is nothing in the purely native authorities of the time to suggest that the moral standard of the people was particularly low. We have already glanced at the opinions of Keating and Lynch on the Irish people of the previous generation. In common with the clergy, the poets dwell on drink more freely as a theme than sexual looseness. . . .

Generally speaking, the relations between men and women were very much what they are and always have been. One has only to read the "Love Songs of Connacht," many of which were composed in the seventeenth century, to realize that. They fell in love with all the romance and ardor of their forefathers and of their descendants. Some people were fickle, some constant; there were men without moral principles and women of easy virtue as there are today, and there were just as certainly men and women of high character. The differences lie rather in the circumstances and surroundings than in themselves. We can, in fact, feel reasonably sure that the average man and woman of the time were decent people, the same essentially as the average man and woman of today.

One is struck by the way in which le Gouz in 1644 accepted as a not very startling fact the exaggerated accounts of the massacre of vast numbers of Protestants in Ireland three years before: such an idea horrified men in the seventeenth century little more than the contemplation of statistics of road fatalities does in the twentieth. So, too, the accepted conception of what constituted decency was different at that time from our notions on the subject at the present day, just as the standards in this respect of two highly civilized nations may differ now. In France, for instance, a man may relieve himself or a woman suckle her baby unscreened without comment, whereas in England these things are regarded as outraging the proprieties. In Japan a professional prostitute may marry and become respectable; in fact if we go outside the Christian countries, instances of such discrepancy could be multiplied *ad libitum.* We know, for example, that in the seventeenth century a certain unpleasant habit was regarded as an unforgivable sin.[18] The commonly accepted word for this is in some dictionaries, but it is stated to be "not in decent use," and there is no convenient polite synonym for it—such as 'eructate' for 'belch.' Both Farewell and Moffet assume the reader's acceptance of this view, and I presume this is what Fynes Moryson had in view when he said: "I would name a great lord among them, who was credibly reported to have put away his wife of a good family and beautiful, only for a fault as light as wind (which the Irish in general abhor), but I dare not name it, lest I offend the perfumed senses of some whose censure I have incurred in that kind." [19]

An English traveler in 1635 was rather shocked when he saw in Waterford "women in a most impudent manner treading clothes with their feet; these were naked to their middle almost, for so high were their clothes tucked about them"; [20] and Fynes Moryson described as remarkable a somewhat similar scene he witnessed, which from our modern point of view would have seemed considerably more indecorous.[21] Barnaby Rich, too, noted something of the kind, but like John Dunton in Iar Connacht at the end of the century,[22] he was more offended by the proximity of food to the woman's bare thighs than by her nakedness.[23]

To the Irish of the seventeenth century, however, mere nakedness—in its proper place—did not seem any more indecent than the exiguous bathing costumes of today do to us.[24] The habit of sleeping naked dates from early times. It was quite general in Ireland in the seventeenth century; but it was not peculiarly Irish. Wright's *Domestic Manners of the Middle Ages* gives many woodcuts illustrating this custom, several of them belonging to the seventeenth century, from which we may see that ladies of quality in England slept naked,[25] just as the lower orders of society did; and, of

[18] See Dunton's 3rd Letter, Appendix B, p. 359. Dineley is even more explicit on the subject, he says that it "is so abominated by an Irishman that he either quarrels, or flies from you and crosseth himself"; Page 262 of original MS. (in National Library, Dublin). This passage and others which throw much light on the personal habits of the people, were considered unprintable and omitted from the published edition of his *Observations.*

[19] Fynes Moryson, *The Commonwealth of Ireland* (Falkiner), p. 284.

[20] Brereton's *Travels,* p. 160.

[21] *Description of Ireland* (Falkiner), p. 226.

[22] See Appendix B, 2nd letter. The incident he describes very closely resembles that mentioned by Moryson.

[23] *New Description of Ireland,* p. 40.

[24] See *Dublin Scuffle,* p. 401.

[25] See woodcut on p. 411,' op. cit.

course, it is well known that the practice persisted even among quite respectable people well into the nineteenth century.

The sleeping accommodation, where small houses and large families
were concerned, has been the subject of frequent comment by travelers
and others. "Beds for the most part of the common people," says Dineley,
"are of mere straw and that scarce clean, some have ticking stuffed with
straw, without sheets, nay they pull off their very shirts so as not to wear
them out. These cabins abound with children which, with the man, maid
and wife, sometimes a traveling stranger, or pack-carrier, or pedlar or
two; aye nine or ten of them together, naked, heads and points." [26] A
description of the same custom written in 1841 is so much to the point
that I venture to quote it in full: "The floor is thickly strewn with fresh
rushes, and stripping themselves entirely naked, the whole family lie down
at once together, covering themselves with blankets if they have them,
and, if not, with their day clothing; but they lie down decently and in order,
the eldest daughter next the wall, furthest from the door, then all the sisters
according to their ages. Next the mother, father, and sons in succession,
and then the strangers, whether the traveling pedlar, tailor or beggar.
Thus, the strangers are kept aloof from the female part of the family; and
if there is an apparent community, there is great propriety of conduct. This
was the first time my friend had seen the primitive but not promiscuous
mode of sleeping [A.D. 1799]. He has, however, often seen it since." [27]
Wright states that the taste for domestic privacy grew up in England in
the sixteenth century among the upper classes, with a consequent alteration in the accommodation provided in their houses,[28] but such changes
occur gradually, and as a rule came to Ireland later than to England.

Referring to the question of nakedness and morals, the remarks of
Philip Luckombe, author of a "Tour" in 1779, are of interest. The *Tour*
is one of the best of its kind, though not, of course, as important as
Arthur Young's or entirely free from the customary condescension of
such writers. "From the promiscuous way these people lie together," he
writes, "a suspicion naturally arises in a stranger's mind, that incest is
unavoidable amongst them. Yet upon the strictest enquiry, I find the fact
to be otherwise. They are bred up in such an abhorrence of the turpitude
of this crime, that I am inclined to think it is as infrequent here, as among
more civilized nations. The better sort of people seem rather surprised
that I should entertain such an opinion; which only shews, that what we
see practiced in our infancy, though ever so unnatural, makes no impres-

[26] *Observations*, p. 21.

[27] Rev. Caesar Otway, *Sketches in Erris and Tyrawley*, p. 32. Cf. Dunton, Letters
2 and 3, Appendix B. Otway's descriptions of housing and other domestic conditions
in 1798, as well as sleeping accommodation—see pp. 28 and 29 of his *Sketches*—are
remarkably similar to those of Dunton exactly 100 years earlier.

[28] *Domestic Manners*, p. 442.

sion. A little reflection, however, will remove even the ground of suspicion. Bred up from childhood together, their wonted and innocent familiarity is carried on step by step, without impure emotions being excited. One of these poor souls is no more influenced by the nude bosom of a sister, than in a more affluent state he would be at seeing it covered with guaze. There is no indecency in mere nakedness." [29] This was equally true of an earlier generation. . . .

In 1699 a pamphlet appeared entitled *A Trip to Ireland*.[30] Whether it was printed in Dublin or London is not known, but its authorship is attributed to the celebrated or notorious Tom Brown.[31] For sheer scurrilous abuse this booklet outdoes anything else of the kind I have seen. Dunton could be outrageous enough in his descriptions of the country and its inhabitants, but if his favorable comments were mostly reserved for people whom he regarded at least as his social equals, he does not leave the reader with a perpetual bad taste in the mouth as does the author of *A Trip to Ireland*. This man, who frequently, after the manner of the period, uses without acknowledgment whole passages of the most pornographic parts of Dunton's recently published *Conversation in Ireland,* has nothing good to say of anybody or anything, except the nobility of English origin, for like all his kind he was a toady; he attributes to the Irish "the cruelty of a Spanish inquisitor, the lechery of an Italian, the levity of a Frenchman, the cowardice of a Savoyard, the perfidiousness of a Scotchman, the ignorance of a Muscovite, and the rebellious temper of a Dutchman." Yet surprisingly we find him offering evidence for the defense in the matter of drunkenness. "Drinking," he says, "is not so much their vice as some of their neighboring nations, unless their so excessive smoking be reckoned in, to which both the men and women are so generally addicted, yea, the very children, too, that an infant of their breeding shall take more delight in handling a tobacco pipe than a rattle, and will sooner learn to make use of it, than another shall of its sucking bottle." A work so contemptible as this is of value to us less for any light it throws on the question of drunkenness than as an example of the semihumorous and wholly obscene sort of scribbling which had a considerable public at the end of the seventeenth century. . . .

[29] *A Tour through Ireland, interspersed with Observations on Manners, Customs, etc.,* Dublin, 1780, pp. 164, 165. It would appear that several pages of this book, including the passages here quoted, were taken almost verbatim from Thos. Campbell's *Philosophical Survey of the South of Ireland* (1777, p. 149).

[30] Sub-title: "Being a description of the Country, People and Manners, as also some select Observations on Dublin."

[31] See Bradshaw Collection, Hib. 4. 699. 2.

PHILIPPE ARIES

Families and Homes

Since everything depended on social relations, one is bound to wonder where people met. They still often met outside, in the street. Not only by chance, because towns were comparatively small, but also because certain streets or squares were promenades where at certain hours one met one's friends, as one does today in Mediterranean towns. The teeming crowds of the Corso or the Piazza Major were to be found in squares which are now deserted or crossed by pedestrians who, even when they loiter, are unknown to one another. The present-day tourist finds it hard to recognize the Place Bellecour at Lyons in this description of it given by an Italian traveler of 1664, the Abbé Locatelli: [1] "Men and women were walking about arm in arm, holding one another as one holds a child. . . . A woman gave her arm to two men, a man his arm to two women. Unaccustomed as we were to these manners [the good priest came from Bologna where people were more reserved than in Lyons], we thought we had entered a brothel . . . I noticed how gay they all were, and at the entrance to the promenade, I saw them take each other by the arm, which they held bent like the handle of a basket, and they walked about in this way." The surprise felt by this seventeenth-century Bolognese at the sight of this laughing population walking about arm in arm is the same as that which we experience today when we mingle with an Italian crowd.

People met in the street; where did they forgather? In nineteenth-century France, and modern France too, the men often gather together in the café. Contemporary French society remains unintelligible unless one recognizes the importance of the café: it is the only meeting-place which is accessible at any time, as regular as a habit. The English equivalent is the "public house" or pub. The society of the sixteenth and seventeenth centuries was a society without a café or pub: the tavern was a place of ill repute reserved for criminals, prostitutes, soldiers, students on the spree, down-and-outs, and adventurers of every sort—it was not frequented by

Philippe Aries, *Centuries of Childhood: A Social History of Family Life,* trans. Robert Baldick (New York: Alfred A. Knopf, Inc., 1962), pp. 390–404.

[1] Locatelli, *The Adventures of an Italian priest,* edited by W. Blunt, London, 1956.

decent people, whatever their station in life.[2] There were no other public places except private houses, or at least certain private houses: the big houses in either the town or country.

What do we mean by a big house? Something very different from the meaning we would give today to the same expression. A house today is said to be big in relation to the density of its population. A big house is always a house with few people in it. As soon as the population density rises, people say that they are beginning to feel cramped for room, and the house, comparatively speaking, is no longer as big as it was. In the seventeenth century, and also in the fifteenth and sixteenth centuries, a big house was always crowded, with more people in it than in little houses. This is an important point, which emerges from all the investigations into density of population made by demographic historians.

The population of Aix-en-Provence at the end of the seventeenth century has been studied by means of the capitation register of 1695.[3] In the light of these analyses, a sharp contrast can be seen between the poor, densely populated districts and the rich, less populated districts: the former had little houses with few people in each house, the latter big houses crowded with people. Some houses contained three or fewer than three occupants, while others contained twenty-five people (two masters, six children, seventeen servants) or seventeen people (two masters, eight children, seven servants).

This contrast was not peculiar to the seventeenth century or to Provence. A recent article on Carpentras in the middle of the fifteenth century gives the same impression.[4] Twenty-three families of notabilities comprised one hundred and seventy-seven people, or 7.7 people to each house; 17.4 percent of the population lived in houses containing more than eight people. One noble had twenty-five people in his house. The cathedral architect lived with fourteen other people. It is a delicate matter to draw conclusions about the birthrate from these figures. But they show clearly that the houses of the rich sheltered, apart from the family proper, a whole population of servants, employees, clerics, clerks, shopkeepers, apprentices and so on. That was the case from the fifteenth to the seventeenth century in the greater part of Western Europe. The houses in question were big houses, with several rooms on each floor and several windows overlooking the street, courtyard or garden. Taken by themselves they formed a veritable social group. Beside these big, crowded houses there were tiny houses containing only married couples and probably just a few of their

[2] But Lagniet, in his *Proverbes,* depicts a tavern in which a child does not seem out of place.

[3] J. Carrière, "La Population d'Aix-en-Provence à la fin du XVIIe siècle," *Annales de la Faculté des Lettres d'Aix-en-Provence,* 1958.

[4] R. H. Bautier, "Feux, population et structure sociale au milieu du XVe siècle," *Annales E. S.,* 1959, pp. 255–68.

children, the youngest. In the towns, these were houses such as are still to be found here and there in the old districts, houses with only one or two windows on each floor. According to Paul Masson, it seems that the house with two windows was considered at Marseilles to be an improvement on the house with one window: "The apartments on each floor are composed of two rooms, one overlooking the street, the other overlooking a narrow space separating the backs of these houses from those of the next street." [5] Often the two windows lighted only one room. Thus there were only one or two rooms in these urban lodgings. In the country, the little houses had no more than that, and when there were two rooms, one of them was reserved for the animals. They were obviously shelters for sleeping and sometimes (not always) eating. These little houses fulfilled no social function. They could not even serve as homes for families. The housing crisis after the Second World War has taught us something of the effect of housing on the family. Admittedly people were not as sensitive about promiscuity under the ancien regime. But there has to be a certain amount of space or family life is impossible, and the concept of the family cannot take shape or develop. We may conclude that these poor, badly housed people felt a commonplace love for little children—that elementary form of the concept of childhood—but were ignorant of the more complex and more modern forms of the concept of the family. It is certain that the young must have left at a very early age these single rooms which we would call hovels, either to move into other hovels—two brothers together, or husband and wife—or to live as apprentices, servants or clerks in the big houses of the local notabilities.

In these big houses, neither palaces, nor yet mansions, we find the cultural setting of the concept of childhood and the family. Here we collected all the observations which have gone to the making of this book. The first modern family is that of these notabilities. It is that family which is depicted in the abundant family iconography of the mid-seventeenth century, the engravings of Abraham Bosse, the portraits of Philippe de Champaigne, the scenes by the Dutch painters. It is for that family that the moralist pedagogues wrote their treatises, that more and more colleges were founded. For that family, that is to say for the whole group it formed, a group which comprised, apart from the conjugal family, not other relatives (this type of patriarchal family was clearly very rare) or at the very most bachelor brothers, but a houseful of servants, friends and protégés.

The big house fulfilled a public function. In that society without a café or a "public house," it was the only place where friends, clients, relatives and protégés could meet and talk. To the servants, clerics and clerks who lived there permanently, one must add the constant flow of

[5] Paul Masson, quoted by J. Carrière, op. cit.

visitors. The latter apparently gave little thought to the hour and were never shown the door, for the seventeenth-century pedagogues considered that the frequency and the time of these visits made a regular time-table, especially for meals, quite impossible. They regarded this irregularity as sufficiently harmful for children's education to justify sending them to college, in spite of the moral dangers of school life. The constant coming and going of visitors distracted children from their work. In short, visits gave the impression of being a positive occupation, which governed the life of the household and even dictated its mealtimes.

These visits were not simply friendly or social: they were also professional; but little or no distinction was made between these categories. A lawyer's clients were also his friends and both were his debtors. There were no professional premises, either for the judge or the merchant or the banker or the business man. Everything was done in the same rooms where he lived with his family.

Now these rooms were no more equipped for domestic work than they were for professional purposes. They communicated with one another, and the richest houses had galleries on the floor where the family lived. On the other floors the rooms were smaller, but just as dependent on one another. None had a special function, except the kitchen, and even then the cooking was often done in the hearth of the biggest room. Kitchen facilities in the towns did not allow of many refinements, and when there were guests, dishes were bought ready-cooked from the nearest caterer. When Hortensius, Francion's master, wanted to entertain some friends, he told his servant: "Go and ask my neighbor the tavern-keeper to send me some of his best wine together with a roast. Now he said this because as it was already very late, and seeing that the latest to arrive had brought a hurdy-gurdy, he realized that he would have to offer supper to all the people in his room." Francion went out with the servant. At the tavern-keeper's, "we found nothing to suit us and we just bought some wine. We decided to go to the cook-shop on the Petit Pont. The servant bought a capon, and as he also wanted a sirloin of beef, went into all the cook-shops to see if he could find a good one."

People lived in general-purpose rooms. They ate in them, but not at special tables: the "dining table" did not exist, and at mealtimes people set up folding trestle-tables, covering them with a cloth, as can be seen from Abraham Bosse's engravings. In the middle of the fifteenth century the humanist architect Alberti,[6] very much a *laudator temporis acti,* recalled the manners of his childhood: "When we were young . . . the wife would send her husband a little jug of wine and something to eat with his bread; she dined at home and the men in the workshop." He must not be taken

[6] P. H. Michel, *La Pensée de L. B. Alberti,* 1930.

literally, for this custom was still common in many artisan and peasants homes at the time he was writing. But he contrasted this simple custom with urban usage at the time: "the table put up twice a day as for a solemn banquet." In other words, it was a collapsible table, like so many pieces of furniture in the early seventeenth century.[7]

In the same rooms where they ate, people slept, danced, worked and received visitors. Engravings show the bed next to a dumb-waiter loaded with silverware, or in the corner of a room in which people are eating. A picture by P. Codde (1636) shows a dance: at the far end of the room in which the mummers are dancing, one can make out a bed with the curtains around it drawn.[8] For a long time the beds too were collapsible. It fell to the apprentices or pages to put them up when company was expected. The author of *Le Chastel de joyeuse destinée* congratulates the youths "dressed in the livery of France" on their agility at setting up beds.[9] As late as the early seventeenth century Heroard wrote in his diary on March 12th, 1606: "Once he [the future Louis XIII] had dressed, he helped to undo his bed." March 14th, 1606: "Taken to the Queen's apartments, he was lodged in the King's bedchamber [the King was away fighting] and helped to take his wooden bed round to the Queen: Mme de Montglat installed her bed there to sleep there." On September 8th, 1608, just before setting out for Saint-Germain, "he amused himself by undoing his bed himself, impatient to leave." [10] Already, however, beds had become less mobile. Alberti, in his regrets for the good old days, wrote: "I remember . . . seeing our most notable citizens, when they went off to the country, taking their beds and their kitchen utensils with them, and bringing them back on their return. Now the furniture of a single room is bigger and more expensive than that of a whole house used to be on a wedding day." [11] This transformation of the collapsible bed into a permanent piece of furniture undoubtedly marks an advance in domesticity. The ornamental bed, surrounded by curtains, was promptly seized upon by artists to illustrate the themes of private life: the room in which husband and wife came together, in which mothers gave birth, in which old men died, and also in which the lonely meditated. But the room containing the bed was not a bedroom because of that. It remained a public place. Consequently the bed had to be fitted with curtains which could be opened or drawn at will, so as to defend its occupants' privacy. For one rarely slept alone, but either with one's husband or wife or else with other people of one's own sex.

Since the bed was independent of the room in which it stood, there could

7 Père du Colombier, *Style Henri IV et Louis XIII,* 1941, p. 49.

8 P. Codde, reproduced in Berndt, 187.

9 *Jardin de Plaisance,* edited by Droz and Piaget, p. 93.

10 Héroard, op. cit.

11 P. H. Michel, op. cit.

be several in the same room, often one in each corner. Bussy-Rabutin tells how one day, in the course of a campaign, a girl frightened by the troops asked him for protection and hospitality: "I finally told my servants to give her one of the four beds in my room." [12]

It is easy to imagine the promiscuity which reigned in these rooms where nobody could be alone, which one had to cross to reach any of the communicating rooms, where several couples and several groups of boys or girls slept together (not to speak of the servants, of whom at least some must have slept beside their masters, setting up beds which were still collapsible in the room or just outside the door), in which people forgathered to have their meals, to receive their friends or clients, and sometimes to give alms to beggars. One can understand why, whenever a census was taken, the houses of notabilities were always more crowded than the little one-room or two-room apartments of ordinary folk. One has to regard these families, for all that they were giving birth to the modern concept of the family, not as refuges from the invasion of the world but as the centers of a populous society, the focal points of a crowded social life. Around them were established concentric circles of relations, increasingly loose towards the periphery: circles of relatives, friends, clients, protégés, debtors, etc.

At the heart of this complex network was the resident group of the children and the servants. The progress of the concept of childhood in the course of the sixteenth and seventeenth centuries and the moralists' mistrust of the servants had not yet succeeded in breaking up that group. It was as if it were the living, noisy heart of the big house. Countless engravings show us children with servants who themselves were often very young. For example Lagniet's illustrations of a book of proverbs— a little servant is shown playing with the child of the house who is only just starting to walk.[13] The same familiarity must have existed in poorer families between artisans and laborers and their young apprentices. There was not a great age difference between the children of a big house and the servants, who were usually engaged very young and some of whom were foster-brothers of members of the family. The Book of Common Prayer of 1549 made it the duty of heads of houses to supervise the religious instruction of all the children in their house, that is to say, of all the "children, servants and 'prentices," The servants and apprentices were placed on the same footing as the children of the family. They all played together at the same games. "The abbé's lackey, playing like a little dog with sweet little Jacquine, threw her on the ground just now, breaking her arm and dislocating her wrist. The screams she gave were quite terrifying." So wrote Mme de Sévigné, who seemed to find this all very amusing.[14]

[12] Bussy-Rabutin, *Mémories*, 3 vols, 1704.
[13] Lagniet, in *Proverbes.*
[14] Mme de Sévigné, *Lettres,* August 19th, 1671.

Sons of houses went on performing domestic functions in the seventeenth century which associated them with the servants' world, particularly waiting at table. They carved the meat, carried the countless dishes in the French-style service which has now gone out of fashion and which consisted of offering several dishes at once, and poured out the wine, carrying glasses or filling them. The manuals of etiquette devoted a long chapter to the subject of waiting at table, and genre pictures often showed children performing this service.[15] The idea of service had not yet been degraded. One nearly always "belonged" to somebody. The handbooks of the type of *The Courtier* advised the *gentilhomme particulier* or minor noble to choose his master well and try to win his favor. Society still appeared as a network of "dependencies." Whence a certain difficulty in distinguishing between honorable services and mercenary services reserved for the menials: this difficulty still existed in the seventeenth century, although the servants were henceforth placed on the same footing as the despised manual workers. There still remained between masters and servants something which went beyond respect for a contract or exploitation by an employer: an existential bond which did not exclude brutality on the one hand and cunning on the other, but which resulted from an almost perpetual community of life. Witness the terms used by moralists to denote the duties of a father: "The duties of a good father can be placed under three principal heads: his first duty is to *control his wife,* the second to *bring up his children,* the last to *govern his servants.*" [16] "Solomon gives us some very judicious advice on this point, which contains all a Master's duties to his servants. There are three things, he says, which they must not lack: bread, work and scoldings. Bread because it is their right; work because it is their lot; scoldings and punishment because they are our interest." "There would be very few servants who behaved badly, if they were fed properly and paid their wages regularly." But wages were not paid as they are today. Listen to Coustel: prodigal parents "place themselves in a position where they are unable to *reward their servants,* to satisfy their creditors, or to help the poor, as is their duty." [17] Or Bordelon: "There are reciprocal duties between servants and masters. For their services and their submission, give them *compassion and financial reward.*" [18] A servant was not paid, he was rewarded: a master's relationship with his servant was not based on justice but on patronage and pity, the same feeling that people had for children. This feeling has never found better expression than in Don Quixote's thoughts when he awakens and considers the sleeping Sancho: "Sleep, you have no worries. You have committed the responsi-

---

[15] Helmont (1623–1679), "Child waiting at table," in Berndt, no. 365.
[16] De Gérard, *Entretiens,* vol. I, p. 153.
[17] Coustel, op. cit.
[18] Bordelon, op. cit.

bility for your person to my shoulders; it is a burden which nature and tradition have imposed on those who have servants. The valet sleeps while the master sits up, wondering how to *feed him, improve him and do good to him.* Fear [of a bad harvest, etc.] does not affect the servant, but only the master, who must support during sterility and famine him who served him during fertility and abundance." [19] The familiarity which this personal relationship produced can be seen in Molière's comedies, in the language of the maidservants and valets when they are speaking of their masters. In those rooms intended for no special purpose, where people ate, slept and received visitors, the servants never left their masters: in the *Caquet de l'accouchée,* dialogues between a woman who had just had a child and her visitors, the maidservant joined quite naturally in the conversation. This was not only true of the middle class, but of the nobility as well. "Madame la Princesse [de Condé]," writes Mme de Sévigné, "having conceived an affection some time ago for a footman of hers called Duval, the latter was foolish enough to show signs of impatience at the kindness which she also showed young Rabutin, who had been her page." [20] They started a fight in front of the princess. "Rabutin drew his sword to punish him, *Duval drew his too,* and the princess, stepping between them to separate them, was slightly wounded in the breast."

This familiarity was undoubtedly beginning to disappear from adult relationships, and the moralists most concerned to ensure good treatment for servants also advised the greatest reserve when dealing with them: "Speak very little to your servants." [21] But the old familiarity remained between servants and children or youths. The latter had played since infancy with the little lackeys, some of whom were personally attached to them and sometimes served them at college; a genuine friendship could arise between them. Molière's valets and the valet in Corneille's *Menteur* are well known. But a forgotten stage valet, the one in Larivey's *Les Écoliers,* expresses the feeling he has for his master with a more sincere emotion: "I was brought up with him and I love him more than any other living person."

The historians taught us long ago that the King was never left alone. But in fact, until the end of the seventeenth century, nobody was ever left alone. The density of social life made isolation virtually impossible, and people who managed to shut themselves up in a room for some time were regarded as exceptional characters: relations between peers, relations between people of the same class but dependent on one another, relations between masters and servants—these everyday relations never left a man by himself. This sociability had for a long time hindered the formation

[19] *Don Quixote.*
[20] Mme de Sévigné, *Lettres,* January 23rd, 1671.
[21] Bordelon, op. cit.

of the concept of the family, because of the lack of privacy. The development in the sixteenth and seventeenth centuries of a new emotional relationship, or at least a newly conceived relationship, between parents and children, did not destroy the old sociability. The consciousness of childhood and the family postulated zones of physical and moral intimacy which had not existed before. Yet, to begin with, it adapted itself to constant promiscuity. The combination of a traditional sociability and a new awareness of the family was to be found only in certain families, families of country or city notabilities, both nobles and commoners, peasants and artisans. The houses of these notabilities became centers of social life around which there gravitated a whole complex little world. This equilibrium between family and society was not destined to survive the evolution of manners and the new progress of domesticity.

In the eighteenth century, the family began to hold society at a distance, to push it back beyond a steadily extending zone of private life. The organization of the house altered in conformity with this new desire to keep the world at bay. It became the modern type of house, with rooms which were independent because they opened onto a corridor. While they still communicated with each other, people were no longer obliged to go through them all to pass from one to another. It has been said that comfort dates from this period; it was born at the same time as domesticity, privacy and isolation, and it was one of the manifestations of these phenomena. There were no longer beds all over the house. The beds were confined to the bedrooms, which were furnished on either side of the alcove with cupboards and nooks fitted out with new toilette and hygienic equipment. In France and Italy the word *chambre* began to be used in opposition to the word *salle*—they had hitherto been more or less synonymous; the *chambre* denoted the room in which one slept, the *salle* the room in which one received visitors and ate: the *salon* and the *salle à manger,* the *caméra* and the *sala da pranza.* In England the word "room" was kept for all these functions, but a prefix was added to give precision: the dining-room, the bedroom, etc.

This specialization of the rooms, in the middle class and nobility to begin with, was certainly one of the greatest changes in everyday life. It satisfied a new desire for isolation. In these more private dwellings, the servants no longer left the out-of-the-way quarters which were allotted to them—except in the houses of princes of the blood, where the old manners endured. Sébastien Mercier noted as a recent innovation the habit of ringing for the maidservant. Bells were arranged in such a way that they could summon servants from a distance, whereas they had previously been capable of arousing attention only in the room in which they were rung. Nothing could be more characteristic of the new desire to keep the servants at a distance and also to defend oneself against intruders. It was no longer good form in the late eighteenth century to call on a friend or acquaintance at any time of day and without warning. Either one had days when one was "at home," or else "people send each other cards by their servants." "The post also takes care of visits. . . . The letter-box delivers cards; nothing is easier, nobody is visible, everyone has the decency to close his door." [22]

The use of "cards" and "days" was not an isolated phenomenon. The old code of manners was an art of living in public and together. The new code of manners emphasized the need to respect the privacy of others. The moral stress had been moved. Sébastien Mercier was quick to observe this change: "Present-day custom has cut short all ceremonies and only a provincial stands on ceremony now." Meals were shortened too: "They are much shorter, and it is not at table that people talk freely and tell amusing stories," but in the *salon,* the room to which people withdraw: the "drawing-room." "People are no longer in a hurry to drink, no longer torment their guests in order to prove that they know how to entertain, no longer ask you to sing [the old concerts over dessert of the sixteenth and seventeenth centuries]." "People have abandoned those foolish and ridiculous customs so familiar to our ancestors, unhappy proselytes of an embarrassing and annoying tradition *which they called correct.*" "Not a moment's rest: people tried to outdo each other in politeness before the meal and during the meal with pedantic stubbornness, and the experts on etiquette applauded these puerile combats." "Of all those stupid old customs, that of blessing someone who sneezes is the only one that has lasted down to the present day." "We leave it to the cobbler and the tailor to give each other the sincere or hypocritical accolade which was still usual in polite society forty years ago." "Only the *petit bourgeois* now employs those tiresome manners and futile attentions which he still imagines to be correct and which are intolerably irksome to people who are used to society life."

The rearrangement of the house and the reform of manners left more room for private life; and this was taken up by a family reduced to parents and children, a family from which servants, clients and friends were excluded. General de Martange's letters to his wife between 1760 and 1780 enable us to gauge the progress made by a concept of the family which had become identical with that of the nineteenth and early twentieth centuries. The family had invaded people's correspondence and doubtless their conversations and preoccupations too. [23]

The old forms of address such as "Madame" had disappeared. Martange

[22] Sébastien Mercier, *Les Tableaux de Paris,* edited by Desnoitères, p. 194.

[23] *Correspondance inédite du général de Martange,* 1756–1782, edited by Bréard, 1898.

addressed his wife as "dear *maman*" or "my dear love," "my dear child," "my dear little one." The husband called his wife by the same name that his children gave her: *maman*. His correspondence with his wife was full of details about the children, their health and their behavior. They were referred to by nickname: Minette and Coco. This increasingly widespread use of nicknames corresponded to a greater familiarity and also to a desire to address one another differently from strangers, and thus to emphasize by a sort of hermetic language the solidarity of parents and children and the distance separating them from other people.

When the father was away, he kept himself informed of all the little details of everyday life, which he took very seriously. He waited impatiently for letters: "I beg you, my dear little one, to write just a few words." "Scold Mlle Minette for me for so far neglecting to write to me." He spoke of the joy of seeing his family again very soon: "I look forward to being with you once more in our poor little home, and I should like no responsibility better than that of arranging your room and making our stay pleasant and comfortable." Here we already have the modern taste for domesticity, contrasting the house, the object of enthusiastic pottering, with the outside world.

In this correspondence, questions of health and hygiene occupied an important place. Hitherto people had worried about serious illnesses, but they had not shown this constant solicitude, they had not bothered about a cold, a minor ailment: physical life had not been regarded as so important. "I should be so unhappy if I had no news about your health and that of my little girls." "Although what you tell me about the poor health which you and my poor little girls are enjoying is not as comforting as a father's heart might wish. . . ." "I am not very happy about what you tell me about our little boy's pains and loss of appetite. I cannot recommend you too earnestly, dear child, to procure some Narbonne honey for both him and Xavière, and to rub their gums with it when they are in pain." This was the anxiety of parents over their children's teething troubles: it could have interested a few old women in Mme de Sévigné's time, but it had not hitherto been given the honors of a place in a staff officer's correspondence. "My daughters' colds worry me. . . . But it seems to me that the weather finally took a turn for the better this morning." Vaccinations against smallpox was discussed then as inoculation against poliomyelitis is today. "I leave it to you to see to Xavière's vaccination, and the sooner the better, because everybody is satisfied with the vaccination." He advised his wife to drink "Sedlitz water," "the salts of the same name," and lemonade, and also to mix vinegar or brandy with her water, to guard against infection.

One of the girls had got married in Germany. In a letter to her "dear sweet *maman*" of January 14th, 1781, she explained her long silence:

"First of all the two youngest had whooping-cough for two months, so badly that every time they coughed they went purple in the face and the blood came bubbling out of their nostrils. After that illness, my little girl and Xavier caught the worst brain fever you could imagine." The doctors had given up hope of saving Xavier: "The poor child suffered all it is possible to suffer." However, in the end he was saved: "Thanks to the Supreme Being, all three have been returned to me." Nobody would now dare to seek consolation for losing a child in the hope of having another, as parents could have admitted doing only a century before. The child was irreplaceable, his death irreparable. And the mother found happiness in the midst of their children, who no longer belonged to an intermediary region between existence, and nonexistence: "The company of my little ones is my sole delight." Here we see the connection between the progress of the concept of childhood and the progress of hygiene, between concern for the child and concern for his health, another form of the link between attitudes to life and attitudes to death.

Considerable attention was also paid to the children's education, the importance of which was fully recognized: "Above all I urge you not to waste a minute that can be given to the children's education; double or treble their lessons every day, especially to teach them how to stand, walk and eat" (an echo of the old manuals of etiquette). The three children had a tutor: "Let the three children profit by his tuition and let the two girls in particular learn how to stand and walk. If M. H. can give them grace, he can consider himself a clever master."

Martange ran into financial difficulties. He dreaded the consequences: "The sorrow of being unable to give them the education I would have wished has given me some bitter moments of reflection." Whatever happened, the "masters' fees" had to be paid. We are a long way here from the laments of the moralists of the 1660s, who complained that schoolmasters were not paid because people did not realize the importance of their work. "I should sell my last shirt, if I had nothing else, to see my children on the same level as all the others of their age and rank. They must not be brought into the world to humiliate us with their ignorance and behavior. I think of nothing else, my dear, but of repairing my fortune to ensure their happiness, but if they wish to ensure mine, they must work hard and not waste time." Martange was worried when his children were vaccinated, in case "the time taken by vaccination is lost by their masters." "Use your stay in town to give them a little of that education which my [financial] misfortunes have so far prevented us from obtaining for them."

Health and education: these would henceforth be the chief preoccupations of all parents. One cannot help being struck by the extremely modern tone of his correspondence. In spite of the two centuries which separate us, it is closer to us than to Mme de Sévigné, who lived only a century earlier. In Mme de Sévigné, apart from the maternal solicitude of a good grandmother, what appears above all, at odd moments in her life, is an amused interest in the caprices of childhood, what I have called the first attitude to childhood, the "coddling" attitude. This attitude is almost entirely absent from Martange. He treats everything much more seriously. His is already the gravity of the nineteenth century, applied to both little things and big: Victorian gravity. In the seventeenth century, when he was not a subject of amusement, the child was the instrument of matrimonial and professional speculation designed to improve the family's position in society. This idea is relegated to the background in Martange: his interest in education seems much more disinterested. Here children as they really are, and the family as it really is, with its everyday joys and sorrows, have emerged from an elementary routine to reach the brightest zones of consciousness. This group of parents and children, happy in their solitude and indifferent to the rest of society, is no longer the seventeenth-century family, open to the obtrusive world of friends, clients and servants: it is the modern family.

One of the most striking characteristics of this family is the concern to maintain equality between the children. We have seen that the moralists of the second half of the seventeenth century gave timid support to this equality, chiefly because favoring the eldest son often drove the younger children into false religious vocations, but also because they were ahead of their times and foresaw the future conditions of family life. We have seen from their writings how conscious they were of going against public opinion. Henceforth, from the end of the eighteenth century on, inequality between the children of one family would be considered an intolerable injustice. It was manners, and not the Civil Code or the Revolution which abolished the law of primogeniture. The families of France would reject it out of hand when the Ultras of the Restoration restored it, inspired by a new concept of the family which they incorrectly attributed to the ancien regime: "Out of twenty well-to-do families," Villèle wrote to Polignac on October 31st, 1824, "there is scarcely one which uses the power to favor the oldest or some other child. The bonds of subordination have been loosened everywhere to such an extent that in the family, the father considers himself obliged to humor his children." [24]

Between the end of the Middle Ages and the seventeenth century, the child had won a place beside his parents to which he could not lay claim at a time when it was customary to entrust him to strangers. This return of the children to the home was a great event: it gave the seventeenth-

[24] J. Fourcassié, *Villèle*, 1954.

century family its principal characteristic, which distinguished it from the medieval family. The child became an indispensable element of everyday life, and his parents worried about his education, his career, his future. He was not yet the pivot of the whole system, but he had become a much more important character. Yet this seventeenth-century family was not the modern family: it was distinguished from the latter by the enormous mass of sociability which it retained. Where the family existed, that is to say in the big houses, it was a center of social relations, the capital of a little complex and graduated society under the command of the pater-familias.

The modern family, on the contrary, cuts itself off from the world and opposes to society the isolated group of parents and children. All the energy of the group is expended on helping the children to rise in the world, individually and without any collective ambition: the children rather than the family.

This evolution from the medieval family to the seventeenth-century family and then to the modern family was limited for a long time to the nobles, the middle class, the richer artisans and the richer laborers. In the early nineteenth century, a large part of the population, the biggest and poorest section, was still living like the medieval families, with the children separated from their parents. The idea of the house or the home did not exist for them. The concept of the home is another aspect of the concept of the family. Between the eighteenth century and the present day, the concept of the family changed hardly at all. It remained as we saw it in the town and country middle classes of the eighteenth century. On the other hand, it extended more and more to other social strata. In England in the late eighteenth century, agricultural laborers tended to set up house on their own, instead of lodging with their employers, and the decline of apprenticeship in industry made possible earlier marriages and larger families.[25] Late marriage, the precariousness of work, the difficulty of finding lodgings, the mobility of journeyman labor and the continuation of the traditions of apprenticeship, were so many obstacles to the ideal way of middle-class family life, so many obstacles which the evolution of manners would gradually remove. Family life finally embraced nearly the whole of society, to such an extent that people have forgotten its aristocratic and middle-class origins.[26]

[25] J. Ashton, *La Révolution industrielle*, p. 173.
[26] H. Bergues, P. Ariès, E. Hélin, L. Henry, M. Riquet, A. Sauvy, J. Sutter, *La Prévention des naissances dans la famille, ses origines dans les temps modernes.* Institut National d'Études démographiques, Cahier no. 35, 1960. Cf. also R. Prigent, *Le Renouveau des idées sur la famille.* Institut National d'Études démographiques, no. 18, 1954.

SUGGESTED READINGS

ANCIENT

FRANK F. ABBOTT. *The Common People of Ancient Rome: Studies of Roman Life & Literature* (New York: Scribners, 1920)

J. P. V. D. BALSDON. *Life and Leisure in Ancient Rome* (New York: McGraw-Hill, 1969)

C. M. BOWRA. *The Greek Experience* (London: The New English Library, 1957)

JEROME CARCOPINO. *Daily Life in Ancient Rome,* tr. by E. O. Lorimer (New Haven: Yale University Press, 1940)

FRANK COWELL. *Everyday Life in Ancient Rome* (London: B. T. Batsford, Ltd., 1961)

VICTOR EHRENBERG. *Society and Civilization in Greece and Rome,* Martin Classical Lectures, Vol. 18 (Cambridge, Mass.: Harvard University Press, 1964)

MARIO A. LEVI. *Political Power in the Ancient World,* tr. by Jane Costello (New York: The New American Library, 1965)

FERDINAND LOT. *The End of the Ancient World and the Beginnings of the Middle Ages* (New York: Barnes & Noble, 1953)

HAROLD MATTINGLY. *The Man in the Roman Street* (New York: Norton, 1966)

U. E. PAOLI. *Rome: Its People, Life and Customs,* tr. by R. D. MacNaghten, (New York: McKay, 1963)

C. E. ROBINSON. *Everyday Life in Ancient Greece* (Oxford: Clarendon Press, 1933)

M. I. ROSTOVTZEFF. *The Social and Economic History of the Hellenistic World,* 3 vols. (Oxford: Clarendon Press, 1941)

M. I. Rostovtzeff. *The Social and Economic History of the Roman Empire,* 2nd ed., rev. by P. M. Fraser, 2 vols. (Oxford: Clarendon Press, 1957)

Henry A. Treble & K. M. King. *Everyday Life in Rome in the Time of Caesar and Cicero* (Oxford: Clarendon Press, 1930)

T. G. Tucker. *Life in Ancient Athens: The Social and Public Life of a Classical Athenian from Day to Day* (New York: Macmillan, 1913)

LaRue Van Hook. *Greek Life and Thought: A Portrayal of Greek Civilization* (New York: Columbia University Press, 1924)

P. Walcot. *Greek Peasants, Ancient and Modern: A Comparison of Social and Moral Values* (New York: Barnes & Noble, 1970)

MEDIEVAL AND RENAISSANCE

Marc Bloch. *Feudal Society,* tr. by L. A. Manyon (Chicago: University of Chicago Press, 1961)

Prosper Boissonnade. *Life and Work in Medieval Europe,* tr. by Eileen Power (New York: Harper & Row, 1964)

Christopher Brooke. *The Structure of Medieval Society* (New York: McGraw-Hill, 1971)

Jacob Burkhardt. *The Civilization of the Renaissance in Italy* (New York: Modern Library Edition, 1954)

G. G. Coulton. *Life in the Middle Ages,* 4 vols. (London: Cambridge University Press, 1928)

Genevieve D'Haucourt. *Life in the Middle Ages,* tr. by Veronica Hall (New York: Walker & Co., 1963)

Eleanor S. Duckett. *Death and Life in the Tenth Century* (Ann Arbor, Mich.: University of Michigan Press, 1967)

Wallace K. Ferguson. *Europe in Transition 1300–1520* (Boston: Houghton Mifflin, 1962)

Margaret Hastings. *Medieval European Society 1000–1450* (New York: Random House, 1971)

Denys Hay. *The Medieval Centuries* (London: Methuen & Co., 1964)

J. Huizinga. *The Waning of the Middle Ages* (New York: Doubleday, 1949)

Robert S. Lopez. *The Birth of Europe* (London: Phoenix House, 1967)

Henri Pirenne. *Economic and Social History of Medieval Europe,* tr. by I. E. Clegg (New York: Harcourt Brace, 1937)

R. W. Southern. *The Making of the Middle Ages* (New Haven: Yale University Press, 1953)

James W. Thompson. *Economic and Social History of Europe in the Later Middle Ages,* 2 vols. (New York: Frederick Ungar Publishing Co., 1928)

EARLY MODERN

Maurice Ashley. *The Golden Century: Europe 1598–1715* (London: Weidenfeld & Nicolson, 1969)

TREVOR ASTON, ed. *Crisis in Europe 1560–1660* (New York: Doubleday Anchor, 1967)

PHILIPPE ERLANGER. *The Age of Courts & Kings: Manners and Morals 1558–1715* (New York: Harper & Row, 1967)

HENRY A. F. KAMEN. *The Iron Century: Social Change in Europe 1550–1660* (London: Weidenfeld & Nicolson, 1971)

HUGH KEARNEY. *Scholars and Gentlemen: Universities and Society in Pre-Industrial Britain 1500–1700* (Ithaca, N. Y.: Cornell University Press, 1970)

BELA KIRALY. *Hungary in the Late Eighteenth Century* (New York: Columbia University Press, 1969)

DOROTHY MARSHALL. *The English People in the Eighteenth Century* (London: Longmans, Green & Co., 1956)

ROLAND MOUSNIER. *Peasant Uprisings in Seventeenth Century France, Russia and China* (New York: Harper & Row, 1970)

IVY PINCHBECK & MARGARET HEWITT. *Children in English Society,* vol. I: *From Tudor Times to the Eighteenth Century* (London: Routledge, 1969)

A. L. ROWSE. *The Elizabethan Renaissance: The Life of the Society* (New York: Scribners, 1971)

HENRI SEE. *Economic and Social Conditions in Eighteenth-Century France,* tr. by Edwin H. Zeydel (New York: Knopf, 1927)